193578

Creating
An Industrial Civilization

Creating An

A Report on the Corning Conference

HELD UNDER THE AUSPICES OF THE AMERICAN
COUNCIL OF LEARNED SOCIETIES AND CORNING
GLASS WORKS, MAY 17-19, 1951, CORNING, NEW
YORK

HARPER & BROTHERS

Industrial Civilization

Edited by Eugene Staley

with the collaboration of

ROBERT L. CALHOUN   ERIC LARRABEE   REUEL DENNEY
FRANCIS CHASE ROSECRANCE   LAWRENCE K. FRANK
DAVID RIESMAN   JOHN A. KOUWENHOVEN
IRWIN T. SANDERS   WILLIAM F. WHYTE

PUBLISHERS, NEW YORK

Contents

v

PART II. Background Papers

Appendix

Introduction

THE SIGNIFICANCE OF THE CORNING
CONFERENCE

by the Editor

Nearly one hundred leaders from the world of industry and the world of learning—from management, labor, government, arts and professions, science, and humanistic studies—met in a conference on "Living in Industrial Civilization" at Corning, New York, on May 17-19, 1951. What they talked over, earnestly and intensively, in roundtable groups of twenty to twenty-five each, was not how to produce more goods, make more profits, get higher wages, nor even how to resist the world challenge of communism—though the discussions had some relevance to all these matters. Their concern was to take a candid look at our industrial civilization from the standpoint of *human values*. How good, in human terms, is this industrial life we have created? What has man lost and what has he gained since he has given up making products with his hands to make them by machine? Where do we go from here?

The Conference brought to a focus several significant trends in the industrial and intellectual life of mid-twentieth-century America. The fact that it took place under the joint sponsorship of an industrial corporation and a national organization for humanistic research testifies both to the growing sense of public responsibility of industry and to a growing sense of responsibility on the part of the "intellectuals"—philosophers, historians, social scientists, psychologists, and humanistic scholars generally—to relate their studies of man's past and his creative spirit to the practical problems of today's civilization. A perceptive journalist saw in the Conference "a dramatic demonstration of American concern for the individual, of American emphasis on the value of personality" and also a symbol of "the awakening at long last of Americans to the need of putting thought before action in meeting their problems."*

There are those who still repeat the old charge that the American people, and especially their business leaders, are solely "materialistic" in outlook, not interested in things of the spirit or in a well-rounded human life. Those of us who participated in the planning of the Corning Conference, observed the roundtables in action, listened to earnest conversations in corridors, lounge, and dining room, must doubt this as of today, whatever may have been true in the past. The very holding of the Conference belies the charge. Appropriately, the Voice of America sent a sound truck to record for foreign listeners a side of American life that is too little known abroad.

Even the "materialistic" achievements of America are seen in much truer perspective, in this writer's opinion, when they are explained not merely in terms of abundant natural resources and a highly developed material technology, but also in terms of human attitudes and the ability to cooperate. In the last quarter century, especially, there has been a truly remarkable growth in the attention paid to "the human factor" in American industry. It is no exaggeration to say that the productivity of this country is due as much to a highly developed, steadily advancing *social technology*— that is, skill in human relations—as it is to material technology. Those who have helped to bring the ECA "productivity teams" of management and labor representatives from Europe to study American industrial methods report that it is this human-relations side of American know-how which impresses the visitors more than anything else.

Perhaps the real "story" in the Conference, therefore, is the fact that it took place. One of the members from abroad, Antonio Carrillo Flores, of Mexico, said that "a conference of this kind under private sponsorship simply cannot be conceived in my country." He made this remark in the course of explaining that the govern-

* Malvina Lindsay, Washington *Post*, May 23, 1951.

ment has to play a larger role in economic development in Mexico than in the United States, partly because private initiative does not show the sense of public responsibility there that it does here. Another conferee, Sir George E. Schuster, British financier and distinguished public servant, stated that he found the Conference "the most encouraging event since the end of the last war."

A line of thought developed in one of the roundtables put the Conference in the broadest setting of all. It was pointed out in the group on "Confidence in Life in Industrial Civilization" that man has become self-conscious about the development of his own culture. Realizing now that human institutions can be shaped and molded, he faces for the first time in history the necessity of consciously guiding his future. Lawrence K. Frank suggested that the Conference theme might well have been not merely "*Living* in Industrial Civilization" but, more dynamically, "*Creating* an Industrial Civilization." This suggestion has been adopted in the title of this volume. Julian Huxley added the note that the main preoccupation in the Western world during the last hundred years has been in building the industrial side of our society; "Now, isn't that going to turn into building a world humanist society based on industry, which is a little different thing?"

ORIGINS OF THE CONFERENCE

The way in which the Conference came about is significant.

The officers of Corning Glass Works, planning for celebration of the firm's centennial in 1951, realized that the last one hundred years had coincided with the rise of a whole new system of life in America. The years 1851 to 1951 had seen amazing changes in technology, growth of factories, cities, and towns, rise of large business corporations, of trade-unions, of new government activities, and new problems in human relations, from the family at one end of the scale to global politics at the other.

They asked: What has this growth of "industrial civilization" in America done to *human beings*? Would it not be a good idea as part of an industrial centennial to do a little accounting in human value terms and, on that basis, to take a look back and a look ahead? Perhaps this effort would help us to see what human problems deserve greatest attention as we move into a second century of modern industry in America. Perhaps it would strengthen this country and its allies in the competition now going on between the methods and ideals of free industrial society and those of totalitarian industrial society.

Might not a conference in which men of "action" and men of "thought" are brought together for common consultation on these questions lead not only to interesting discussion but also to practical consequences in terms of a new awareness, new experiments, new research, of benefit to all?

The increasingly close relations between the natural sciences and industry in the last one hundred years have produced amazing results. What might happen if representatives of the humanistic studies—studies of man, his nature, his feelings, his systems of thought, his modes of expression, his creations—were brought into closer relations with persons concerned with industry?

The officers of Corning Glass Works therefore turned to the American Council of Learned Societies Devoted to Humanistic Studies, the national coordinating and planning organization in this field. They asked the ACLS to join in holding a conference to explore these questions and to undertake responsibility for planning the program. They made it clear that Corning Glass Works would impose no restrictions on selection of subject matter and personnel which seemed best suited to the joint purpose.

The ACLS, on its part, had been championing the idea that humanistic research and scholarship is not an end in itself, but that it should be practiced with the definite purpose of aiding puzzled modern man to understand his problems and potentialities, to keep worthy goals in view, and to choose new ways more wisely in the light of the great human achievements and struggles of the past. It saw in the Corning proposal a unique opportunity and a challenge to try to bridge the gap that so often separates those who devote themselves to the science and learning of man and those who make decisions and carry responsibilities in the practical world.

BASIC IDEAS

The Conference planning started from the fact that there is more to living than making a living. Modern technology and modern industry have brought enormously higher levels of consumption. But the way people live in order to produce things is as important as the things they produce. Modern industry makes more than the objects that come off its assembly lines: it makes living conditions for human beings.

The planners, therefore, thought it essential that the Conference should note certain humanly important changes which have been wrought by modern industry and by the science, technology, and social organization on which industry rests. It should give attention to changes in the nature, conditions, rhythms, and personal relations of daily work; to changes in the amount of leisure, and the opportunities presented for its use; to changes in the relation of the individual to his family, to his local community, and to broader communities; and to changes in the attitudes, expectations, hopes, and fears with which men face life's problems and mysteries.

The Conference should ask: How do the men and women who make up modern industrial society feel about these changes and about the life they lead today? Can we discover new ways to increase the meaningfulness of life for modern man? To enhance human satisfactions? To decrease the tensions and conflicts that threaten our civilization?

The Conference was to be focused primarily on the human problems of industrial civilization within the United States. There were several reasons for this decision. Industrialization and its attendant technology have reached their highest level in the United States. This is the case history most readily available and best known to us. Nations all over the globe are now seeking to acquire American "know-how" and to imitate American productive methods. Furthermore, through ECA, Point Four, the Fulbright and other exchange programs of government, through the international activities of business and the philanthropic work of great foundations, Americans are voluntarily engaged in exporting their technology and industrial methods. It seems appropriate, therefore, to pause and examine—as a whole and with stress on its human consequences—this product which is in such demand for export.

Thus, while the Conference was not a conference on international relations or on development of less-industrialized areas as such, the issues it raised have a direct bearing on fundamental problems in these fields as well as on living in the United States.

THE ROUNDTABLE INQUIRIES

The intent of the Conference planners was to provide an opportunity to *confer*. Though there were general sessions featuring formal speeches, the main emphasis was on discussion, and particularly on the roundtables.

The general topic was broken down into four areas for roundtable discussion:

ROUNDTABLE A. *Work and Human Values in Industrial Civilization.*

What have been the outstanding successes and failures of industrial society from the point of view of the human satisfactions or dissatisfactions in work?

ROUNDTABLE B. *Leisure and Human Values in Industrial Civilization.*

What gains and losses in human terms have arisen from increased leisure and from such influences as the movies, radio, TV, books, crafts and hobbies?

ROUNDTABLE C. *The Individual's Sense of Community in Industrial Civilization.*

What are the outstanding gains and losses, from the point of view of human values, resulting from the changed relations of individuals to groups or communities ("belonging") under modern industrial conditions?

ROUNDTABLE D. *Confidence in Life in Industrial Civilization.*

How have modern industry and science and the attendant reorganization of human living affected the individual's confidence in life (security, faith)? What has happened to his peace of mind, his feelings about the future of himself and his loved ones, the assurance with which he confronts the universe? What gains or losses in human values do these changes imply?

Each conferee was assigned to one of the four roundtables, which met simultaneously. A "background paper" for each roundtable was circulated in advance of the Conference, but there were no papers read in the sessions themselves. Summaries of the spontaneous, give-and-take discussions of the roundtables and of the speeches and discussions of the general sessions appear in Part I of this volume. The background papers are printed in Part II.

GUIDE TO THE SUMMARIES

In order to make the discussion summaries useful and interesting for a broader public, the rapporteurs and the editor have tried to present the main themes that emerged rather than to give a verbatim record. Related passages which were separated in the original discussion have often been brought together in the summaries. To convey some of the flavor of the roundtable interchanges, and for the sake of accurate presentation, frequent use has been made of direct quotations. These were based on the stenotype record, and each conferee has subsequently been given an opportunity to approve or correct remarks attributed to him.

The opening session of the Conference took place at 5:30 on Thursday afternoon, May 17, 1951. It consisted of three brief statements welcoming the members and informing them on the origins, aims, and procedures of the Conference. An evening session the same day presented a spokesman for industrial management and a spokesman for organized labor on the topic "Human Values in Industrial Civilization." These two general sessions are summarized in Chapter 1.

On Friday evening a general session was devoted to "Living in Industrial Civilization: Views from Abroad," with a panel of observers of the American scene from Great Britain, India, and Mexico. The summary appears in Chapter 4.

The final general session convened on Saturday morning at 10:30. Two spokesmen from each roundtable presented brief commentaries on the Conference theme as seen in the perspective of their roundtable's work. Then there was discussion from the floor. This session is reported in Chapter 7.

Each roundtable met briefly following the opening session on Thursday afternoon, largely to get acquainted, and then held working sessions all Friday morning and Friday afternoon and part of Saturday morning. The total discussion time was some seven to eight hours. The agenda for each roundtable asked it to isolate the major current problems in its field, to evaluate the efforts that have been made toward solving these problems, and to indicate where we need to go from here.

The roundtable discussions are summarized in Chapters 2, 3, 5, and 6, and the respective background papers appear in Chapters 8, 9, 10, and 11. Readers will no doubt have their own preferences among the roundtable summaries. Those who are interested in a quick look at some modern thinking on the relation of organizational techniques to the workers' sense of participation in industry and trade will enjoy Roundtable A. For anyone who wants provocative observations on the changing role of leisure in modern society, spiced with repartee and a verbal slug-fest on radio and television, Roundtable B is recommended. If it is analysis of community problems and instances of successful efforts to revitalize community spirit that one is looking for, he should turn to Roundtable C. In Roundtable D, on the other hand, one will find the broadest humanistic outlook of all, together with some down-to-earth observations on such concrete topics as how to get stockholders, workers, managers, and the consuming public to have more mutual understanding and confidence.

A BEGINNING

The invitation to Conference members said: "It is hoped that this Conference will prove important as a *beginning* of a process rather than an end. Of course, no one expects that in two or three days of discussion we can come up with a neatly packaged array of 'solutions.' The Conference will be a success in the eyes of its planners if it produces some small gains in:

1. *Identification* of some of the main problems of human values in industrial civilization;
2. Increased *appreciation* of their importance;
3. Better *acquaintance* among people who come at these problems from different angles;
4. *Stimulus* to further exploration by subsequent discussion, by practical experiment, and by research."

To what extent the Conference will in fact turn out to be a starting point for significant further thought and action remains to be seen. The aspect of the whole experience most remarked upon afterwards by those who attended, and in most appreciative terms, was what Walter Paepcke in the Roundtable on Leisure referred to as the "cross-fertilization" achieved by bringing together persons from many different backgrounds to discuss broad, common problems in a humanistic setting. Another member called the Conference "a great experiment in better communication among groups." Certainly, as the reader will realize, what went on in the new Corning Glass Center on those May days had little to do with the chemistry of glass, but much to do with the chemistry of the human spirit.

This whole volume is a product of an imaginative enterprise which was conceived and jointly executed by two organizations— Corning Glass Works and the American Council of Learned Societies. "Authors" of it in a broad sense are the officers and planning committees of the two organizations; their regular and special staffs who labored long, hard, and devotedly to set up the conference on which the book is based (anyone who has been in on the running of a conference of this magnitude knows what I mean); the roundtable chairmen, background paper writers, and rapporteurs whose essential and arduous but unobtrusive function it was to provide a framework within which effective group communication could go on; and, of course, the conferees themselves, including the speakers and panel members, who gave so generously of their time and enthusiasm and special competences to generate the ideas recorded in these chapters.

To put these ideas on paper for a broader public is much more than a mechanical task. Probably no two people hear a discussion in quite the same way, and no two would pick the same themes for highlighting. All of us who were present at the conference, and readers who find this report stimulating, will be grateful to the rapporteurs for the comprehensions and skills which they brought to the problem of seizing and interpreting such a wide range of important subject-matter.

In addition, it is a pleasure to make special acknowledgement:

To Eric Larrabee, Associate Editor of *Harper's Magazine*, not only for his work as one of the rapporteurs (the brilliant presentation of the conference setting and the general sessions is due to him) but also for his very helpful advice and assistance in general editing.

To Shirley Duncan, of the American Council of Learned Societies, for the extraordinary skill and meticulous care with which she contributed to shaping the form of the text and to checking its content.

To Stanford Research Institute, my regular employer, for arrangements which made possible my part in the conference planning and in the preparation of this volume.

EUGENE STALEY

Part I

Conference Discussions

1

Human Values in Industrial Civilization

GENERAL SESSION

Eric Larrabee, rapporteur

If a justification were needed for the representative American institution of conference holding, it might be said that the conference allows no idea to be put before it in disembodied form. This is the story of a conference. In it observations will be found only in conjunction with live personalities, with their relationships to one another, and with the heat and humor of the conversations amongst them. Naturally this will make for confusion in the account, since—in spite of the formation of various cliques, cabals, and underground resistance movements during the sessions— there were nearly as many discrete notions presented as there were participants. The Corning Conference, however, imposed its own equations on these tangential tendencies and rode a rising curve to climax.

The generic excitement of the occasion will appear only fitfully in these pages. Information can scarcely have been available to the organizers of the Conference, if in fact it exists, as to the critical mass of ideas and individuals it is necessary to assemble in one room before a release of energy takes place; but in the event, the planners planned well. It is the conviction of at least one delegate that we did not leave the subject as we found it, that a variety of hesitant and hitherto unformulated intangibles were given sub-

3

stance, and that the contents of this record—lest the reader be discouraged by its specificity—are of wider consequence than may first appear.

Attention is directed to the fact that the Conference as such reached no conclusion, recommended no course of action, and took no formal steps to perpetuate itself. No "six point resolution at the end saying, 'Go out and do these particular things,' " will be found in this volume. (The quotation is from the closing remarks by Charles E. Odegaard, executive director of the American Council of Learned Societies and chairman of the Conference.) Nor was it the intention of the planners that any such conventional response to the demands of a conference situation be sought. Periodically, there may have been efforts by determined persons to locate the deliberations in a stabilized context—"the given problems of American culture in the given terms" was David Riesman's phrase for it—but for the most part these seem to have been circumvented and neutralized by equally determined colleagues. Automatic deference to the jargon of compromise was held to a minimum. At the same time, the semantics of the questions raised were subtly altered by the manner in which they were answered, shifting the axis of social inquiry—in the direction of new data and new meanings—by a number of degrees.

This is not to say that a hundred-odd delegates left Corning on May 19, inflamed with a common vision precisely applied to their particular areas of competence, or even that the rapporteurs of the several roundtables are agreed on a single "sense of the meeting." This is far from the case. The author of the general sessions' report respectfully differs even with Mr. Odegaard's modest conclusion that "this Conference has proved that there is really a common basis of interest between active policy makers on the one hand and the academicians interested in the humanities and social studies on the other." I would submit, to the contrary, that it revealed "common bases of interest" which sharply cut across the nominal boundaries of attitude or caste. Either the reader must be prepared to encounter businessmen and labor leaders differing with other businessmen and labor leaders, with academics and journalists on both sides and at odds with one another, or he will have his preconceptions unsettled. (Among the ironies, you will find an earnest defense of highbrow culture by a shrewd manufacturing executive and a massive denunciation of American education by a mild-mannered college professor.) The inviting conclusion, to the extent that it concerns the subject matter of "Living in Industrial Civilization," is that the distinctions between so-called scholars and so-called men of action are either imaginary or inadequate.

CHANGE IN TERMS: NEW LINE ON OLD BATTLES

A major shift in perspective is epitomized in the minor change in the phraseology noted by Mr. Staley in his introduction. Initially, as Mr. Odegaard described the sequence of events, he and his fellow members of the planning group had characterized the chosen topic as "Life in Industrial Civilization" but, finding this too static, had substituted "Living in Industrial Civilization"—"to indicate that there was a dynamism here." In his final summary, Mr. Odegaard indicated that, "thanks to the imagination of Lawrence K. Frank," there had evolved "an even better topic, and I wish it had occurred to us earlier . . . 'Creating an Industrial Civilization.' "

MR. ODEGAARD: One of the things that is evident from your discussions, gentlemen, is that industrial civilization is still evolving—and revolving—at a rapid rate. It is not a terminus which has been reached, with a static and mechanical character. It is an ongoing process of development, and great changes have been taking place—yes, taking place in the past twenty years in this country and in other parts of the world. There is no reason to think that these changes will not continue. . . .

Now, oddly enough, when it comes to our generalizations, we still rely on a whole series of stereotypes, stereotypes which we helped to create and to perpetuate by using them about ourselves, and stereotypes which are carried along by foreign observers. I think this Conference suggests the desirability of our really looking at ourselves to see some of the things which we have done; and this, I think, will perhaps give us the degree of confidence that many think we have lost.

. . . We have to know ourselves better, to look in the mirror of life in America, not the stereotype but a vision that comes of self-analysis and observation. . . .

This rephrasing of title implied a marked redirection of the lines which the Conference might have been expected to pursue. In several of the documents placed before it (reprinted here in Part II) the static approach—and the consequent necessity of reaching static conclusions—was built into the assumption that the "given problems of American culture" should be approached by preference in the "given terms," or that these problems—lack of a sense of belonging, "spectatoritis," or the backwardness of the social sciences are examples—do in fact exist. What are the problems? What is being done? What can we do? This dialectic of problem solving, whatever appeal to practicality it has, runs the risk of overgeneralizing in its first step, of taking for granted too many hypotheses which subsequent discussion might properly challenge. A case in point is the frequently invoked contrast between the humanistic studies to which the ACLS is devoted, on the one hand, and the purely physical sciences, on the other. This comparison lay so close to the heart of the Conference's subject matter that it was independently introduced on at least three separate occasions by an academic administrator, a labor leader, and a businessman —Donald K. David of Harvard, A. J. Hayes of the International Association of Machinists, and Amory Houghton of Corning Glass.

MR. DAVID: There can be no doubt that, within our lifetimes, the physicists, chemists, and biologists have demonstrated that those who are working—at least, in part—as scholars can apply their knowledge effectively to the solution of practical problems. . . . Can the scholars in the social sciences match these performances?"

MR. HAYES: I must add that the lag between the breath-taking advance in the physical sphere in industry and the snaillike pace of our social science in the same area indicts us, I think, as a civilized society . . .

MR. HOUGHTON: There are many of us who feel . . . that there is a lack of equilibrium between the great advances made in the scientific field and those made in the humanistic field.

Far from accepting Mr. David's contrast at face value, the Conference proceeded to question this "lack" of sophisticated cultural machinery and to ask if there was not already in existence—to use Mr. Staley's pertinent phrase—"a highly developed, steadily advancing social technology" which ought to be minutely examined, and which might be found to rival the technology based on the natural sciences in usefulness and complexity. That these new traditions and techniques need not have been conceived by "scholars" in the narrow sense of the word went without saying. On an issue that was thematic to all four roundtables the question could be reduced to the specific one of whether in actuality the inarticulate members of industrial society do not have a greater "sense of participation" than is generally assumed by those who talk about the need for it. ("Has the modern industrial production system," asked Sir George E. Schuster in the Roundtable on Work, "created a state of affairs in which the great bulk of the people cannot find any satisfaction in their work? *Is that really a fact?*") The record shows that a healthy proportion of the common stereotypes which cluster around these questions—though not always, nor invariably with success—were resisted and brought to book.

Much credit for this effort devolves upon the visitors from abroad, especially the representatives of nonindustrial cultures, in whom a skeptical curiosity and fresh awareness was both pronounced and inevitable. Here, again, it cannot be said that as a group they adopted an identifiable position, unless it lay in skillfully evading another stereotype and near-unanimously failing to satisfy the perennial American appetite for abuse from outsiders. (The pressure on this score was overt, as you will see.) From these by-no-means neutral observers, nonetheless, there came an unusual percentage of the most acute penetrations into the matters of amorphous knowledge and concrete ignorance about industrial America which the Conference was gently compelled to recognize, however reluctantly, as objects of primary interest.

Forced by its own dynamic to redirect attention to a multitude of objective though unclassified facts, to a process of development already in progress, the Conference was fortunate in the presence of a distinguished British philosopher of "process," Lancelot Law Whyte, who counseled humility before the equal failure of scientists and philosophers to provide us with "a sufficiently accepted view of ourselves." This theme was echoed by Margaret Mead—herself a self-constituted alien ("Every time I come back to this civilization from the South Seas, I am surprised it works at all")—in the most inclusive definition entered in the transcript. "What this Conference is," said Miss Mead, "is an experiment in making the necessary inventions to make self-consciousness bearable to Americans. . . ."

Miss Mead's epigram will help to illuminate whatever unintentionally mysterious moments may have occurred; for even where the Conference conversations seem to veer blindly into the dark, they reflect a unanimous preoccupation with the discovery of acceptable interpretations and the successful achievement of Conference aims. Though there are multidimensional ambiguities in the thesis that Western self-consciousness can be or should be made bearable through such a ceremonial folk festival as this one, the members of the Conference themselves did not act as though they suffered from a lack of confidence or of a sense of belonging where they were. An act of faith in the virtue of roundtables and amiable argument was willingly performed at Corning in May, 1951. The atmosphere in which the Conference took place was such that its participants engaged themselves enthusiastically in the game of ideas, ran broken-field through each other's vulnerabilities and biases, to emerge triumphant at the close with carefully collected evidence of cooperation, contact, cross-fertilization, or other trophies of contemporary good intentions and concern with synthesis.

LANDSCAPE WITH FIGURES

Corning, a town of some eighteen thousand people, lies in the valley of the Chemung River, in the west-central portion of New York State, a few miles north of the Pennsylvania line. The glass works, which occupy the south bank of the river, come at the first

level below the tierlike parallel streets that rise up the valley wall
on a plan common to many nineteenth-century American towns—
first the factory, then the shopping thoroughfare, the railroad
station, the churches, and finally rows of residential districts in
ascending order of worth and circumstance. Erastus Corning,
after whom the village was named in 1837, is memorialized in a
stone clock tower opposite the Baron Steuben Hotel, where the
Centerway bisects the main streets and leads across the Chemung
to the new Glass Center where the Conference was held. This
clock tower, an imposing monument to the tasteful theories of its
time, had been sandblasted to such a startling whiteness for the
occasion of the Centennial that some citizens were worried lest
the conferees might think it had been recently constructed.

"And they planked down full-grown trees out there," one
Corning lady was overheard to say to her companion, "that cost
five hundred dollars apiece." Her reference was to a row of six
poplars, still wrapped in their protective burlap, standing parallel
to the street at the southeast corner of the aggressively shiny
structure of which the Conference made first public use. Friendly
concern and curiosity about the opening of the Glass Center, and
the Conference that preceded it, was not limited to this lady, nor
to the cost of landscape gardening around the Corning company's
Centennial showplace. It was made evident to the visitors in
memorable ways, from the substantial representatives of local
businesses who served as substitute chauffeurs, to the number of
times one heard the objection (informally expressed) that
strangers, no matter how welcome they might be, were getting in
to see the community's newest building ahead of those whose
center it was intended to become—a complaint which both casts
a sidelight on issues the Conference tended to neglect and helps
define Corning as a town whose major industry is significant to
its people in a social as well as economic sense.

The Glass Center will ultimately serve in three capacities: as a
museum, an exhibit of manufacturing processes, and a community
recreation hall. In function it is adventurous; in design it is an
achievement of handsome competence by the architectural firm

of Harrison, Abramovitz and Abbey, which was represented at the Conference and enjoys renown for its work on the Rockefeller Center and the United Nations buildings in New York. The low-lying, rectangular spaces in which the purposes of the Glass Center will be pursued have been surrounded architecturally with heroic-scale panels of glass and steel construction in the manner of Mies van der Rohe, forming a severely decorative box of novel appearance for western New York but by no means out of key with its surroundings.

From the corner of Fulton Street and the Centerway a variegated slice of the American man-made landscape is visible—buildings of the Fuller Construction Company (which built the Center), a Quonset hut bowling alley, a State Armory constructed of red brick in a style that might be called Rosicrucian Gothic, a group of postwar "garden" apartments in Contractors' Colonial, the Corning ballpark, and a row of garages advertising used cars and "job-rated" trucks (at one roundtable a disconsolate college professor, staring glumly out the tall glass windows, indicted the latter as representatives of "highway culture").

One additional American quality of the Glass Center lay in the fact that it was unfinished as the Conference began. Three days of roundtable discussions on the human aspects of industrial production could not have been more appropriately located than at this center of activity, as squads of craftsmen—glaziers, painters, carpenters, electricians—raced against a deadline to finish the building for the scheduled formal opening. Fortunately, as Mr. Amory Houghton, chairman of the board of the Corning Glass Works, observed when he accepted the keys from the architect in the final ceremony, he had not been given them a day earlier—there would have been no door to unlock. Yet presentably finished it was, with doors installed—black glass, to keep light out of the velvet-lined entrance hall in which the first casting of the Palomar 200-inch mirror glows roundly in the dark—by the time the Conference ended on Saturday.

"Credit for the conception and execution of the project," said Mr. Houghton, speaking of the Conference and Glass Center together, "belongs in the main to my cousin, Arthur A. Houghton, Jr. . . ." The latter, before turning over the proceedings to Mr. Odegaard, explained how his two ideas had in a sense a joint inception. In the Glass Center, he said, "we are seeking to present a rounded picture of a single industry in all its many aspects— historical, scientific, aesthetic, utilitarian, humanistic—indicating its past development, its present impact on society, its future potentialities. In particular, we are concerned with the humanistic aspect of the industry—that is, its relationship to those working in it and those for whom its products were designed, namely, the community at large." It was this conception of the Glass Center, with its facilities for the widest investigation into the history of work in one material, that led by a natural transition to "the necessity of effecting a closer correlation between the academic humanists in this country and the men of affairs."

Generously mapping out the grounds of respect on which the scholar might meet the businessman, Mr. Odegaard extended these divergent viewpoints to encompass a contrast between the material and spiritual aspects of the "distinctive mode of production known as industrialization." He submitted that Americans in particular, by subjecting themselves "to the kinds of discipline and the altered way of life which industrial production requires," had succeeded in molding "a culture whose material benefits are now the envy of men everywhere."

MR. ODEGAARD: It does not detract from the virtues of the United States if we note that Americans have been much preoccupied with material benefits. Our generation is still very close to those generations of our forebears who came into a wilderness. . . . In a new country which provided no human inheritances from the past, and with labor relatively scarce, men's imagination was greatly challenged by the problems of material existence—and Americans rose amazingly to this challenge. . . . But we are far less conscious of the psychological, emotional, and spiritual consequences of industrialization.

Without implying that we can or need to forsake this mode of production, it would seem reasonable to ask ourselves what are the results for human happiness and welfare in these very real, even if intangible, aspects of living in industrial civilization. . . . Though we aspire to as rational a view as possible, we hope to get beyond an external and impersonal view to a realization of what it means to men as individuals, as human beings. . . . We seek the voice of Everyman. There are no universal experts here. . . .

MANAGERIAL EVOLUTION

After brief meetings of the roundtables and adjournment for dinner, the Conference reconvened Thursday evening for the only two formal addresses it was to hear. The speakers had been selected in the apparent hope—expressed by Dean Donald K. David of the Harvard School of Business Administration as he introduced them—that they would represent the extremes of two conventionally opposing views: management and labor. "Our conflicts," said Mr. David, "lead to our dynamic way of life. . . ." The choices, in this respect, had paradoxical results, since both men (Gwilym A. Price and A. J. Hayes, presidents each of Westinghouse Electric and the International Machinists Union) were far more remarkable for the areas in which they saw eye to eye than for those in which they didn't. To an audience that was anticipating a fight, they might have seemed either painfully enlightened or statesmanlike to a fault.

Both, for example, were insistent in their endorsement of industrialism as such. Mr. Price reviewed a number of American achievements which he believed to be "the fruits of production. They are the product of the machine, which was supposed to be digging the pit deeper and deeper for the masses. In our discussions, then, let us not ignore or undervalue the material blessings of modern industrialization, inseparable as they are from the spiritual aspects. They are, moreover, their own justification. . . ." Mr. Hayes was equally fervent. "I am quite willing and eager to testify," he said, "that the industrial processes in the United States are literally—marvelous. On every hand and at every turn we see the miracles of their creation. . . ."

If there was an intrinsic difference between the speakers, it lay not in the fact that they came from two competitively organized social groups but in the necessity for one to speak of management's hopes for the future and the other, of labor's fears from the past. "I suggest," began Mr. Price, "that we begin with the understanding that we mean here *American* industrial civilization; that we are discussing the conditions of 1951, not of earlier times. . . ." But Mr. Hayes did not follow suit. On the grounds that this Conference was celebrating the past century of industrial development, he directed his comments to that period of time— "one hundred years . . . from 1851 to 1951 . . . I want to review, in outline, some of the injurious and socially bad things our industrial growth has done. . . ."

In figures of speech that were characteristic of the period he was describing, Mr. Hayes drew the memories of his listeners back into the past through pictorial images. The camera, a natural chronicler of industrialism, had come into use within the period and recorded with impartiality both the "vulgar display of wealth" and the "heart-rending contemporary scenes of tiny children shut up from sunlight at work. . . ." He referred to the company towns which "remained as a permanent characteristic of some of our basic industry on through the early years and into our contemporary society," prevailing "in the steel industry, in parts of the coal industry, and in some sections of textiles until fifteen or twenty years ago." He described the "soot and grime and smoke-filled air" of the "environment designated by industry as home-sites for its labor force." He asked whether a conference such as this one should not concern itself with "a human aspect of this phase of industrial development," the contrast between the "different rewards accruing to those who bought their way of life from their relationship to industry. . . . Does life on the hilltop and in the gutter of a common society have anything to do with the story of man?"

Mr. Price was willing to admit that it does, for he readily agreed that the effect of industrialism had been "deep, abrupt, and sometimes deplorable." He, too, felt that "large sections of our cities are not fit to live in," and he conceded that "the modern industrial structure has robbed some employees of their sense of individual enterprise." Mr. Price, in fact, as a representative of industrial control, wanted to give a sense of enterprise back to the employees. "So far as we can, we in management must restore it. We must keep our people informed of our plans, our policies, our hopes for the future, and of their place in them. We must give them recognition, a genuine sense of participation, a true feeling of identification, a realization of opportunity."

It was implicit in Mr. Hayes' remarks to the Roundtable on Work the following day that he disagreed at this point not on what should be done but on who should do it. Clearly he regarded Mr. Price's position and a good part of the discussion at his round-table as revivals of paternalism in modern dress.* Though disposed to agree that the industrial worker lacks a "sense of participation" or "sense of importance," Mr. Hayes was rescued just in time by a sound instinct that warned him to fear managers when they come bearing employee relations. He seemed to recognize that the problem he and Mr. Price were discussing might all-too-easily degenerate into an open and undignified struggle over the privilege of lecturing the American workman about his own greatness. Neither Mr. Hayes nor Mr. Price was disposed to evade the verbal trap or to ask whether the lack of "sense of participation" is actually as reprehensible and widespread as we suppose. Instead they both turned for a scapegoat to that class of society which is logically held to be responsible for words and their meanings—the intellectuals.

Mr. Hayes made clear what he meant by a "humanitarian" problem. "The activities and influence of the humanists in our society," he said, "never have kept pace with our industrial progress. . . . In this audience there are many humanists and social scientists. Well, maybe you have the answer as to the uneven record made in our society by the influence of your branches of study—the humanistic and social fields—as compared

* Mr. Hayes' words will be found at greater length on pp. 45-46. "We in organized labor . . ." he said, "take the position that these people must be given a feeling that their job is important . . . and that they really are impor-tant. . . . I think they are important, and I think our big problem is to show that to them. . . . That's a humanitarian problem."

with physical science." (Here, again, is the familiar antithesis, posed elsewhere by Mr. Hayes, and also by Mr. David and Mr. Amory Houghton.) Furthermore, in his peroration, Mr. Hayes did not miss the opportunity to accentuate an implied contrast with Thomas Jefferson, "a humanist and social scientist who was native to this continent and who left his mark on our culture."

But it remained for Mr. Price to do the real hatchet work in deploring the tendency of educated people to visualize industrialism in terms of Charlie Chaplin's *Modern Times*—or, as he put it, "the assumption almost unconsciously but commonly made that all American workers are employed at putting a nut on a fender as it passes by on an assembly line."

MR. PRICE: Of course that is not true. It ignores the 10 million workers in agriculture, the 4½ million professional people, the 6½ million proprietors and managers, 3½ million salespeople, 7½ million clerical workers, and most of our 7 million craftsmen and foremen. Perhaps 11 million out of 63 million now employed are so-called operatives.

Not all of these eleven millions, of course, work for big companies. Of those who do work for big companies, not all work in large plants. Of those who work in large plants, not all work on assembly lines. Of those who work on assembly lines, not all put nuts on fenders. And of those who put nuts on fenders, it may just possibly be erroneous to assume that they are all unhappy while and because they are doing it.

I sometimes feel like asking the gentlemen who write about the tensions and frustrations of our industrial workers: "Have you talked, really talked, to any lately?" . . . It is sometimes presumptuous to assume that someone else is in trouble and that we must do something to fix him up. Bernard Shaw once wrote: "Do not do unto others as you would that they should do unto you. Their tastes may not be the same."

THE TREASON OF THE CLERKS

Mr. Price reserved a place in his little list of those "responsible for the ills of modern society" for the "liberal intellectual," who has "lifted a lid from a Pandora's box and loosed forces on the world that he did not expect, does not understand, and cannot control." Mr. Price thought it deplorable that "in a crucial fifty years of our civilization, the authors of our books and plays, our other molders of public opinion, have only recently produced anything like effective opposition to the ruinous concepts of the extreme right or left. It is ironic that the distinguishing mark of so many of our best educated, most articulate, most cherished people has been an appalling ignorance of our traditions and of the simplest economic truths. That ignorance has given rise to . . . events that reduce the bad effects of the machine to relative triviality."

Mr. Price: In examining our industrial civilization, many of us, I think, make one basic assumptive error. . . . We do not realize to what extent capitalism has changed in the past generation, the past decade, even the past few years. . . . *Fortune* magazine has described the change. "What has happened," it writes, "is that American capitalism has changed and developed beyond the ability of the historians to catch up with it; that its transformation, perhaps because people rarely see in perspective what is occurring before their eyes, has escaped the full awareness of even most businessmen; that most of the popular books, the great books even, that have furnished Americans with their stereotypes about capitalism are now obsolete. . . ."

Ownership and initiative are broadly dispersed in American capitalism. Management is becoming a profession. Corporations today support a wide variety of material benefits that they could not afford at a lower production level. They are persistently, even painfully, aware of public opinion. They are continually self-critical. American business enterprise has demonstrated that it can correct its faults, withstand abuse from both its friends and its enemies, and continue its dynamic transformation and growth. . . . The problem is not easy or simple, but please credit us with trying. . . .

On this issue Mr. Hayes could take a firm stance at the opposite side of the bargaining table and, while conceding that improvements had been brought about, deny that "capitalism" could claim the credit. "Let me point out now," he said, "that as regards any and all of the undesirable industrial practices I have described, the workers themselves and those individuals and

organizations in society outside of industry were unable to eliminate or significantly to improve these conditions until there was
organized action on the part of the labor force." Anyone who
possessed even the smallest knowledge of the history of organized
labor in the past century, he felt, would recognize that "a review
of the obstacles set up to prevent organization, the appalling
sacrifice made to achieve organization by the membership, must
indicate a compelling need for such an organization." He did not
trust, in short, the new managers who are "painfully" aware of
public opinion and anxious to represent their job as a "profession."

MR. HAYES: I want to pick up for a minute that dream of freedom
of the early American pioneer which I said was lost for the wage-
earning population of early history. . . . The United States was a
common man's country. The American dream inspired and inflamed
the minds of ordinary plain people. That's why they came here from
all the lands in all the world at every opportunity. They came to
Colonial America as indentured servants and to the United States as
immigrant labor. You know the price they paid.

The industrial system and the capitalist economy growing out of
it was new under the American sun. The new order changed the face
and the culture of the United States, and as it did so it exploited, and
often mercilessly, both the natural resources and the working population of the nation. . . . With all the progress we have made I know
that behind the façade of improvement in industry and elsewhere the
same old forces of greed and evil lie in wait to reassert themselves. I
am familiar with the wide areas of industry and in agriculture where
exploitation like that I have described is rampant still. And I know how
thin the economic foundation is on which our higher paid, better
treated industrial workers stand.

Here Mr. Hayes stood on solid ground, though it was not quite
the same ground that Mr. Price was attempting to capture. It
may be true, Mr. Price might have responded, had their discussion
been a give-and-take instead of two set speeches, that "as human
beings we are not much better than we were prior to the miracles
of the machine age, and as a community we seem in some ways

to be worse," but the assumption he wished most to question was "that industrialization—and industry—are alone or even chiefly the cause of the present-day moral and spiritual ailments of mankind."

MR. PRICE: It is assumed that these evils of our industrial civilization have resulted chiefly from industrialization. In seminar language, mass production destroys the skills of the worker, eliminates the traditional satisfactions of this workmanship, changes for the worse his traditional values and his behavior. We are told that the human stresses created by the machine result in profound individual and social dissatisfactions, tensions, and frustrations.

These words express an attitude on which many conclusions about our industrial civilization and its human values are based. Both the attitude and the conclusions should be questioned and re-examined, for many of them—I believe—are wholly or partly wrong.

In the belief that many assumptions about industrialism derive from nostalgia for preindustrial times, Mr. Price now undertook to construct a position which was later to be occupied by Mr. Harrison and by John E. Burchard, dean of Humanities and Social Studies at the Massachusetts Institute of Technology, in the proceedings of the Roundtable on Community. All three were members of a small minority who sallied out from the bastions of industrial technology to counterattack obsolescent forms of social organization and to stand by their urban preferences.* It fell to Mr. Price, as a businessman, to pose the issue in terms of the accuracy of modern historical scholarship and to link (as D. W. Brogan was to do a day later) the European-American past with the Asiatic, or nonindustrial, present.

MR. PRICE: There is all too little truth in the picture of the happy, creative artisan of other centuries who loved the product he created and was one with his environment. To the extent that he existed at all,

---

* "The implication seems to be," said Mr. Burchard, "that there is something evil and bad for human beings in a change from a Gothic society or a Greek society to a large and complex society, or that the village of five hundred is the only community in which human beings are basically going to be happy and content and can live. I would say the evidence for this is pretty thin." (See page 122.)

he was one of a very small minority. His fellows were underpaid and overworked; they died young. We cannot believe that men were never uprooted or unemployed . . . that all workers were at peace with their fellows, up to the time James Watt discovered the uses of steam and Eli Whitney fitted together a set of interchangeable parts. Nor did men begin to be frustrated, insecure, unhappy, and tired of dull jobs only after Henry Ford had laid down the first assembly line forty years ago.

Some tend to forget that in the fine preindustrial cultures of the past a small privileged class lived on the destitution of the great submerged mass of humanity. If we would see history as it really was, we need only visit China today, or India, or Russia. These peoples, living in the main by spinning-wheel agrarian culture, share one passionate desire—to acquire adequate food, clothing, and shelter. They will get even that minimum only through industrialization, for only industrialization can produce enough to provide broad and varied distribution of goods and services to all classes. They will get it, too, only under that system of free wages and prices known as democratic capitalism. But that is another story and another speech.

HOW NOW, SPIRITUAL VALUES? OR MATTER OVER MIND

The reader may have noticed that Mr. Price is relying, for the impact of his arguments, on a "humanitarian" disposition in his listeners toward the provision of food, clothing, and shelter for the two-thirds of mankind who have never had enough of them— and away from the ancient abuses of early industrialism which furnished Mr. Hayes with most of his ammunition. (Mr. Price also seemed to take for granted the reaffirmation of the American missionary spirit which reveals itself in Point Four or the Marshall Plan, which assumes that it is manifestly our twentieth-century mission to civilize the "backward" peoples of the planet materially instead of spiritually, and which formed the basis for Friday evening's panel discussion—see Chapter 4.) In this sense both speakers were in debt to the tradition of "liberal intellectualism" which they professed to disparage but which had nonetheless drawn narrow limits around their unspoken terms of reference.

The growth of that tradition, for example, might have had a

large part in providing Mr. Hayes and Mr. Price with an audience that could receive them as equals and would not expect each merely to call the other names. Mr. Hayes did not even lock horns with Mr. Price's idol, "democratic capitalism," but injected only the most moderate reminder that "the economic system which grew along with industry, which we and the textbooks used to call capitalism and which we now sheepishly refer to as free enterprise, had a habit of slowing down or coming to a halt during our one hundred years." If it would only work reliably, Mr. Hayes seemed to be saying, he would be for it; and he strongly emphasized the resistance of American workingmen—as a result of their successful efforts to organize and the productivity of the industries they participate in—to the appeal of other systems, especially "the Kremlin's promise of a new deal on earth. . . ." Mr. Hayes, in brief, was also willing to abandon the dream of pastoral contentment and to take as a starting point for further deliberation in this Conference the proposition that industrialism is the rock on which a civilization worthy of labor's allegiance might be founded.

MR. HAYES: Freedom and dignity and a good life are not confined to a homestead on the land. They are possible in an industrial civilization, and moreover they are possible for all the people who contribute constructive effort to industrial enterprise. . . . Under the American form of government the capitalistic, profit-making system and its industries can be made to take cognizance of the human equation in labor relations and with respect to human welfare. We have had enough experience during the past hundred years with such matters, in my opinion, to believe that this is true. . . . Therefore we struggle for equality of status, for economic security. And in the struggle we have improved the whole United States.

We have shifted the levels of discourse of both management and labor, in other words, until now both are able to move within the "liberal" vocabulary with such familiarity that they can attack intellectualism on its own terms. Industrial society has brought into existence a set of institutions which presuppose that men in Mr. Hayes' and Mr. Price's shoes can agree on ultimate ends and will walk rapidly (how fast is too fast?) in the direction of agreement on the means to reach them. They differ only where they believe it healthy to differ, within a rigidly formalized structure or over issues of largely historical interest, and even in disagreement they employ a common language of political manipulation in the presence of the public—especially the intellectual public, which accepts the same clichés and eagerly identifies itself with the "profound spiritual crisis" which Mr. Price allowed that we share "with all of Western man."

Though he had challenged an academic stereotype of mass production, Mr. Price did not inveigh against the allied article of faith which holds that far too often—in Mr. David's words— "we stress the productive aspect of our industrial civilization and ignore the fact that people have to live in it too." Mr. Price had shown himself conscious of how little stress the "productive aspect" often receives in contrast to the continual emphasis on the absence of "spiritual values." In this instance he was willing to allow his academic hearers to bear the burden, for he indicated in another context how aware he was that our "profound spiritual crisis" was a function of increased communication and more leisurely attention. "Our ancestors," he said, "would never have learned of international calamity in time to be worried about it and would have been too tired from their toil if they had heard. Our cares and our worries now are global." In any event, it was clear that when faced with how difficult it is "to distinguish between the material and the spiritual," Mr. Price would prefer to see us aim for "a spiritual gain built on a material base." His endorsement of technology was categorical. "Many of you know," he said, "that the machine, which created the problem in the first place, is the answer to the problem. Peter F. Drucker has correctly described the unskilled worker as an engineering imperfection. . . . Those of you who went through this great glass works today saw that the common laborer has almost completely given way to trained specialists who supervise the work of the machines and to employees who design, set up, service, and repair the machines."

It was possible, one might add, that a large number of "human values," and many of them improvements on their predecessors, had already been embedded in the texture of the civilized industrialism still growing in the Western world. Perhaps the difficulty in rationalizing this location of emphasis lay in artificial antitheses, or in the static words we use, or in the fact that academic disciplines are still too blunt an instrument to disentangle the delicate filaments of live experience. This query was left with the Conference as its first session closed. "I don't think we fit into any particular category," said Mr. David, speaking of modern industrial civilization. "Isn't there something new; isn't there something basic which perhaps we are trying to develop?"

2

Work and Human Values in Industrial Civilization

ROUNDTABLE A

John A. Kouwenhoven, rapporteur

Perhaps it should be said at the start that the rapporteur believes that some of the wisest things his colleagues said, and some of the most illuminating conflicts between them were not recorded in the stenotype transcript of the roundtable's deliberations—for the simple reason that some of the most fruitful "conferring" was done elsewhere than at the roundtable. In a sense this is regrettable, since there is no record of the ideas and attitudes expressed in informal conversation. But in another sense it is a testimonial to the wisdom of those who set up the Conference. If the participants preferred to say their say over coffee, or cocktails, or dinner, or to carry on impromptu discussions in the halls of the splendid new Glass Center, in the homes of hospitable Corning citizens, or in the Disc Room at the hotel, this was precisely what the sponsors of the Conference had foreseen. The officials of the ACLS and of the Corning Glass Works had made generous allowance for the fact that ideas, like other commodities, can sometimes be exchanged more readily through the black (or gray) market than through the more respectable channels of trade.

Our "above the counter" business began when our chairman, Douglas McGregor, president of Antioch College and specialist in industrial relations, called the meeting to order and asked the members of the roundtable to suggest ways of coming to grips with the problems assigned to us: namely, (1) to isolate the major current problems in our field, (2) to evaluate what has already been accomplished toward solving them, and (3) to indicate where we ought to go from here.

A number of suggestions were made, and it may be well to record here not only the subjects raised for discussion but also, in somewhat abbreviated form, the words in which they were proposed. Only by liberal quotation from the actual transcript of the discussion can the rapporteur avoid giving the impression that we dealt abstractly with abstract problems—which certainly was not the way we dealt with them, even when the problems were abstract. It may be true that the ideal way to solve the problems of "work in an industrial civilization" would be to deal with them in the light of pure, impersonal reason. But if our roundtable's experience proved anything, it proved that they cannot be dealt with in quite that way.

THEME AND VARIATIONS: IS DIRTY WORK AT THE CROSSROADS?

The first suggestion came from A. J. Hayes, president of the International Association of Machinists, who thought that we should begin by considering that portion of our problem which, in his view, actually creates the greatest trouble.

MR. HAYES: I think our greatest problem lies with those who have the most unimportant tasks in industry, those people on production lines, the ditchdiggers, those who perform very simple operations. Those are the people who feel rather unimportant in so far as the whole scheme of things is concerned. . . . They are told that their jobs do not require much skill, that anybody can be taught to do their work in a few hours. Those are the people, it seems to me, that develop complexes. They develop complexes because they are not convinced that they are making a worth-while contribution to society. To cover up these complexes, they develop certain habits that they pass on to others whom they influence.

Though there is an over-all problem of which this is only a part, it appears to me that, in so far as the attitude of workers is concerned, the greatest problem lies with those who perform the least important operations in a plant or wherever they may be working. . . .

Yale Brozen, professor of economics at Northwestern University, proposed that we begin from a somewhat broader point of view. Our roundtable, he observed, was concerned with "work and human values," which implied not only the problem of satisfaction in work but also, and more implicitly, the problem of how the organization of work in industrial society affects our values. He called attention, for example, to Gandhi's attacks upon factory organization and upon those forces which tend to treat man as a machine to be used as a mere element in the productive system.

At this point, appropriately enough, the stenotyping machine broke down and the discussion came momentarily to a standstill. During the interval there were a number of jokes about the machine's domination of mankind, but when the necessary repairs had been made, Mr. Brozen continued.

MR. BROZEN: In order to preserve such values as the mastery of one's own circumstances and the family basis of social structure, the Province of Madras in India has taken Gandhi's views and enacted them into legislation designed to prevent the further factory production of textiles and to maintain and promote cottage-industry production. By so doing they hope to preserve a set of values inherent in the cottage-industry method, values which would vanish, they fear, if people were to have to live in the mill organization. . . . Similarly, in this country, Jefferson suggested that what we needed, if we wanted to preserve the values inherent in democracy, was a kind of society with a different sort of work organization than that characteristic of the factory.

We might ask, then, whether the factory is the essential mode of work organization for modern industry or whether we cannot work out systems of organization which would preserve more of the elements of cottage industry and preserve, therefore, a better basis for the kinds of values that are necessary if the people are to remain democratic, the kind of values that we think of as being inherent in small-town life and family farming.

Still another approach was suggested by Theodore C. Blegen, historian and dean of the Graduate School of the University of Minnesota. He proposed that we begin by deciding what we meant by "work."

MR. BLEGEN: It is quite obvious that work is not just the immediate job that a man is doing—the technical job. I think of work as involving a certain sense of dignity or importance that the workman carries into his whole life as a human being. It is a sense of identification with something worth-while. You are not through with work when you leave your immediate job and go home. You carry it out into the community. . . .

Sir George E. Schuster, bringing to the Conference his experience in British industry (he is director of the Westminster Bank, and a member of the Government Committee on Industrial Productivity), proposed at this point that we adopt Mr. Hayes' suggestion as a way of limiting the discussion.

SIR GEORGE SCHUSTER: It seems to me Mr. Hayes has put his finger on what is the crucial problem today. Has the modern industrial production system created a state of affairs in which the great bulk of the people cannot find any satisfaction in their work? Is that really a fact? I think we might discuss that. If it is a fact, how are you going to change that very undesirable state of affairs? That leads us on to what might be a focal point of our discussion. Can, you counteract that unfortunate state of affairs by some method of participation? . . . If we accept that as something worth discussing, then I suggest that we could fruitfully spend our time in discussing the technique, the method, the logistics of participation. . . .

George C. Homans, associate professor of sociology at Harvard University, emphasized that two different—though related— kinds of problem were involved: the problem of the worker's immediate satisfaction in his job and the problem of relationships between groups of people within an organization.

MR. HOMANS: In some cases it is not so much a problem of the immediate satisfaction in one's job as it is a problem of how to relate the particular group of persons to other persons in an organization.

I would like to emphasize that we have two kinds of problems, the problem of job satisfaction and the problem of adequate social organization in industry. I think they are related, but I think they are two different kinds of things.

Elliott Jaques, of the Tavistock Institute in London, agreed with Mr. Homans and pointed out that there are two aspects of group organization which are especially important in considering human values inside industry, as well as in the other aspects of community life.

MR. JAQUES: First, there are problems of authority in industrial organizations. . . . I refer to authority at any level, not just the relationship between the president and his divisional heads. There are so many social factors involved—relationships between people—and these might bear scrutiny. What are the experiences that people have, particularly in large-scale organizations of perhaps over a thousand people? There is the question of giving orders and instructions, of running an organization effectively; and questions of methods of participation also come in.

At this stage the roundtable's rapporteur, John A. Kouwenhoven, professor of English at Barnard College and contributing editor of Harper's Magazine, suggested that if we wanted to get the diversification of outlook suggested in Mr. Jaques' remarks, and yet still concentrate on specific problems, as Mr. Hayes and Sir George Schuster proposed, we could not limit our view solely to the assembly line.

MR. KOUWENHOVEN: We must remember the man, for instance, who works for a large advertising company, who frequently, in my experience, has the symptoms you referred to, Mr. Hayes: the feeling that the job he is doing is essentially not important. There are other people in other areas who feel that way. All I am suggesting is that we bear in mind that a lot of people who work in our civilization don't think their work is significant in any respectable—or socially approved—value system. . . . These problems aren't confined to one area. The foreman and the fiddle player can come up with as many complexes as the assembly line worker, and at least as juicy ones.

MR. HAYES: I think that all of these things run through the entire problem that we have. However, compatibility on a group production line certainly is not the answer to the major problem, in my opinion. . . . People can get along with one another and still be working on jobs that they feel are very unimportant. Those jobs affect them mentally, and this affects their lives after they leave the work jobs. That is what I assume we are trying to struggle with here: human satisfaction in work. . . .

MR. HOMANS: I really wasn't exactly referring to compatibility of the group on the job. I was thinking of what I call the structural problem. Take the foreman, for instance. . . . Whether or not he likes the job, the structure of the organization sometimes puts him in certain relationships to other people which make it difficult for him to handle the situation. The question I was raising is: how do we structure our organization so that these problems in personal relationship can be handled? . . .

CHAIRMAN MCGREGOR: I wonder if we haven't suggested to ourselves a line of development for our discussion. We might begin by focusing on that group of jobs which might broadly be thought of as the semiskilled, unskilled group, including not only the operator's job in the factory but the comparable jobs in all types of organization. Beginning there, we might ask ourselves questions about the convictions that have already been expressed around the table—what you might call the basic assumptions that we have about that kind of work. Is work at that level unsatisfying? What are the kinds of dissatisfaction that exist there? I think that we tend to be a little naïve in looking at those jobs. Because we wouldn't like to do them, we assume immediately that they must be troublesome and unhandy for the people who are doing them.

At any rate, what are the satisfactions of work? What are the impacts on values for that group of people? We will inevitably get to the various other things suggested here, to the broader values and relationships, to the problem of organization and structure. . . .

LAWRENCE A. APPLEY (president, American Management Association): How specific are we when we use the term "Industrial Civilization"? If "the problems of industrial civilization" means problems that have been introduced by modern machines, then that definitely limits us in the nature of the problem. While I acknowledge the problem of the menial task in the common laborer's job, that was not created by industrial civilization; that has existed ever since the beginning of man. If you are speaking specifically of the problems created by a modern industrial civilization, the two problems which come to my mind are: the problem of the machines in relation to the man and the problem of business organization in relation to the man. The man who is wielding the pick and shovel, digging a ditch, has been doing that for many, many centuries; it didn't start with industrial civilization. But the problem has been increased due to the fact that he never sees or hears from the guy who planned the ditch and no one can come up and thank him for his part in the building, say, of a skyscraper.

EVERETT C. HUGHES (professor of sociology, University of Chicago): I wonder if the questions are, after all, so separated. What we mean by an uninteresting or low-skilled job is a relative matter. I assume that it means the job that is the least interesting in a particular organization and is considered so by the one who does it or by other people. Certainly there are things which in history have been defined at times as dirty work, or uninteresting work, which, in other settings, become more interesting. In hospitals nowadays the nurses are making a great fuss about sweeping floors. They didn't use to make a fuss about sweeping floors. They used to do it as an initiation rite in becoming nurses, expecting to become the right-hand man of the doctor and save the doctor from mistakes. In other words, they had a role definition, not a task definition, of their job. Now they are having trouble because they are delegating the sweeping to nurses' aides, who have no hope of becoming nurses. These nurses' aides find this work uninteresting, and they don't do it with as much vigor as the people who had at least a prospect of becoming something important.

So it would seem to me that as we get into this question of uninteresting work, we are inevitably getting into the question of organization and what kind of futures and prospects people have before them. The job ceases to be a thing by itself. It becomes part of the organization and part of a man's view of himself and what he is worth. I think of the case of the surgeon, who used to be a pretty low fellow. There wasn't anybody who did such messy work as the surgeon. But surgery has risen from low to high prestige. Is any work monotonous or uninteresting in itself? Or does that depend upon the organization and the attitude of the people in general? I don't know the answer to that.

MR. HAYES: I think that the effect of plant organization, and of the general treatment of the people who do the work, is important; and I think that is what we are struggling with now. Certainly, there are people who are always going to be sand hogs and ditchdiggers, regardless of what we may do about them, and we can't compare such jobs to those of skilled mechanics or artisans. However, it seems to me that what we are trying to do is decide how we can give a feeling of importance to people who help do that work today, and in the future, how we can give them a feeling of dignity. . . . We in organized labor . . . take the position that these people must be given a feeling that their job is important, that it is one of the cogs in the wheel, and that they really are important. . . . It is the psychological effect of the organization of the plant itself and the treatment that these people receive, the things that they are told by their supervisors, the respect in which they are held by management, that are important. . . .

MR. BLEGEN: Do we not come back to this basic question of what work is? I was much impressed by two phrases I have just heard, one "a role definition of a job," and the other "a task definition." It seems to me that much of what you say, Mr. Hayes, centers about the concept of the job as a role rather than a specific task, as Mr. Hughes was saying.

FRITZ J. ROETHLISBERGER (Wallace B. Donham professor of human relations, Harvard University Graduate School of Business Administration): It seems to me that all these topics are related. I can hardly imagine that one of them can be discussed without the others. I don't know how you can discuss the satisfactions and dissatisfactions of work without bringing in participation, authority, the machine and its bigness, work and how we define work. So why don't we begin with just one? By just starting with satisfaction and dissatisfaction, you are going to become involved immediately in all these other problems.

THE A, B, C'S OF WORK

By this time most of the major and minor themes that were to be developed by the roundtable had been stated or implied. From then on we kept coming back to a few basic and closely related questions:

(1) Assuming that work in industrial civilization breeds more dissatisfactions than it should (and, despite a few tentative objections, a majority of the roundtable took this for granted), what are the principal causes of dissatisfaction?

(2) What values, social and individual, determine the satisfactions and dissatisfactions of work?

(3) Can the dissatisfactions be reduced or eliminated by creating a sense of participation?

(4) Can participation best be achieved by changes in management's attitudes toward the worker or by changes in the patterns of work organization?

Of all these questions it was the last that received the most persistent attention—especially the patterns of work organization. We eased into it almost at once, and we came back to it frequently in the course of our three roundtable sessions. It first arose in this way:

At one point, we had apparently agreed that the problems of work have to be met head-on, and cannot simply be evaded by providing increased satisfactions in leisure-time activities. As Lou R. Crandall, president of the George A. Fuller Company, put it, no man's work should be mere drudgery.

MR. CRANDALL: Whether we are thinking of a man in a large advertising agency, or in engineering design, or at work on a menial job, the problem is the same and the cure is the same. We have to make the work interesting. . . . You have to stimulate interest or you are not going to get the final product.

But how do you make a job interesting?

Joseph R. Strayer, chairman of the Princeton University Department of History, thought it was possible only if the worker were convinced "that the end product is going to be important." If the end product does not justlfy the means, people will lose interest even in a job which requires a certain amount of skill. This assumption was promptly challenged by Mr. Hughes.

MR. HUGHES: I know that it is one of the articles of faith of our civilization that man must "believe in" the product of his labor, but it might be true that there are kinds of work which cynics can do. I like my work and I think that we all of us here are happy in the sense that Chesterton spoke of: "Happy is the man whose work is his hobby." I certainly would find it intolerable if my work were an unmitigated bore all day. But maybe a man can do his work with a slightly cynical attitude. I have known slightly sardonic characters in industry. Maybe we are naïve in assuming that everybody's work can be interesting.

MARTIN JOOS (professor of German, University of Wisconsin): Mr. Chairman, perhaps I should speak at this point. I worked some years ago with the Western Electric Company making telephone equipment, making parts and assembling parts. It struck me as I watched it years ago that there was dissatisfaction in that factory. In all too many cases, the product of one man's job went from him to a stockroom from which it was drawn, possibly a month or year later, to be assembled further. The people who were working on that kind of job didn't have quite as happy faces as the people who, having done their job, passed the product on to men at a neighboring bench to be worked on further. You have a role identification of the job, instead of a task identification, when you know that the man who is going to work on that thing next is depending on you to do your work.

CHAIRMAN McGREGOR (to Mr. Worthy): Jim, do some of the things you are doing at Sears tie up with what we are talking about here?

JAMES WORTHY (Personnel Department, Sears, Roebuck and Company): It ties up in several ways. I am thinking about Mr. Appley's comment on the importance of the machine in this picture. It seems to me that it is not just the introduction of machinery into productive processes which creates this problem. More particularly, the problem is created by the way work processes are organized around the machine. The whole question of work organization—the relationship of the worker to his job, to his fellow workers, and to supervision—is the real problem. Introduction of machinery, of course, has made necessary a great many changes in work organization, but I think the work organization is the basic problem.

At the chairman's suggestion, Mr. Worthy then described, with the aid of some blackboard charts, two alternative methods of organizing the processes of production. Taking as his example a shop where the operation involved three different processes, Mr. Worthy proceeded to give a descriptive analysis which can be paraphrased somewhat as follows:

Suppose we call the three processes "A," "B," and "C." Process "A" might be punch press; process "B" might be another type of machine; process "C" might be assembly. Suppose, further, that this particular shop has enough volume so that three units each of "A," "B," and "C" are necessary.

One way to organize the shop would be to group together the three "A" processes, the three "B" processes, and the three "C" processes, with some kind of supervision over each group and with general supervision on a still higher level.

On the other hand, this work could be organized in an ABC, ABC, ABC pattern, with supervisors in charge of each group, responsible directly to a single executive.

These two patterns of work organization, Mr. Worthy observed, will produce quite different results so far as training people on the job is concerned. With the ABC method, the individual supervisor has control over all three of the processes involved in turning out the complete product. This is not true of the AAA pattern, where each supervisor is concerned with only a single process. The supervisors in the ABC pattern have a high degree of responsibility, and this in turn affects the attitudes of all the people working in the group. Furthermore, the individuals in the group have an opportunity to see much more of the total process that is involved in production and thus have a greater sense of the significance of their work than do those working in the AAA pattern, where related processes are grouped together, abstracted from the total business of producing the particular product or service, and set up as independent departments.

If people were machines, if we didn't have to worry about their finding significance in their work, it would make less difference how we organized work, said Mr. Worthy. But they are not machines, and it is often exceedingly difficult for them to find significance in their work if, like machines, they are set to perform isolated tasks, without context and therefore without significance.

Finally, Mr. Worthy noted that the size of an organizational unit has a great deal to do with how people feel toward their jobs and toward management. The ABC type of organization will consist of three small units, each with a high degree of integrity. The AAA type of organization, on the other hand, necessarily embraces the whole shop, which makes it much more difficult to carry on the work of the organization on the basis of spontaneous relationships between the people involved.

THE OLD REFRAIN

The stenotype record of the discussion that followed Mr. Worthy's remarks suggests that some misunderstandings might have been avoided if we had at once related his AAA and ABC patterns to what William F. Whyte, professor of industrial and labor relations at Cornell, had said in his background paper about "Tall vs. Flat Organization" (see Part II, p. 232). For Mr. Whyte's paper makes it clear that what is involved in the discussion of these types of organization is not simply an argument over principles of administration but—in an important and practical sense—the question of how to provide those "satisfactions" in work which we had been discussing.

Mr. Whyte observes, for example, that in tall organizations (which would include those developed in Mr. Worthy's AAA pattern) people work under close supervision and therefore become preoccupied about complying with directives and about jockeying for position within the political structure of the organization. In that situation it is, as Mr. Whyte says, extremely difficult to develop the kinds of management attitudes and methods that increase the sense of participation of the workers—or of anybody else in the organization, for that matter.

In the roundtable discussion, however, there seemed to be a feeling that by discussing organization we had got away from the problems of job satisfaction and participation, and for a while we wandered all over the lot in an effort to find home base again.

In the process, happily, several other aspects of the problem were suggested. Harold Boeschenstein, president of Owens-Corning Fiberglas Corporation, called attention to the necessity for having people in management—all the way down the line—who are trained to "understand the importance of the human equation."

MR. BOESCHENSTEIN: Whether he be an industrial engineer or a foreman, he has to understand that part of his problem is getting the best out of his people. . . . You have to have properly trained people who understand that that is one of the most important things, if not *the* most important, if you want to continue to get results.

MR. WHYTE: I won't deny the importance of properly trained people, but I think sometimes we try to solve this problem through putting too high requirements upon the administrative and "human relations" skills. Without the proper organizational setup, you require really remarkable people to make it work to satisfaction. The problem is to develop the organization in such a way that, with a reasonable degree of intelligence and skill, people can find the satisfactions we have been talking about.

MR. BOESCHENSTEIN: I am not disagreeing with Jim Worthy at all. I agree with him. I say that training is part of the answer to the problem.

MR. WORTHY: Absolutely. But there is a further point. The way in which the plant is organized will profoundly influence the kind of people who come up in that organization and achieve positions of importance. You will find a somewhat different kind of person coming to the top in the ABC type of organization than you do in the AAA type of organization. In our own company, for instance, we find that those units which are organized on the ABC pattern produce a far higher output of promotable manpower than do the others. . . .

So we were back to organization again. But the exchange between Messrs. Boeschenstein, Whyte, and Worthy reminded us that there are two theories of how to get good men in all levels of management. One emphasizes the value of providing the kind of organizational pattern that permits or encourages them to develop; the other emphasizes the need for training them in approved techniques of dealing with others. The latter came up for discussion again at a later session, but meanwhile Temple Burling, psychiatrist from the School of Industrial and Labor Relations at Cornell, made the cautionary observation that the policy of doing to others as we would be done by often creates unexpected problems elsewhere in an organization. By increasing the status or the importance of one undesirable job, we in effect diminish the relative status of another.

MR. BURLING: Somebody has to be low man on the totem pole. I saw this problem in a mental hospital where some of the psychiatric staff thought it would be good to raise the morale of the help by giving them psychiatric training. The nurses sabotaged the plan, however, because they thought their relative status would be lowered.

For a little while the discussion moved off on a new tack. Langbourne M. Williams, Jr., president of the Freeport Sulphur Company, reminded the group that our roundtable was supposed to assess the "outstanding successes" as well as the outstanding failures of industrial society with respect to the human satisfactions in work.

MR. WILLIAMS: Dr. Burling, I think, made the very good point that always at some stage there has to be the low man on the totem pole. We must accept the fact that there will always be at some stage that low man. We are doing an enormous number of things to make that man as satisfied as he can be under the circumstances, but I think it is worth noting that dissatisfaction is a positive good for human progress. . . . It's the man who is anxious and eager to improve the lot with which he is dissatisfied who accounts for a great deal of the progress that has taken place throughout the world and in this country.

With respect to the human satisfactions, I wonder if it isn't worth raising the question of what we have done to permit the dissatisfied man to change his role in life. I have the feeling that in this country, more than any other place, it is easy for the dissatisfied man to change his relative position on the totem pole. I wonder if that is worth throwing into the discussion when we are assessing the outstanding failures and successes; because if we concentrate wholly, as we have tended to do, on dissatisfactions, we miss some of the total picture. You will always have dissatisfactions. We must recognize that.

There were several comments on this point by Mr. Joos, Mr. McGregor, Mr. Whyte, Mr. Blegen, and Mr. Jaques. But there seemed to be general agreement that there was a flexibility in our industrial system which frequently makes it possible for those who are dissatisfied to advance. As Mr. Hayes pointed out, however,

"There are people who will always be common laborers . . . who will always do the menial tasks"; and it was their problems which led the group to return, over and over again, to the discussion of ways and means of creating what Sir George Schuster called "the proper system of participation—in which everyone has the chance of understanding why the business is run as it is, and everyone feels that he has some chance of using his own know-how in determining how his own job should be done." And that, in turn, brought us back to the A, B, C's of organization.

CHALLENGE AND RESPONSIBILITY

Thus far, in an effort to give some of the flavor of the round-table discussion, the rapporteur has relied heavily upon direct transcripts from the stenotype record. But that record runs to a total of almost two hundred typewritten pages; and it will be necessary, therefore, to summarize briefly most of the remainder of the discussion.

The Friday afternoon session began with a point which Mr. Appley had introduced just before the morning session ended: namely, the change which has taken place in the pressures upon management, and in the criteria by which management is judged, during the past thirty years. During the years when we had to build up physical plant (railroads, telephone and telegraph systems, skyscrapers, etc.), the great managers were the producers and builders. Now that we have obtained at least the minimum of our physical needs, and have more time to live, we are less interested in the mere necessities of life and more interested in the satisfactions we can get out of being alive. Management, therefore, tends to be judged increasingly upon its competence in providing satisfaction in work and in handling human relations.

The responsibility of good management, in this new situation, was summed up by Sir George Schuster as the necessity to create an organization which is "human, adaptive, and elastic, so that it opens up to each individual the maximum opportunity for self-realization according to his own ideas and ideals."

SIR GEORGE SCHUSTER: It is no use to try to write a code of ten or twenty commandments, which every industrial manager ought to carry out. What we have to do is create a living, adaptive organism which will be ready to meet the constantly changing problems of our society as they arise. . . .

The question was, however, what steps management should take to build such an organization.

Several suggestions were made. Mr. Williams, for example, called attention to the value of geographical decentralization, whereby even large companies can spread out their activities in small plants, located in small communities where the workers can remain at least part-time farmers and gardeners. Sir George Schuster agreed that such decentralization is a good thing where it is possible but pointed out that it is not a practical solution in highly industrialized centers. And Mr. Joos noted that, when it has been tried in such cities as Detroit where the tool and die workers were moved out to the country, it simply skimmed the cream off the labor force and left the unskilled workers behind in a worse mess than they were in before. With those reservations, however, it was agreed that geographical decentralization—as demonstrated by the DuPont company and others—could be an effective step toward a more agreeable and adaptive industrial pattern.

Mr. Appley then made two suggestions: first, that top management should clarify its own philosophy of management and make certain that everyone in the organization, down to the foreman and supervisors, really understands that philosophy; second, that management should study what each worker is doing, what he can do, and what help he needs to do better, and then provide that help in so far as management can provide it. He called attention to the fact that only about 16 per cent of the companies in this country make use of the available programs and procedures of employee training, orientation training, presupervisory training, training for promotion, and so on, though such training is designed to help people get the satisfactions that come from doing a job well. Some of the participants questioned whether these training programs would do much good unless the company's organizational pattern was such as to encourage genuine participation, but it was generally agreed that training programs and procedures could well be more extensively used than they are.

There was some discussion of the degree to which management, as such, is responsible for creating satisfactions in work. Mr. Brozen, for example, warned against the danger of loading management with "the responsibility for being benevolent" and mentioned the possibility that the worker "may not want to realize his maximum capacities in his job. Maybe all he wants out of the job is pay." Gwilym A. Price, president of the Westinghouse Electric Corporation, suggested that labor unions should share the responsibility, since some of them have discouraged interest in work by enforcing rules that "tend to create mediocrity, with everybody doing jobs on the same level."

MR. PRICE: I am not objecting to seniority. I think there should be such rights; but I think that management should be able to reach in and pick out a good person for promotion. . . . Somehow the ladder of opportunity must be kept open, and I think there is a great area here for union-management cooperation. If we don't keep the ladder open, we are going to have a class of managers made up altogether of the young engineers who come out of our technical schools, and we will lose something that is very valuable.

Over and over again the question of promotion came up, both as a sign of health in the recruiting of management and as an element in the problem of job satisfaction. Dr. Burling, for example, noted that it is all very well to say that a man should be enabled to do the best he can, so that he can be promoted, but "only one man in a group can do the *best* job. Many men are doomed never to be promoted, and it is important that they be able to find satisfaction in other terms than climbing the ladder."

To this Mr. Worthy replied that he had found, in surveys of employee attitudes, that in units where no one has been promoted for a long time dissatisfaction is general. But in other departments, where there have been promotions, there is usually little dissatisfaction. From this he concluded that not everyone wants to be promoted, though almost everyone wants to feel that promotion is a possibility.

THE CHICKEN OR THE EGG?—A DIALOGUE

Following the afternoon recess, Mr. Worthy was again asked to describe some of the comparative studies he had made between enterprises organized in the "flat" and "tall" patterns. When he had finished and had answered a number of questions from various members of the group, the chairman raised the following question:

CHAIRMAN McGREGOR: There is a point that interests me very much in connection with this. You pointed out a series of correlations between organizational structure and managements' philosophy of dealing with people. The implication that one tends to draw, I think, is that if you set up an organization in a certain way you impose a certain philosophy upon everyone in it. I wonder if the opposite isn't more likely the fact, that given a certain philosophy of how to deal with people, the structure results, so to speak.

MR. WORTHY: Precisely.

CHAIRMAN McGREGOR: So it isn't the structure that determines the philosophy; it's the philosophy that determines the structure.

MR. WORTHY: Yes. If you conceive of your job as a manager as that of doing the thinking, assisted by a staff that you gather around you, making the decisions, issuing orders to people that they must carry out; if you think of your job in that way, you'll tend to set up the AAA (tall) type of organization. If you think of your job more in terms of the over-all task to be accomplished, and see yourself accomplishing that task by surrounding yourself with capable people and then relying on their initiative, judgment, and abilities to cooperate with you to get a job done, then you tend to set up the ABC (flat) type of organization. . . .

MR. BOESCHENSTEIN: Who handles your personnel situation in a store, the hiring and handling of people?

MR. WORTHY: That's usually the assistant manager. He's likely to be spread pretty thin because he has a lot of different functions he's responsible for, of which personnel is only one.

MR. JOOS: So, to a large extent, he has to take the word of the department managers on personnel problems.

MR. WORTHY: Well, remember this is a fairly small unit, with only one hundred twenty-five or one hundred fifty people in it. In that size of operation, the manager and the assistant manager will know the whole organization pretty thoroughly. You don't need any system of merit ratings and periodic reviews and all of that stuff to know who's doing a good job and who isn't. The evaluation of people is something that happens pretty much automatically.

MR. KOUWENHOVEN: Mr. Chairman, aren't we back then to something that we touched on once before, that one of the peculiar problems of an industrial civilization is largeness? In order to cope with that, one of the most efficient devices is apparently the type of decentralization Mr. Worthy has described. There is further evidence of this in the history of some of our biggest companies—the shift from the kind of executive who made Standard Oil, for example, into a great corporation, to the kind of executive who now operates it. Standard Oil of New Jersey at present is run on a decentralized pattern, much like the one Mr. Worthy has just described, with Eugene Holman sitting at the top of the pile, like your store manager, having men under him who are almost absolutely responsible for the part of the business which they deal with.

MR. WORTHY: I might say there are two kinds of decentralization: there is geographical unit decentralization, but there is also decentralization within the unit itself.

MR. KOUWENHOVEN: Yes; I'm talking about your kind.

CHAIRMAN MCGREGOR: I think the point is that they have to be differentiated. Mr. Williams was pointing to a kind of decentralization which didn't necessarily involve this kind at all. This is another concept.

MR. KOUWENHOVEN: Both of them are obviously products of a specifically industrial necessity.

MR. WORTHY: There's no necessity about this.

MR. KOUWENHOVEN: I think there is.

CHAIRMAN MCGREGOR: Well, I can point to a comparable organization—size and so on—that hasn't decentralized in this sense at all. It's done the opposite.

Mr. Kouwenhoven: Why, then, does Mr. Worthy prefer this one? Is it, as you said earlier, that the ABC organization tends to be more profitable because it can weather a depression or slight recession of business more easily?

Mr. Worthy: No, I don't think it's quite that rational and clear-cut. Basically, I think it's the way the president of a company sets up the over-all organization, the way he works with it. Whatever type of organization he sets up, he will tend to surround himself with people, in all key spots, who can function in that type of setup. And people coming up through the organization will likewise tend to be the same kind of person and to run their own units pretty much along the same kind of lines the organization as a whole is being run on.

Mr. Kouwenhoven: If it is just a matter of personality, if there is no inherent advantage in the pattern, then it isn't of any value to any-one else.

Mr. Worthy: I think there's something else. . . . If I thought the problem were basically a personality problem, I would be pessimistic about the future. I think to a certain extent it *is* a personality problem, that certain types of people will tend to set up their organizations in certain kinds of ways. But I think that a lot of people who might, if left to their own devices, set up a more decentralized, a more "per-missive" kind of organization, don't do so because of the patterns of thinking that have been encouraged by the scientific management movement. I think that "scientific management" has moved in a direc-tion which makes effective decentralization within an organization, within a unit, practically impossible.

SCHOOLS AND AUTHORITY

Unfortunately the roundtable did not get on to the question of why a permissive type of organization is "proper." If we had done so, we might have been face to face with the problem of values, which we kept sidestepping. At all events, it was clear that we were skirting the edge of a fundamental problem, namely, the relation between the form that industrial processes assume and the social context in which they operate. These are deep waters, and some of us found ourselves beyond our depth when Mr. Joos launched into an account of the psychological experiments which

Alex Bavelis of the Massachusetts Institute of Technology has undertaken in this area. But the point Mr. Joos was making was that the Bavelis experiments suggest that the mere "pattern of communication" may make the man who occupies a certain position in that pattern into a dictator, though the same man, in a different position or in a different pattern, would not be one. Also, some patterns of communication seem to be better than others for solving problems and maintaining morale. The experiments have admittedly not yet produced conclusions which can be applied outside the laboratory, but Mr. Joos' account of them did serve to direct our attention to the relationships between industry's own internal problems and those of society at large.

Sir George Schuster, for example, pointed out that the round-table had given relatively little attention to the outside influences that affect people's attitudes toward work and toward the possibilities of satisfaction in work. There were three such influences which, he felt, deserved special consideration: (1) compulsory national service; (2) the different types of union organizations; and (3) the kind of education we give young people before they enter industry.

Although it was agreed that all these "outside influences" upon the problem of work are important, education was the only one that the roundtable had time to consider at all. Mr. Hughes felt that the schools are no longer providing an apprenticeship for work-situations, as they once did.

MR. HUGHES: We get almost universal agreement in industry that no matter what people learn in school, they've got to learn something new when they get to industry. . . . Yesterday I asked a man out here in the Corning company's north plant, where they're making glass tubing, what they had to teach a young engineer when he came down there to help make glass, and this man said that they had to teach him everything. It probably isn't true, but they certainly have to teach him some things. . . .

I thing anybody who will talk honestly and with knowledge about the American schools at this moment will say that most—perhaps half, probably more—of our youngsters, from the age of about thirteen or fourteen up until the time they quit school, are getting an excellent lesson in restriction of effort; an excellent lesson in doing nothing. And I have an idea that this may have a rather profound effect on their attitude toward work. There's a restriction of production. The teachers don't really expect them to do any work, and they don't expect to do anything. The whole thing is a frightful sag.

Not everyone shared Mr. Hughes's bleak view of the school system, but there was some speculation as to the connection between the way schools are organized and their success, or lack of success. Mr. Jaques spoke, for instance, of a school he had recently visited, in which morale was high, and in which the pattern of organization, the relationship between principal and teachers, resembled the ABC pattern which Mr. Worthy had described.

MR. JAQUES: I think there's something very important here. If you look at the kinds of things that are happening in the schools and the kinds of things that are happening in industry, I think it becomes quite clear that what we're talking about is one of the basic problems of Western society: how to achieve an adequate or satisfactory interaction between problems of authority, on the one hand, and of participation, on the other. That problem has been dealt with for hundreds of years in the field of political science and government. But I think it is exceedingly striking that the relationship between legislative action, or policy making, and executive action—the carrying of authority and responsibility in an effective way—is now being dealt with in the field of industrial organization, school organization, and so on. In other words, it's coming into the subsystems, the smaller systems in our society, and developing there along much the same lines as it did in political science and government over a long period of time.

Mr. McGregor made a similar point, at a later stage in the discussion, when he called attention to the fact that in our culture as a whole—in schools, colleges, and in social relationships generally—we are focusing more and more attention on the nonmaterial values of living.

CHAIRMAN McGREGOR: We people in management are getting the problem dumped in our laps, so to speak, because external events—

things that are happening in our culture as a whole—are changing people's ideas about what is valuable, what is important.

It does, in fact, seem to be true that in all the areas of contemporary experience, as David Riesman (of the Roundtable on Leisure) recently pointed out in his book, *The Lonely Crowd*, there is an increasing demand for a high degree of sensitivity to other people, a high degree of awareness of others' interests and needs. Regardless of whether we welcome or regret this increasing preoccupation, it is probably being forced upon us, as Sir George Schuster observed, by the nature of the industrial process itself.

SIR GEORGE SCHUSTER: I think you get a valuable illustration by comparing World War II with any previous war. Never has warfare been so highly mechanized, and yet never has it been so important to take account of human factors. I think one of the reasons is that if you're working with highly complicated machinery, you've got to have a high degree of human cooperation. That, I think, is one of the features of the development of modern industry; and perhaps, in this cooperation, we are getting at least some compensation for the diminution of the single craftsman's job. I think it is to some extent true to say that the job of craftsman is being transferred in industrial society from the individual to the group, and I think that is one of the reasons why we are being forced now to give greater consideration to the problems of human relations, of collaborative effort.

COUNTERPOINT

It undoubtedly came as a surprise to several members of the roundtable that at this point in our discussion, just as the Friday afternoon session was coming to a close, Mr. Hayes raised serious objection to what he spoke of as "a tendency here this afternoon to imply that there are some who must decide, for the masses, what the plain people want or what they should have."

MR. HAYES: There are too few, apparently, among those who are in a position to do something, who really understand how the masses feel as human beings; too few who realize that they feel that they have a right to be heard and make some sort of determination as to the type of life that they would live. They feel that they have a right to be considered as human beings, the same as the select class, the same—let me say not the select class—the same as the more fortunate. I hope I am wrong.

But I certainly think that I know something about the people we're talking about. I've lived with them; I've been one; I've worked with them for many, many years. . . . I think that our problem is: How can we make these people feel that they're human beings? How can we make these people feel that they are important, that they make a contribution?

CHAIRMAN McGREGOR: I think it's more than that, Mr. Hayes. I think it's not how can we make them *feel* that they're important and that they're playing an important part, but how can we *make* them important. And I think we've been addressing ourselves to that question.

MR. HAYES: I think they are important, and I think our big problem is to show that to them. . . . That's a humanitarian problem. It isn't up to us to say that we know what kind of organization is best for you; we know what's best for your wife and we know what's best for your family; we know what's best for your environment; we know how you can best contribute to the social welfare of the country; we know how you best can contribute to the company; and so on. I think that's been one of our fundamental mistakes. There are too many of us who have become inflated with the idea that we, as the more fortunate, have a special obligation to take care of the less fortunate. . . .

Mr. Hayes may, as a number of his colleagues felt, have misinterpreted a good deal of what they said, just as they, in turn, may have misunderstood his position. At all events, what Mr. Hayes said served to remind some of us of a statement which Mr. Jaques had made earlier in the day:

MR. JAQUES: Just wishing for an adaptive and cooperative community won't get us anywhere. It is clear, as seems to be agreed around this table, that unions and management are anxious to improve relationships. The fact that relationships do not improve more rapidly than they do is not to deny the strength of the wish. The wish is very strong indeed.

The point I would like to make is that there are a lot of difficulties inside us that stand in the way of achieving these wishes. We have been talking about the workers' satisfactions and dissatisfactions. Is it not true, in part, that we are using the workers to talk about ourselves?

TO BE CONTINUED

At the final session on Saturday morning, Chairman McGregor announced the selection of Sir George Schuster and Mr. Worthy as our roundtable's representatives in the panel discussion that would take place at the final general session of the Conference. He then suggested that we use the remaining time to air any points of view or questions which had not been brought up before.

One of the subjects discussed was the role that research could play in guiding those who are concerned with the practical problems of industry. Sir George Schuster made the point that research in industrial sociology and related fields is of little use unless management takes an interest in it from the beginning and co-operates in carrying it out. He suggested that what we particularly need is a series of case histories of what happens to the life processes of industry when you introduce changes in organization or other new factors into the flow of work processes.

Mr. Homans noted that astonishingly few research studies have been made and that most of these have been descriptive. He suggested that the time had now come for more experimental studies, such as the classic experiments in which Mr. Roethlisberger and others pioneered some years ago at Western Electric.

MR. HOMANS: If the kind of thing Mr. Worthy talked about yesterday is right, as we believe it is, then we ought to get a chance, for instance, to try out different ways of organizing small groups and larger groups and see if we can get any effective check on the results.

It was agreed that such research would be valuable only if it were undertaken with the aid and counsel and understanding of management and only if management cooperated in applying the results. Some of the problems involved in accomplishing this were described by Mr. Jaques in an account of the work the Tavistock

Institute has done over the past two years in cooperation with a large engineering firm in England. [It is not possible to give even a suggestion, here, of the complex interrelationships between problems of participation and problems of authority which Mr. Jaques and his colleagues discovered. Fortunately, however, Mr. Jaques' book, *The Changing Culture of a Factory*,* makes this material available to a wide audience.]

Several other points were raised briefly. Mr. Strayer commented upon the fact that, in all our discussions, nobody had mentioned "the intervention of government in the work situation," though government had in fact intervened in many ways and would probably intervene further. To which Mr. Joos added that it was his impression that government intervention was treated like the weather: "You take it into account, but you don't try to change it."

Mr. Blegen pointed out that, though we had talked about the schools (which, in his opinion, are contributing to a better understanding of the interrelationships that are so important in our social and economic system), we had overlooked other important aspects of education, including the whole adult-education movement. And Mr. Kouwenhoven added a reminder that industry itself is a powerful educational force, as witness the Glass Center in which this Conference took place.

Here, again, we came back to the problem of ambivalent values, which had underlain so much of our discussion throughout the three roundtable sessions. For there was, after all, something characteristically ambivalent, perhaps characteristically American, about the fact that we met to discuss the problems of "living in an industrial civilization" in a magnificently contemporary building whose museum and library, plus facilities for observing glassblowers at work, were established to preserve and to celebrate the techniques and products of a handicraft culture which industrialism has all but destroyed.

In closing our roundtable discussion, Chairman McGregor urged

* Elliott Jaques, *The Changing Culture of a Factory: A Study of Authority and Participation in an Industrial Setting*, London: Tavistock Publications, Ltd., 1951.

all of us to remember that, in spite of the fact that we had not achieved any clear-cut conclusions on the subjects we had considered, all of us would probably find that we had carried away some ideas, some points of view which would be useful to us.

CHAIRMAN McGREGOR: I want to urge you not to be discouraged by the immediate, surface impressions of frustration. I think there are a lot of things that will filter in our minds and take effect as time goes on. I commend to you especially the very thoughtful background paper by Bill Whyte, which was the basis on which our discussion started. I think perhaps you will find, since we have talked together, that a rereading of that paper will be a profitable experience.

MR. PRICE: My friend Harry Higgins from Pittsburgh and I were talking last night about the Conference, and he said, "Bill, did you get anything out of your conference today?" He has been sitting in the "B" group, the Roundtable on Leisure. I said, "No, Harry, these academic fellows just frustrate me and put me in a state of hypertension. They keep an idea going back and forth, and lose me completely." But I am pretty sure that in days and months to come a lot of the things that were said today will be valuable. At present I don't know just what I have got out of it, but I suspect I have gained a lot more than I now realize.

3

Leisure and Human Values in Industrial Civilization

ROUNDTABLE B

Reuel Denney and David Riesman, rapporteurs

We think that this record will have meaning for all who are interested in the changing role of leisure in modern life. Is leisure leisureful if it becomes a problem? Do we need training for competence in leisure? Are the mass media of communication and entertainment that fill the leisure hours of so many people doing a proper job? All these themes and many others were touched upon by this roundtable in a discussion that was deliberately unsystematic and exploratory.

The record shows the spirit of a roundtable, under a genial chairman, that was both productive and easygoing. At all the points at which the participants harried the agenda and asked the chairman for guidance as to the proceedings, the latter repeated that "the wish of the roundtable is the wish of the roundtable." It was up to the participants to do what they wanted, and they generally did just that.

This summary groups together passages which pursued the same topic, even when they were separated by other comments in the original discussion. We hope that the liberal use of direct quotes will nevertheless preserve some of the conversational flavor, while highlighting the major lines of thought and the most suggestive ideas. The discerning reader may find that some of the ideas are new in the literature of the subject.

THE ROLE OF LEISURE TODAY

LEISURE: TIME, OR STATE OF MIND?

William C. DeVane, dean of Yale College and director of the Division of Liberal Arts at Yale University, tried to pin down the subject of discussion. He observed that there was leisure at various times in life. The leisure of the child is a different thing from the spare time that modern industry provides for the active worker, and that again is a different thing from the enforced leisure of the retired worker. John W. Dodds, professor of English and director of Special Programs in Humanities at Stanford University, thought Mr. DeVane's point an important one; leisure for his 15-year-old son is something quite different from leisure for him. He added that leisure could be considered as an attitude of mind rather than merely spare time. David Sarnoff, chairman of the board of the Radio Corporation of America and director of the National Broadcasting Company, agreed that leisure is a state of mind. He went on to emphasize that we ought to distinguish also between leisure in a normal world and leisure in an abnormal world full of tensions and war clouds:

MR. SARNOFF: If we are discussing the problem of leisure at the present time, we are discussing merely the problem of how to escape from the things that are troubling us all day, how we can forget the problems of the day when we are through struggling with them in the office and elsewhere. But if we are discussing leisure in a normal atmosphere, where we have done the day's work and it has no more than the usual problems, then the question is how best to utilize that leisure, how to advance happy living, how to advance education and culture and better understanding.

Mark Starr, educational director of the International Ladies' Garment Workers' Union, AFL, distinguished between leisure for an elite and leisure for all, pointing up the modern problem of leisure.

MR. STARR: Our problem today is leisure for the mass. There has always been an elite in every civilization which has enjoyed leisure.

Sometimes they have used it to make people put up the Pyramids; sometimes they have used it like Plato, whose leisure depended on the slave class. Someone was doing the dirty work of the world. Our problem now is that we don't need a slave class any more; we have so harnessed our technical resources that leisure is now within the reach of a greater number of people than ever before. . . .

LEISURE AND OUR CONSCIENCES

Running through the whole discussion was something that the chairman, Lynn T. White, jr., president of Mills College, called "an ambivalence of attitude" toward leisure. In a conversation with another roundtable member the night before, he said, a mutual sense of guilt at taking part in a roundtable on leisure had come out.

CHAIRMAN WHITE: We said, "Ha, ha, I have no leisure; why am I involved in this?" It was a sense of guilt and, at the same time, a sense of pride. In other words, we feel leisure is a cultural value. Theoretically we would rather like to participate in it, but we are sort of proud that we are such responsible members of society that we really have no time for leisure.

This ambivalence was related to a deep division of opinion that gradually appeared among members of the group. One idea was, as Chairman White put it, "that leisure is leisure, and that it is perfectly all right to do nothing either to improve yourself or to justify your existence to society." Another view was that leisure is to be used constructively for some purpose, not for mere idleness. Miss Santha Rama Rau of India, author, and student of both Asian and Western cultures, first put the issue acutely:

MISS RAMA RAU: I am wondering why leisure is a problem at all. Surely, nowhere else in the world do people fuss about what to do with their spare time. I think it is rather sad that some kind of guilt has been built up in this particular society so that people feel that they should be productive in their spare time. Production rolls with such a speed that now you feel you are useless unless you are making a bookcase or turning out a car or whatever you do. I think it is unfortunate that respect is gone for the man who simply sits in his rocking chair and thinks, if he happens to feel like it, or does nothing if he happens to feel like it. I think that is really the sickness underneath all of this. . . . So long as leisure is considered as a problem, it is certainly never going to be solved. What is wrong with lying on the beach and relaxing?

Charles B. Fahs, director for the Humanities, The Rockefeller Foundation, agreed with Miss Rama Rau and thought that we tended to overemphasize the distinction between leisure and work or between leisure and good forms of activity. Partly because of a linguistic difficulty, we have a problem and start worrying about what should be done during leisure time. Mr. Dodds and the chairman agreed that Americans evidently have a Puritan conscience on the subject of leisure—the very existence of a roundtable on the topic suggested that.

OUGHT WE DO SOMETHING IN OUR LEISURE?

When Mr. Sarnoff confessed that "of all the problems which trouble me in the world at the present time, leisure is the least of those," Walter P. Paepcke, chairman of the board and chief executive officer, Container Corporation of America, spoke up for "exactly the opposite point of view."

MR. PAEPCKE: I think our fault today is that we are so busy with the urgent that we do not have time for the important; that we are always telephoning and seeing people and thinking and doing this and that, and when we come home in the evening we are dead tired.

Mr. Paepcke felt that our civilization will probably go down as similar to that of the Romans, not the Greeks. We will be known for our aqueducts, our roads, our laws, and for other concrete developments, but not for our philosophical, cultural, or artistic achievements. We have a somewhat distorted picture of success, not honoring the humanities or philosophers sufficiently.

CHAIRMAN WHITE: Mr. Paepcke is identifying leisure with the entirety of cultural activity.

MR. PAEPCKE: If I were a painter, I would say anything I do after I finish my painting is my leisure time. If I happen to be in the paper mill business and I go home from that, anything I do after that is my leisure time. I think we are confusing leisure with idleness.

MISS RAMA RAU: As I said before, what is wrong with doing nothing?

MR. PAEPCKE: I think there is something wrong with that. I think if we do a little thinking, or if we are being of some good to ourselves or to our neighbors, that is one thing . . .

MISS RAMA RAU: You cannot be good to yourselves or to your neighbors if you do it under any kind of compulsion. If you happen to feel that you want to do nothing but lie on the beach and get a sunburn . . .

MR. PAEPCKE: Then you might as well say that if one likes to get drunk, then it is all right to drink until ten or eleven.

MR. SARNOFF: Suppose you have done a useful day's work and you are engaged in creative work, and you have used your creative facilities for eight hours a day on your job, what is the matter with doing nothing after that? Why do you have to create any more that is useful or anything else?

Mr. Paepcke then stressed the importance of continuing one's education through life, and Reuel Denney, assistant professor of social sciences, University of Chicago, picked up one of Mr. Paepcke's earlier points.

MR. DENNEY: I agree with Mr. Paepcke's idea that leisure after work may come by looking at the works of man, his artistic achievements. After a day's work, leisure does not come easily, and one of the ways to get it is to be involved in an appreciation of someone else's work. This taking a look at how other people do things is a way of moving oneself toward the do-nothing state. It is like a kid who watches the garage mechanic; he can stand and watch fascinated for a long time because somebody else is working very well.

Mr. Denney's defense of the passive watcher seems to have escaped Mr. Sarnoff or not to have satisfied him, for, being worried by the implications of Mr. Paepcke's remarks, he took off by asking the chairman whether he would mind a "little frank discussion." Once assured on that, he defended the business career from Mr. Paepcke's observation that it was not a total way of life. Mr. Sarnoff felt that if a businessman did a good job at work he did not need to apologize either for that or for what he did afterwards. If he wanted to read a book or listen to a symphony, that was fine too. Mr. Sarnoff thought that there was no need to feel that he *had* to. If he uses his leisure in such a way that he has a happy state of mind, brings a happy atmosphere into his home and to his friends, and doesn't make trouble for his wife and his children and his community, that is the most useful thing he can do with his leisure.

Mr. Dodds: You wouldn't argue that leisure should not be spent in mental and challenging pursuits, would you? The charge is brought against educators that they are always wanting to improve somebody's mind. There is nothing against it, I suppose?

Mr. Sarnoff: Certainly not, but I would not want to impose an obligation to do it.

Mr. Dodds: We are never going to legislate it. Obviously, nobody is going to do the same thing all the time as a leisure pursuit. I am a little surprised to discover a person in your profession saying leisure doesn't make any difference; it doesn't need to be discussed.

Mr. Sarnoff: I stand by that position; I would still sell radios whether you define the issue or not.

Mark Benney, author and social scientist, London School of Economics, observed in this connection that the British, through taxation policy, were enforcing a self-improving attitude toward leisure. They were, in effect, "nationalizing" leisure, with no entertainment tax levied on what the government thinks are good plays, whereas, of course, gambling is taxed, saloons are taxed, the music halls are taxed. [Note that on the day the Conference opened it was reported that the House of Representatives in the American Congress had voted to exempt the Metropolitan Opera, symphony orchestras, and ballet from the admissions tax.] Mr. Benney then turned to the issue of the Puritan conscience, asking why some people at the table seemed to define leisure as leisure and others as work which has to be done in order that one may get on better with his neighbors.

Charles H. Sawyer, director of the Division of the Arts and dean of the School of Fine Arts at Yale University, identified himself—and this took a fair amount of courage—with the Calvinist position. "Leisure for what?" was his question. He suggested that most of us need leisure as pauses for reflection. Some need it as a relief from monotony, and possibly looking at one of Mr. Sarnoff's television shows helps in that respect. Other people want leisure for the enrichment and the enhancement of the individual, and Mr. Paepcke had suggested leisure for contributions to the community itself. Mr. Sawyer regarded all these uses as important.

"HAPPINESS" AND SATISFACTION

The chairman turned next to Howard Mumford Jones, professor of English at Harvard University. Like a few others, Mr. Jones had come prepared not only with a viewpoint but with facts and figures. The viewpoint was that business civilization had substituted happiness for satisfaction—the latter being better. The figures to back up Mr. Jones' position were drawn from his content analysis of the ads in the *Saturday Evening Post*. Of 167 faces he found 114 that were smiling or laughing; eight blissfully asleep and obviously happy; six men blowing smoke rings—well known, he said, to be happiness. It was plain that Mr. Jones was against this smiling, fatuous happiness. He found, indeed, the whole system of advertising to be one great vacuity that induced its readers not to look for anything else in leisure but this vague happiness.

Mr. Starr, who qualified, in the chairman's words, as "another spokesman for the Puritan conscience," felt that one could possibly get happiness by Miss Rama Rau's method of loafing in the sun but not for long by the fake happiness depicted in the ads which Mr. Jones had counted up.

MR. STARR: We are spoiling our kids to a certain extent unless we show them that the only real satisfaction is something they do for themselves. One evil that is spoiling our leisure is "spectatoritis." We go and watch the other guys do things. The only real satisfaction comes through putting something of yourself into something and expressing yourself. That means self-imposed hard work and self-discipline, and that is the real enjoyment which leisure can give.

Leo Lionni, art director of *Fortune* magazine, took up the cudgels for the view previously expressed by Miss Rama Rau. Describing himself as "a man with partly Calvinistic, partly Jewish, and partly Catholic background, who was raised for fourteen years in a country where *dolce far niente* is considered one of the most wonderful things in life," he observed that Americans feel sinful about sometimes doing nothing, and at the same time they admire the "poor, underprivileged, and yet happy Italians" for being able to do nothing.

Mr. Lionni: I think the thing that should be explored is whether the incapacity for doing nothing has not caused many bad things in our society. For instance, heavy drinking, I think, is to a great extent due to the incapacity for doing nothing. . . .

LEISURE AND WORK

There was considerable discussion on the relations between leisure and work in modern society. Is the distinction really as sharp as we sometimes seem to imply—or, as Charles B. Fahs had suggested, do our words mislead us? Is there a trend toward a more "integrated" life in which the work and leisure of industrial civilization merge into each other again, as in more primitive cultures?

Robert T. Stevens, chairman, J. P. Stevens & Company, testified that the greatest satisfaction in his thirty years in industry [textiles] had been to be "just a very small cog" in an effort to improve the status and standards of that industry. The industry was once a sore spot.

Mr. Stevens: Thirty years later, as I go about this industry and see those plants, the air conditioning, the lighting, the vastly improved wage scale, the shorter hours, the more leisure, the happiness of the people, for my money that is the thing in business that I have got the real kick out of. It is true that, as I have gone along, it has provided my family and myself with a livelihood, but that was not the satisfaction which I have derived from a thirty-year experience in an industry which has started to come along.

CHAIRMAN WHITE: Do I interpret correctly . . . you feel your fun has come from your business primarily?

MR. STEVENS: Correct. . . . If a person, after doing his job, goes home and still during the course of an evening finds satisfaction in trying to think about how he can do that job better and, particularly, if it will benefit other people, is that leisure or is that work?

Mr. Paepcke suggested that this applied mainly to people in management. Would a clerk get such satisfactions? Suppose Mr. Stevens had been making out bills of lading for the last thirty years, or sending invoices, or writing dunning letters, like 95 per cent of the people in business? Mr. Dodds at this point wondered whether management also ought not to be included in the "circle of sympathy." He observed that the manager is often as much fettered outside of working hours as the person who punches a time clock. And Mr. Starr added, "A worker can drop his problems with the time clock. Management cannot forget so easily, especially if management is having a tough time."

It is difficult for one person to tell another how to enjoy his leisure, said Henry B. Higgins, president, Pittsburgh Plate Glass Company, who described his own idea of leisure as being happily occupied in some voluntary activity. From the variety of literature that clutters his desk he picks out something to take home to read in the evening—perhaps something on the administration of a hospital. "I think I am doing it in leisure; that is a leisure activity; Mrs. Higgins thinks I am working!"

Eric Larrabee, associate editor of *Harper's Magazine*, and David Riesman, professor of social sciences, University of Chicago, both spoke of a strong tendency to haze over the distinctions between work and play.

MR. LARRABEE: If you take the usual prototype of the unfortunate advertising man who can no longer distinguish between his business and his free time and pursues his contacts as avidly at cocktail parties as anywhere else—if we regard this as a poor development (which again comes back to Puritanism) but if we do regard it as poor— should we be trying to stop it?

Mr. Riesman suggested that the distinction between the passive leisure of the masses and the active leisure of the classes might to some degree lie in the eye of the beholder. As an analogy in the sphere of work behavior, he drew on the experience of one of his students who had spent summers working in one of Mr. Paepcke's container plants. The student had taken a boring job stacking corrugated board as it came off the assembly line—the kind of job that many a visiting French intellectual would feel degrading—and he discovered to his surprise the amount of control that even the occupant of such a job had over its activities. The workers appeared to be able to vary the job by varying their own time-and-motion patterns, as well as by their ability to stop the work when they felt like taking a holiday. This ability gave them a feeling of control which none of Mr. Paepcke's managers could, in turn, control.

MR. RIESMAN: And contrary to the impression that one would have, these men in the factory got a good deal of leisure in their so-called worktime, and they enjoyed their opportunities to cuss the company, enjoyed their physical agility, their craftsmanlike work, even in a job that appears to the observer to be routine.

One of the most interesting things about industrial work is the fact that people personalize the machines they work with. Wouldn't you agree, Mr. Higgins and Mr. Stevens, that people in the plants do not feel each machine is the same?

MR. HIGGINS: That is quite right.

Mr. Riesman also suggested that the person who has learned manual skills in his work may participate more actively than the intellectuals realize when he is watching a sport.

MR. RIESMAN: Let me again recur to the student who suddenly realized that if men were as graceful in their work as these men in the container plant, when they watched wrestling on television they didn't watch it as intellectuals would, but they were aware of the movement of the bodies and it therefore became an active experience.

From still another viewpoint, Mr. Riesman added, so long as people, like some of the participants, insisted that leisure should be occupied in a highly strenuous and active way and in communal or family pursuits, many would be driven to seek refuge from leisure in their work. Paradoxically, since time in the office is defined as work, play in the office during that time may have a certain freedom.

Mr. Starr, who had previously defined leisure as "activity outside that which is necessary to earn your living . . . our own choice," made the point that "some of us are happy enough to have work in which we take pride and which we also enjoy doing." In his view, that is a good working definition of Paradise— "to get a living doing what you think to be important." He also agreed with what Mr. Riesman had said about manual workmen on seemingly boring jobs. But he added a practical note from his own experience as a mine worker.

MR. STARR: I was working underground and hewing away at the coal. Often my thoughts were far, far away. I could do my job so automatically that there was release; but that did not deny the fact that I was in danger and dirt and darkness for twelve hours, and when I got an eight-hour day, that meant I could go home. . . .

Mr. Benney observed that the *work* of one class becomes in time the *leisure aspirations* of the one lower down. "The office worker of England is encouraged to take up the occupation of the upper middle class, and you find that the pleasure of the aristocrats becomes the leisure pursuit of the middle classes in England."

Chairman White drew on his knowledge as a medieval historian to remark that the feudal aristocracy of the Middle Ages could not distinguish between its work and its leisure. The work was to stay fit to fight in a certain highly developed manner on horseback, and leisure activities were much the same. "I am wondering if we are not developing an industrial society in which the machine is putting more and more of us into the position of the noble, where it is harder and harder for us to distinguish our function from our fun?"

JOBS AND HOBBIES

Mr. Benney raised a question about the relation between a man's work and his hobbies. Why do so many corporations ask a man to indicate on a job application blank what he does with his spare time? Personnel departments evidently assume that "what the chap does with his leisure time is an important part of his personality and what they want him for."

Mr. Benney: This is what I would like to talk about: It may be that the brighter boys know that there are certain kinds of leisure which are more highly regarded in management circles than others, and not only will they say they indulge in them but they will, in fact, indulge in them, not necessarily because they like them.

Mr. Starr: You don't think if a fellow wrote down "None of your damn business" that he would get the job, do you?

Mr. Benney: Suppose he said nothing?

Mr. Sarnoff: I don't know that the personnel manager determines employment on the basis of hobbies, but it does furnish some additional information that is useful to the personnel department.

Mr. Dodds: If he says drinking? [Laughter.]

Mr. Sarnoff: If he said it, that would solve the problem, but he doesn't say it; you have to find that one out.

Mr. Benney: But there is a system of values of what is a good activity and what is a bad one.

Mr. Sarnoff: We encourage our executives to go out and play a game of golf once in a while. We think a lot of business is done on the golf links.

Mr. Paepcke suggested that the main use of hobby information on application blanks is not so much to determine whether or not to hire the person but to help keep him happy after he is hired.

Mr. Paepcke: I know that in our own company we do list the hobbies; if someone says he likes music, our policy is to take some ten or twelve seats every Thursday night for the Chicago Symphony Orchestra throughout the year. We let them draw lots out of a hat, and they are the ones who are given the tickets. If they say they like bowling, a bowling club is organized. If someone says he likes poetry, if there is some advertisement to write or something which has to do with writing, we would ask somebody like that to do it rather than someone who likes lacrosse.

LEISURE AND HOME LIFE

MR. SARNOFF: On the basis of our experience, the single most important factor determining whether a man is really a satisfactory employee, either as a wage earner or as an executive or a clerk, is determined by his family life. If he has a normal, happy family life, a good home, he is a satisfied, normal fellow. If he hasn't got it—if he has a nag for a wife, for example—he can have all kinds of recreations and all kinds of abilities to fish or to write poetry; but he isn't going to be worth a damn because he isn't normal, and he isn't able to keep his mind on his work. So the most important factor about leisure, in my opinion, is what kind of a home has a man—or a woman, for that matter—got to go to after he is through with his daily work.

On the relation of family life to leisure, Chairman White instanced "the perfectly extraordinary development of leisure occupations connected with the home" on the Pacific Coast.

CHAIRMAN WHITE: I think the symbol of that is the circulation of *Sunset Magazine*, which now has about half a million circulation. It covers the three Pacific Coast states and is devoted exclusively to barbecues, lath houses—just everything imaginable around the house. It is a puttering magazine, and obviously there is a prodigious amount of puttering going on on the Pacific Coast at the present time.

Mr. Larrabee added that it is a glamour magazine also, glamorizing a particular kind of house, of which the barbecue is a good symbol; and Mr. Denney pointed to the "inspiration" this was providing to the rest of the country.

MR. DENNEY: The notion of California culture that turns up in all kinds of ads, the articles about it, and the kind of feeling about California and its domestic life that goes with the migration into California are certainly indications of its importance as a model.

MR. DODDS: If many more people come, there won't be room for another lath house!

MR. LARRABEE: Mr. Riesman suggests in his paper, and Mr. Denney also, that the home has become a machine for consuming leisure. Although Americans tend to sneer at the idea of the home as a machine, they have been happily active in making it just that and enjoying it very much. The supposedly gadget-mad American is a man who gets a great deal of pleasure our of the simple devices of his "interior" life.

The style of architecture of California has impressed itself on the minds of people all over the country, so that they imitate it in climates to which it is not adapted and in cities where these houses have no reason for existence at all. That is another example of the time lag between the inventiveness of the people themselves, who are presented with more leisure in which to exercise it and with the number of sources of information they have, and our ways of getting at this and describing what it is and explaining it to each other.

This led to observations on the importance of food and cooking, not from the nutrition standpoint but as a focus of leisure interest. "Thousands of kinds of cookbooks—Chinese, Italian, everything" have appeared in recent years, Mr. Larrabee noted. Mr. Riesman reflected on the "redefining of the role of the sexes," as it becomes obligatory for the man to be a good cook not only in the camp with other men but also in the back-yard grill and the Sunday kitchen.

AFTER WORK: THE RETIREMENT PROBLEM

Repeatedly the roundtable came up to the problem of the elderly in our society and that special kind of leisure known as retirement. But each time it backed away, partly out of a feeling that the subject of "geriatrics" has been receiving so much attention lately and is such a large topic in itself that a general group like this one could do little with it in a brief session. However, the importance of the problem was recognized, and it was one of the subjects on which the roundtable definitely urged the need for further study.

Mr. Starr referred to the situation in the coat and suit industry where, thanks to enlightened management and progressive unions, a man can retire at sixty-five. "It is not made compulsory. If it were made compulsory, we would kill a lot of the old men, because they know how to do nothing but work." Mr. Starr regarded this as a great indictment of our educational system and of the narrow life to which these men have been confined hitherto. His union, with the aid of Columbia University and the Federal Security Agency, has started a research project on the relation between leisure time and the prospect of old age, both among those who have not yet retired and among those who have.

To Mr. Higgins, the problem of retirement seemed the most acute problem of leisure that we have today, and in his view it is becoming more and more acute. Mr. White was inclined to agree.

CHAIRMAN WHITE: This is perhaps the most critical area of the whole problem of leisure. In the very first half hour of our roundtable, there were several members who felt it was so complex that the word "geriatrics" should no longer be mentioned at the table. I have rather regretted that. I don't quite know what we could do in a short time, but we might be able to define the areas of our ignorance.

As examples of our ignorance, Chairman White suggested that "we simply do not know what can be done to make retiring people feel they are still significant in our society. I think we do not know how we can build attitudes during the more active working periods in people's lives which will sustain them in the period of retirement. Perhaps we have to glamorize leisure as we have not."

Both Mr. DeVane and Miss Rama Rau pointed out that preparation should begin at an early stage for the late and important stage of retirement. Miss Rama Rau spoke in this connection of competence in the use of leisure, which requires specific attitudes and a specific training of the mind.

PREPARING FOR LEISURE

Millard O. Sheets, artist, and professor of art at Scripps College, had early alluded to a division of the American people into those who participate actively in their recreation and leisure activities and those who simply want to be entertained. He thought that there was a tendency for less personal participation all the time, and that this has something to do with a sense of frustration and lack of satisfaction. In turn, he traced some of the difficulty to "a lack of fundamental experience early enough to enjoy many of the cultural and real activities of leisure."

Miss Rama Rau felt that there is a problem in American culture in the lack of capacity for enjoyment on the part of adults. No child, she said, is without capacity for enjoyment and for spending its time amusing itself over things which leave grownups standing with astonishment. The children certainly do not lose that capacity even through their early school days. "From my experience in American colleges, they don't even lose it at college." But at some point in an American's life, in her view, his capacity for enjoyment seems to go.

Miss Rama Rau: Where does this thing happen? At what point in the life of Americans do they suddenly become incapable of feeling cozy in their leisure time, of enjoying themselves in whatever it is, whether it is constructive or nonconstructive? Somewhere it happens, because if it did not happen somewhere, why, then, would there be this terrible feeling when retirement comes that suddenly life is over?

These questions of competence in the use of leisure and the ability to play kept coming up in the roundtable in application to all ages and many different types of leisure situations but most acutely, perhaps, in connection with the retirement problem. Mr. Higgins believed that a tremendous educational effort should be made with people before they reach the age of fifty. He felt that few people could acquire new ideas for the use of leisure after that age. Perhaps at thirty or thirty-five one ought to develop an interest in some activity which he could enjoy when he reaches retirement age.

Mr. Higgins: I have known many, many people who have gone to seed when they have retired, simply because of the absence of ideas about the employment of their time. My own company leans over backward to keep men as long as we can, because we have had too many like that. They have not committed suicide, but they have died quickly.

MR. LIONNI: In Italy people don't commit suicide when they stop working.

MR. STARR: A conference the other day came to the conclusion that one should begin to prepare for old age in the prenatal period.

COUNTRY IDEALS IN CITY CIVILIZATION?

Mr. Benney traced part of the difficulty to the fact that our environment has changed as a result of modern industrialism and the rise of cities, while our ideals of leisure activity have tended to persist. This analysis belongs to what might be called, he said, "the ecology of leisure."

MR. BENNEY: Most middle-class professional people inherit a set of values which includes an attitude toward leisure based on a survival of rural, upper-class attitudes. The old aristocratic sports—hunting, shooting, fishing—were good things to do, and living in town was something to be avoided. But the majority of people have to live in towns. And towns have been built by the Puritan conscience: they are meant for business and not pleasure.

The result is that there are only limited kinds of leisure which can be undertaken in towns. There is the leisure Mr. Sarnoff provides in the home, and other leisure activities in the home. There are the mass entertainments that go on in large buildings.

We have to remember that the town planning background, tied to our Puritanical value system, has encased us in our peculiarly urban limitation of leisure activity. At the same time we institute a whole set of conflicts in how to find pleasure in the city, because we say to the poor worker how happy we would be if he would go swimming, fishing, or hunting and all that sort of thing which comes down from the rural and aristocratic past. Meanwhile, the town worker is listening to soap opera. And to attain a sense of participation he increasingly becomes interested in entertainment about entertainment; he wants to know more and more about the people who entertain him.

CHAIRMAN WHITE: He reads the movie magazines.

PARTICIPATION VS. WATCHING

Mr. Starr, Mr. Sheets, and others had deplored "spectatoritis" and an alleged trend toward forms of leisure that involve less personal participation. But not all members were convinced that this trend is a reality.

Mr. LARRABEE: The specter has already stalked the table of the moronic American who is entirely a watcher and never participates. I know of no evidence whatever that this is actually a true statement of the country today. It may not be a nation of Sunday painters, but it is well on the way to becoming one. You can go to the art supply stores on 42nd Street opposite Grand Central and see how they are booming. They have developed much of their new business since the war. And there was a time a few years ago when musical instruments were in very short supply.

There is an argument—quite a reasonable one—by a psychologist who has examined reading habits that a number of widely circulated publications in this country deliberately adopt policies contrary to those of their readers in order to establish an active relationship. A man can say "I certainly disagree with that"—and when he has done it he has had a satisfying experience.

Mr. Riesman, as noted earlier, also contended that we tend to underestimate the activity of the spectator (e.g., the manually skilled watchers of a wrestling match). Also, we tend to have "vested interests in other people's leisure."

Mr. RIESMAN: Mark Starr wants other people in their leisure to turn out for the very interesting and worth-while educational operations of the Ladies' Garment Workers' Union. Mr. Sheets wants people to turn Sunday painters. . . . We must speak of active and creative leisure, not only with reference to the Sunday painters and so on, but also with respect to the increase in the capable and competent critics of the media. . . .

Mr. DENNEY: Speaking of spectator skill, one of the problems of leisure arises because people may be trained early in their lives to work and to use their leisure in ways which are not necessarily useful to them later in their lives. Some of the goods and processes in the entertainment sphere today are beyond the vocabularies of criticism we have to deal with them. . . . For example, the cliché is sometimes used that television is "only vaudeville." The issue there to me is not whether some of TV is vaudeville or is not, but the implications of the use of the term "vaudeville." Apparently the word is supposed to carry with it some kind of meaning for the bad. But we know that there was vaudeville; and some of it was very good and some very bad.

Mr. Larrabee: I think I can give you another example of that, and it ties in with the question of competence in leisure. Certainly the most universal American leisure activity is going to the movies. There are in the country, say, several hundred movie critics who attempt to provide a machinery for judging this occupation and for providing the movie-goer with ways of making decisions. There is apparently no effect of the critics on the audience. The pictures which the critics praise are left alone; the ones they run down are magnificently attended. If it is desirable that there should be greater competence, then what you are asking for is a vocabulary of movie criticism, which as yet does not exist.

SELF-FULFILLMENT

Mr. Sawyer, speaking as a museum director, returned to the question of "vested interests in other people's leisure" and pleaded guilty to a concern for the way in which people spend their leisure.

Mr. Sawyer: It is a definite problem of values. Admittedly all of us who are concerned with this are trying to impose a conviction of values on other people. We think we are doing it for good and legitimate reasons. We may not be.

Mr. Dodds took the view that anybody who is concerned about our civilization will be concerned to see that "each individual, to the extent of his intellect and capacity and condition, is able to arrive at as great a degree of self-fulfillment as he could in that civilization—the highest degree of spiritual well-being, personal poise." The use a man or woman makes of his leisure time would contribute to or detract from that self-fulfillment. A humanist surely has some responsibility to aid the individual to arrive at a maximum of his inner resources; and, if this is so, the use of leisure time becomes quite important. There are kinds of satisfactions, inner ones, "which it seems to me it is our job to stimulate and encourage, if not to impose."

INTEREST IN ART IN AMERICA

Miss Rama Rau had implied that America is unsympathetic to artists. Mr. Riesman thought that this view was dated, and that the mass media were in part responsible for a new and more favorable view of artists (of which more below). When Miss Rama Rau countered that perhaps this was more an interest in glamour—the life of the movie star—rather than artistic self-expression, she drew a rapid-fire of contrary evidence from those around the table who were professionally associated with the arts and education.

MR. LIONNI: There has been an incredible increase in art in the last ten years. Frankly, I think it is going to pose an enormous problem.

MR. DEVANE: Music, also.

MR. LIONNI: There are close to ten million people in this country painting pictures, and maybe we are really on our way to the kind of thing Miss Rama Rau is talking about that exists some places in Asia.

CHAIRMAN WHITE: The number of people trying to write poetry, whether they succeed or not, is another example. In my own undergraduate student body, it is statistically phenomenal how many of the kids are trying to write poetry now.

MR. SHEETS: The third highest group on the GI Bill studied art in one form or another, and the support, particularly in the West, has been enormous.

PRIVATE LEISURE VS. LEISURE IN MASSES

It was Mr. Jones who, pointing to a garage across the street as a symbol of what he called "highway culture," deplored the tendency to commercialize any leisure habit which gets established. He also deplored the loss of the ability and the opportunity to enjoy the more primitive forms of leisure activity and to enjoy them in private.

MR. JONES: If I go, let's say, camping, which used to be a simple matter when I was a kid, and I go, let's say, to a lake in New Hampshire or Michigan, I immediately find myself involved in a vast commercial enterprise of rented canoes, rented houseboats, rented this and that. Or I send my child to a professional camp. It is no longer the amateur camp, it is the professional camp.

As any leisure activity expands, it becomes captured by persons who quite honorably contribute to it. This means that the individualism, the magic of the savage—this return, if you like, to the primitive— becomes more and more impossible, even in the case of the Sunday painter. How the exploitation of art materials immediately pyramids!

Mr. Higgins failed to see what was wrong with commercial supply of leisure materials, and Mr. Denney warned against exaggerating the response of leisure habits to commercial stimuli. But Mr. Jones pressed on.

Mr. Jones: I don't mind the Sunday painter in the least except that there is more and more of him. Edith Wharton, in one of her novels, talks about the American women who "hunt culture in packs," and in that sense you notice that if archery is set up, presently we hunt it in packs. . . .

Mr. Lionni did not see where all this was so bad. For instance, in the artist's materials section of Gimbel Brothers in Philadelphia he had seen a dozen women, fifty to sixty years old, eagerly painting. They were making horrible paintings, but they looked very, very happy. And he doubted that European women, who would not dream of being so undignified as to participate in that kind of activity, were better off because they chose "to be very lonely at home with all kinds of neuroses."

Mr. Jones then spoke of the rows and rows of cars leaving Boston on Saturday afternoon, fiercely driving down to the Cape and back again in order to be leisurely.

Mr. Larrabee: Isn't this where Riesman and Denney have spoken of the casual attitude toward leisure on the part of the people who never had it before and suddenly get a great deal of it? If this acceleration in numbers is a result of enlarging the leisure market, then that is simply *friction*.

Chairman White: That is, we are the *nouveau riche* of leisure and are misusing it.

Mr. Larrabee: Or you are the aristocrats and are resenting it. [Laughter.]

Mr. Lionni and Mr. Sawyer, pointing out that temperaments differ, thought that many people must like the crowded beach and the crowded weekend. Some people are happier in groups and would not enjoy Walden Pond. Mr. Paepcke noted that today more people are earning enough money to take vacations away from home. He and his children used to ride all alone up to Estes Park; now they go behind a busload of 28 schoolteachers from Nebraska who are making a hot 6-day trip, but the unhappiness of the three is offset by the happiness of the 28.

MR. BENNEY: What seems to me to be really important is that there are 165 million people in the States and a good many want to do the same thing as the others do. I was staying with some friends on the North Shore of Long Island, and we wanted to go swimming. We drove along that boulevard—you know, past the beaches—and we came to Jones Beach, and I was fascinated by that sight. I thought it was a sort of paradise for mass entertainment, and I wanted to stay there; but no, they wanted to go up and up until there were fewer and fewer people, and then they felt O.K. They were afraid of the mob. That seems to me to be a kind of residual value that we can't afford any more in an industrial world. We have to face up to the fact that a lot of people want to do the same things as we do. The rest of us are a little old-fashioned in accepting from our silly aristocratic forebears who made our culture for us the notion that there is something good about exclusiveness in leisure.

JONES' BEACH VS. THE JONESES' BEACH

Mr. Jones continued to bemoan the crowds driving to Jones Beach: "It means the majority eventually steadily diminishes the area in which the minority can enjoy itself. I rather object to the notion that anybody who likes to get away from the crowd occasionally is representing an acquired aristocratic characteristic. I think that in our urban society it is almost a necessary piece of social therapy that every individual at some time or other shall have an opportunity to retire into privacy of some sort."

Mr. Sawyer suggested that this was not an issue of social class, but rather of individual temperament, and that there was a good deal of variability both within individuals and among them.

Mr. Riesman added that we must not make the mistake of reading our own limitations as well as our capabilities into people of different class origins. To illustrate, he observed that people growing up in the lower class, that is, in the noisy society where there aren't doors, learn privacy in other ways than the door—the door being the characteristic institution by which the middle class got privacy—and that the mechanism of privacy differs with one's training and education. "Maybe the noise of the radio is the way you shut off the noise of the mother-in-law."

Miss Rama Rau noted that there are many leisure activities we have all learned to enjoy in public more than in private. She, for instance, would much rather see *South Pacific* in a crowded theater than to be the only person in the theater. "I imagine that as this civilization keeps on being more successful—and I suppose it will—one will learn to appreciate more and more things in those terms."

MR. JONES: I can't imagine anything more dreadful than a completely socialized existence.

MR. LARRABEE: You want Jones' Beach as opposed to the Joneses' Beach.

FLEXIBILITY

Mr. Starr contended that the individual, if he is ingenious and intelligent enough, can develop new forms of enjoyment when his previous outlets become overcrowded. Mr. Riesman, too, emphasized the need for flexibility. Our industrial civilization moves so fast that we have to be "fast on our feet."

MR. RIESMAN: When you grow up in a small town, as so many Americans have done, and you have gained your feeling of competence in leisure in a garden and you are then living in an apartment, what are you going to do? Have a flower pot? Is that how you are going to retain your competence? It seems to me that here is a problem which education has hardly touched, namely, to teach people to be so fast on their feet that they can move their whole emotional life away from a field which has been closed off. . . .

Mr. DeVane and Mr. Dodds spoke of the need for developing besides flexibility, inner personal resources that are unshaken and unseduced by the changing environment.

Mr. Jones through it all held to his point that our culture is losing something important that it formerly had. "My head," he said, "is bloody but unbowed on this matter of privacy."

LEISURE AND THE COMMUNITY

Mr. Starr, alluding to the "emotional debauch when a Kefauver investigation comes," suggested that a wise use of leisure would be to "get back to our communities and our neighborhoods and clean up the political life of our country." As already reported, Mr. Sawyer, Mr. Higgins, and others saw in community service activities one satisfying use of leisure. Various speakers had stressed the need for personal "inner resources," and Mr. Sawyer observed that the individual can get these needed resources in part by contributing to the community. But it was Mr. Sheets, the painter, who presented the roundtable with the most sweeping view of leisure in relation to the community.

Giving an account of his experience with city planning, both in a large city (Los Angeles) and a small community (Claremont), he suggested that the inability of the planners to get the community to accept their plans was due to the ignorance and apathy of citizens as well as to vested interests. Consequently, he felt that there was a great need for more effective education for social responsibility and for the improvement of fundamental taste. If the artists were seriously interested and concerned about their society, he said, they might contribute substantially to this job. But the artist lives in a large vacuum, and, "as for actually serving life in the most useful and dramatic and dynamic way, I think the arts fail very definitely."

He also placed part of the blame on the public schools and, in turn, on the colleges which teach the teachers. Good taste, social responsibility, and their application to community decisions might be taught to children before the responsibilities of adult life forced them into the fixed patterns of the man who has a vested interest in a home or a business. But the teaching of art in the schools is so utterly banal and lacking in vitality that a high school boy would naturally conclude that art is a sissy business.

Mr. Starr came back later to Mr. Sheets' "dim view of teachers and teachers' colleges" and observed that the high schools were doing an increasingly good job in developing a sense of social responsibility and participation in civic affairs. He felt that with greater leisure we can give a greater amount of time, care, and concern to the well-being of the community.

Mr. Sawyer carried on the theme of the community aspects of artistic expression by suggesting that it might be a good idea to devote space in the Corning Glass Center "to a great laboratory of craftsmanship of the arts in general, where people would participate." This kind of leisure activity, encouraging group participation, would be a healthy part of the community process. Such space—and of course this might already be in existence—should include a place for music and other communal arts, as well as for the more individual arts.

Such concerns worried Mr. DeVane. "I detect," he said, "running through these comments, a certain dread and fright of leisure." And he went on: "Various people are busy about community projects and other worthy causes which may be devices to destroy what leisure we might get. This is perhaps an unfair comment, but it seems to me we are worrying a good deal about this busy-work to save ourselves perhaps from boredom."

LEISURE AND THE ROUNDED PERSONALITY: ASPEN

Chairman White asked Mr. Paepcke whether it was a philosophy of leisure that had led him, a businessman, to embark on the unusual adventure in community development at Aspen, Colorado, where both sports and cultural activities are emphasized. Mr. Paepcke replied that what had interested him in this little mountain town was that in the old days it had seemed to have in a rounded way the three important things in man's life: economic opportunity (from mining), physical recreation (provided by the mountains, the fishing streams, and the game), and cultural

activities (represented by education, religion, singing societies, ·
ballet societies, literary societies, and an opera house and theaters).
The town had begun to decline in 1893 and by 1945 it had only
500 people.

MR. PAEPCKE: So I thought it would be interesting if one could
have a revival or renaissance, a rehabilitation, of a community which
had been founded apparently on those principles. We began with
the recreational side—skiing and so on—which incidentally also helped
on the payroll side. Youngsters, instead of having to leave town and
go to Texas or California, were able to stay there because they could
earn some livelihood. Next we got into the cultural.

Mr. Paepcke here developed the idea that we are too specialized
and that this is one of the reasons we are having trouble solving
our social and humanistic problems. People in the labor group, in
government or business, the educators and the artists, all tend to
associate with their own kind, even in their leisure time. Cross-
fertilization is needed to dispel distrust and to build more understanding. One of the theories at Aspen was that some good might
be accomplished by bringing together people from these different
class groups to discuss things related to our American heritage
and to participate in common cultural experiences.

MR. PAEPCKE: If I just associate with my friends—most of whom
are Republicans, and when they hear a lecturer, it is Bob Taft or
someone like that—there are no souls saved. I think labor, generally
speaking, has been on the Democratic side. Educators are a little
on both sides. So it seems to me we ought to have cross-fertilization,
bringing together the wiser representatives of all these various groups.

Queried further about the leisure aspects of the Aspen venture,
Mr. Paepcke spoke of providing vacation opportunities for employees of his company. The aim was to combine "food for the
body and food for the minds."

MR. PAEPCKE: If the average employee takes his two weeks' summer
vacation fishing or playing golf, and in the evening playing bridge
or canasta, and drinking and ending up by singing "Sweet Adeline," I
don't think he has had a very good vacation.

Again, who am I to tell him what sort of vacation he should have? But any number of people have come out to Aspen the last two or three summers, have had the chance to exercise and to come back brown, have had a little stimulation of the cultural and discussion type in many cases, and have said "We always thought a vacation should be complete loafing, and we have only realized recently how nerve-racking loafing could be."

SHOULD AMERICAN LEISURE BE VIEWED WITH ALARM?

There was a division in the roundtable between those who wanted to worry seriously about the leisure problems of American culture and those who felt that either those problems were not the real ones or that to consider them in the customary way is unrewarding. The professional humanists, such as Messrs. Sawyer, Sheets and Jones, were at one with the labor and management representatives in insisting that leisure is a problem either for the elderly or for others. The certainly less preoccupied and possibly less conventional view, that leisure may be more of a problem for those who worry about it than it is for those who spend it, was represented at the Conference by Larrabee, Denney, Benney, Lionni, Riesman, Miss Rama Rau, and in some ways by our chairman. When the former group woke up to the view of the latter group, there was a distinct shock. Indeed, some found themselves startled at the possibility that some of the people at the roundtable didn't really think that leisure was a problem, at least in the socially moralized terms in which it had been stated by many.

MR. FAHS: I am thoroughly confused; I have difficulty figuring out what we are trying to do.

It seems to me there was a basic assumption in the beginning that there was something wrong in our society which a different use of leisure might cure; and it seems to me we have had two approaches to a definition of what was wrong. One of them was inadequate time given to public service activities and the other was maladjustment in people over retirement age.

Both of these seem to me to be legitimate problems, and both are something we could discuss in terms of leisure activity.

MR. LARRABEE: Hasn't the point of the discussion been that our society is *not* in a crisis and that it is *not* suffering?

MR. FAHS: In other words, the implication is that the leisure activity is perfectly all right?

MR. LARRABEE: It is certainly outracing our efforts to keep up with it and localize it here at this table. . . . Or doesn't it answer Mr. Fahs' question to say that the course of this discussion has been on the question: Does industrial civilization stultify the grace of living or does it not?

MR. FAHS: Which side are you on?

MR. LARRABEE: I think it does not. If there is actually in existence this disproportion between the phenomenon and our effort to explain it, that is a far more serious problem. It means the instruments we have been using are failing to analyze our subject.

MR. FAHS: That is a purely scholarly interest then.

At this stage in the discussion it was clear, as Mr. Starr observed, that Mr. Riesman and Mr. Larrabee were indeed highbrows in disguise, engaged in that most highbrow activity of defending the lowbrows. Doubtless Mr. Denney and Mr. Benney also were in this category. This quartet, fighting a two-front war against the Joneses on the one side and the Sarnoffs on the other, were unable to switch roles when it appeared that the highbrow had no effective advocates at the table. This appears as the greatest and most glaring defect; there was no real snob. The firmest voice for high culture, appropriately enough, was Mr. Paepcke, the businessman. Yet even he and Miss Rama Rau, who also defended it, did not emphasize the possibility that the advances of America in the field of high culture were as extraordinary as any of the other advances discussed in the course of the Conference. This indeed was one job of the Roundtable on Leisure, and we fell down on it.

FIND THE PROBLEM

Mr. Riesman thought that the concern of Mr. Fahs and others "as to where we are going, what does this add up to?" perhaps stemmed from a failure to appreciate the difficulties of the enterprisers of the roundtable.

MR. RIESMAN: This Conference is a unique enterprise, in which people with different backgrounds, different interests, and different skills come together. This is the very point Mr. Paepcke was making—about the cross-fertilization of areas of widely diverse experience. It is so new that some of us get the feeling: "Well, what is the problem of the table? How can we best spend our time here in these limited hours?"

My guess is that a reading of the record will show that we did reasonably well on one enterprise, namely, to see whether the problem that has been put to us is the real problem or not.

It is the commonest experience of the academic person, when an industrialist comes to him and says, "I have problem A," to find that it isn't problem A, it is some other problem.

I think what some of us have been saying about leisure is of the same order—not that there are no difficulties, but that the difficulties do not lie with industry or with industrial civilization per se. This is not the source of standardization. If I'm wrong about this important point, I would like to be corrected. For if we think the difficulty is in the wrong place, then we will have the problem Mr. Sheets was talking about of unstrategic intervention. Then as a result we will perhaps be more gloomy than I think we need to be about leisure. . . .

MR. BENNEY: It seems to me that one of the real purposes we are achieving around this table is not necessarily to solve problems that exist, but to help us orient ourselves to problems which will probably exist. We now have a lot of leisure, both here and in England; we are likely to get a lot more. We are going to get a lot more Jones Beaches soon; we are going to get a lot more mass entertainment of one sort or another, and it is going to have more and more effect on the people of the kind we are vaguely anxious and worried about. Now is the time to try to anticipate what the problem will be in ten, fifteen, or twenty years' time.

MR. LARRABEE: Could our discussion here also be likened to a jam session in jazz music? If the freedom of the individual within a group, within a community, is the old Emersonian American problem, haven't we demonstrated here a variety of extemporizations on the theme? It may have seemed to wander away, as it does in most jazz music, but there is a possibility that if you superimposed one on the other they might harmonize.

CHAIRMAN WHITE: It seems to me that this afternoon's discussion has gone along extraordinary and, to me, quite unexpected lines. We began with emphasis upon the tremendous importance of leisure, of achieving privacy in leisure. We have come full circle with emphasis upon the tremendous importance of using our leisure, not for the search for privacy but for the search for the good community. We passed through the intermediate phase of admitting that we don't know how to achieve privacy because so many people—once you discovered a technique for privacy, such as trout fishing, for instance— so many other people discover it simultaneously that you no longer achieve your privacy. So you must be sufficiently flexible and take up digging mud pies or something like that until the crowd catches up with you.

It seems also that we are extraordinarily puzzled—and I think rightly —about how we shall go about achieving the sense of community (which, I believe, is staked out for another roundtable) through our use of leisure, and how we will improve the community. Here again it seems to me it goes without saying that complete flexibility of mind is in order. This notion of cross-fertilization through leisure is really the key, so far as I see it, to the achievement of a better community, especially in this country where we have such extraordinarily diverse regional traditions, religious, and ethnic also.

But Mr. White did not want a leisure program à la Mussolini. He feared that too much cross-fertilization would tend to make us "merely synthetic personalities, lacking the rough corners, the obtuse convictions, and the other things which I think a great many of us value. In other words, I think too much of this may lead to a kind of tolerant, cosmopolitan stereotype."

THE BATTLE OF THE MEDIA

Verbal brickbats began flying in the direction of the radio and television industry within the roundtable's first hour, and other mass media of communication were not exempt. A vigorous defense sent some of the bricks flying back in the direction of educators who found fault without studying the facts or the technical problems and without offering constructive suggestions. The exchanges were good-natured, even when vigorous; and at the end there was agreement at least on the proposition that the issues require much more and much deeper study than they have been given up to now.

Chairman White later looked back on the discussion of the media and saw in it the same deep-going division of opinion that had manifested itself in the argument on the usefulness of leisure (self-improvement and community improvement vs. "What is the matter with lying in the sun?"). In regard to the mass media, some roundtable members held that they were not improving people sufficiently. The reply from the other side was, "Well, let mass media improve the people who want to be improved; but after all it is snobbishness, it is coercive and undemocratic to insist on improving people who do not have a passionate interest in being improved." There is a difference in value structure here, said the chairman, which permeates the foundations of our society.

HIGHBROW, LOW NECKLINE

"One thing which makes leisure a problem," in the view of Mr. Starr, "is that the mass media are at the present time used perversely." He launched into an attack on the media and the hucksters for their social irresponsibility. He saw the newspaper proprietors as profiting from headline hysteria, and he called for a consumers' council on radio and motion pictures that would "let intelligent people like Mr. Sarnoff know what we are thinking about." The mass media have a great opportunity to teach the wise use of leisure, and also to destroy social illiteracy.

Like Mr. Jones, Mr. Starr deplored the false standards of the radio advertisers. He put his point in terms of the moral problem of a person like himself, a parent, who has to explain to his growing daughter (whose standards are still in a formative stage), "Look, that guy will blart and blart about somebody else's coffee tomorrow morning, and say that it is the best in the world, as he is blarting about the particular firm that is paying him today." To Mr. Riesman's query, "Who does believe the ads, really?" Mr. Jones replied, "I don't think the point is who believes the ads. The point is the particular world which is created in the consciousness by this totally false world."

What Mr. Starr had further to say about the wrongs of radio had best be quoted in his own words.

MR. STARR: Highbrows should insist on their rights. A highbrow is as important as a low neckline. We all know women have mammary glands. We are tired of having that fact dragged continually into our living rooms for our kids. While some lowbrows are right and proper, and so are low necklines, highbrows ought to stand up for themselves and ought to shout about a good idea if they have one. The people who own mass media should be more aware than they are of the tremendous responsibility that is theirs, because here is leisure coming in, and it is being degraded.

EDUCATORS AND DEMOCRATS

Mr. Dodds, who also indicated his dissatisfaction with the programs and the commercialism of radio, nevertheless reminded the group that "educators have vested interests in other people's leisure."

MR. DODDS: Mr. Sarnoff has threatened to turn on the educator. I wonder if you would ask him to do so?
CHAIRMAN WHITE: Turn!
MR. SARNOFF: Reference has been made here to the imbalance between the sexes around this table and I would like to make reference to the imbalance between the lowbrows and the highbrows and classify myself as one of the lowbrows. I don't see as many businessmen around here as I do educators and artists and publicists. I think the time has come for a little plain speaking, and I would like to take Mr. Starr on for a little massage. [Laughter.]
The trouble with intellectuals that I find here is that at heart they are not democrats. What they really want, when they talk about mass media of entertainment and views and information, is to impose their views upon someone else. They want the people to listen and to look at the kinds of things which interest them and which they think are good for the people.

If you gave the masses only the kind of things intellectuals and educators think they should have, continued Mr. Sarnoff, there would be small audiences. Even where there is a choice between the good and the bad, as in the press, the tabloids have a far larger circulation than the better newspapers. "What can I do about the fact that if I put Toscanini across from Jack Benny, Toscanini would have an audience of 2 or 3 million against 20 or 25 million for Jack Benny?"

Mr. Sarnoff advised Mr. Starr to check through the daily or weekly radio programs that are published, select the ones he wants to hear, and listen to them. When he goes to a show on Broadway, he takes the trouble to find out what the name of the show is and to inquire what other people think about it. But when people turn on the radio, they want to have the thing they are interested in right away; and if they turn the knob and do not like the program, "then radio is no damn good."

At this point Mr. Riesman intervened to argue that criticisms of radio should not take the line of highbrow vs. lowbrow but should be more specific. He made a specific criticism, namely, the radio and television reporting of the MacArthur reception in Chicago. A group of some fifty University of Chicago students had stationed themselves as observers at various points along the line of the parade and at Soldiers' Field. They all reported that for the spectator this was a parade, interesting, no politics in it, no ideologies—just good humor, a day off—leisure, if you like.

MR. RIESMAN: While this was going on, students monitored the radio and television, and here there was real distortion. Radio and TV gave an impression of a much more excited, much more passionate, much more interested audience than there actually was. For instance, at Soldiers' Field, according to the best estimates, there were 30,000 people; the place was two-thirds empty. The television and radio announcers built it up and talked as if there were 100,000 people there. That was a distortion. There I am on your side, Mr. Starr. . . .

Mr. Riesman added that these distortions had to be examined in terms of the glamorizing effect of the media.

Mr. Sarnoff replied that he would not claim that everything is 100 per cent perfect or that radio and TV do not have some element of distortion. Then he turned to the positive accomplishments of these media. In this connection he cited the stations allocated to labor, to the public information programs, and the great development of the Metropolitan Opera and symphonic music.

MR. SARNOFF: I maintain that since the advent of radio more people in the United States are interested in good music than ever before. More people are buying records, for example—and we know something about that because we sell them. The field of good, classical, recorded music is many times as great as it was before the advent of radio. Also, there are more people interested in chamber music; there are more people interested in discussions of scientific matters and in discussions, certainly, of politics and of news, in the whole war effort, both sides of which are being reflected over the air in debates of all kinds. I don't mind telling you in the confidence of this little family circle that I do not like a great deal of what is on the air, but I exercise the privilege of an American citizen of turning it off and of selecting the things I want to hear and look at.

Mr. Sarnoff went on to say that he welcomes criticism when it is helpful but that some important educators, in his experience, have made the least contribution to the development of the new media. "They have shown not only a disinterest but an incompetence in handling these new media—and I speak from knowledge and not from hearsay." University stations for the most part are as dry as dust. The educator does not know how to expose his knowledge. "The average good teacher is not necessarily a good showman, and education to the masses has to be dramatized." Mr. Sarnoff spoke in specific terms of prominent educators, among them some outspoken critics of radio, whom he had brought into NBC in staff positions or as advisers, and whose practical contribution to developing better programs had been disappointing. "The educators, in general, have been sitting around criticizing and doing little to contribute to the development of these new media."

THE BATTLE RESUMES

The chairman made sound conciliatory remarks—pointing out that many in the academic world do not feel that general indictment of the mass communications industry is justified by the facts, and also that indictment of a profession, such as the educators, is probably only partially justified—and thus sought to end the battle of the media. Mr. Starr was content to say nothing, but the chairman had not reckoned with Mr. Jones.

The latter entered the fray as a resident of Greater Boston who pointed out that Mr. Sarnoff spoke from the point of view of New York, which was rich in cultural programs, whereas the level of symphonic and similar programs had steadily sunk in Boston in the past fifteen years. For instance, the station which broadcast classical music had disappeared, and likewise the Lowell Cooperative Broadcasting Institute was having a hard time retaining a TV channel.* Then he indicted radio commercials as an insult to the American intelligence. While he confessed to liking Jack Benny and Fred Allen himself, he stated his concern about the "constant atomization of radio programs as they become smaller and assume us all to be so scatterbrained we can't listen to anything for more than twelve minutes."

Naturally enough, Mr. Sarnoff rejoined with an account of what was actually available in Boston; he pointed out also that Harvard and the Massachusetts Institute of Technology could have had a frequency several years ago for nothing if they had been willing to spend a little money to develop educational radio. Mr. Jones corrected him by saying eight of the Boston colleges are united in the Lowell Cooperative Broadcasting Institute.

Mr. Sarnoff: What is your audience?

Mr. Jones: Pretty good.

Mr. Riesman: General Sarnoff to General Jones: How many divisions have you?

Mr. Sarnoff continued the battle, making the point that sponsored programs of a given content were always more popular than sustaining programs with the same content.

* "Since the Conference, there has been a significant change in the Boston radio situation, the Lowell Institute having acquired an FM channel. I should be glad to indicate that my statements were of last spring." (Letter from Howard Mumford Jones.)

THIRD PROGRAMS AND SUBLIMATIONS

MR. BENNEY: It seems to me I might be able to contribute something useful to this discussion by saying something about my impressions of BBC, to which I am an ardent listener. The development of the BBC, of course, is very different from radio here because it is a public operation and there is no competition. From the beginning of British radio there has been among the administrators a sort of uneasy feeling that they have to give the public what it wants; but what the public seems to want is perhaps not what it ought to want, and therefore we ought to try to make radio a little bit better than what it wants.

Recently the experiment was undertaken—and it is still in an experimental stage—of putting a Third Program on, which is just about as highbrow as it is possible to conceive as a radio program. It is really tops. If you want music, you not merely get good music but experimental music, the very latest thing that has just come off the sheets, and you get research into sixteenth-century little-known organ music. You get the poets really having their fling. There has been a development of verse radio drama which is something, probably, which has not hit the States as yet.

The interesting thing about this is: what effect has it had on the other programs? One or two of the Third Program programs that were conceived entirely for a highbrow audience have graduated into the Home Program and the Light Program just by their sheer entertainment value; but apart from that, the Light Program has definitely deteriorated. My suspicion is that all the uneasiness which went into building up the program which aimed at being relatively intelligent and trying to improve mass standards of radio has now been channelized off on this other program. The radio producers now feel that they can get away with almost anything on the Light Program because their consciences are absolved by having the Third Program.

It seems to me that Mr. Sarnoff is also in danger of this thing. He feels that, provided he is putting on the Boston Symphony or the Metropolitan Opera, his conscience is absolved about what goes on the other programs. That is perhaps inevitable. . . .

Mr. Sarnoff said that he was close to the BBC and had the highest respect for the job it is doing; but he thought that the BBC programs, including the Third Program, would be washed up in the United States in about thirty days. He said, moreover, that the BBC would be regarded in the United States as a monopoly and as undemocratic, because the BBC does not provide the kind of freedom of political discussion and debate which American radio provides. On this Mr. Benney had reservations.

Mr. Denney also took exception to some of the things Mr. Sarnoff had said about the BBC. "I don't agree that something like the British Third Program in the United States would fail. Because, for one thing, I am not quite sure what 'failure' means. And how long would Mr. Sarnoff give it to succeed?" He also argued that British radio was more free than had been suggested. And he observed that commercial broadcasters often asked educational radio to prove its competence in advance of a chance at the channels. Commercial radio, by contrast, had proved nothing in advance, everything by experiment and practice.

MASS MEDIA AND HOME LIFE

In an exchange between Mr. Sarnoff and Mr. Larrabee on the state of family life in America, Mr. Sarnoff expressed alarm over the divorce rate, while Mr. Larrabee maintained that more divorces are a reflection of the higher marriage rate.

MR. SARNOFF: Do you take the position that our home life, by and large, is no different than it was twenty years ago?

MR. LARRABEE: It is extraordinarily better.

MR. SARNOFF: Would you credit the mass entertainment industry with any contribution to that?

MR. LARRABEE: In good part.

MR. SARNOFF: It keeps people at home by stretching out the four walls so they can hear and see things beyond the wall?

MR. LARRABEE: Absolutely.

MR. SARNOFF: Then what are you kicking about that for?

It was only later that Mr. Larrabee made the point that entertainment and fiction not only enlarged home life; they also defined it. Mr. Larrabee said: "Aldous Huxley once remarked that the reason home life in Germany was so bad was that they had no good novelists to tell them how to behave. You can apply that to the situation in this country today. In the slick magazines and soap operas—except for a burden of crisis in the latter which I could do without—you will find useful and accurate descriptions of the different kinds of life that are available to the people who read and listen to them. But in the novels which are successful and respected in this country now, and encouraged by the educators, you will find a long-drawn-out development that culminated recently in James Jones' book *From Here to Eternity* and that bears little resemblance to any American experience I have seen myself or believe exists."

Chairman White, however, was horrified by the introduction of prize fighting and wrestling via television into the living rooms all over the United States.

"BLOODFACE"

CHAIRMAN WHITE: May I say, on the matter of sadism and mass media, as the father of small children I am infinitely puzzled. I believe that this is the most brutal age since the sixteenth century anyway, and I think that kids need a certain insulation, a certain callousing, perhaps, to defend themselves. Our kids are getting that callousing, I feel, from television because no evening passes without about three murders and seventeen beatings.

Margaret Mead asked me to tell you the "Bloodface" story. I don't tell this just as a fond father, but as a sociological and psychological event in my own family which she thought was significant.

The kids invent playmates. They have had quite a series of them, and one day (the twins were a little under five) Mrs. White detected a new entity in the house, and it wasn't Poddy, who had been around for some time; it was obviously somebody different.

They said, "This is Bloodface."

Mrs. White gathered herself together and smiled sweetly and said, "Are you inviting Bloodface to Catherine's birthday party tomorrow?" —Catherine being slightly older.

"Oh, no," said the twins, "he would drip on the carpet."

Bloodface was in and out of the house a great deal. We kept him off the carpets, just on the linoleum and the hardwood floors where he could be mopped up now and then. One day the twins were sitting in

their high chairs drinking milk, a vacant chair between them, and it
was clear that Bloodface was sitting in the vacant chair.

Mrs. White asked if Bloodface was drinking his milk too. "Oh, no,"
said the twins. "He doesn't drink milk. Nothing but tomato juice."

This is clearly an invention out of their television experience, perhaps no worse than the giant in *Jack the Giant Killer*, who said,
"Fe-fi-fo-fum, I smell the blood of an Englishman."

Neither Mrs. White nor I feel it is wholly bad, because we feel that
probably in the middle of the twentieth century above all it is necessary to be conversant with Bloodfaces. But we don't know very much
about this kind of thing.

THE TELEVISION CULTURE

Mr. Riesman observed that he and Mr. Denney and some of
their colleagues had been interested for some years in studying mass
media, and recently they had tried to raise the small sum of
$3,000 so that six of them could get television sets and study
the television culture.

MR. RIESMAN: For instance, there is a man named Studs Terkel—
I don't know if he is one of your men, Mr. Sarnoff—who produces
shows which are like what jazz used to be: everybody improvises his
role, no rehearsed script; everybody in the cast puts in his two cents'
worth. It is a very interesting and spontaneous thing.

Yet it has proved difficult to find friendly support for such a small-
scale, nonmarket-research study which is interested in the culture that
walks into our living rooms, interested in such a question as Lynn
White raised as a father.

Incidentally, I didn't like Mr. Starr's remark about the low neckline.
I think the more censoring of sex, the more sadism; and I like sex
better than sadism.

Turning to a concern voiced by Mr. Dodds, Mr. Riesman
suggested that there might be a tendency to overestimate the
power of the mass media producer. He suggested that Mr. Sarnoff's
very activities at the roundtable indicated that his industry was a
vulnerable industry; as a result, it also appeared that Mr. Sarnoff
was not bored. The impact on the industry of the people seems,

he continued, to be considerably greater than general discourse around the roundtable often would indicate. "People simply won't believe how sensitive the industry is." Some of the industry's defensiveness was actually the result of the energy of the Mr. Starrs and the Mr. Doddses, who, in viewing the industry with perhaps more alarm than is justified, nevertheless perform a constructive function and allow more interesting things to be done with the media as a reaction to the criticism.

CHAIRMAN WHITE: I love the concept of Riesman using Starr and Dodds against the General here. This has great dramatic possibilities.

MR. SARNOFF: Having had so much to say, which was merely to ball up what they had to say about me—it is all in good, clean fun—I think I would like to make one constructive contribution if I am allowed:

Mr. Riesman is struggling in an effort to raise $3,000 to get six television sets to study the television programs.

I would be very happy to give you—or to lend you—six television sets if you will really study and tell me what comes up.

MR. RIESMAN: That's a bargain!

CHAIRMAN WHITE: Closed!

RESEARCH NEEDED

Mr. Benney had suggested that a useful project for the roundtable might be to "try to define our areas of greatest ignorance in the field of leisure." This might help to stimulate and guide research. Mr. Sarnoff probably expressed the general view of the group when he said, "I assume we weren't expected to do more than state the problems; we couldn't be expected to suggest solutions in a Conference that lasts only a day and a half or so. If we can emphasize the existence of the problems, the importance of them, and that they will continue to increase rather than diminish, perhaps we will have done all we should be expected to do."

Mr. Sarnoff presented a brief statement which he had drafted and which received the approval of the roundtable. It covered two items shown by the discussion to be subjects worthy of attention by foundations and institutions concerned with humanistic and social research.

The statement referred to is as follows:

"Leisure is a subject that poses a number of social problems which will increase as the area of leisure increases with the advance of technology.

"For example, modern media of mass communication, such as movies, radio, television, theaters, newspapers, magazines, with their varied forms of entertainment, information and education, exert their influences upon society chiefly during hours of leisure. As hours of labor diminish and hours of leisure increase, the influences of such media are bound to increase. Question: How much that is factual do we know about the influences of such media upon society and its attitudes and behavior?

"A second example: With the increase of retirement, accelerated by pension and social security benefits, what can be done to make the life of retired persons free from a feeling of frustration and uselessness, and how can the remaining years of their lives be made normal and satisfactory to themselves, to their families, and to the communities in which they live?"

OTHER SUGGESTIONS FOR STUDY

The following, in condensed form, are other suggestions for research which were put forward by various members under the stimulation of the roundtable's exploratory talk:

1. Organized sports and their effect upon the psychology of our society. (Benney, Denney)

2. The historian of language might make a contribution to the study of sports and society by watching the penetration of sport into the language and how the words become classified. (DeVane)

3. Comparative study of the films and the sports of different countries, from the standpoint of the way in which these serve as

indices of culture patterns and as influences shaping the culture patterns. (Riesman)

4. The role of gambling in connection with organized sports, and why it seems to meet some need. (Starr)

This led to interesting comments on gambling as it appeared in street games played by London children, which Mr. Benney had been studying. He had found class differences in the attitude toward taking chances. In a discussion on gambling which took off from this point it was emphasized that it is hard to study the meaning of gambling in society if the approach is limited to moral condemnation.

CROSS-FERTILIZATION

As the hands of the clock moved to the appointed hour and the chairman dutifully sought to adjourn, Mr. Paepcke made a final comment.

MR. PAEPCKE: I think we spent a profitable time in discussing leisure and the problems of the mass media. We spent little time on geriatrics. But I think many other things came up which are of broader scope. I, for one, would think that this type of conference is of considerable value. I don't know whether we call this leisure or not. I would classify it as that under my definition, because I am not plying my Container Corporation trade while I am here. I, for one, would love to see more of this cross-fertilization among people in labor, business, government, education, sitting around a table discussing things, not as class groups but as representatives of the various classes meeting in a group. I think that is extremely important.

MR. DEVANE: You have to underlay cross-fertilization with the knowledge of what goes on in any social conversation. What would a group of businessmen be talking about? What would a group of professors be talking about?

MR. SARNOFF: The professors would be talking about the businessmen and the businessmen about the professors!

CHAIRMAN WHITE: I think they ought to be talking about each other more.

4

Views from Abroad

GENERAL SESSION

Eric Larrabee, rapporteur

The persuading of three visitors from other countries to limit
their Friday evening remarks to adverse comment had been attempted by the moderator, Philip D. Reed, chairman of the board
of the General Electric Company and president of the International Chamber of Commerce, before the meeting began. Mr.
Reed confessed that beforehand he had asked the members of
his selected panel to provide him with outlines of what they
planned to say. "I looked them over," he said, "and, my goodness,
they were saccharine indeed. They were so friendly, so diplomatic,
so kind, that I have taken the very personal liberty of asking them
. . . if they would just dig down deep for all the things they really
have in their minds about America: things they don't like, that
are unsound, that they would not care to see develop in their own
countries. . . ."

Though he accepts responsibility for it, Mr. Reed's desire for
criticism is not a personal idiosyncrasy. Future historians, in fact,
might find it possible to extrapolate from his remarks a pattern of
American attitudes toward foreign visitors at mid-century. Accustomed as they have been since the start to employ the distress of
traveling Europeans as a vehicle of self-examination, the citizens
of the United States may seem to have come by this time not only
to expect, but to demand, that the inmost antipathies of each
visitor be revealed to them. One may also identify another Ameri-

can characteristic in Mr. Reed's assumption that "down deep" in the minds of his panel members lay their true bitterness, admiration, or affection for America being by implication a superficial attribute. To be sure, Mr. Reed occupies in this instance a truly "personal" position, since he (together with Mr. Victor G. Reuther) is American co-chairman of the Anglo-American Council on Productivity, an organization which has done more than any other to put the outsider's enthusiasm for the social underpinning of American industrialism on the written record.* The Productivity Team Reports on American techniques, prepared by representatives of both management and labor from the industrial counterparts in England, contain such extravagant praise for the psychological sources of our abundance that American readers run the risk of taking them too seriously or not seriously enough. Mr. Reed's connection with the Council should be remarked, since his admonition to the panel—"I want them to leave out the nice things. We know about those"—might have been misconstrued by the audience, many of whom did not share his special familiarity with a favorable verdict on industrial civilization in the United States.†

As it turned out, two of the three guests wished to compliment Americans on things most of us did *not* know; one by saying that we misrepresent ourselves abroad as more successfully mercenary than we are, another by asking what had become of the optimism

* The Anglo-American Council on Productivity, established in 1948 as part of the program of the Economic Cooperation Administration at the initiation of Sir Stafford Cripps and Mr. Paul Hoffman, maintains an office at 2 Park Avenue, New York City. Its publications form a unique though ambiguous source of contemporary documentation for the subjects discussed in this chapter.

† The result of Mr. Reed's admonition was in fact misinterpreted in a newspaper account of the Conference. Though Mr. Carrillo's prepared text expressed so deep an admiration for the North American industrial culture that he could not suppress it even by leaving out (at Mr. Reed's request) the most flattering sections, his remarks were reported in the New York *Herald Tribune* under the headline: "Mexican Cites His Country's Mistrust of U.S." A more striking example of American determination to be abused could scarcely have been invented. Mr. Carrillo wrote a dignified correction which was subsequently printed by the *Herald Tribune*.

with which we have long been thought to be infatuated. None denied that the world wanted industrialization, that the United States stood for the most advanced form of it in the eyes of mankind, or that the American life was in the large a pleasurable one to live—all statements that, while very possibly true, would be the first to be examined in a genuinely astringent analysis of our failings. Thus was Mr. Reed's appeal resisted by these unwilling devil's advocates, who were (in order of their appearance) D. W. Brogan, historian, Fellow of Peterhouse (Cambridge) and of Corpus Christi (Oxford), author of *The American Character, The Development of Modern France, Politics and Law in the United States, American Themes,* and other books; Santha Rama Rau, daughter of an Indian ambassador to Japan and to the United States, student of contemporary cultures in both East and West, author of *Home to India* and *East of Home;* and Antonio Carrillo Flores, director-general of Nacional Financiera, Mexico's agency for financing economic development, formerly dean of the National School of Law in Mexico City, Mexican representative on the Inter-American Economic and Social Council, and economic delegate to the United Nations General Assembly.

While all three may have agreed with Mr. Reed that "you build on criticism," they did not seem to follow him in thinking "that compliments don't do anybody any good." Not only did Mr. Brogan, Miss Rama Rau, and Mr. Carrillo scatter compliments lavishly, but they periodically lapsed into ambivalence so phrased as to reveal what they did not "care to see develop in their own countries" and to contradict Mr. Reed's belief while satisfying his request. "I feel, very frankly," remarked Miss Rama Rau at one point, "that the American way of life is an excellent thing, but I feel it's an excellent thing for Americans." Mr. Brogan, with an important reservation which was not clearly delineated until later in the evening, chose the same friendly means of being unfriendly to Mr. Reed. "The American businessman," he said, "is very much to blame, in a way he doesn't think he is, because he talks as if American know-how were a thing in itself, whereas in fact it is but an aspect of the total American society. . . . That is why the impact of America on the world is at the moment far more deeply revolutionary than most Americans, I think, realize."

COCA-COLONIZATION: A CAUSE THAT REFRESHES?

During the evening the three speakers performed in sequence and thereafter amplified their remarks, in response to questions from the moderator and the floor, in their several ways. Rather than attempt to follow them chronologically, this report will treat their words as extemporizations around the dominant melody of American industrial civilization as viewed from abroad—is it desirable for other peoples, and if so on what terms? This particular session must therefore be set somewhat apart from the Conference as a whole; it fell more directly under pressure from immediate events of which everyone was conscious (the Marshall Plan, Point Four, and the technical assistance programs of the United Nations) and raised issues of methodology that had been left outside the purview of the roundtables proper. The primary need for an "accepted view of ourselves," in Lancelot Law Whyte's words, might be concealed by agenda questions which presumed a "spiritual crisis" in the West; but no evasions needed to be entertained— least of all by a Scotsman and two descendants of the ancient Indian peoples—in comparing the views of American industrial civilization accepted by others and by Americans themselves, and in considering the relevance of American self-understanding to the consequences of American hegemony.

For it was strikingly apparent that in the minds of these three, in contrast to many of their American colleagues in the Conference, the material components of American industrialism were assumed to be inextricably enmeshed with an all-pervasive and paralyzingly aggressive doctrine of the spirit. This potent "civilizing" force for good or ill, moreover, was understood to have an impact on every department of living, from childhood within the family through the furthest reaches of philosophy and art, including on the way the four flourishing fields of inquiry in which the roundtables cultivated their uncertainties about industrial culture.

Here doubts were set aside, and when the voice of nonindustrial culture (needless to say, the misnomer "backward" was not applied) was lifted in meditation, asking what the chances were of survival in the face of the powerful American synthesis of human diversity, one wondered if the doubts had needed to be raised to start with. Assuming that they did, however—and this assumes the need to overhaul the Western juggernaut and make it more efficient still—new dimensions of the "problem" were revealed by placing it in the hands of sympathetic individuals who came from the outside but had each been partially "converted" to America.

MR. BROGAN: It is true that the whole Western world is a pupil of the United States in all the making of a modern society. Not that all, or even perhaps most, of the basic inventions are American, but that everywhere in the world it is America that is doing it the way that the rest of the world wants to imitate.

I saw on my last visit to Paris what I should never have thought of seeing in my lifetime—French workmen drinking Coca-Cola. [Laughter] I took this so seriously, coming up on the train from New York on Thursday night, that for the first time in my life, out of my thirty visits to America, I drank Coca-Cola—neat. [Laughter] . . .

MR. CARRILLO: We want all the benefits of industrial civilization. . . . Mexico, like other Latin-American countries, is a very poor one; and we have been convinced, and we are convinced, that only through industrialization can we get a better standard of living for our people. We know, at the same time, that material well-being is not enough, but nevertheless it is a condition for the happiness of our people. . . . So we know, not only from a point of view of spiritual solidarity but also of a sound selfishness, that the only window open to us to better the conditions of our countrymen is the United States. We accept that fact. . . . We believe that there is a fundamental decency, that there is a fundamental soundness, in the industrial civilization of the United States. . . . And I can assure you that to reach that conclusion demands, on the part of a Mexican, a greater emotional and rational effort than probably from any other foreigner. . . .

MISS RAMA RAU: I had planned to start off by saying what advantages I thought my country and my continent could get from the kind of industrial civilization you have over here; but I've decided not to itemize them, partly because you all know a great deal more about it than I do and partly because Mr. Reed isn't going to be happy unless this meeting ends in a free fight. [Mr. Reed: Hear, hear!] So I assume you will take my good intentions for granted.

I do feel that my nation in particular, and all of Asia at this particular moment, finds itself in a curious and an interesting position . . . this is the first time that my people have had a chance to choose what it is they are buying in the way of industrialization. In other countries it is something that has just happened, and people have either tried to keep up with it, or have just come by it, or have managed to control it. We have a chance, I hope, to profit by your mistakes. . . . Being essentially a selfish and nasty-minded person, I rather hope that we can manage to keep what is in our civilization without losing the advantage of yours. Whether this can be done I don't know, but I hope that all of you will help us in the future to see whether or not it can.

It is no less curious that both Miss Rama Rau and Mr. Carrillo should use the same word to describe themselves ("selfish") as it is that both, no more than amateur historians, should share with the professional (Mr. Brogan) a degree of historical-mindedness which lifted this session far above the ordinary in its insistence on proper context and perspectives. Miss Rama Rau, contrary to her protestation of ignorance—"the only qualification I have is that I have lived about equal parts of my life in an industrial and a nonindustrial civilization"—showed herself indeed "a gentleman and a scholar," as Mr. Reed had said, when she seized upon a feature of the argument which few other speakers had had the wit to recognize—the fact that the character of industrialism varies greatly from nation to nation, according to the time at which it arrives and the speed at which its marriage to earlier institutions is consummated. On this aspect of history Mr. Brogan was especially eloquent and especially successful in returning to American hands the responsibility for those nations which are in process of remaking themselves, over the objections of American and non-American alike, in the American image.

Mr. Brogan: I think the whole question of the American approach to nonindustrialized countries, like India and Mexico, is that it is not merely an American attitude but the attitude of all the other existing countries who have forgotten what it is like *not* to be industrial. That's to say, the novelty and impact of industry has been forgotten in America because it happened a long time ago. It has been forgotten in England because it happened a long time ago. . . .

The Industrial Revolution struck England first of all, or Britain first of all, and it wasn't accidental. It took place there because of the institutions which made it possible—such as the legal system of that time, the comparative fluidity of the English social structure, the fact that anybody could enter business (a French nobleman couldn't enter business; it was against the law), and so on. The Industrial Revolution came first to England, or to Britain, and came to a country which had not only invented the Industrial Revolution but was ready for it; and then it came to America, to a society which was even better fitted for it. Now it is coming into Asia, which hasn't really asked for it, except that it wants to increase its standard of living, and that means that every kind of impact is hitting Asia at the same time—that is to say, industry, Western ideas of law, the breakdown of the family, and so on, all are arriving in Asia in the same package at the same time. Now that is a kind of strain which Europe hadn't got to undergo. . . .

To take an example of that, no historian nowadays would dare say that the Industrial Revolution began in 1776, but you can determine when it arrived in Japan, and to a date. You can tell when it arrived in India almost to the year. . . . The significance of all this seems to me that not only America, but Britain, France, Germany—all the countries of the Western world—are unconsciously brutal, if you like, in their approach to countries where these things didn't occur spontaneously. We just ignore the fact of India's having a lot of teething pains. They have the bad factories; we had, too—the child labor; we had that, too—the epidemics; we had that, too. What we *don't* realize is that this whole thing is coming at one time from the outside into a society which, strictly speaking, in certain respects, didn't ask for it— and perhaps isn't asking for it yet. That is one reason why the problem, since it is America they want to copy, is above all an *American* responsibility to see that this kind of impact is not accidental. . . . The great problem—and it is a very great problem indeed—is how the world, which is becoming more and more Americanized, is to avoid being assimilated to the American way of life completely and how it is to take over from America not only the making of Coca-Cola or atom bombs but the values of American society which have come from the fact that both Coca-Cola and the atom bomb are American productions. That is the kind of thing that puzzles and worries me. . . .

"SHE TALKED OF ASIA . . ."

"It may be very wrong," Mr. Brogan had said, "it may be very foolish, but all these peoples, for various reasons—perhaps all of them foolish reasons—want what America can give, but not quite on American terms. They want it on their own terms." The truth of Mr. Brogan's statement was illustrated by both Miss Rama Rau and Mr. Carrillo, yet most of all by Miss Rama Rau, whose affection for the Indian institutions menaced by advancing industrialism was poetic and persuasive, clothed in as great elegance as the sari in which she herself was dressed. In one instance she called these institutions, perhaps unintentionally, "the things we are going to lose," yet clearly she did not greet the inevitable with enthusiasm. "She talked of Asia," Mr. Brogan later remarked, "as Americans talk of Europe."

MISS RAMA RAU: You at the moment are concerned with a way of life. We are concerned with the means of life. These I am certain you can provide for us, with all the attendant advantages. As to way of life, we have been concerned with this for some five thousand years now, and it doesn't come to us as any shock. But it is fairly recently that it has occurred to America that this thing they have built up during the last couple of centuries that they call "the American way of life" is an exportable commodity, that this is something they ought to try to sell to the rest of the world. I think they rather plunged into this with all kinds of good intentions and enthusiasm, without quite bothering to determine how the outside world feels about taking it over. . . .

We on the other side of the world have ways of life of our own, and cultures of our own, and attitudes and human values of our own, that are in their own way important, and I would hate to see them go. . . . We may be illiterate—and 90 per cent of us in Asia are—but we are by no means uneducated. We are a people with thousands of years of civilized history behind us. We are people who have created great strengths and great cultural institutions of our own, and we would like to preserve them.

Miss Rama Rau grouped the institutions she described under four general headings: the family, art, the basis of livelihood, and philosophy. On two of these points she would later be questioned from the floor, and over her hopes for subdividing industrialism Mr. Brogan was to dash an unpleasantly cold shower of skepticism. Yet before the controversy is entered it must be seen what Miss Rama Rau was defending, and for what reasons.

Her definition of the Oriental family—"a complete structure of culture and morals and individual behavior"—could have been applied, though Miss Rama Rau did not so apply it, to the corresponding force which starts to break down the large "clans" into individual couples and their children "as soon as industrialization comes to a country. . . ." Instead, her attention was concentrated on the structure of Indian family life in which she had been raised, which "involves at least three generations, possibly four . . . all kinds of aunts and cousins and great-uncles and nieces and strange relatives that no one has ever seen or heard of, that drift in and out of the family group." This family unit is essential to the process of growing up in Asia, Miss Rama Rau argued, since out of the stories told by a grandmother, the experiences of a great-aunt, or the work and the world of a grandfather "comes the basic familiarity that any child has with the culture of his country. . . . It is not only an important thing in the human sense, but it is also our education." Her perception of the weaknesses of family life in the West—expressed in terms which the Roundtable on Leisure, to its great detriment, largely ignored—made life in a traditionally organized society seem almost attractive by contrast. Miss Rama Rau praised Oriental institutions as superior to ours on our own scale of values.

MISS RAMA RAU: As soon as you start spreading affection thin over a number of people in the family, you lose the chances for the intense relationships between parents and children which you get over here. They can, of course, be successful relationships; but increasingly, I understand, these things become more and more corrosive. These frictions, these deep tensions that exist within families in an industrial civilization, are on the whole unknown in Asia; because when you have, say, ten or twelve or fifteen—or, as there were at one time in my family, twenty-five—people living in the house, you can't fuss about whether the immediate relationship between, say, mother and son is going to start affecting the psyches of both of them. You can't worry about whether the mother goes out to dinner one night, because there will always be people in the house whom the child is used to, and consequently that kind of intensity doesn't operate. . . .

The child loses the distance between the generations, in this sense— that no teen-ager in Asia, for instance, is going to fuss if he or she is asked to take care of two small children in the afternoon. That is something natural. He has got to learn to incorporate even the small child into his work or play . . . and this is something that he does without resentment, that fits quite naturally into his social pattern, and that makes the step into adulthood a great deal easier. . . .

In America it seems to me that you have an enormous gap between the concept of the individual, which is an important one, and the concept of the nation, which is an important one. In between the child gets nothing to work on. In Asia you work in a series of concentric circles . . . so that by the time the child is ready to leave his family he already has a sense of his rights and responsibilities, his duties, his privileges, within the small group where he is already at home and happy, and eventually in the broader social unit.

American readers who feel the impulse to interrupt Miss Rama Rau at this point with examples of the intermediate social institutions of a thousand kinds including the "gangs" of childhood which our society has created to bridge the gap between the individual and the nation-state will have to hold their peace, for the challenge was not accepted by any member of the Conference.* Perhaps her devastating use of the "intensity" of Western family relationships† to disorganize resistance is responsible, in this case, for the fact that her opposition (as it later developed) steered

---

* A number of these were described in the Roundtable on Community, however, by Louis Wirth, who had made an investigation of "voluntary associations" (see page 128). "This was in Chicago. . . . We studied about thirteen thousand of these organizations. . . . There are probably at least fifty to a hundred times that many."

† Cf. *The Lonely Crowd: A Study of the Changing American Character*, by David Riesman in collaboration with Reuel Denney and Nathan Glazer (New Haven: Yale University Press, 1950), pp. 36-255.

clear of the mundane details of every-day life in which the West is traditionally self-sufficient and engaged her instead over art and philosophy, which have been for long a privileged sanctuary of the East in campaigns of intellectual propaganda. Certainly an unusual reversal of the anticipated roles took place when John E. Burchard and Reuel Denney spoke from the audience to defend the "human values" of Western thought against the charge assumed by the calling of a Conference to deplore their neglect. (Mr. Burchard asked whether Oriental art was "experimental"; Mr. Denney's speech, which is regrettably missing from the transcript, was described after the meeting by one of his colleagues as "a historic moment—for the first time the Americans are talking back.") Yet Miss Rama Rau's remarks were cogent, and she argued for each example of an Eastern custom on the thoroughly Western grounds of social responsibility, an unanticipated victory for pragmatism over the competing philosophies of ultimate ends which have been a staple Asian article of export.

MISS RAMA RAU: I remember a Balinese mother whom I once talked to telling me that the reason why the West was abnormal was that Westerners were not artists, and she said: "Of course, you can understand it very easily, because if you push children around the way they do, and make them sleep when they aren't sleepy and eat when they aren't hungry and generally persecute them, you get only depressed individuals who cannot create art and are therefore not human beings."

It is not so wild as it sounds. In most parts of Asia, with the exception of the highly industrialized ones, the creation of art is a natural and an essential part of any human being's activity. It is considered as essential to his growing up, to his normality, as his work is considered essential to his livelihood. . . . We heard yesterday that the man who turns a nut on a fender might very easily be happy, even if he does not have the feeling of a complete process in his mind—that this tiny operation might be enough for him, even if he does not have a feeling for the complete car.* Well, that may very easily be true, but I think

* See p. 15. Notice that Miss Rama Rau's grasp of the wholeness of human activity has caused her to enlarge the dimensions of Gwilym A. Price's argument but to mistake its import. He was suggesting two things: (1) that the

the thing that one forgets is that in Asia the cycle is not considered to be from the beginning where you start to make the car to the point where the car is complete. The cycle is of a different sort, and it is a cycle of life. . . .

Once in Assam, which is a fairly remote part of India, I was talking to some hill women who examined my sari and immediately said, "Where were you educated?" I told them in England and America, and they said, "Well, they're very nice. They do give you a good education there, don't they?" So I said I had enjoyed it, without quite seeing what the connection was. They said, "We wouldn't be able to weave this kind of material here." I said, "I didn't weave it, I bought it in a shop." They were horrified, absolutely horrified, that a woman existed who didn't know how to weave her own clothes.

Extend that further, and you will see that this fundamental knowledge of how to grow the things you eat, how to build the things you live in, how to weave the things you wear give you a kind of security, a kind of feeling for the basic necessities of life, which in Asia is considered important and which I think you lose when you are simply turning the nut on a fender, however pleased you may be with the job.

And lastly I come to a point which I have some difficulty in expressing, because I am even more ignorant about it than I am about industrialization, and that is the question of philosophy.

In Asia, and in my country in particular, the philosopher—and by that I do not mean the man who studies various other systems of philosophy, I mean the man who quite simply sits in his chair and thinks [laughter]—is a respected man and a necessary member of society. It is considered a perfectly good, sensible occupation for any human being. It is considered more than that. It is considered a rather necessary part of anybody's activity, regardless of what else he does.

---

stereotype of the industrial worker who merely puts a nut on a fender is a caricature and not a true representation of the actual tasks of American workers; (2) that a failure to participate in the "complete process" need not prevent a worker from having a "feeling" for it. This latter distinction was often lost sight of in the Conference and is incapable of resolution short of asking the workers themselves. This was the method suggested by Mr. Price: "I sometimes feel like asking the gentlemen who write about the tensions and frustrations of our industrial workers: 'Have you talked, really talked, to any lately?' " Harry H. Cook in the Roundtable on Confidence, wanted "more people right out of the ranks to participate in meetings of this kind." Mark Starr made a similar point in the final session: "Why not import a few and really find out what they are thinking?" (See pp. 197 and 207.)

And I think that concern with and respect for philosophy is something rather serious that is lost in the West.

". . . AS AMERICANS TALK OF EUROPE"

If only it had been possible to map out for each roundtable this stern and lucidly expressed indictment of the Western world, a number of dead ends and detours might have been avoided in the process of resisting it. Admittedly, every one of Miss Rama Rau's generalizations can be substantiated from American sources, so large is the literature in which we disparage our virtues for not being those of the mature European societies by which we instinctively measure progress—our government for not yet being English, our music for not being German, our cafés for not being French. It seemed likely that Miss Rama Rau had been impressed by the low value put on the indigenous vernacular culture by a vast majority (as Mr. Price had lamented) in the hierarchy of higher learning in America. This is partly what Mr. Brogan meant when he said that Miss Rama Rau had "talked rather like a Wellesley graduate, if I may say so," and it is a large part of what Mr. Carrillo meant when he said that it was necessary for Mexicans to discard European preconceptions in order to understand the United States.

MR. CARRILLO: The history of Mexico is a rather curious one. We are Indians. I personally am of Indian forebears. Then we got three centuries of domination by Spain; then we had the French philosophy. French philosophy dominated the cultural program of Spain all through the nineteenth century. In 1928 I studied law in French books. And after the French, or the European, framework of our culture at the beginning of the century, now we have come to accept the fact that not only the material aspects of the industrial civilization, but also the cultural aspects of the United States, are those in which we must be more interested. So we have a new effort to make. We have to accustom ourselves to abandon, more or less, the European ideas of the past generation.

Yet it is much easier to call for a cultural farewell to Europe, as Americans have been doing for more than a century, than it is to make this necessary family parting come to pass. In separating the "material" from the "cultural" aspects Mr. Carrillo himself had fallen into that philosphical rut of dividing every unity into two opposites which pervades Western thought and which has been called "the European dissociation."* It is a tribute to the power of Miss Rama Rau's early environment that she nowhere adopted the same alternatives but rather showed—in her considered fear that industrialism could not be imported selectively—that she viewed our civilization as, like her own, "a complete structure of culture and morals and individual behavior"—no matter how little she liked it. Since many Americans do not do themselves an equal justice, and since he had observed the uneasiness which the pressure of an inadequately organized tradition still exerts on Europe-oriented Americans, Mr. Carrillo interpreted the symptoms of incomplete independence as a loss of enthusiasm.

MR. CARRILLO: I fear that some of the optimism that was considered a basic characteristic of this great country is not so strong as it used to be. . . . The idea, which undoubtedly still has validity, that there are more frontiers to conquer in the realm of technology and material progress apparently is not accompanied by a strong conviction that you are going to be able to tackle the social and human problems created by the tremendous economic and political power of the United States. I should be very happy to know whether this doubt is justified. Perhaps it will be dissolved before the end of this Conference.

Mr. Carrillo was partially answered the following day by Charles E. Odegaard, who concluded in a phrase already quoted that "this Conference suggests the desirability of our really looking at ourselves to see some of the things which we have done; and this, I think, will perhaps give us the degree of confidence that many

* Lancelot Law Whyte, The Next Development in Man (New York: Henry Holt and Company, 1948). "Western man stands out as a highly developed but bizarre distortion of the human animal. . . . The history of European man can only be understood as the development and disappearance of his characteristic dissociation . . . between deliberate activity organized by static concepts and the instinctive and spontaneous life. . . . Europeans could speak of little else. Their language tells the persisting story of two distorted and incompatible tendencies. . . ." (Pages 64, 122-124.)

think we have lost." Yet to the extent that Mr. Carrillo's question itself separated "human" values from "material" problems it was either unanswerable in the American context—or already answered within the definition he had earlier established of "material well-being" as a "condition for happiness." Certainly his own fears for the American future, using "American" in the sense that includes two continents, were shaped by a primary concern for our industrial abundance and what we chose to do with it. This part of our responsibility, Mr. Carrillo reminded us, involved not a hemisphere but a planet.

MR. CARRILLO: The productive capacity of the United States . . . will have to be used to raise progressively the standard of living of the people. The hope of the Latin-American countries, which provide much of the raw material for the operation of the enormous American economic machine, is that they may share in the benefits of this increase in production through a more equitable relationship between the price of their products and that of the manufactured articles made from these raw materials. If, on the other hand, the growth of production does not result in a situation of progressive stability and well-being but in a new depression, then the situation of the free world bristles with peril.

TOO LITTLE MATERIAL, TOO MANY SPIRITS

The question of long-range prospects for "progressive stability and well-being" led two members of the Conference to ask from the floor for a discussion in this connection of what one of them, Julian Huxley, called "probably the most important problem before the whole world at the present moment"—that of population. "Do you think," asked William F. Whyte, "that it will be possible to achieve an increased standard of living in Mexico and India by this industrialization which we are discussing in this Conference without a conscious and deliberate program of population limitation?" The question was addressed to both Mr. Carrillo and Miss Rama Rau, neither of whom undertook to answer it with a categorical yes or no. Miss Rama Rau felt that population was only one of many problems and that a balanced program would inevitably encompass increased education and expanded agricultural resources; Mr. Carrillo, on the other hand, was convinced that "there is no way out through agriculture."

In driving the representatives of these two industrially immature nations to the wall, over an issue with serious political and religious implications for their compatriots, the Conference may have been demonstrating the Western quality of being "unconsciously brutal" that Mr. Brogan had described for the explosive increase in population resulting from a lowered death rate is only one of the many initial impacts of industrialization which lie behind us and make a vaguely superior attitude possible. As an American attitude, of course, it suggested an examination of an actual American policy. "I would like to know very much," said Mr. Huxley, "what is happening in Japan. I am told that the American occupation in Japan has managed to persuade the Japanese to adopt a rather drastic population limitation policy, and I understand that that could be done in India also."

Margaret Mead thought it unlikely that India could be so influenced. She pointed out that we had not had any such sudden success in Japan where the idea had had historic precedent.

Miss MEAD: Japan—for many, many generations—has been limiting its population to the size of its islands. . . . This is a civilization that for hundreds of years has been impressed by the relationship between population and land supply, and the head of each family was charged with the task of never letting the members of the family exceed the land supply of that group. . . . We ought not either to encourage or to discourage ourselves, whichever we want to do with it, by using this recent Japanese experiment as a model in understanding other sorts of civilizations.

What we want to do with it, as Miss Mead had offhandedly inquired, was the unanswered question, for the American reaction to an embarrassment we no longer faced would in great part determine whether our influence on Asia could avoid, in Mr. Brogan's term, the weakness of being "accidental." It required, first of all, the closer look at ourselves which Mr. Whyte had tried to take before he shifted the burden of proof to India and Mexico. "In the

United States," he said, "as we have been industrializing, at the same time we have had what I consider an undercover program of population limitation. This is something that we don't discuss very openly, but it has been going on." Was it possible to ask others to speak frankly until we did also? Was it our desire to be completely understood? Was it possible—since American civilization was at best half-intelligible to Asians, Europeans, and Americans alike—to send technical missionaries out into the nonindustrial world without causing more angry, deracinating upheavals than any party to the bargain was prepared to face?

"There is one danger," said Mr. Brogan, "which I think Americans who have this external responsibility ought to remember: that a great deal of American industrial life can be exported in the sense that the institution can be exported, but what you want exported is what makes it tolerable or admirable in America." As far as Miss Rama Rau's or Mr. Carrillo's points of view were concerned, Mr. Brogan foresaw the same difficulty. "You can import American things, but they suffer a sea change, and they become something different. In the description of American society, as seen from outside, quite often the real values of American life disappear in that transfer." It appeared to Mr. Brogan that not only European but American ideas about Americans were responsible for these misapprehensions; and of the two, he thought the latter were the most to blame. "American propaganda for Europe, for example," he remarked, "is based on a feeling that Americans have about themselves—that they are extremely hard-boiled and severe people, who know exactly what they want to do and do it for simple-minded, straightforward, selfish motives. [Laughter] And a great deal of American presentation of itself to Americans is quite like that. Anybody knows it exaggerates the degree both of selfishness and, ah, of competence." [Laughter]

YALE CLUB PRAGMATISM: "NO FREE LUNCH"

Mr. Brogan addressed himself with care to the proposition that had attracted the major attentions of his colleagues, making it clear that he found himself in a diametrically opposed position—

and that he feared Mr. Carrillo and Miss Rama Rau might be inviting disappointment. This chapter will be concluded largely in Mr. Brogan's words, which go a great distance toward resolving the conflicts so far encountered and which initiate the first full-scale effort of the Conference to define industrialism in terms of the attitudes that make it work. Mr. Brogan was also the first speaker to state firmly the proposition that American technology is not a neutral agent, that it will not function in a vacuum, and that it generates "spiritual" values wherever it operates.

MR. BROGAN: The impact of America on the outside world, in Latin America and still more in Asia, is far more revolutionary than most Americans think, because we think of it as the arrival of Cadillacs or Coca-Cola or anything else, without realizing that they are bringing in the same ship—so to speak, in the same package—they are bringing a whole series of ideas, habits, and concepts, which must all hang together. Otherwise you won't have industrialization, and you cannot help but break down a great deal of what Miss Rama Rau wants to preserve. I don't think—in fact, I don't think it is best to think—that India or Mexico can get the benefits of industrialization without having to give up many of the things which they both treasure.

Mr. Brogan suggested that the institution of the family and the respect for a particular kind of philosophy were good examples of this, since they varied so conspicuously from one country to another within the Orient and Occident alike. The kind of Indian philosophy that Miss Rama Rau had talked about did not exist in China, while "the American family hardly exists in the English point of view, the English family hardly exists in the French point of view, and so on." This led Mr. Brogan to the parenthetical observation that the most permanent revolutions were not necessarily the most "noticed and conspicuous" ones, and that "perhaps one of the great events of history" took place when "the French Revolution prevented France from being industrialized as quickly as she would have been without the Revolution."

MR. BROGAN: I will get back to answering the question. I don't think you can have American know-how in technology without having

American know-how in a great many other things. How many of these things are necessary I don't know; but I am quite certain, no matter what Americans say or do, when they bring a single effective American machine, effective factory, effective economic institution into any country, they bring with it, whether they know it or not, a whole series of things which are revolutionary. I don't see any way that can be avoided.

I think industrialization is never got free. There's a great remark made by a great unknown American pragmatic philosopher—the Italian immigrant who used to clean shoes, and still cleans shoes, outside the Yale Club (that is no doubt where he picked up the philosophy). And he was asked after forty years in America what he had learned about life from observing Grand Central Station and the Yale Club. He thought a moment and said, "There is no free lunch." [Laughter]

Mr. Brogan succeeded far beyond the achievement of other members of the Conference, in describing those social qualities of American know-how which are half-consciously transferred—and which had to be transferred—along with our purely physical and technical machinery.

Mr. Brogan: I think all these great concepts of a total society have got to be watched very, very carefully. The American weakness in exporting its culture—and I use that word in the widest possible sense—is sometimes to export just a bit of it, and sometimes to export a sort of fully packaged show, as I believe the radio says. The second is probably the wiser of the two, but awfully difficult to get over. The reason why things go wrong with American generosity, for example, is that the rough edges are left on with the product. America is not a tidy country, as you may have noticed. [Laughter] Sometimes people go away and leave things. . . .

A great deal of the American know-how is in itself a consequence of the American legal system—an important system—and when you get an industry into another country you get different results, because you don't bring the different methods, from the American high school to the Supreme Court of the United States. Well, I'll give you a simple example: you don't bring into England, for example, one of the things that makes American industry go. I understand Americans like to cut ethical corners rather finely—that is to say, many things work very well in America because people don't obey laws. . . . When you get into another country, you bring with you adjustments of that kind into a society in which the adjustments—the looseness of the edges, so to speak—of the American society are not present. That is often why American machines don't work as well in English hands as they do in American hands.

"The problem here," as Mr. Brogan had said at the start, "is not really what's wrong with America—a rich subject [laughter]—but what is the kind of industrial society in which people in America live and people in England live"—in other words, industrialism for its own sake, setting aside the historical circumstances in which we were familiar with it. This he tried to make clear to his American listeners by disentangling from their own industrial history those elements which were fortuitously American, and on which we should not pride or impugn ourselves unduly. Nobody, after all, really knew what industrialism in any other sense was like. "Nobody is used to living in this new society at all," he said. "It's new to all of us. Yet, in America, it starts with an immense advantage, which you can't export. American industrial society is almost as old as the United States—that is to say, roughly speaking, foreshortening history a bit, American characteristics became free in America soon before there was real industry. This was a new land. . . ." Many American characteristics, as Mr. Brogan went on to say, were thus a consequence of a unique experience.

MR. BROGAN: One side of the American problem, which falls in the history of the United States and the immense flowing of people into this country, is the creation of a unified society inside it. I think the success has been great, but the question is what kind of success. Part of the price is the uniformity, the one hundred per cent American attitude which has to be made, instead of coming quite spontaneously, as it often does in societies where the unification process began a long time ago. . . .

I was very struck, in reading the preliminary papers, by the amount of unnecessary effort spent in American communities in treating national conditions of unity—the amount of irrelevant stress on race problems, for example; or the role of the school not as an educational institution in the narrow old-fashioned sense, but as a unifying force. I think it is highly desirable in America that this should be done, but rather a special American problem which doesn't exist in the same way in France or England. And I sometimes think that possibly too much effort is spent in American schools in creating a unified national personality. One can be too unified in many ways, and you can have too uniform a society.

Here, again, was one of the "simple concepts which fit the American pattern perfectly well, but don't necessarily fit the European societies into which they are brought," when Americans try to build up their kind of communal unity in a "society which has its own communal unity and doesn't require that particular kind of importation." Mr. Brogan had observed this in "discussing American policy in Bavaria, where there was the simple assumption that what happens in Connecticut will do equally well for Bavaria."

MR. BROGAN: Well, it isn't true; and what Bavaria needs is not the sense of American virtues that can be brought in by a few handbooks, brought in by people, or issued to any population. . . . And there is the danger—as the whole world goes flocking to America for leadership, for technical know-how, for political leadership—that sometimes a sort of disillusionment comes over the countries that come to school in America, either directly or indirectly. When you export your technology, with extremely valuable social attributes—such as great flexibility, social flexibility, mobility of population (which is a thing Americans don't realize is so extraordinary: people move two thousand miles for a job)—you also bring with it not only the obvious blots on American society, like color prejudices, but you also bring with it the simple, straightforward ways of doing things which are valid, let us say, in Dayton, Ohio, or in Los Angeles, or New York, or in Corning. And yet coming into a European society, which was sometimes better but also based on a spontaneous or a standing tradition, some of the very best things that Americans do are spoiled in the way they are done. And I think this goes back to the final remark here. . . .

You can't give the best that America can give to the outside world—namely, not only how to make this new society but how to live inside it—unless there is more, shall I say, humility before the job, more objectivity, more realizing and facing this problem. . . . I have been moving around Europe a great deal recently in the few times I am not in the United States, and there you see people behaving badly to America, ungratefully, resentfully, foolishly—but humanly. And if only Americans would accept the fact—that people can be very foolish, very ungrateful, very stupid, and yet be human beings who deserve not only to be treated as human beings but could possibly be integrated into the whole modern economy with a little more adjustment.

Adam Smith was quoted here today, this afternoon. I remember the comment—Adam Smith was a Glasgow man, a statement which covers a great deal of ground [laughter]—and Walter Bagehot's comment on that great man was: "He saw the whole progress of history as the promotion of the human race to the rank of Scotsmen." [Laughter]

Well, there is a certain American danger of seeing it the same way and, as a Scotsman myself, I will not say which idea is more foolish than the other. [Applause and laughter]

5

The Individual's Sense of Community in Industrial Civilization

ROUNDTABLE C

Irwin T. Sanders, rapporteur

The Roundtable on Community not only talked about a sense of community; it provided an illustration in itself of the way a sense of community develops. When the roundtable assembled at the brief introductory session on Thursday afternoon, its members represented widely different backgrounds in industry, labor, publishing, university teaching and research, and public service. At first, many of the members talked unsurely, as to strangers, and even at cross-purposes. By the concluding session on Saturday morning, a group loyalty and understanding had been built and communication was easier. Members knew fairly well which fellow members agreed or disagreed with them. When there were disagreements—and there were bound to be some fairly fundamental ones in a group like this—there was a disposition to explore the opinions of others without condemning them as misguided, ignorant, or unprincipled.

This sense of community came about because the members communicated with each other—fifty-five thousand words' worth—in surroundings that helped develop confidence and mutual respect. They were all working toward the common goal of constructively investigating a major issue of our time, and they thought the task at hand more important than the winning of converts to any particular brand of thinking. Especially helpful in the growth of this group, or "community," spirit was the background paper by Francis Chase Rosecrance, associate dean, School of Education, New York University, which challenged, though not necessarily channeled, the thinking; the ability of the chairman, Shepherd L. Witman, executive director of the Cleveland Council on World Affairs, to keep the discussion moving along amiably and meaningfully; and the "corridor chatter" between sessions which gave members a chance to air in more detail with small groups those points which they thought needed explanation.

Running through the sessions were five major themes or queries, and these form the framework of the summary that follows. The first had to do with definitions: What are we talking about when we discuss *sense of community* in *industrial civilization?* The second was an appraisal of trends: What has been happening to our sense of community, and why? The third and fourth dealt with problems: What are the main community problems that we face today? What may be done in a practical way to increase the sense of community and to meet these problems successfully? The fifth, and final, theme might be called "notes for future reference"— points listed by members when, toward the end of the session, the chairman asked "What have the roundtable discussions left unsaid?"

DEFINITIONS

"INDUSTRIAL CIVILIZATION"

D. W. Brogan, professor of political science at the University of Cambridge, England, made the point that the roundtable ought to talk about "the whole industrial complex" and the way it affects people and their sense of community, whether the people live in big cities or small towns. The chairman, Mr. Witman, referred also to agricultural, rural communities. Are they not also, in their modern form, an aspect of industrial civilization? Wells Bennett, dean of the College of Architecture and Design, University of Michigan, observed in reply that the mechanization of farming has been an important part of industrial development; and David E. Lilienthal, consultant to management in New York and Washington, and former chairman of the Atomic Energy Commission and the Tennessee Valley Authority, expanded the point.

MR. LILIENTHAL: I think agricultural life has been at least as profoundly affected in all the senses which we are discussing here by industrialization and technology as has city life. . . . Electricity, radio, the telephone and modern highways, which are some of the evidences of technology, have completely changed agricultural living in most parts of the country, whether there is large-scale farming or not. . . .

Sidney Painter, professor of history, Johns Hopkins University, felt it would be hopeless to try to sort out aspects of present-day American society which are to be considered "industrial" from those which are not.

The group agreed, therefore, that for its purposes "industrial civilization" would mean life as it is lived in twentieth-century America, whether in the city, the small town, or the countryside, and that the roundtable should not attempt to divorce industry from the whole of society, even for discussion purposes.

"SENSE OF COMMUNITY"

The group also wrestled with the meaning of *sense of community*, never becoming precise but arriving at a working agreement. The accepted conclusion was that *sense of community* means a sense of belonging, which, in turn, is based on participation of people in common efforts, perhaps in a factory, in some civic affair, or in several communities of interest.

There was agreement that communication (contact) was necessary for a sense of community and that, through working together on common projects, people from many walks of life could build up a sense of belonging to a larger whole. The emphasis was upon belonging, participating, communicating with others, though the members of the group differed considerably as to the area within which a community could effectively exist.

Here there began to emerge a persistent difference in point of view among the members. Some, like Baker Brownell, professor of philosophy, Northwestern University, held that the desired sense of community could exist only when people met each other intimately through several interests, so that they could know each other as "whole men," not just in specialized, fleeting, or casual contacts. Those who took this view were likely to be most interested in ways to rebuild the cultural and economic bases of the small-town community or to develop local neighborhood communities in metropolitan areas. Others, like John E. Burchard, dean of Humanities and Social Studies at the Massachusetts Institute of Technology, held that the lives which human beings are able to lead within the more specialized contacts of city living are not necessarily lacking in satisfactions. They pointed to the "sense of community" that develops around specialized work activities, as in a factory or a professional community, and they viewed with considerable skepticism the alleged human advantages of small-town communities or of preindustrial conditions. Still others, of whom Wallace K. Harrison, architect, was the most outspoken, preferred for themselves the relative anonymity and freedom of big-city life; they did not like too much of those all-round human contacts which others regarded as the great virtue of the village. Still another line of thought, stressed by Mr. Lilienthal and others, cut across all the preceding views and at the end seemed to be rather generally accepted in the roundtable. It was that a sense of community these days need not—indeed must not—be confined to the small neighborhood but can and should broaden in scope until a person has a fellow feeling for people even across the seas, as well as for his nearer neighbors.

ATTAINMENT OF COMMUNITY IN RURAL AND URBAN AREAS

The chairman asked whether it might not be easier to achieve a worth-while sense of community in rural than in city areas.

CHAIRMAN WITMAN: Is it true that the rural area has the simplest organization? They are all farmers, and they live in small compact units in which everybody knows everyone.

MR. BURCHARD: But doesn't necessarily love everybody. Don't think it is all love.

MR. PAINTER: You don't have a simple community. You have farmers and you have farm laborers; you have country lawyers; you have the man who has been a farmer, or would be if he had enough energy to farm. You have, it seems to me, just as complicated stratifications.

MR. COGHLAN: Don't forget the village atheist.

MR. BROWNELL: And the village idiot.

MR. PAINTER: And the village drunk, who in our farm area was always the deputy sheriff. [Laughter] It seems to me fully as complicated.

Ralph Coghlan, former editor of the editorial page, St. Louis *Post-Dispatch*, now with the office of the Defense Mobilization Director, had been reading the background paper. He quoted a passage which said, "In the older rural community the neighbors would drive by the land and comment on the height of a neighbor's grain, the straight, clean rows of cultivated corn, the number, size, and quality of his cattle and horses."

MR. COGHLAN: That sort of thing is lacking in our big communities. . . . In other words, what I am thinking about is the day-by-day living in an industrial community on the part of the average person. How can we make that person feel that he really belongs? . . .

MR. BURCHARD: It seems to me in our nostalgia for the village that all of us left, apparently, and to which none of us has returned . . . We are getting confused as to what the farmer was doing when he looked at the grain and the cows. They were all technicians, and that was admiration for their professional skill. Nowadays we have different communities from the ones we have been talking about, and those are the communities of our work. In these communities we test our skill, as people once did on the farm. Mr. Coghlan, as a journalist among other journalists, has certain standards of pride. These journalists talk about their common work interests. Businessmen talk about theirs; educators talk about theirs; and so do people who work in factories. . . . After all, a man is in the plant a great many hours a day, and maybe that is his community. . . .

THE COMMUNITY OF WORK

Mr. Brogan: I just want to agree with Dr. Burchard. I think the community may be a great many things including a plant and not a town. . . .

Mr. Brogan then spoke of a visit he had made to Clydebank, which has John Brown's, the most famous shipyard in the world, and also the biggest Singer plant in Britain, employing some 15,000 people. He had given a lecture on America and, to connect it with local interests, had made several references to shipbuilding; but to his surprise there was hardly any show of interest in this. The local librarian later explained, "the people from John Brown's never come to lectures."

Mr. Brogan: What the community is in Clydebank, apart from John Brown's and Singer's, I don't know; but I know what it isn't. It is not the public library, and it is not other things of the same kind. That is what I think we might bear in mind: that in a modern industrial community the community may in fact be the factory itself. It may be the nearest approach to the community that there is. Whether it is a good community—that isn't the question. It may be a real community. I don't think it is any use to evade that in a modern industrial society. . . .

Harcourt Brown, professor of French language and literature at Brown University, drew attention to another kind of "community of work."

Mr. Brown: In many communities where there is a university, the university will form a community entirely apart from the local industries, and the university people are very much aware that their only possible community is themselves. I think most of the academic men will have probably experienced that.

Returning to the notion of the factory community and Mr. Brogan's instance of Clydebank, Mr. Bennett observed that the size of the plant makes quite a difference. The factory mentioned in Clydebank and the Corning Glass Works in Corning are quite different in this respect from, say, a small planing mill. The group's rapporteur, Irwin T. Sanders, head of the Department of Sociology at the University of Kentucky, noted that even the larger industrial plants are not complete communities.

MR. SANDERS: Do the people who work in a plant send their children to school in a plant? Or do they go to church in a plant?

MR. BROGAN: I didn't mean they did any of these things in that sense, but at John Brown's they are actually doing it in a sense because the plant deeply affects education through large contributions of time and money. . . . I am not certain there is a community which covers all the activities of any individual at all. There are cases when it is so; there are cases when it isn't so. A man can be a member of four or five different communities. . . .

COMMUNITY AND PERSONAL FREEDOM

Some people, and they were represented at the roundtable, do not want to be forced into a "sense of community" by the accident of neighborhood or any compulsion; they value the freedom to be alone and to choose their own "communities."

MR. HARRISON: I happen to be a maverick. I don't happen to like the community. I live in New York, and the one thing I prize and love is the fact that I can be by myself. It is the one city on earth where I know I can be by myself and nobody bothers me.

MR. BROWNELL: You are suggesting there is no community there?

MR. HARRISON: No, I am suggesting I have my own community, and it is freedom. It is a freedom from these restraints that people are talking about putting on me and—being just a maverick—I say that I think we must consider this seriously from the point of view of education, and, in thinking of education, we have to think of the freedom involved in any community efforts. There must be a desire to do something on the part of the people. We must create this desire in order to get anything really done. I don't believe there is any group effort worth-while unless that desire happens to exist.

CHAIRMAN WITMAN: Perhaps it is less that you don't believe in communities than it is that you don't believe in other people's communities.

MR. HARRISON: I don't believe in anybody making me join a community.

WHAT HAS BEEN HAPPENING TO OUR SENSE OF COMMUNITY?

The attempt to explain historically what has been happening to our sense of community raised the most lively issue of the round-table. Two schools of thought emerged. One tended to hold the Industrial Revolution accountable for a regrettable loss of neighborhood association and for many of the social problems that confront us. If our civilization is to achieve the best in human values, this group thought, we must find ways to recapture this personal quality in our community living.

The other school argued that the Industrial Revolution had brought in many more constructive values than it had destroyed, that the traits of the old neighborhood are passing—a fact which we may as well recognize—but that there are other ways in which human beings can achieve the personal satisfactions they require.

These issues, of course, were never completely resolved; but a certain amount of common ground did appear in the course of the discussion as the following record will show.

MR. BROWNELL: It seems to me we have a profound problem in the sense that the kind of industrial civilization that we are developing tends to divide people on the basis of many different activities. . . . That is a simple but a fundamental point. I prefer the community where the people are organically related in the terms of many activities connected with a full life rather than in terms of specialized contacts with many different people. . . .

Later Mr. Brownell elaborated on this theme. He spoke particularly of "the fragmentation of life." The human being gets broken down into various specialized functions and loses his wholeness. Some members of the roundtable tended to accept that increasing fragmentation of life and to justify it; but, in Mr. Brownell's view, this tendency toward fragmentation is disastrous to human values.

MR. BROWNELL: Modern technology must meet this problem somehow. I think it will have to be done through modern technology, not by repudiating modern technology. But it isn't being done now. To me it seems extremely important that the community is a type of organization or a type of association of people who are not fragmented.

Other roundtables in the Conference were dealing with "Leisure and Human Values in Industrial Civilization" and "Confidence in Life in Industrial Civilization." Mr. Brownell suggested that the fragmentation of life had an important bearing on both these other topics.

MR. BROWNELL: We have not been discussing leisure here, but one of the great problems of today is unquestionably the fact that leisure is segregated from work. Much of it has to be, I know. Still, life in which leisure is segregated from work and made into a different function is not entirely good.

In the same way, I would say that one of the great reasons for our lack of confidence or religious interest is this almost fatal fragmentation and segregation of the different functions of our lives. We don't put people together. We are not living with whole people.

This is an extremely important question. It underlies, I think, this whole Conference.

Mr. Burchard was not willing to accept without more evidence the assumption that our specialized and complex society is as inferior in human values to the simpler preindustrial society as Mr. Brownell seemed to think.

MR. BURCHARD: The implication seems to be that there is something evil and bad for human beings in a change from a Gothic society . . . or a Greek society to a large and complex society, or that the village of five hundred is the only community in which human beings are basically going to be happy and content and can live. I would say the evidence for this is pretty thin. The trend toward urbanization is there. It certainly shows the desire for the individual to escape from this village in which he was born and in which there could be no anonymity. Why do people leave the village? Because they are dumb? Not necessarily.

Mr. Lilienthal observed that the roundtable might give some attention not merely to the defects of industrial civilization but also to ways in which human values, and especially the individual's sense of community, had been increased by modern industrialism. Industrial civilization has broadened the individual's sense of responsibility toward others at the same time that it has increased the individual's need for others. Keith S. McHugh, president of the New York Telephone Company, agreed.

MR. McHUGH: Mr. Chairman, Mr. Burchard, and Mr. Lilienthal have stated precisely and better than I can the questions I have about this. I started off having some serious questions about two sentences in the opening paper which will illustrate what I mean: "Unfortunately, the new technology is also responsible for many less desirable features of modern life," and another sentence, "Perhaps the most serious evil resulting from industrial civilization is the loss of the sense of meaning of life for the individual and his fellows." Both seem to be accepted a priori as springboards for this whole discussion, and I find myself with great difficulty accepting them. . . . I have no doubt that industrialization has had something to do with a lost sense of community, but there are many other causes that have had something to do with it—loss of moral and spiritual values, for example. No one has mentioned the family, the only group, I believe, that history shows has always hung together as a community from the earliest days.

Mr. Lilienthal then spoke further of the effects of industrial civilization, basing his remarks on observations over a period of fifteen years or more in a relatively unindustrialized region—the Tennessee Valley—where new industrial activities were coming in.

MR. LILIENTHAL: These industries varied greatly in their outlook— all the way from the manufacturing plant which came as a kind of refugee from other communities that it had milked without carrying out its community responsibilities, to the large, modern, progressive viewpoint represented, for example, by Corning. . . . My own experience in the Tennessee Valley has been that the infusion of a new industrial enterprise into a community has brought with it more positive values than existed in the community before and has stirred those enterprises that were already there. Modern management, in respect to community responsibility, bears no more resemblance to that of twenty-five years ago than the modern policies in respect to labor organization bear to the policies of twenty-five years ago. It would be fruitless to dig up that past if we are talking about what should be done today. . . .

The nostalgia about the small community and about the isolated community or neighborhood, I think, is quite a false one and will not stand inspection. The great point about the sense of community as influenced by modern means of communication is how broad it is. If I now, because of industrialization—as I believe to be true—have a sense of responsibility for people in India or people in other parts of the United States, I think this is a great evidence of the broadening of the sense of community; and it can be attributed directly, I think, to industrialization.

Mr. BURCHARD: Hear! Hear!

Mr. McHUGH: Check.

John M. Gaus, professor of government at Harvard University, suggested that perhaps it was commerce rather than industrialization as such which had been most responsible for the larger world outlook. He and Mr. Brown spoke of the wide-flung contacts of the seacoast towns of Maine and Massachusetts in the old days of the clipper ships, before modern industrialism.

Mr. LILIENTHAL: Let me select an illustration. Fifty or seventy-five years ago in the state of Indiana a taxpayer in Porter County (which I know better than any other part of the state) . . . would have resented the idea that he had any obligation to take care of the poor kids in Brown County, which was then an impoverished part of the state. We now have a feeling of responsibility, a sense of community with kids everywhere in the United States and elsewhere. Whether it is commerce or whether it is because industrialization has accelerated commerce is a fine point I wouldn't even want to argue. The fact that the change in the physical basis of our life, which I have been describing as industrialization, has raised moral standards and has also extended our sense of responsibility seems to me, at least, to be something that ought to be indicated in our report. . . .

Mr. HARRISON: Mr. Chairman, I would like to make two points in backing up what Mr. Lilienthal has said about this. Number one, I think we ought to take industry off the hook. I don't think the problems we are talking about stem only from industry. They are problems of the whole community. Industry, as near as I can see, has helped us out to some extent.

Number two, we must realize that we are living in a modern world where there are going to be new kinds of approaches and where we must utilize the various means that we have at hand to solve these problems. We have a bigger, a wider, and a richer field of experience to work in for the future. The thing that has impressed me more than anything else in this discussion has been the fact that, while I do like to close my door in New York, I certainly think a lot more about Iran and Korea and a few other places today than I would have twenty-five years ago. These wider responsibilities have come into every man's life through our media of communication—the press, the radio, the movies, and everything else. . . .

A certain confusion was evident in this part of the discussion between "the industrial revolution" or "industrialization"—in the broad sense which the historian uses to denote the major trends which have characterized our modern, industrial society—and "industry" in the sense of particular firms or management as a group. Mr. Rosecrance cleared up this point and then went on to make some statements about moral values in present-day living which were then challenged by skeptical Mr. Burchard.

MR. ROSECRANCE: I was glad to have industry taken off the hook. As a matter of fact, throughout my background paper I might have used the phrase "living in twentieth-century civilization," realizing that the chief characteristic of twentieth-century civilization is an increased amount of industrialization. But by no means have I thought at any time that industry was "on the hook," so to speak. . . .

Let me illustrate some of the changes that have taken place. When I was a lad, thrift was something which was highly valued; and I think my father had a relative assurance that if he saved his money he would be able to have a safe old age. I ask you, does a person who values thrift now have that same assurance?

Or, let us take the kind of thing which was preached to me in our college chapel: service to mankind as the duty of all of us, no matter what kind of profession we went into. That was presented as the acme of every person's life. At times I think—I am speaking now for the college students whom I see—that their notion today about their objective in life is to do the other fellow before he does him.

I could go on with this kind of thing to say that religious, moral, and spiritual values have weakened. I doubt if there is a man around this table that doesn't want them strengthened. I would be interested in hearing how we could have them strengthened. . . .

MR. BURCHARD: I have yet to see any evidence, regardless of churchgoing, that there is any diminution in the sense of responsibility of, say, the citizens of this country, the parents of children. I think there is a good deal of evidence of psychology in the basic attitudes of these boys in college who often talk very differently than they are going to act later. They all have to go through all kinds of stages. I am sure Mr. Rosecrance can remember all kinds of stages he had to get over. I don't think you can make a case to show that, as a people, the people of the Western world are basically any less idealistic than they were when they all went to church and had it preached to them, because many a man took that sense of obligation only on Sunday between half past ten and noon. It is just my opinion . . . but I think that society is amazingly idealistic. . . .

Also, even if it isn't true that today's society is idealistic, the last thing one could blame for this would be industrialization. One would probably have to blame increasing knowledge.

Louis Wirth, professor of sociology at the University of Chicago, commented further on the alleged decline of moral and spiritual values. In his view, it was the character of the moral content of our thinking that had undergone change.

MR. WIRTH: I would say that the allegiances of people nowadays are more "contrived" than "traditional." In the old days, we had allegiance to kinship groups and immediate neighbors. Now we feel a linkage with the most remote causes, the most indirect appeals, to which we are all subject.

I think what Mr. Rosecrance is pointing out is that we are living in an age which the old German poet, Schiller, spoke of as the age of "die Entzauberung der Welt," the disenchantment of the universe. In other words, allegiances today are put more on a secular basis, and we don't give these allegiances credit for being moral obligations just because they are secular. . . . But in practice there is more concern about the health of the community today than before; there is more concern about dependency, about children, about recreation, about all these other things in the average American community. . . .

It is evident from this brief summary of the discussion that, while there were decidedly different points of view in the round-table and these were maintained, there was also some meeting of minds. Those who felt that the sense of community had been dying out or that there has been a loss of a central meaning in life under modern conditions also thought that the modern technology of organization and intelligent planning could be brought to bear to give people a view of the whole community and their significant part in it. On the other hand, those who took a more optimistic view did not argue that all is well or that "nature should take its course." They, too, agreed that much needs to be done and that action needs to be based on a fair assessment of the present situation, regardless of how we got that way.

WHAT IS THE SITUATION TODAY?—THE PROBLEMS

At an early stage in the discussion the roundtable began to address itself to the appraisal of problems related to a sense of community. Somewhat later the group grew restive under the *problem*, or negative, approach and decided to devote its attention more specifically to consideration of what could be done. Nevertheless, the preliminary discussion of problems proved highly important because of the way it stimulated thought, raised issues, and eventually led to an agreement as to the use of terms.

The background paper had, of course, raised a number of problems which were in the minds of members. Some of these were emphasized and some new ones added in the discussion summarized below.

APATHY, NARROW INTERESTS VS. PARTICIPATION

MR. WIRTH: If I were to put the problem as I see it . . . we have political apathy as over against the urgent need for participation. We have segmentation of interest—which I think is not to be bemoaned but taken as a fact—as over against the integrated needs of life. We have spectatorism as over against the important urge and need for being identified with something important. These I think could be spelled out in great detail.

I think they arise from the fact that where you have large numbers of people with different origins living in diverse ways, impersonally related to one another in an anonymous fashion, you find them pursuing personal and individual rather than common or group ends. . . .

Mr. Wirth spoke of the need for organization in our modern, highly segmented life and also of the tendency of the number of organizations to mount. He illustrated these points with an example.

Mr. Wirth: Some years ago, some students of mine and I undertook a study of what we called "voluntary associations." This was in Chicago. We found that there are as many organizations as there are conceivable human interests. We studied about 13,000 of these organizations. I am sure that we only scratched the surface. There are probably at least fifty times to a hundred times that many.

I came across one organization that particularly interested me. . . . It was in the telephone book until World War I started, when the boys apparently dispersed. It was intriguingly called "The Independent Organization of Unorganized Independents." I think that calls attention to the pull in two directions that we all feel. We know that without belonging to these organizations we are paralyzed, we are impotent, we are negligible. Yet we fear the dominance and the monopoly of our loyalties that these organizations wish to exercise over us. As an old teacher of mine put it, "What a man belongs to constitutes most of his life career and all of his obituary." [Laughter]

The background paper rather bemoans the fact that this is so. . . . To me, the segmentation of life, the fact that individuals are interested in highly segmented, personal, individual, or small group problems and interests, ranging from a poker club to a political party, cannot be talked out of existence. We have to take it as material upon which to build a community.

ARCHAIC LOCAL UNITS

A number of members of the roundtable presented as a problem the inadequate adjustments that have been made in our local political structures in order to fit them for modern industrial life. Ted F. Silvey, staff executive of the Congress of Industrial Organizations and secretary of the National CIO Community Services Committee, raised the issue.

MR. SILVEY: We are attempting to operate in a highly industrialized society with the political structure that was suitable to a primitive, colonial society. . . . I can best show what I mean by referring to the towns of northern New Jersey around the Newark area. There must be sixty of them. Those towns and the prevailing county and township governments were built for the 1740 period. They still operate pretty much, I guess, the way they did in those days, except for the implications of transportation and communication that are imposed on them.

This is one thing that prevents the individual from functioning effectively in his community. He may live in Montclair and work in Newark; he may belong to organizations in Garfield; he may work in Kearny and live in the Oranges and belong to organizations in Rosedale and go to church in some other place. . . .

Perhaps the way to deal with the situation would be to make northern New Jersey a whole city; call it the City of Northern New Jersey, with one government, one community, one transportation system, one system of communication, one sewer system. At present these are all fragmented. But when the legislature in Trenton is asked to do anything about it, of course, you run up against real estate interests, and rural interests as against city interests; and everything is in conflict with each other in such a way as to frustrate completely the individual who might wish to belong to anything anywhere in this mixed-up cosmopolitan arrangement. . . .

MR. GAUS: May I raise a question in there, Mr. Chairman? It seems to me what has just been said rather illustrates almost too much sense of community. The fact of the metropolitan region is, I think, present all over the world. But, embedded in the suburban and municipal and other jurisdictions, we have a set of loyalties that people won't give up quickly; otherwise the problem would have been solved long since. . . . Nevertheless, at bottom, there is a real sense of the community in these local suburban districts that I assume is one of the objectives that we are trying to achieve.

MR. COGHLAN: Mr. Chairman, St. Louis, as you possibly know, is a city that is hemmed around by a restrictive boundary line that was established some fifty years ago which forbade it to grow to the west.

It can't grow to the east because of the Mississippi. In the course of time, the western part of St. Louis has grown up in small communities. It really is one city, but this artificial line shuts off the new communities.

Well, as Mr. Silvey pointed out for northern New Jersey, there obviously would be a great many advantages in making this a thoroughly metropolitan area—that is, in the matter of common sewers, common police, schools, and so on. Over the past twenty years, numerous attempts have been made to draw those outlying communities into the city proper. But that movement has been strongly resisted by the members of the small communities. . . .

In such situations small community life in suburban communities is greatly prized by these people who like to have their own schools and their own school administrators. They like to be able to know who the mayor is and to be able to speak to him on the street; they dread being drawn into a large city where that sense of community would be lost.

REJECTED PEOPLE

Mr. Silvey also raised another problem—that of people in the community who feel rejected for one reason or another.

MR. SILVEY: The people who are rejected may be at any economic level. I think first, though, of the Negro people and the frustrations that they have to suffer. Because of their high visibility, their rejection follows them constantly in all the daily life they have.

Then I think, also, of the rejection that is felt by very rich people, particularly because they know they are so useless to society. There is a tremendous organization manipulation to prove to them that they are not useless; but if they have got any sense at all, they know how useless they are, and they therefore feel rejected. . . . The sons of rich men who turn radical try to compensate for their uselessness by joining the Communist Party and giving some of their fortune to it. The best example, of course, from the community standpoint is the rich man who, escaping the clownishness and the joining or being used by the Communist Party or some foolish group, does constructive things with his time and money. I am thinking, for example, of Marshall Field, who has been through a whole cycle and came out to do some very useful things.

What can be done to reclaim people who feel that they are useless or who feel that they are rejected by society, so that they may be embraced in the community, both to add to their value in society and to achieve their own redemption as members of the community?

THE COMMUNITY OF MAN AND NATURE

MR. BROWN: I have a question. I don't know whether it has anything to do with this group . . . except that it does bear on the problem of the effect which being brought up in an industrial civilization may have on a human being. Mine is the general question about the larger community in which we live, which consists of plants and animals and geography and nature as a whole. Our perspective here, unfortunately, is almost entirely within the human frame of reference.

I am much interested in the other because of my interest in nature. I spend a good part of my life attempting to escape from industrial civilization and living in the Canadian woods. I do that every summer for a considerable period of time and that, to my mind, is about the best part of the year for me. . . . I don't particularly like industrial civilization. I think these things that are being done to it are palliatives, and I am rather distressed when I see the spread of our tremendous cities and wonder what they are going to be like in the year 2051, which is just one hundred years from now. What is going to be left of our natural background—plants and animals, birds? What is going to be the picture?

CHAIRMAN WITMAN: There is a point on which I am not clear. Are you suggesting that the best way to handle civilization is to move into the Canadian woods?

MR. BROWN: No, only two or three people should do that. [Laughter]

MR. BURCHARD: Will you note that Mr. Brown doesn't want to do it all the year round.

MR. BROWN: I can't afford to.

PRACTICAL MEASURES FOR IMPROVING THE SENSE OF COMMUNITY

The area of greatest concern to the roundtable was that of practical measures. In what ways may people gain more sense of community? It had already been pointed out that a sense of community must, in the final analysis, be achieved within the individual. He is the one who must put together in some kind of sensible arrangement all the different segments of his life. But it also seemed apparent that social groups—whether management or labor, civic groups, or special interests—could have some part in making the task easier for the individual.

One approach is to improve the physical and economic setting so that people will have a pride in their surroundings. This calls for conscious coordination and planning by industry in partnership with others interested in sound community life. As concrete examples of what can be accomplished when people pull together, the group heard from some of its members about the encouraging community accomplishments in Pittsburgh and Toledo.

HOW IT WAS DONE IN PITTSBURGH

Edward R. Weidlein, president of the Mellon Institute of Industrial Research, gave a firsthand participant's account of a remarkable recent renaissance of community action in his home city.

MR. WEIDLEIN: Mr. Chairman, I might tell you what we have been doing in the city of Pittsburgh and Allegheny County, which is the most highly industrialized center in the world. We do not want to hold ourselves up as an example of perfection, but I do believe that since World War II the city of Pittsburgh has been attracting more attention than any other city in the United States as an example of real accomplishment in community development.

We had a small group of people at the start. . . . We all realized that there are many different organizations within a community, and that everyone is so much interested in his own that there exist conflicts with other interests. We had a peculiar political situation, in that we had a Democratic administration in the city of Pittsburgh and in Allegheny County and a Republican administration in Harrisburg. We needed funds from the state. We had a Democratic administration in Washington, and we needed funds from the federal government.

Also we have the same problem that Mr. Coghlan described for St. Louis. The city of Pittsburgh is a small center in itself. It is surrounded by many communities which are also local-minded. . . . We organized the Allegheny Conference for Community Development, which takes in the whole county, consisting of one hundred twenty-eight communities besides the city of Pittsburgh. We conceived the idea that we were either going to get cooperation—all pulling together and working together—or, as Mr. Mellon said, "We give it back to the Indians and move someplace else."

We first united the political groups, which we didn't believe we could do. . . . We have had no interference from these units. . . . All has been done entirely for the development of the community. The result was that we put eight bills through the legislature enabling the authorities to go ahead and wholly revamp the program for the city. This included the smoke abatement project for the largest area that has even been covered by an ordinance of this type. The railroads started to object to it in the beginning, but they finally came through wholeheartedly. We have practically all the railroads dieselized at the present time. We have eliminated the smoke nuisance from the city of Pittsburgh. It is amazing to see what that city is today as compared with what it was even three years ago. The county ordinance has been in effect only two years this October.

We have the various cooperating groups—the steel mills and all others—on research programs to eliminate dust and dirt from the atmosphere. We have a five-year program set up; it has been operating for two years. A report is made to the smoke committee of the progress of these research activities.

Summarizing briefly: We have the stream pollution program going; we are dealing with mass transportation; we have a parking authority; we have set up a sewage disposal system for the whole county; we have a park development project—a beautiful layout to which the State and the Federal Government have contributed; and we have a slum clearance plan with the authority to go in and clear out any objectionable area.

The whole community is working together, and before any rebuilding program is started it is tied in with the complete redevelopment. Formerly we had difficulties if a highway or a thoroughfare was to be put through in any one place—a department store would object because the people might be taken away from its area. Now these varying interests have forgotten all about their differences. They are working together and pulling together. . . .

CHAIRMAN WITMAN: Tell us why we shouldn't all move to Pittsburgh. [Laughter] But you have all the communities in this particular picture.

MR. WEIDLEIN: We have the complete program set up. The Business Council raises the necessary money for all these things. We have a regional planning association, which is a research organization. All the various groups today are pulling together and working together. We have a cleanup campaign going on right now, to be carried out each ensuing year. The only city that is ahead of us in this respect is Memphis. But we have been second for the last three years, and with the cleanup campaign we have taken an enormous amount of real junk out of the city of Pittsburgh. . . .

CHAIRMAN WITMAN: May I raise this point, Mr. Weidlein: the key here is coordination, is that correct?

MR. WEIDLEIN: That is the whole idea.

CHAIRMAN WITMAN: What worries me now is this: according to Mr. Weidlein, Pittsburgh has done the task. It is all accomplished. What happens to the individuals since the community effort is over?

MR. BURCHARD: Those of us who have lived in Pittsburgh know they have not finished.

MR. WEIDLEIN: In my own organization, I was running into difficulty, just as the universities were in getting good professors and like the industries in obtaining good young men to come to Pittsburgh. Nobody wanted to live in Pittsburgh. Today, every person is proud to live in Pittsburgh. . . .

MR. COGHLAN: May I ask for clarification? At any point in your Pittsburgh movement was this thing taken to the electorate for confirmation?

MR. WEIDLEIN: No, we did not have to do this. It was necessary to get the bills through the legislature, and so, of course, we had to work with the representatives in the House and the Senate in Harrisburg.

MR. COGHLAN: May I make this point then: that possibly what you have done is a triumph of leadership rather than participation on the part of the individual?

MR. WEIDLEIN: It took participation on the part of the individual. For example, in order to put over the Allegheny Smoke Ordinance, a group of 18,000 clubwomen joined forces. The influence of this group helped put the bill through in Harrisburg. We have over two hundred million dollars' worth of development work going on in Pittsburgh today. It is all being properly taken care of—not from taxes—and the people of Pittsburgh are proud of it. . . .

THE EXAMPLE OF TOLEDO

Next the roundtable heard about another outstanding achievement of community betterment in an American city. The member who told the story was William E. Levis, chairman of the Executive Committee of the Owens-Illinois Glass Company.

MR. LEVIS: I think there is a definite pattern for community improvement, and Mr. Weidlein pretty much stated it in the Pittsburgh case. One principle is that you have to set your sights high enough to have a problem that is really difficult of accomplishment to really attract your better community talent. I would like to relate three or four specific instances from our experience in Toledo.

We started out in Toledo with the city management form of government. We accomplished that by a study, a survey, the getting in of the experts. Then we turned to the community chest, because we had never reached our community chest goal for a period of ten years. We tried to enlist the strongest people in the community, we did advertising, we spoke at every possible meeting that we could get together. The result was that we accomplished our goal almost 100 per cent and that revived the interest of many people who had taken a defeatist attitude.

Then we found that our city finances were bad, and we started on a city income tax project of one per cent. Because of a referendum insisted upon by the CIO, it was necessary to have a special election just on this one issue; and it was won almost three to one against this opposition. With the new tax, the city authorities got themselves out of debt. Then DiSalle, whom you know, really went to work on the management-labor program, and we got on with those particular problems.

Now, there was one project that the citizens of Toledo never hoped to accomplish, and that was to get a new union station. [Laughter] They finally got a promise of a million-dollar union station, which rose to three and a half, but which we finished at almost nine million dollars. For this project the whole community turned to, with the head of the two papers as the chairman. It was really terrific. There were all kinds of meetings, including a tea for the ladies where there was an attendance of 48,000 people. Only because it was a difficult program did it really challenge the people who wanted to build that community. . . .

I repeat, in Toledo we accomplished things because we set our goal high enough to do those things that the people didn't think could be done. We had challenging tasks, and all the women's clubs and the Legion posts and the church societies and everybody else had a focal point around which to rally. . . .

COMMUNITY COUNCILS

The group then sought to draw some general lessons from these two examples of community effort and from other experiences of members. Mr. Lilienthal pointed out that, as the reports of Pittsburgh and Toledo indicated, in some communities we were no longer trying to find a devil—plutocracy, greed, the boss, or industry—but were trying to solve the concrete problems of smoke abatement, recreation in relation to juvenile delinquency, and other community problems by making use of technical people who are for the most part the product of our industrial civilization.

Among the essentials in the development of a stronger sense of community is to find means to increase participation on the part of the people. Several ways were proposed: to bring people into the decision-making process, to use community councils, to promote self-surveys, to provide local events such as community drama, and to help people develop interests outside their jobs.

Mr. Rosecrance: One way—not the only way, but sometimes a useful one—to activate citizens in local communities and to get them to work together in the solution of local problems is through a type of voluntary organization known as the community council. Such a community council is to be distinguished from the council of social agencies or the community chest. Representatives of the social agencies, of the chambers of commerce, of educational groups, of welfare groups, of labor groups, of racial groups—if those exist—are all brought together into a community council thinking about local problems, beginning perhaps with the most noncontroversial issues. . . .

Marion B. Folsom, treasurer of the Eastman Kodak Company, commented that the situation varies from city to city. Some need a community council and some are accomplishing that same purpose in other ways.

Mr. Folsom: In some communities you find you don't need any over-all council because the various agencies are doing a good job. In Rochester during the war we set up a postwar planning council which had one particular, specific job to do there. When that was done, we went back to the previous situation without a community council, because we thought the other agencies in the community would do the job. There was no reason for having a superorganization all the time. . . .

Mr. Brogan expressed doubt that the community council type of organization is desirable at all. Some of the best results come from competition in a society, and the idea of a community council ignores the fact that there may be no single community purpose at all. The interest of the people may be more concretely related to one plant or to the interests of those living on the same street. "If you start with the idea that unity breeds community, I think you may end up with just another wheel, a fifth, sixth wheel."

Chairman Witman: Is there any comment to that?

Mr. Rosecrance: Yes, I would like to comment. In the first place, I do not have in mind that in a great city like Rochester, New York City, or Chicago you can have one community council that will solve all the problems for all the city. I am perfectly aware of the fact that great cities have neighborhoods. I know one neighborhood which has just a simple problem. The problem is how to get the garbage collected. It is collected in other neighborhoods, but it isn't collected well in that neighborhood. Now, the people, the citizens of that particular neighborhood have a problem. I think they might well have a neighborhood council to work on the business of how they can get the garbage collected.

Neither am I thinking that one should put in a community council when there is another organization, such as a chamber of commerce, already doing the job adequately from an over-all point of view. I would want to be certain that it was really doing the job well.

There is no magic about names. I don't care whether you call it the chamber of commerce or the council of social agencies or what. What

I am interested in is the solution of problems—the solution of problems without legislation, without referring the problems to the state capital, without referring them to Washington. I believe we have a tendency in this country to wash our hands of our local problems. That was shown by the Kefauver Committee. We allow or expect someone else other than ourselves to tackle the local problems.

Frederic W. Ecker, executive vice-president of the Metropolitan Life Insurance Company, again stressed that different methods of organizing to deal with community problems are needed in different communities and especially that the factor of size is important.

MR. ECKER: Might it not assist us if we looked at these things from the standpoint of the size of the community involved? It seems to me that the approach must be quite different in New York City from the approach in some much smaller town.

Mr. Wirth, carrying further Mr. Lilienthal's point about the use of technical experts in the solution of community problems, noted that it is important to identify these problems carefully and to establish a priority among them. He also thought that participation by the people might be increased through self-surveys and through giving people a sense of achievement in a successful execution of concrete projects—be it in traffic, housing, or health. This calls for the development of leadership which can transfer from a completed project to a new need. He continued:

MR. WIRTH: Some of the problems involve the manipulation of physical things—houses, streets, buildings, utilities, and so on. Some of them involve the generation and modification of attitudes and sentiments and ideals and ideas. The techniques are not the same. . . .

That raises the question of the neighborhood. I happen to be one of those who believes that the neighborhood is not the ideal unit around which to build a modern metropolitan society, although I do think that the local area has certain functions to perform. But I don't believe in a self-sufficient series of neighborhoods because, in reality, they never exist, as Mr. Brogan has stated. They shouldn't perhaps exist, because you do narrow and provincialize your life. . . .

Mr. Brownell felt that the group might be ignoring an important element in Mr. Rosecrance's suggestion about community councils. The very being of a community depends upon the co-ordination of different functions, and the community council is essentially a coordinating device. Meeting separate problems one at a time is not going to give you a community. Community consciousness develops out of the inner, organic relationships of one person with another, not in terms of a segment or of one function but in terms of many functions.

Mr. Sanders went on to deal further with the problem of segmentalization and the possible role of the community council in counteracting it.

MR. SANDERS: There are two ways of looking at this sense of community, and I think some of us are looking at it from one way and some from another. This whole matter of segmentalization has to be resolved within the individual in the end. He is the one who has to put these segments together so they have some meaning for him. There we can toss the problem back to the school, to the church, to the family. . . .

Then, there is the other side: looking at it from the standpoint of the way the community is put together. It seems to me all these techniques are important, and we could extend that list two or three times with little difficulty. An essential principle here is that many of our problems or handicaps in community life today arise from the fact that there is no communication among the various people in the community. This group is going along its way, and another group is going along its way. They are not in conflict; they are just not in contact. I would say that oftentimes a simple justification for a community council would be just to afford contact.

SMALL-TOWN RENAISSANCE

Up to this point the discussion of practical measures for building community spirit and increasing the individual's sense of participation had been mostly in terms of large cities. But the round-table had Mr. Brownell to remind it that America, even in this industrial age, does not consist solely of Pittsburghs and Toledos. Mr. Brownell knew his small towns. He had actively participated in a noteworthy experiment designed to explore the possibilities for rebuilding the cultural and economic basis of life in smaller places (see *Small Town Renaissance: A Story of the Montana*

Study, listed in the bibliography pp. 322). He spoke of his work in Montana—"in little places of 80 people, 500 people; no town over 5,000"—and described concretely the case of Darby.

MR. BROWNELL: Darby has about six hundred people. And I would like to suggest that the future of Darby is far more important to this country than the future of Pittsburgh, Toledo, or the rest of them. If we are going to let Darby go, we are lost.

Mr. Brownell emphasized that he and his associates in Montana's university system who were engaged in small-town experiments had not taken the initiative in Darby. The Darby people asked them to come in and help with a job of community self-analysis, as they had done in other places.

MR. BROWNELL: We formed what we called a study group. We made it clear that the study group was not an action group. We didn't go in to try to do something primarily.

Secondly, the study group was distributed. The membership was free, of course, but we canvassed sufficiently ahead of time to know that the membership came from all groups in Darby. That is, the women's club might have liked to have a study group of their own. We said, "No, we want people who aren't members, and we want people from both sides of the tracks so there will be a representative group."

Well, the study group met, mostly they met weekly, to consider problems as they emerged. The group didn't meet primarily to handle any specific problems. Among the problems that emerged out of the discussion of that study group several were especially important:

One was that Darby was just about to become a ghost town. The lumber company that had been in there had cut out the lumber and had gone off and left the piles of debris over all the region, cluttering up the valleys. The ranchers had their little ranches, but they weren't taking care of the streams. Darby probably couldn't exist much longer unless Darby herself did something about it.

A second problem was that the school system of Valley County, where Darby is, has more children per family than any other county and, as is always the case, also had the lowest income of any county in the state.

What was done was this kind of thing. First of all, they decided they wanted to have a community drama. I knew nothing about community drama, but I was able to borrow a man who could help coach them. He came down there to live. They put on a community drama which was more or less a symbol of the entire history of Darby, with the emphasis on conservation—the necessity of forest conservation and the like. It was a tremendous success. There were many more people at the show when they put it on than there were people in Darby. They came from all over. In a town of 600 there were 120 people on the stage at different times. Everybody took part. It went on and on until four o'clock in the morning, and the point is that Darby became aware of itself. . . .

Then another thing happened: A man who is a logger, a lumberjack most of the time, named Danny Gray, was appointed chairman of the committee to study the possibilities for businesses of various sorts in Darby. Danny Gray went at this with remarkable energy and judgment and came up with a recommendation for some ten or fifteen different businesses which he thought might succeed. For example, you couldn't buy lumber in Darby. You had to go seventeen miles to get it. Here you were right in the lumber region and you couldn't get corral posts.

Well, the net result after the study group closed was that various people began working on these different possible projects. One man started a plumbing and well-drilling enterprise. Another put in a small planing mill; he had a little bit of capital. Somebody else financed a garage mechanic who had come back from the Navy. A total of about fourteen little businesses developed there within a period of some three years, employing about 75 more people than had been employed before. That makes a big difference in a little place like Darby.

In other words, Darby became aware of itself, and being conscious of itself as a community, pulled itself up by its own bootstraps and is now—unless we have a crash of some sort—probably a going community. It isn't going to be a ghost town, in all probability.

CHAIRMAN WITMAN: Where did it get its start? Who started its pulling itself up by its own bootstraps?

MR. BROWNELL: Their own suggestions. They asked us to come down. I did nothing but lead the roundtable. I did bring experts from the university to advise them on school taxes when that problem came up.

CHAIRMAN WITMAN: But the initiative to get you down there came from inside the town?

MR. BROWNELL: Yes. They knew we would be available if they wanted us. The point is, to back up Mr. Rosecrance's point of view, that the important thing isn't so much to start with specific problems to answer as to get communities to become aware of themselves. To get people to pulling with each other is the fundamental thing. That, I think, we are inclined to ignore.

COMMUNITY RESPONSIBILITIES OF INDUSTRY

What can and should industrial organizations do to help develop a sense of community? Should a corporate enterprise consider itself a "citizen" and give attention to its community responsibilities? The businessmen in the roundtable were quick to answer in the affirmative, and they referred repeatedly to a new attitude of management in this respect which had developed notably in the past twenty-five years.

MR. McHUGH: Perhaps I can add a little bit to this discussion out of experience. None of you normally think of the telephone company as coming into a community. Chances are we were there when you were a little boy, in some form or another. The fact is, though, that we operate in my company in most of the cities and towns and villages in New York State, and the Bell System operates in some six thousand communities all over the country. The impression that you make on a community when you expect to live there forever using that in a foreseeable sense—become important. . . .

Now, these things that Dr. Wirth has described so well, seem to me to come automatically to your thinking when you are planning that kind of operation. I don't think we described them to ourselves perhaps as precisely or as well; but no one can be in a community, work there and live there, have property there, be dependent upon the market of that consumer group to produce business, without being conscious of these things and giving them great attention.

As far as business is concerned, community participation comes down finally to two rather fundamental things: one, the corporate conduct of the business, which has great influence upon what the town thinks about you; and second, the conduct of your people, that is to say, the kind of people that you have and what they do as individuals in the community. It is a little hard to tell which has the more influence. I suspect the conduct of the people has more than the corporate conduct, although either can get you in great trouble or can redound with great benefit if they are done well.

Of course, that leads in turn to perfectly normal things to think about: What kind of buildings will you design so that they will be a credit to the community instead of an eyesore? Where are you going to locate them? Obviously, the questions of transportation, the labor market, schools, hospitals, all the rest of it enter into this. What shall be your course of corporate conduct with respect to being a citizen in that community? We think that is extremely important not only because of this "foreign ownership" element which is, in small communities especially, always a point that may arise, but because we think we need the cooperative action of the citizens in order to give good service in the community.

As for the participation of our personnel, when we put a manager in a town, we say to him in effect, "This is your town. No matter where you came from, or what your previous experience may have been, or what your other loyalties may be, you are going to be loyal to this community. It is yours, and that is just as much a part of your job as it is to give good service in the community."

We try to say to our people, "The company is going to try to be a good citizen in this community and take part in all general purpose activities affecting the welfare of the community. But you as individuals ought also to take part in the activities of this community. You girls, you chief operators, you ought to take part in the women's activities. You men, you ought to become part of your church and school and local affairs."

So that, as Mr. Lilienthal says—and I know my associates in other lines of business think and feel this same way—managements of business today give as much thought and care to community responsibility as they know how to give. They may make mistakes—we all do—but it can't be said that they don't try to become an integral part of the community and yet at the same time not appear in any sense to dominate it, because that is just as bad on the other side.

Mr. Levis took up this theme and agreed emphatically with Mr. McHugh. Industry is managed today, he said, by people who are much more public relations minded than they used to be.

Even five years ago technical people were largely responsible for community contacts. Now community contacts are increasingly being made the responsibility of personnel people or public relations people. He referred again to the Toledo experience. The effort at civic improvement was inspired by industrialists who believed that their investment in the community was declining in value. But they knew if they were to sponsor the job alone they could not possibly accomplish it, "so they started with the city fathers and with labor and the churches and the public." And, he repeated, they set their sights high enough really to challenge people.

MR. McHugh: I think industry can do a lot about this, Mr. Chairman, and is doing a lot. Mr. Levis said in effect that he wouldn't think of having one of his plant managers who was wholly an engineer—an operating man—any longer. As a practical matter, if he couldn't get any other kind of fellow to do the job, chances are he would supplement him with a right-hand man who would be thinking about community problems in order to make certain that the manager really took these factors into account.

I think industry can add to its teaching and training program with its own people some subject matter, if it is not already there, which makes them more apt to be critical in a constructive way of what is going on in their home towns and their communities, more apt to be party to a group which will start to think about and do something about community problems, and more constructive in their approach.

LEADERSHIP PROBLEMS

Mr. McHugh went on to the problem of developing better, more farsighted leadership for community efforts.

MR. McHugh: Most of our community problems don't get anything done about them until they get fairly bad. . . . If the streets get holes in them to the point where the springs of your car are broken, you will get a group together sooner or later to do something about it. If our government gets bad enough, although we are all patient about this question, sooner or later a group will get together and do something about that. . . .

Now, then, what happens? First there is a leader, and he doesn't necessarily have to be a prominent businessman. He may come from any walk of life. It may happen to be a woman who gets concerned about what she thinks is wrong with the community. He, or she, begins to talk about it.

What we need, then—and this I don't know quite how to accomplish, although I have some ideas about it—is a way in which to develop better leaders for our communities from a wide variety of walks in life. We need men and women who, a little earlier than others, will see these things which are important to the community—men and women with a little stronger purpose, breadth and scope, who can lead. . . .

So, it would help us a lot in meeting our community problems if you gentlemen in the academic world could find some sort of school for leaders in the community problem field. It would be helpful also to have some sort of communications system for leaders, if nothing more than an exchange of information about some good things that have been done, here, there, and yonder in other communities that might be facing similar problems. This would build an awareness of the problem itself, which may be vague as it is just beginning to encroach on our sensibilities; and it would be an encouragement to know that there is someone else who might have other sources of information or expert knowledge that would be applicable to our local problem.

LOOKING AHEAD

Mr. Folsom, citing particularly his experience in the Committee for Economic Development, agreed completely with Mr. McHugh that businessmen are increasingly aware of their community responsibilities; and he, too, stressed the importance of developing leadership which could take the long view and spot emerging problems before they had become acute.

Mr. Folsom: It is difficult to get business or corporation people to work on the long-range problems, because they don't see immediate needs. . . . There are tax problems facing local communities and metropolitan areas, problems relating to metropolitan districts, the consolidation of services, and other long-range problems which don't appear for a number of years but do appear in the acute stage when it is too late to do much.

It is relatively easy to get people to tackle immediate problems, but there is trouble in getting top executives to work on the long-range problems. That is the main purpose of the Committee for Economic Development on the national basis, trying to bring college people and experts together with business people to see if we can get answers to some of the national problems.

We feel there is a great need in the local communities for that same approach, and we have actually set up on an experimental basis ten units over the country in which we have business leadership sitting down with college leadership. They tackle on a research basis the problems of that immediate community, bringing to bear both the theoretical approach and the practical approach.

The roundtable looked specifically at one type of situation requiring foresight and community planning: the coming of a new industrial plant to a fairly small town in a rural area. Mr. J. B. Ward, of Corning Glass Works, told why Danville, Kentucky, had recently been selected by his firm as a plant site. His presentation led to considerable speculation as to the nature of the changes that would take place in Danville as a result of industrialization. Mr. Folsom described what did happen in Kingsport, Tennessee, after Eastman Kodak Company located there over thirty years ago. Owing to the vision of one man, there was careful community planning well in advance of the industrialization, with the result that, in many ways, Kingsport is now considered a model small industrial town. Various members raised questions about the costs of such planning and how they are to be borne by small towns where citizens see no need for such measures. No solution was found, although Mr. Gaus did indicate that many state agencies, such as state planning boards, could provide helpful services upon request from the communities.

Throughout this discussion of techniques, the roundtable had constantly in view—reminded by Chairman Witman and others —the purpose of all these suggested practical measures; a better life for the people of the communities, and the enhancement of human values which comes with the individual's sense of community participation.

CONCLUDING THOUGHTS

One of the most helpful periods of discussion came toward the end of the session on Saturday morning. The members knew that adjournment was near; a short summary of what had been presented thus far gave many a feeling of accomplishment but also made members of the group realize how much more needed to be said on the general topic assigned to our roundtable. The chairman called on one member after another to make a final statement, perhaps to indicate some of the things the roundtable had necessarily left unsaid. The statements continued to reflect differences of opinion, but they showed that earnest concern had replaced any early wonderment as to the importance of a sense of community in our industrial society.

Douglas Haskell, architectural editor of *Architectural Forum*, seconded by Mr. McHugh, introduced an issue which was recognized as one of high importance, though there was no time for extended discussion—the planning of industrial communities to include the minority groups, particularly Negroes.

Mr. Haskell: Now, I hope that the policy of not employing certain kinds of people is a fading attitude of industry, but I know it has been a major source of friction that we have hardly talked about. We have hardly talked about Detroit and Chicago and the trouble that comes up between races there, some of which arises out of the fact that industry not long ago played one racial group against another and created that situation. . . .

It seems to me that one of the promising suggestions that was made in proposals concerning the new towns that are going to be needed— new steel towns, industrial towns—was the idea that this time an attempt should be made for industry and its work force to get together and plan the housing part, the residential part, the living quarters of the town together, If that can be done, taking in all the kinds of people at work, not excluding foreigners, not excluding Negroes, then I think we will have something to be proud of. I don't think that has had nearly enough discussion.

Mr. McHugh: Picking up the point that Mr. Haskell made. I

would like to say to him that I don't know in detail what is going on in Detroit and Chicago, but I can tell you that something real is happening in New York on matters of both color and religion. I think enormous progress has been made in that area, faster progress than one would have any right to believe possible. In my judgment, that is not due to the enactment of a Fair Employment Practices Law in New York State, except that the law has influenced some people on the fringes of the question. The main results have been achieved by people who have the feel and the spirit of the thing and who are not too much concerned with the detailed letter of the law. I only ask that in that area, that you do not expect miracles to happen all at once. You must take them to get that job done right.

Mr. McHugh also mentioned that the roundtable's lack of attention to issues concerned with God and religion seemed to him "an extraordinary omission for people who are talking about improving the community. There is still no working substitute for faith and hope in its final effect upon the improvement of the lot of man." (The Roundtable on Confidence was devoting itself with great earnestness to these very topics. The record of its discussion amplifies and supplements Mr. McHugh's point that there is no substitute for faith and hope, and it also suggests the close connection between these qualities and the individual's participation in a healthy community life. See Chapter 6.)

Harold S. Buttenheim, editor of the *American City Magazine*, recalled that in earlier stages of the roundtable's discussion the so-called "functional" view of the community, emphasizing the individual's sense of kinship with others who share his profession or hobbies or interests, had been contrasted with the "geographical" point of view which thinks of community relationships as existing within a localized area.

MR. BUTTENHEIM: I wonder if it wouldn't be well to stress that both points of view go along side by side, and that both are essential —not just one replacing the other. . . .

Another point deserves mention. There are plenty of values created as a result of city planning which can be paid for by the increase of community values which that planning produces, if we would only adopt some method of recovery for the community of the values that the community creates.

Other concluding statements touched upon a variety of topics:

MR. BENNETT: I hope our final report keeps an even keel so that we don't appear to be leaning toward the industrial combination. I know we don't. On the other hand, we don't want to appear too dubious.

MR. WIRTH: I have a list of points. It would be too long to talk about them in detail. I will just read them off.

(1) We have not talked about the problem of standardization that is created by industrialism. I think our communities tend to look as though they were cast out of the same mold. That is not true in some other civilizations.

(2) I think we ought to emphasize that goodness of communities is not synonymous with bigness.

(3) I think we should emphasize also that there is no problem in any community in America which hasn't somewhere been solved in a fairly satisfactory way, and, as John Gaus earlier said, we need to make that knowledge available to other communities.

(4) The main point, as I see it, is that a good community is one that is a good place in which to live and to work and to give expression to all, or if you will, to realize the American dream.

(5) We need bench marks, and a community requires as much an inventory and assessment of its condition every year as the human body requires a medical examination once in a while; but we don't do that in our communities. Part of the need is to discover not only what our vital interests are, but how they conflict. Conflict is not bad in itself, only bad if it is resolved by violence. If we systematically assess our community situations we might find that we do subsidize slums, crime, and a lot of undesirable things when we might be subsidizing the opposite. With proper inventories and assessments we ought to be able to foresee crises.

(6) Recommendations are needed in the field of administration. We can do a lot in every community to make our district health department coincide with the district fire department, a ward, or some other boundary, so that in local life we can get some coincidence of these responsibilities. You can run a community effectively only if power is more or less coordinate with responsibility. Most American

communities are not self-governing; they are dependent upon states in which the urban communities are underrepresented.

(7) For almost every function that communities carry on, there are some specialized technical, sometimes national, organizations which have taken responsibility in that field. We can make it possible for communities to get access to the fund of experience and the expert knowledge of these national organizations.

MR. ECKER: I don't think quite enough has been said about the advantages of the improvement of certain cultural aspects of cities and the outlets they give people.

The only other point I would bring out is my impression from what we have been doing that there is no single answer to these questions. It is a matter of all parts of our community bearing a share of getting things moving and planning a part of the improvements.

MR. PAINTER: It is clear enough from what is going on that we have the knowledge, and the means can be found. The chief difficulty seems to be that not enough people have a feeling of responsibility, of doing something. I think attention should be devoted to convincing more people that they have a real responsibility for this sort of thing. While you will get twenty people who will sit around a table and talk about it for every one who will get fired with enthusiasm, the more twenties you have to sit around the table, the more of the others there will be.

MR. BROWN: I think we should give greater stress to what the scientists call the ecology of the situation. These lie beyond the industrial society. They are matters of habitat—weather, food supply, climate. I am afraid perhaps I am ending in the clouds, but I think it is the necessary place to end.

MR. LILIENTHAL: You are ending on the ground. [Laughter]

Finally, there were some comments on the method of the discussion and of the Conference itself, with suggestions that the plan of bringing together people with quite varied backgrounds for discussion of common problems might well be carried further, not only on a wide geographical basis such as that of the Conference at Corning, but in local communities as well.

MR. LILIENTHAL: The last question in the prospectus says, "What can the Conference accomplish?" I think someone ought to try to answer that. Maybe just a short answer. I think the record is entitled to some reactions as to whether it is worth doing or whether it is worth doing this way.

MR. COGHLAN: I am particularly impressed with this meeting and the fact that it is under the auspices of a private corporation, which indicates to me that corporations are becoming adult in the sense of social relations.

CHAIRMAN WITMAN: My own point of view is that it is probably too early for us to give any kind of precise evaluation to what has been done, but certainly, from where I am sitting, it looks as though it is a good thing.

I think the procedure which was developed here, that of putting together diverse elements into a conference, certainly has validity. Second, I think that no matter what the outcome of the Conference in terms of our individual judgment of its value, the example to the country of an industrial concern taking the leadership and trying to fuse the fields of social science and humanities and industrial affairs is one which, from my point of view, deserves a commendation and can become, I trust, an example to other industries and firms on a large and small scale.

This sort of thing might well be understood, it seems to me, at the community level and become a practical experience in the development of the very thing that we have been talking about in this particular roundtable.

MR. McHUGH: Mr. Chairman, before we adjourn, I would like to say for one, how much I have personally enjoyed the opportunity of discussion here, especially with the academic people, and how much I think we are all indebted to the really fine objectivity of our chairman and to the extraordinary reporting and summation ability of our rapporteur.

CHAIRMAN WITMAN: Thank you, I can tell you that it would not have been done if there hadn't been such a remarkable panel of people.

6

Confidence in Life in Industrial Civilization

ROUNDTABLE D

Lawrence K. Frank, rapporteur

The group that met as the Roundtable on Confidence was faced with a difficult task. Its problem was basic but intangible. Has modern man, in the process of industrializing his society, gained or lost confidence in himself and in the universe? What kinds of confidence are desirable, and what can be done to restore or build up the desirable kinds? As members of our group, we had distinguished leaders of thought in philosophy, social psychology, and political science; practical decision makers from the top levels of industrial management and organized labor; and able interpreters from religious life, government, and the creative arts. They brought to a focus on the common topic the oldest and the newest findings from such fields of study and action as religion, mental hygiene, social security, and industrial relations.

At the outset, chairman Frank W. Pierce, director, Standard Oil Company of New Jersey, engineer and long-time specialist in industrial relations, invited each member to state briefly some of the ideas that seemed to him most pertinent for the roundtable's consideration. This round robin developed into a major enterprise which resulted in exposing a great many facets of our central problem.

Later, on the recommendation of a special steering committee, the roundtable turned to practical measures by which to meet some of the problems that had been raised. It searched especially for measures that might be taken by management, trade-unions, and other factors in industry but also looked more briefly at things that might be done in the fields of education and family life.

Finally, the group drew from the varied resources of its membership a series of suggestions designed to indicate more clearly where future studies bearing on problems of confidence in life should be directed, and it also took note of the need for putting existing knowledge to more effective use through better-trained leadership and through better communication.

No summary can convey the sense of intellectual excitement that gradually built up in the roundtable as we found ourselves, toward the end, really making some progress in the difficult task of establishing mutual communication among members with such diverse backgrounds. It would not be accurate to say that all was clear and agreed by the end of the final session; but certainly we had a definite sense of accomplishment, and it seemed to be the unanimous sense of the roundtable that more of just this kind of effort is needed.

FACETS OF THE PROBLEM

NATURE OF THE CONFIDENCE WE WANT

One of the roundtable's members, Robert L. Calhoun, professor of historical theology at Yale Divinity School, had defined the topic in a background paper circulated prior to the Conference:* "It is the problem of personal morale, working faith, active confidence that human life is worth living." He had repudiated false confidence based on wishful thinking and overprotection. His definition and warning seemed to meet general approval, and several members reinforced the warning, among them Seward Hiltner, researcher in religion and mental hygiene from the Federated Theological Faculty of the University of Chicago, and

* See p. 323.

William Ray Dennes, dean of the Graduate Division and professor of philosophy, University of California.

MR. HILTNER: It is . . . possible to have one level of confidence which is essentially like whistling as you pass the cemetery, and . . . a good deal of discussion about confidence may unwittingly be at this level. . . . In that sense, it is not only hypocritical and false, a kind of façade, but actually tends to undermine the very structure upon which a true confidence might be built. . . .

There is a . . . deeper level of confidence which is closely allied with what we mean by faith. . . . The kind of approach we should make to this more general confidence would be similar to that which we make in regard to faith when we talk about the road to true faith being through creative doubt. This has to do with the gathering of strength to confront obstacles instead of trying to dodge around them on the ground that it might be bad for morale. . . .

MR. DENNES: We have learned a good deal in the last thirty years about ways to induce extraordinarily high degrees of confidence through illusion and propaganda. Basic to any really enlightened discussion of these themes is a distinction between factors that substantially justify confidence and devices that merely induce it. On these problems we cannot hope to reach firm ground, or even to reach an intelligible analysis of the issues involved, until we have achieved some agreement: (1) on the nature of value and (2) on the kinds of concrete values the realization of which we shall regard as constituting satisfactory human living.

HAVE WE MORE OR LESS CONFIDENCE TODAY?

Philip D. Reed, chairman of the board, General Electric Company, asked early in the discussion, "Is it true, as the background paper seems to imply, that people have less sense of confidence in today's industrial civilization than they had in some earlier period?"

MR. REED: Are we talking about more improvements, or are we talking about restoring something we have lost as a result of industrial civilization? . . . You know, we create markets and we sell our products by building demand. A great invention is made, a new product appears which people have not heard about. It is presented, it is seen, it is advertised, and then people begin to want it. I am inclined to think that this business of confidence in life and the things that as of today we think we require, we require because we have created a demand for them ourselves. Because as we have progressed, as material and spiritual resources perhaps are broadened, we find ourselves wanting things we haven't wanted before because we didn't know about them. . . .

Mr. Reed's question never got a clear-cut answer, but at least two members offered support of his tentative suggestion that we are not really worse off than before but are demanding more of life today because more can be had.

Else Frenkel-Brunswik, research psychologist, Cowell Memorial Hospital, and lecturer in psychology, University of California, remarked on the tendency to romanticize life in other times and places and to exaggerate the degree of confidence felt by people in preindustrial cultures.

Miss Frenkel-Brunswik: When we talk about the disintegration of our times, we should make some kind of comparison. Recently I analyzed some material from a tribe in India, and all my romantic ideas about India disappeared quickly. . . . The degree of distrust found in certain of their stories that I analyzed is much greater than in comparable stories of our own culture. . . .

Antonio Carrillo Flores, legal scholar and director-general of the Nacional Financiera, Mexico's agency for financing its national development program, had no doubt about the reality of the human advances made possible by industrial civilization.

Mr. Carrillo: Some of the remarks I have heard here convey to me the impression that the United States is living in the best period of its history, and that nevertheless some of its people are not satisfied. That is undoubtedly encouraging, because if they were satisfied, I am not sure that the progress would go on. So there is a constructive aspect in the dissatisfaction of living in the best period that the human race has ever known. . . .

THREE MAJOR THREATS TO CONFIDENCE

Laurence Sears, professor of American political philosophy, Mills College, suggested that lack of confidence may spring from situations which are too great for man to meet, either individually or collectively. What are the major situations that impose strains on our confidence in life today? Mr. Sears listed three: (1) the threat of war, (2) economic insecurity which comes with depressions, and (3) "the fact of change itself—rapid change, too rapid for us to cope with, change in political and economic institutions, change in our values, change in our basic loyalties."

MR. SEARS: It seems to me that today war and depression are as essentially mysterious and terrifying, because they are uncontrollable, in the feeling of the ordinary person as a typhoon is to a primitive native. What we do doesn't matter. I hear that reiterated over and over again from my students. What difference does it make what I do? And I suppose one immediately contrasts that with the great scientific control over the course of nature. To what extent is lack of confidence due to loss of a sense of personal significance in the control of our destiny as we face the things that concern and frighten us? In so far as this is true, what institutional forms and patterns can be established which will restore to us this sense of mastery and, therefore, of confidence?

THE THREAT OF WAR

The chairman guided the discussion away from the war problem as such, but the existing state of international tensions was in everyone's mind and cast its shadow over all the talk about achieving a more satisfactory industrial civilization. "With the fear of a new war, I don't see how any man can feel confidence now," said Mr. Carrillo, and Meyer Kestnbaum, president of Hart, Schaffner & Marx, was even more emphatic.

MR. KESTNBAUM: If it were not for this great threat of war, I think that we would be in a new golden age. The opportunity for improving life is great with our industrial capacity. We have learned to deal to some extent with the social problems which we have created. But the fact that we must divert the major proportion of our capacity and energy to preparation for war bears heavily on all of the problems that we are dealing with. Our greatest hope would be, of course, to find some way in which we can accommodate ourselves to the pressures that exist in the world so that we could go about our business of improving life for our people and for all the other people in the world.

ECONOMIC INSECURITY AND GOVERNMENT'S ROLE

The bearing on confidence in life of the second of Mr. Sears' three major "situations"—economic insecurity—was a topic which kept bobbing up in the roundtable and brought out more disagreement than any other issue. No doubt there was also a substantial area of agreement, which might have become clearer had there been time to pursue the matter further, but the difference in approach and emphasis was striking.

Wilbur J. Cohen, technical adviser to the commissioner for Social Security, pointed to the greatly increased responsibilities of government in modern industrial society and stressed the consequent need for better citizen participation in civic affairs. Whether we like it or not, we are living in the kind of world where we have to ask government to do many things that individuals or families used to be able to do for themselves. "Government . . . is all of us working together," but in such a big way that it is hard for individuals to participate adequately in group decisions. We must seek to understand and improve the processes by which they do so. "I make the assumption—which may perhaps be challenged— that if we were to look ahead for the next generation or two, we would have to say there will be more assumption of responsibility by government, so that the problem is going to be intensified in the period ahead."

The interest of working people in more security against economic hazards, partly to be achieved through government, was the theme of remarks by Harry H. Cook, international president of the American Flint Glass Workers' Union, AFL.

MR. COOK: I am in the labor movement, have been practically all my life. I am in a position to understand many of the problems of those people who work for wages, and I know that they do not feel that they have been justly treated or that they have got as much out of life as they are entitled to. I do believe in certain things that government should do for the people who need help. We have heard a great deal about socialized medicine. I believe that is a matter that should be taken care of by government for various reasons: one, that many of the people who work for wages are unable to pay the cost of medical attention. I feel, too, that people would feel more secure if they were guaranteed retirement pensions under a more extensive Social Security arrangement by government. One of the reasons I feel that way is that while we have retirement pensions and paid vacations, group insurance, and many things of that kind that are made available by individual industries, they do have the effect of restricting the freedom of people to change their places of employment. . . .

SELF-RELIANCE

The businessmen, on the other hand, viewed with misgiving a tendency to look for security by group action, especially government action. They spoke of the need for self-reliance and initiative. Don G. Mitchell, president, Sylvania Electric Products, Inc., wanted to hear some discussion of "confidence in self." He was disturbed by a survey of college seniors which showed many stating that they would prefer to work for a large company rather than a small one.

MR. MITCHELL: That would not disturb me except for the unfortunate reason they give. It is that "If I work for a large company, the chances of my being laid off in bad times are less." I am talking about college graduates and not manual workers now. That attitude on the part of what should be a leadership group is not what made this country great. People who sought security ahead of opportunity never carried this country from the east coast to the west coast in prairie wagons. Those people had little security. What they sought was opportunity.

MR. SEARS: I confess to have some sympathy for the boy who wants to get into a situation where he is not apt to be laid off in a depression. . . .

SECURITY AND CONFIDENCE

At this point, Julian Huxley, biologist, author, and past director-general of UNESCO, injected a clarifying comment.

MR. HUXLEY: We are really discussing two different things. Confidence is not the same thing as security. Both are necessary, but security in the current sense alone may be bad and may discourage initiative, as Mr. Mitchell pointed out. But all the same, we do need security to remove fears, depression, ill-health, war, etc. . . . To me, confidence is something positive. It is confidence in the free exercise of your capacities, your own and those of society. So it is an outlook for adventure and creativeness. . . . It is essentially a state of mind. . . . Of course, it must be related to the reality of the situation, including war, which is part of the present situation. Otherwise, it is just wishful whistling in the dark, as Mr. Hiltner says. . . . It must have a long-term component . . . be related to some sort of general values, to belief in ourselves and in something outside ourselves.

Subsequent contributions to this theme further revealed the common ground and the differences of emphasis within the group. Mr. Carrillo agreed entirely with Mr. Huxley that security and confidence are different concepts, and he pointed to the positive functions of government in meeting certain of the causes of insecurity in an industrial civilization. All democratic governments have been taking measures in this field and, without falling into the authoritarian pattern, will have to be concerned with it in the future. Mr. Cook said that confidence and security are closely bound together where working people are concerned. "It is hard for the head of a family to feel any great degree of confidence if the family is living under hardships. . . . We must have confidence, and we must have security; and security, I believe, encourages confidence."

George M. Humphrey, president, M. A. Hanna Company, suggested that there could be such a thing as too much economic security. Whether security is a good thing or not depends on how it is generated. "Security that is earned is a good thing. Security that is given without earning and without effort, I am inclined to think, is a bad thing. I am not talking about the sick and the old and the young and the incapacitated."

MR. HUMPHREY: Mr. Mitchell talked about the college boys who want secure jobs. The two motivating things for human beings are fear of consequences and hope of reward. If, by gift, you remove fear of consequences, it no longer serves as an incentive for effort. . . . We ought to organize ourselves so that people have more and more opportunity to earn more, not to be given more. . . . This country is built on risk, activity, endeavor. Any move . . . which is a developing move in a new field, whether it is geographic, scientific, or whatever it is, is involved with risks nobody can measure; and as quickly as you eliminate or minimize the desire of people to take those risks and to move into uncharted and unknown fields you are limiting the development of the society we have built up.

MR. HUXLEY: I think what Mr. Mitchell said and what Mr. Cook said ought to be interpreted from a rather different angle. Mr. Cook said that you could not get workers confident unless they had security. I quite agree. . . . What everybody needs is security to get a minimum, a minimum of freedom from want, a minimum of freedom from unemployment, etc. Until he has that minimum, you are going to have mass pressure in which the individual is not paid much attention. Once you have that minimum, then you can begin building your confidence, which involves a development of individual personality. . . .

RAPID CHANGE

Mr. Kestnbaum picked up the point that Mr. Sears had made about the disturbing effects of rapid change. An industrial society, he said, is a discovering society, capable of great effort and great dynamic power. It is, therefore, subject to changes perhaps more rapid than we can absorb. We have developed airplanes that fly faster than sound and motorcars that go faster than most people can drive them safely. These developments permit and cause rapid changes in the organization of society and give us serious social problems; this is responsible to some extent for a lack of confidence.

MR. KESTNBAUM: When you have the kind of world we are living in, we are condemned to a perpetual struggle. As we develop new resources, new ideas and new capacities, we simply develop new problems. . . . The great job of modern society, as I see it, is to develop the capacity on the part of our people to deal with modern social and economic problems.

This is why we must have new theories about universal education. This is why we must change from a society in which there is a small elite that does the thinking and provides the leadership while a larger group of slaves or followers do as they are told. We have now developed the idea that all people can participate or should participate in determining their destiny. If they are going to do that, we need to pay a great deal more attention to the kinds of thinking, education, social pattern, social standards, etc., that are made available for people as their guides.

Other members, notably Lawrence K. Frank, author and mental hygienist, pointed out that in a world of rapid change our historical institutions and our old assumptions and beliefs have become obsolescent and inadequate. However, this loss of confidence might be a prelude to growth and development in social life and individual personality quite beyond anything we have had in the past.

MR. FRANK: We know that the adolescent comes to a time in his life when he undergoes a considerable period of stress and strain and insecurity, a loss of confidence both in himself and in what he has believed and thought, as he gives up a lot of his childhood assumptions and beliefs and fears. He has to give up his dependence upon parental authority if he is going to grow up and become an adult, and that loss of confidence is a necessary prelude to his growing maturity. From this viewpoint, it would seem to me that, instead of deploring the loss of the past, we might say some of this loss of confidence is a therapeutic, almost necessary, stage in the development of Western culture. . . .

Later Mr. Frank returned to his theme and observed that we have made great advances in technology largely because we have developed new ideas and conceptions, especially in the past forty or fifty years. "Are we still relying on older assumptions and beliefs in the field of human relations and in social life?" he asked. Much of our social thinking has been built upon the analogy of the static, Newtonian theories of physics. Lately, these have been supplemented in the physical sciences by newer, more dynamic conceptions, and perhaps the application of the newer conceptions to the human and social field may give us a new basis for hope and for confidence in life. But our aspirations will have to be translated into new terms.

MR. FRANK: Many of the older goals have become inadequate in the light of what we now think and believe. Isn't it a task, then, of reformulating those goals in terms of our persistent aspirations and using the new ideas and the new technology for that purpose?

BELONGING, CONFIDENCE IN EACH OTHER

Another of the major preoccupations of the roundtable was the individual's relations with his fellow men. It was recognized that a sense of belonging, participation, and a basis for confidence in each other are fundamental to man's confidence in life. Benjamin L. Masse, S.J., associate editor of *America*, national Catholic weekly, called attention to the remarks in the background paper in this connection and added that in his opinion some of the big problems connected with confidence in life in our industrial civilization stem from, first, an absence of status and belonging, coupled with a loosening of family ties, and, second, an absence of a sense of civic responsibility.

FATHER MASSE: I use the term "civic responsibility" in a somewhat wider sense than is customary. I mean not merely a man's relationship to government—local, state, or federal—but also his relationship to economic organizations to which he belongs, to trade-unions and trade associations. . . .

In the view of Donald K. David, dean of the Graduate School of Business Administration, Harvard University, threats to the sense of personal importance derive not so much from the nature of business or economic organizations per se as from the way these organizations are administered. "Subordinate relationships are very important."

MR. DAVID: I happen to be in the business of trying to train administrators. I think we have made some advance, because we have learned that administration has to do with people. . . . We try to make our students aware that a sense of personal adequacy comes to an individual from his relations with a group. . . . We know very well that more effective communication is a method of restoring the feeling of adequacy in our modern world and is most important.

René d'Harnoncourt, director, Museum of Modern Art, called attention to the loosening of family ties in the United States, with the loss of the old feeling of belonging to a clan. Mr. Mitchell spoke of the difference in the feeling of belonging and participation in his firm's factories located in small towns as compared with those in large cities (more on this below), and Mr. Cook stressed the need for a more neighborly attitude of confidence in each other, both in industry and in community affairs.

Mr. Cook: An evidence of what can be done, if we can get a little closer together, lies here in this community. . . . Here in this Corning Glass Works the company has done much for its employees, and it is much appreciated. We established our organization here eight years ago, after fifty years of independence of unions, and I don't believe we have had one day of interruption of production in those eight years; and the reason for that is the splendid attitude of management and the splendid attitude of the workers. They have an understanding of each other's problems and a determination to work together and help each other. Here we are in this building. I am told that everybody worked hard to get it finished in time; the mechanics worked long hours, submitted to a lot of unusual things, and the reason for it was the proper relationship between management and workers. They were not driven; they were asked to help. They had an objective. Everybody worked to gain that objective, and they have done a good job. I believe that can be done in a more national way. It is my observation that there has been a growing lack of confidence, not only in so far as labor and management are concerned, but even in the neighborhoods. People care less, it seems, about their neighbors. They assume a more selfish attitude. That is growing, and I think much can be done to correct it if we can just instill a little more confidence in each other. . . .

Mr. Reed felt that all over the world of late there has been a disintegration of confidence "not resulting from industrial civilization but from moral disintegration, from the acceptance of the doctrine that the end justifies the means."

Mr. Reed: In the jungle it was brute force that was the compelling law. In this civilization I suppose we have learned to obey known rules, we have achieved some moral standards, decency, honor, integrity—

call it what you will. In my view, the past thirty years have seen a substantial weakening of the belief in the acceptance of those fundamental premises on which people have leaned through the centuries and have learned to live together. If that is true, then I think it is a restoration of a moral force, integrity of contract, confidence—as Mr. Cook said—in one another, that is needed.

CREATIVE, INTEGRATED PERSONALITY

Appropriately, it was a member from the field of art who first brought to the attention of the roundtable the role of creative activity in building an individual's awareness of his own capacity and confidence in life. Mr. d'Harnoncourt spoke of the standardization of ways of living through standardization of tools and of the constant exposure to mass media of entertainment that ask less and less for the participation of the individual and give little occasion for the exercise of individual opinion, individual creativity, and other aspects of personality. This, he suggested, is a factor in loss of confidence, for a true confidence requires that the individual be "aware of his uniqueness, which is one of the things that helps you to know who you are."

This thought was developed by other members of the group and soon led to related ideas on the types of individual personalities that we would like to see our society produce and on the value of the well-rounded and integrated personality. Harold D. Lasswell, professor of law, Yale University, a researcher in personality and the political process, urged that we ask ourselves what "goal values" we prefer for our society. He suggested that positive confidence could best be built on a basis of such clarified objectives. Charles Morris, philosopher, of the University of Chicago and Harvard University, took the view that the goals of a society are most fundamentally expressed in the kinds of personalities it admires.

MR. MORRIS: Ultimately the problems of value all come back to the basic question: . . . What kind of person, or what kind of personality, do we wish to approve of? . . . Can we form some sort of picture of man that is compelling and attractive, and can we have confidence in the ability of man to be that kind of person? . . . The ultimate standard by which any institution should be valued is the question: What kind of person does it produce? . . .

Some people are struggling for a mode of life in which all aspects and sides and phases of the human personality can again operate in a unitary way, and I think this urge or feeling for the protection of creativity in a time in which many people feel that they are simply being swept along in a glacier is one of the aspects of confidence in human creativeness that we have in mind. . . .

MR. HUXLEY: However you look at it, the highest possibilities are human personalities and their experiences and capacities. There is where you find the fullest extension of the idea of human dignity and certain aspects of democracy. I think the psychiatrists here would agree that we want a new emphasis on wholeness of personality—integration rather than merely separate achievements in particular fields. . . .

LANCELOT LAW WHYTE, philosopher of science, Great Britain: This word "creative" is horrible, sentimental. It allows all kinds of fancies to come in. But it means something simple and inclusive. It may be found in human relations in terms of the family. It may be found in social relations in terms of some work in the community. It may be in the factory. And the great inventive situations, which created not only American industrial civilization, were born out of exceptional individuals dreaming things which the community had no sympathy for at the time. . . .

If we have any faith, religious or other, in man, it must be a belief in allowing him a certain degree of freedom to discover himself. What comes out will not only be good in the development of his own potential interest but good for the community. . . . Neither the sciences nor the religions have adequately brought within their conception of a man a constructive, creative faculty—creativity in human relations, in thoughts, in experiments, in inventions. This is, you might say, almost the divine mystery. This is the great human fact. With it man can be dignified, can fulfill himself, can escape the despairs that led into this lack of confidence.

If we can create a civilization that gives every individual, man or woman, and the child as he develops, more than we do at present of the opportunities of discovering his own constructive role in whatever group is around him, then I think we will be able to carry on the

Western tradition and make something out of it. . . . And I think the liberal world ought really to be searching. An approach hasn't to my mind yet been formulated, either from the church or from the intellectuals, from the medical or psychological professions. . . .

In this connection Mr. Hiltner made a point which, by implication, set a question mark against Mr. Humphrey's doctrine that "the two motivating things for human beings are fear of consequences and hope of reward."

MR. HILTNER: If the obvious and important positive needs . . . for creative expression, which are difficult to define but which are not quite so difficult to identify, are actually met, you do not require a residue of deprivation to keep people moving productively and creatively in the world. I realize that this notion runs counter to a great many of the stereotypes which have run through our civilization in the past—what Larry Frank calls the Newtonian type of thinking about human relations—but we have begun to get a great deal of evidence on this point, coming in the main from study of children, also from psychotherapy and many other sources. And this has reasonably obvious implications in terms of industry.

Mr. Hiltner also spoke of the problems of older people who lose their opportunities for creative expression and therefore lose confidence. This is a particularly acute problem in American culture; and as the average age of the population rises, it will become still more important. Mr. Carrillo called attention to the benefits of modern industry.

MR. CARRILLO: Mr. Chairman, I am happy that the general idea has come out of our discussion of the importance of the value of the human personality as a basis for confidence in industrial society. And I think it is fair to say . . . that only through the spread of industry and the great productivity that industry has created has it been possible to look back again to the individual and to see in the individual a value in himself, not as an instrument but as a goal. . . .

WHAT CAN WE BE SURE ABOUT?

There was another order of ideas which the roundtable found highly significant as it sought to understand the problems of modern man seeking a basis for confidence in life. Science has upset many of the older ideas about the universe. The great glass disk, original casting for the Mt. Palomar 200-inch telescope, which confronts the visitor as he enters the Corning Glass Center, served to remind the conferees of this. Our earth is no longer viewed as the center of everything; rather, it is a comparatively minor planet circling a minor star. Many cultures have worshiped the sun, but it is less impressive in the light of modern astronomical knowledge about millions of other suns in galaxies and supergalaxies extending perhaps for billions of light-years through space-time. Furthermore, our ideas about man have been upset by modern cultural anthropology, with its discovery that what one society regards as good, honorable, or sacred may be regarded in another society as evil, immoral, or profane.

FATHER MASSE: Another big problem is the absence of certainty with regard to what the author of our background paper calls "the ultimate sorts of moral and religious faith," namely, the growing inability of many people to answer the age-old questions, the whys and whens and whithers of life.

CORNELIUS KRUSÉ, philosopher, of Wesleyan University: Pascal, the great seventeenth-century philosopher and scientist, said, "The contemplation of these infinite spaces fills me with terror." I always think how much ahead of his time he was. We are just catching up with his remark today, because the expansion of the universe has been communicated to people at large; and I think there is a great deal of cosmic fear, a feeling that "I am a stranger and afraid in a world I never made." How do we overcome that feeling? . . . I think that is a terribly practical thing, though it sounds as if it were simply philosophical. I think we have to get somehow the view that we belong cosmically and that the values we cherish most also belong, and they are not obtruded or intruded into the universe. . . . Also, I think that it is terribly important in the field of values that we overcome the prevailing sense of relativity. "You have these values, we have those values. Well, it doesn't much matter which they are." You can't get a sense of belonging cosmically if it is just a matter of each one for himself and the devil take the hindmost. . . . What we cherish most must somehow also belong to the universe, and I think it is helpful in this connection to distinguish between the "thatness" and the "whatness" of truth. *That* truth exists is an absolute. *What* truth exists is not an absolute. So we can mediate between absoluteness and a sense of non-absoluteness.

This problem—whether there are any absolutes and certainties left that we can be sure of—arose again and again in one way or another and at length brought a middle-ground suggestion from one of the roundtable members which some others seized upon and rallied round. Here, selected and condensed, are a few of the thoughts that came out in this phase of the discussion:

MISS FRENKEL-BRUNSWIK: Many of us are concerned over certain tendencies toward relativism and lack of enthusiasm. I think we also have to watch out for the danger of going in the opposite direction in searching for new absolutes and new certainties at the ideological level. Lack of confidence oftentimes makes people look for more firm leadership and for authoritarian solutions. How do we combine belief in basic principles with some degree of freedom in these beliefs as such?

MR. WHYTE: We moderns are facing new responsibilities without that adequate conviction in God that perhaps might have solved the problem for others, without strong individual convictions, certainly without adequate collective convictions. . . . Perhaps most important of all, we lack a balanced, sufficiently accepted view of ourselves, of what human nature is individually and collectively. Another way of saying this is that we lack a unified conception of modern knowledge. The facts that science has brought to light have not been simplified and brought together in a way that can let us fuse our new knowledge with our emotions as a basis for individual and collective action. . . .

MR. HUXLEY: A very important point was raised by Dr. Frenkel-Brunswik. We mustn't think in terms of absolutes. We have to think in terms of trends, in terms of directions, in terms of development toward fullest possible realization.

MR. DENNES: May there not be a third alternative to the two possibilities of absolute goods, absolute values, on the one hand, and the suggestion that otherwise we have simply capricious and arbitrary preferences to base our evaluations on? I think nothing is more important than to explore what may be the much more promising middle ground. . . .

Enough has been done in the past forty or fifty years to make out that some needs are pretty generally basic to human beings. Dr. Mead may correct me on this, but it seems to me that there is a good deal of evidence that certain basic needs manifest themselves in the most diverse cultures and that the blocking of these needs leads to dysfunction and even death. The kinds of activity that satisfy these needs may not be absolute values. . . . After all, I suppose the very existence of the human race on the face of the earth might come to an end with no violation of natural order; if we roasted ourselves to death, the order would simply be different than what it has been for a few hundred thousand years. . . . But as between absolute norms of value and mere capricious and arbitrary whims, there may be an area where kinds of concrete goods which, on pretty empirical grounds, we know to satisfy basic human needs, would give us a degree of . . . basis for value judgment . . . that is perhaps all that we can reasonably hope for. . . .

There is nothing awfully surprising about any of these concrete goods. . . . I mean health, knowledge, love, play, imaginative expression, and work at the kind of job that is fit for a man to do, the kind that enhances and disseminates these basic concrete goods. . . . I think that any sense of personal adequacy has to be grounded in, indeed constituted by, activities of these four or five kinds. . . . And if one asks how to justify these common-sense goods, it may not be possible to justify them absolutely. But may it not be enough to justify them in terms of their effectiveness in satisfying needs that are basic to people generally, to us as one race, as one species?

These goods are not divisive, but are goods such that anybody's achievement of them tends to enrich, on the whole, the opportunities of others. These are problems that deserve to be the subject of continuing study. . . .

MR. CALHOUN: The problem of absolute values vs. values which change from culture to culture, from time to time, from individual person to individual person, has, I think, been helpfully supplemented by Dr. Dennes' comment. Between these two extremes we may find it desirable to focus upon specific values which, in the course of actual experience, we find human beings to require for a full and satisfying life. So, whether we take one or the other of the two abstractly contrasted views about the ultimate reality of our values, we can, at any rate, recognize an emerging community of understanding of what men need in order to be fully, confidently, creatively, productively human beings. . . .

MAN, JITTERY MASTER OF FATE

An underlying theme which came to permeate much of the roundtable's thinking (and made more poignant the search we have just been describing for adequate goals and values of human endeavor) was first stated by the English scientist-businessman turned philosopher, Mr. Whyte.

MR. WHYTE: The unique feature today is that man, both individually and collectively, is for the first time in his history facing the necessity of consciously guiding his own future. . . . We are not only facing that new responsibility, but we are facing it . . . without, apparently, the technique, guidance, conviction, faith, that we need to do it properly. I think we all need great humility about this, because certainly the scientists and the philosophers have failed tragically in meeting this opportunity. I shouldn't be here today if I didn't feel that the humblest of us has to try to contribute what he can.

Mr. Huxley enlarged this idea and, with the biologist's perspective, broadened it into a responsibility for managing organic evolution. Miss Mead stressed the self-consciousness of our era. Mr. Kestnbaum spoke particularly of our use of the new power made available to man by industrial technology, and Mr. Carrillo pointed to the need of positive political and economic goals throughout the free world.

MR. HUXLEY: Our immediate crisis is also something of a long-term nature, as Mr. Whyte has said. . . . We are in the position, in the human species, as if we had been given the job of managing director of the whole future of evolution, including the evolution of our own species, without being asked whether we wanted it or not and without proper training. . . . Suddenly this has come on us, that we are the managing directors for the whole of the future of the world. . . .

This links up with the point that many people around the table have made: the human need for the feeling that you belong to something bigger than yourself. . . . We have just realized properly for the first time that all human species are one and are engaged on a collective adventure of realizing fuller responsibilities and achieving new fulfillments. . . . We have to try to reduce the risk of war, to get an ideology that can do that, resist all attempts to divide the world, and resist all attempts to reduce the importance of human personalities, whether it is done by totalitarian, authoritarian methods or by the subtler but equally disastrous methods which you get in some aspects of a democratic civilization from the tendency to reduce everything to a dead level of mediocrity and uniformity. Unity is not the same thing as uniformity.

The over-all idea that we have to try to get into people's minds, which will give them confidence, is that they are participating both in their own development and in this great joint adventure. They are making a world worth-while for their children to grow up in. That links up with a lot of immediate points—wheat for India, Truman's Point Four, and all that—the idea that the whole human race is linked together in a common adventure. . . . Once we get this over-all view, we have a means of resolving many of our conflicts, such as those which arise between separate individuals in a purely competitive, individualistic society and those which take the form of labor-management conflicts.

MISS MEAD: I agree with Mr. Whyte that the significant thing about this particular period as compared with any other period is our self-consciousness, so that we are able to define the task that we are up against as we have never been able to do it before. This Conference is an experiment in making the necessary inventions to make self-consciousness bearable to Americans, and to a lesser extent to Western Europeans, members of a modern industrialized society. . . .

I am not at all caught by a sense of pessimism and failure. I don't think science and philosophy have failed; I think it is incredible that they have got as far as they have. Every time I come back to this civilization from the South Seas I am surprised that it works at all.

It is a peculiar mixture of Puritanism and engineering that we are using here to define our situation. We have to make it out as awfully bad before we can fix it, which is the Puritanism in our background. And we have got to fix it, which is the modern industry in our background. So we become managing directors. I am sure that if an Indian or a Chinese would define the situation, the figure of speech that would appeal to him would be a different one.

But the principal problem is so to define the present situation that we can make the necessary social inventions. . . . That is what we are trying to do in this Conference . . . and the significant thing is that we know enough to ask whether we can make the necessary social inventions. We are not savages in outrigger canoes, looking at a modern steamship and saying, "Isn't it a pity we can't make that." We are people who know about steamships but aren't quite sure about the particular kind of steamship we are going to need in different times. But we have invented invention, and we ought to be able to ask, "All right, now, what are the necessary inventions to establish the sort of going equilibrium between man and the universe which will give us the kind of moving, integrated society we want?"

MR. KESTNBAUM: It was rather generally assumed through a good portion of history, in Western Europe at least, that there wasn't much hope for this life, that the best we could hope for was happiness in another world. The idea that we can improve the environment in which man finds himself is a relatively modern one, I think less than five hundred years old. And it has developed at a very accelerated pace to the point that, with the rapid advance of technology and science, we have discovered immense power to do many things. . . .

The industrial organization of society has given us this great power and of course has brought with it many serious problems. . . . It seems to me that the industrial organization of society is essentially a kind of tool. It is a means by which we do something. It is a tool for good or for evil, depending on how we use it, and it is useful. Industrial society is not bad per se. I think it is not good per se. It is capable of being put to some strange uses, to some good uses. That depends on other things that have been referred to here—the principles which we use as a guide to conduct. . . .

The only possible confidence that we can have is confidence that we have the wisdom and the intelligence and the goodwill to take this tremendous industrial machine that we have developed and move it, slowly, perhaps, but nevertheless definitely, in the right direction so that we can have a sense of progress and some confidence that, if not we ourselves, at least our children will be able to benefit.

MR. CARRILLO: Our negative convictions seem to be stronger than our positive convictions. This may be an inheritance of the eighteenth and nineteenth centuries. Those centuries, especially in political science, were times of negative convictions. The American Bill of Rights is a list of things that government should not do, and probably that set of negative convictions was enough in the social framework of the age. It is not enough in the twentieth century. If we compare the

American Bill of Rights with the Declaration of Fundamental Rights that was approved by the United Nations in Paris in 1948 . . . it strikes us as a difference between a set of negative convictions and a set of positive convictions. . . .

The main importance of this 1948 document is that it takes into consideration the problems for human life that have been created by industrial civilization. This document is fundamental and is not enough known in the world, though it is concrete and easy to understand. It speaks of the right of a man to raise a family, the right of a man to be informed of what is happening in the world, the right of a man to have a fundamental belief. But the problem is that the Declaration of Human Rights was only approved two years ago, and apparently it has lost its appeal. I don't see the speeches, I don't see the commencement addresses, I don't see much of those positive convictions that people put stress on after the war continuing to have the appeal that they formerly had. Probably there is a sense of failure in the international institutions that were created after the war; probably we were too optimistic in believing that we were going to have one world after the war. But I sincerely believe that unless we go back to the positive convictions that the United Nations fought for during the war, it will be difficult to overcome this feeling of lack of confidence.

PRACTICAL MEASURES

Undoubtedly the main task and the main accomplishment of this roundtable was to turn the problem of "confidence in life in industrial civilization" through many angles, and thus bring its diverse facets to the light. Merely to state problems without knowing the answers is itself a constructive move, for—as the directors of industrial research laboratories are fond of saying—a problem correctly stated is halfway to being solved. But the roundtable from the first showed a strong desire to go further and to find practical measures for dealing with some phases of the problem of confidence. Mr. Huxley proposed that we deal with things that we can do something about relatively soon. Mr. Reed referred to the feeling in business "that on the social side we haven't kept up with the physical and technological side."

FROM "WHO DONE IT?" TO "WHAT TO DO?"

There had been some tendency to allocate blame or credit to industry or labor or government or to deplore the inadequacies of science and philosophy in meeting problems of confidence. As the group got its collective teeth into the question of practical measures, a definite change of mood occurred. A question by Miss Mead marked the turning point.

MISS MEAD: Mr. Chairman, are we in search of heroes and villains here, or are we in search of activity? If we say labor, industry, government, did something . . . and turn them into villains, the opposite of the villain is the hero, and one shifts from one position to the other. If we ask the question instead, "Within this changing industrial society, are there values that we are not looking after but which need to be looked after if we are going to increase the confidence of the whole society?" Then I think we will get out of this sort of "Who done it?" theme.

It was Mr. Kestnbaum who later congratulated the group on the "happy turn" its discussion had taken.

MR. KESTNBAUM: We have got away from the issue of "Who done it?" into an examination of capacities. . . . To find the pattern and the way in which life in an industrial civilization can be improved for large groups of people and to take care of the human friction that is created in any change of the pattern puts great emphasis on the function of leadership and management. They say that when Themistocles was asked to play, he replied, "I cannot play the lute but I can make a small village into a great city." That is what we need now, some people to tell us how to convert industrialism, which has great power, into the force for good in our own country and elsewhere that it can be. If we meet that challenge, I will say again that we are on the verge of a golden age.

CONFIDENCE IN EACH OTHER WITHIN INDUSTRY

As the discussion moved into the specific things that might be done in industry to justify and promote a sense of mutual confidence, a visitor might have thought he was listening to the Roundtable on Work. It is interesting, and probably indicative of certain dominant trends in the thinking of at least a more progressive segment of American industrial leadership, that both roundtables emphasized the need for personal identification in worth-while activity, the sense of participation or "belonging," treating people as individuals rather than as anonymous members of groups or classes, and the advantages in these respects of decentralized organization.

Where the subject matter overlapped, the conclusions of our Roundtable on Confidence confirmed those of the Roundtable on Work. But the "confidence men" (as we cosmic thinkers were nicknamed in the Conference) used a broader perspective and ranged more widely. The discussion touched not only the participation and interrelations of labor and management but also relations with stockholders, industry's community responsibilities, and the importance of good management in business, unions, schools, government, and throughout industrial society. To keep this report within reasonable limits, we must condense a practical, concrete discussion to its most salient points.

Mr. Reed opened with a description of a program begun by the General Electric Company five or six years ago in an effort to give its 250,000 stockholders more of a sense of belonging. The company completely revised its annual report to give much more information in simpler, clearer language. A motion picture was made showing scenes of the various plants and products of the company, and this was shown in a series of meetings over the country attended by thousands and thousands of stockholders. They came not only to see the film but also to see the local management and to ask questions and have them answered. In the past few years, much more interest has been built up in the annual meeting, and it is now held at one of the factories.

Mr. Reed: As these people come in, we put a badge on them, "Stockholder"; and as they go on around the factory on conducted tours, we are glad to have our people, our employee family, see who are the stockholders. They include the teacher down the street—the grocer—just ordinary people. Forty-five per cent of them are women. And the concept of Wall Street owning these great companies is, I think, to some extent put in perspective and corrected by having as many as two thousand stockholders moving around through our plant and shaking hands and seeing their own kind of people who are the employees. Some of the stockholders are of course employees. But the people who come, by and large, are outside people and come from twenty or thirty states.

CHAIRMAN PIERCE: From the standpoint of your aim, is confidence definitely in your mind? Is it an effort to get the stockholder to have confidence in the management, or what is your aim?

MR. REED: I think if we were to use one word it would be "understanding"—mutual understanding. We feel that if our stockholders can have the real facts concerning our company and its policies, our problems will be minimized. We are anxious to get their suggestions, and we get many of them at these meetings, and some of them are critical, of course. We expect that; we want that. . . . The objective is to let them know, give them the feeling that they understand what it is all about, and let the confidence come, we hope.

CHAIRMAN PIERCE: Do you feel that this experience represents just a start and that it is capable of extension and improvement?

MR. REED: Yes, we have just scratched the surface. Each time we see many new possibilities. It is endless in its ramifications and its possibilities.

Mr. Humphrey suggested that the problems of mutual confidence in business are perhaps made to look too complicated by starting out with a large concern like General Electric. In starting any business, the first thing you have to get is the money, and you can't get that unless you have the confidence of some people who are willing to put it with you. But no one man can run an enterprise by himself, so he has to get the confidence of a group who will help to manage; and that group can't run the enterprise without some people to work in it. One of the greatest jobs of management is to get good people to work in the business and to keep them sufficiently interested so that they will stay, thus developing and maintaining a good organization. And the public, which is the final judge, has to be given confidence in the product. These are continuing, everyday tasks of management, and the fundamentals are the same, "whether you are talking about General Electric or . . . about running a cigar store."

EMPLOYEE FAMILIES AND UNIONS

Father Masse then turned from stockholders to employees and unions and the sense of confidence that comes from participation. He addressed a question to Mr. Reed.

FATHER MASSE: Mr. Reed used the phrase "our employee family." I wonder if that expresses the desire of G.E. management or whether is it an actuality, and if so, how that actuality was achieved? If your employees have a family feeling, I presume that their spirit of confidence is strengthened.

MR. REED: The family concept is our concept. To us it is basic. That it has been one hundred per cent achieved is another question. Of course it hasn't. But we often use the expression; we mean it sincerely, and we regard that family as also including our stockholders. In other words, it is an enterprise, a broad enterprise, in which something over 200,000 people are engaged as employees. Another 250,000 people are owners of the enterprise. If we can get that spirit of joint interest, joint participation, of belonging, from the standpoint of both our family of employees and our large family of stockholders, I think we at least set the backdrop against which we can build. . . .

FATHER MASSE: And I wonder whether the average employee in General Electric has this family feeling, feeling of belonging; and if he does have it, I wonder whether he has it directly or indirectly through his membership in the union?

MR. REED: I am obviously a prejudiced witness on this point. It is my firm belief that the average employee does feel that he is a member of the family, that he does have confidence in the objectives, attitudes, and purposes of the management, from his foreman on up to the supervisors and others.

The extent to which there is a sense of divided loyalty, if you put it that way, in his attitude toward the company, on the one hand, and in his relations with his local union leaders, on the other, is something which I would be much interested to have Mr. Cook talk about. It is clear to me—because I deeply believe in unions, the desirability of them—that the employees should have an organization through which they can deal with management. There will always

be, I suspect, until the millennium comes, a certain amount of difficulty in drawing the line in the attempt to hold or get the confidence
of employees on the part of management, on the one hand, and the
union, on the other. This shouldn't be so. At least it shouldn't be to
the point that either management or labor leadership should feel that
it must impugn the other in order to get the confidence of the employee. That, of course, is the case still in this country, and I only
hope and pray that at some stage unions will be so firmly rooted and
doing the kind of job that so clearly contributes to the welfare of the
employee that it won't be necessary to try to build strength by de-
stroying the relationship and the confidence between management
and the employee group. I believe that we can do much better than
we are doing. Whether we will ever reach perfection in that area one
never knows.

Mr. Cook agreed that the "one big family" policy does benefit,
to a large extent, the people who are in that one big family. But
what about the other people who are not in that family and who
do not participate in the retirement pensions, paid vacations, insurance, and other benefits that have been set up by such industrial concerns for the benefit of their employees? And what
happens to the people who leave the employ of such concerns?
We are interested, he said, in a better way of life for everybody.
While individual corporations make a contribution toward the
solution of the general problem, there is still need for extension
of Social Security by government.

Mr. Cook: What I understand that labor wants . . . is the things
that will lead to a better way of life for them and their families. . . .
It is all right to talk about meetings of stockholders and management,
but to understand the problems of the workers you must get down
and meet with them and hear their stories. They do not always tell
them to management.

I am one who believes that in industry we have a mutual interest.
It is wrong for one group, whether it is labor or management, to take
an unfair advantage of the other. I think that we should live together
and try to improve conditions for all of us. . . . I am in the glass
business. . . . We have been, as a union, meeting with a principal
association of the glass business annually since 1888; and we have had

little labor trouble, because we understand each other's problems. We realize there is a mutual interest there to be respected, and we get along quite well.

One of the reasons for that is that many of the representatives of the employers or management came from the ranks of the glass workers' union. They know the workers' problems; they are more liberal in meeting the issues that come before the conferences. . . . We believe that it is time for industry, business, and labor to get a little bit closer together and to respect each other's interests.

PARTICIPATION BY THE LABOR FORCES

Mr. Huxley then asked whether there are ways by which the labor force, as well as stockholders, could be given a greater sense of participation through greater understanding of the objects of a business. While labor obviously cannot participate in the actual process of making management decisions, is it possible to make them understand what the decisions are about?

Mr. Reed responded that his company has a regular procedure by which the local manager talks with small groups of employees from time to time in an effort to give them a better view of the whole operation and to generate their pride and enthusiasm about the whole as well as their specific part. "He goes over the operating statement with them; he explains what the situation is, if the inventory is getting too big. He tells them what his problems are and what he is trying to do . . . and asks for their help. . . . We haven't brought it to perfection by a long way, but we are completely sold on the need for it and the benefits that are derived from it. Again, it is the building of confidence through understanding."

LARGE-SCALE ENTERPRISE AND PARTICIPATION

Miss Mead then pointed out that several types of participation or identification had been mentioned: participation in name-identified enterprises, like that of Mr. Reed's stockholders and employees; participation not in an enterprise, but in an industry or operation, as when Mr. Cook said, "I am in the glass business"; and the other type of identification which Mr. Cook had illustrated by the fact that many of the managers in the glass industry had risen out of the ranks. Miss Mead went on to discuss the question of participation in large-scale undertakings.

MISS MEAD: Mr. Humphrey has said that it doesn't make any difference whether you are running General Electric or a cigar store . . . the principle is the same. But I think there is a difference we ought to cope with here. If you are running a cigar store, you have one employee whose business it is to stay there; and if he goes away and boys break in from the street and steal the cigars, it is obvious that he is exceedingly essential. But if you have five thousand comparable employees working in a large industry, it is terribly difficult to make any one of those people feel as important and as essential as the one man in the cigar store who has to stay there and watch things. . . . How can a large-scale industry design things so each person will feel that he has a role to play that is irreplaceable, even though it may be a simple one?

MR. MITCHELL: Mr. Chairman, may I take a crack at answering that, because I think that Miss Mead has not merely hit upon one of the problems, I think that she has hit upon *the* problem. I was trying to say this morning that you can't consider people as people. You have to consider them as individuals. As soon as you stop considering them as individuals, you get nowhere. . . .

When Grandpa founded the business, he had fifteen employees; and there wasn't a day when he didn't pat each employee on the back and say "Joe, how is the missus today?" And when the old man had a time meeting the payroll on Saturday, every one of the fifteen employees knew it. . . . They were interested in his problems, and he was interested in them. Unfortunately, as industry has grown, no longer can someone in Mr. Reed's position pat 200,000 General Electric employees on the back every day. . . . What can we do? This gets down to the problem of communication, and there is no single answer; but I would like to point a direction that some of us in industry can go to some degree. . . .

DECENTRALIZATION

Here Mr. Mitchell outlined the advantages of decentralized operations in small plants from the point of view of human relations. He was aware that this solution was applicable mainly in businesses where the products are small in size, light in weight, and high in value, so that mobility is possible and production does not have to be concentrated in a single spot. "Mr. Reed can't make Diesel-electric locomotives the way I make starters for fluorescent lamps."

Mr. Mitchell: The greatest reason that I am a fan of this business of decentralization of industry is that we get a little closer to individual contact with the individual employee, and he thinks more of himself as an individual than as a number on the time clock. That is important. . . .

We have a few plants with a sizable number of employees, three or four thousand. It is most difficult in those plants to get this feeling down the line. You have to have a big organization even for two or three thousand employees. Communications are difficult all the way down. The words that management says may get translated down the line pretty closely, but you can bet the meaning is different when it gets down there.

But take a little plant. . . . In Towanda, Pennsylvania, we have 209 employees and a young manager who knows individually every one of those 209 employees and calls them Joe and Pete and Frank and Mary; and if Mary is sick and in the hospital, he goes and finds out how she is. He can do it with 209 employees. I could give you case after case where the labor efficiency in that little plant will make the labor efficiency in the big plant of 3,000 people look silly. There isn't any question about it. The reason is that we have got back some portion of that camaraderie that used to exist between management and labor.

I am not disagreeing with Mr. Kestnbaum, who said earlier that nobody wants to go back to the good old days. I guarantee him that my little plant of 209 employees is more highly mechanized than any plant of 3,000 employees I have ever seen in my life, so there is no lack of efficiency there. It is just a small number of employees. And they are not in the horse-and-buggy days. They have refrigerators and radios and television sets in their homes. But we still get some inkling of that camaraderie, because it is not a group of people known as labor talking across the table with a group of people known as management. . . . In the big plants we try to communicate through the foremen, and in their little groups they do a fair job of it. But talking to the foreman is not like talking to the boss.

UNIONS AND INDIVIDUALITIES

Here, Mr. Mitchell made a suggestion to organized labor. The unions might do more to help management to consider the people in their group as individuals and not merely as a group. Some unions follow this policy; others do not.

MR. MITCHELL: Sometimes the unions do not want us to consider them as individuals. They want everybody to be on exactly the same basis. . . . That doesn't give a person any feeling of belonging, because simply belonging to the union gives no sense of belonging in the great broad sense we are talking about here of belonging to an enterprise—I don't mean belonging to the company either—but doing something that gives you a status in society. . . .

MR. COOK: Doesn't your union set up standards that the workers and members of the union are supposed to meet?

MR. MITCHELL: Oh, yes.

MR. COOK: We find in our industry that if an employer complains of an individual not meeting certain standards, we get after them individually.

MR. MITCHELL: Sure you do, but your union is one of the oldest and, I might say, one of the best unions—from the standpoint of considering the welfare of the individual worker—of any that I have ever had anything to do with. And there are some much newer unions which will eventually, given the right number of years, come to the same conclusion and will act that way. But in the interim period it is difficult. I know why they are doing it. They want the strength to bargain with, you see; and we haven't yet been able to interpret to them that that strength to bargain can still be there and we can still, between us, by some mutual way, take cognizance of the difference in the ability of this person and that person. It is working out gradually, but that is still one of the difficulties in this translation of what management really believes to what the worker thinks management believes. . . .

GOOD AND BAD MANAGEMENT

Mr. Mitchell ended with an assertion that "managements generally are not nearly so bad as the workers think they are; they don't mean to be, anyway." This roused Mr. David, a professional at management training, who countered, "I suspect that some managements are as bad as the workers think they are. There are good managements, bad managements, and intermediate managements."

Mr. David: Obviously, the managements represented around this table are top-flight managements, some of the best in this country, or they wouldn't have been invited to this Conference. That kind of management is the goal toward which I think we have to go. Mr. Cook happens to be the representative of a good union. He manages that union well. We need better union management. . . . One of the great challenges of our time is to apply our knowledge of the social sciences so as to train better administrators, whether those administrators are in our labor unions, in our school systems, in our hospitals, in our businesses, or in our government. . . .

The good administrator must make it possible for his group to participate; he must try to establish a two-way street of communication. . . . His responsibility is not just giving a sense of participation—and we have thrown that word around here a good bit—but actually making sure individuals in the group do participate. . . . This concept of the process of administration is related to the two things which I think we have hit on here: one, real participation and, two, satisfactions that come from being members of the group and in that way building confidence. . . .

And I hope I may say this without embarrassing the chairman. The chairman happens to represent a company which for many years has probably been the leader of all companies in having good management in the sense of having its people feel as though they were participating in the company. Mr. Kestnbaum has also had great success in that area. One without unions; the other with unions. But somehow or other, good management, you can smell it; or rather, let me put it in reverse, you can smell bad management.

Chairman Pierce: We shouldn't leave this question of the professional character of management without really distinguishing between Don Mitchell's situation and that of some of the rest of us where, even though we wanted to, we couldn't decentralize into his size units. That leaves you in the predicament that you must find organization techniques to achieve these ends. One of the things that we have found important in developing a progressive attitude in management is an adult education program to train management at the intermediate levels. We have made great use of the universities, and a number of other companies are doing the same, sending younger management to them to get out of the specialization rut. The universities really have the spark that stimulates management. . . .

WHERE DOES THE CONSUMER COME IN?

Now, Mr. Sears, the political philosopher, raised a new question. Where does the consumer fit into this picture of confidence in industry? The consumer is interested in the prices he has to pay, and his interest is bound up not only with the budgets of individual families but with the economic health of the country and fears of economic depression. We have long assumed, he said, that this problem didn't need to be faced—at least not by any conscious participation on the part of the consumer—because competition on a free market, operating automatically, would take care of it. But is that assumption any longer true, especially in view of what we have seen in the past twenty years? Perhaps the answer is that all of us as consumers are also citizens and have our consumer interests represented through the government. But then we come up against a new difficulty. The consumer is not organized into any effective pressure group, as the various industries and unions are.

MR. SEARS: I am not offering a suggestion or a solution. It is purely a question. How are the vast mass of us who are mere citizens and consumers going to participate in industry at the point that is most important for us? In so far as we do not participate, is this sense of confidence that we have been talking about likely to arise?

The chairman said he would call on a roundtable member "who has to sell a product with a very touchy consumer demand" to deal with that question; and he turned to Mr. Kestnbaum, who commented that the most powerful pressure group in America is the consumer. The consumer sits in the center of the stage, reviews all the products that are offered for his selection, and makes his choice. Our industrial civilization in America, he continued, is consumer-oriented. Despite all our arguments to the contrary, the controlling person in it is the one who buys the products.

There are industries which for one reason or another are monopolistic, but the basic character of the American economy is highly competitive, not only as between companies but as between products. We know that the consumer does in the end get a good break, because, regardless of what political party has been in power, the standard of living in our country has just about doubled every thirty years quite regularly since our country was founded. This has given us a sense of progress which has made one of the greatest contributions to the fundamental question of confidence. With the exception of the period of the depression, which has colored our thinking a little too much, this progress has been uniform and quite striking. It has become, Mr. Kestnbaum concluded, the envy of the world, and also it is one of the most revolutionary things that is happening in the world.

Mr. David suggested that the freedom of choice which we have in this country, based upon our marketing developments and techniques, is perhaps the least understood aspect of our American scheme of things. Mr. Huxley reminded the group that there was not only one depression, there have been a number, and that there is an important interest on the part of all the people in preventing inflation. Mr. Humphrey, from his intimate knowledge of the anthracite coal industry, spoke of the reality of interindustry competition, as illustrated by the rise of oil and natural gas.

Obviously, the issues raised here could have occupied (and have occupied) many a seminar on marketing, monopolistic competition, business cycles, inflation, and government control. The issues were left at this point, Mr. Sears merely noting that, in his view, there was not a real meeting of minds, because different members of the group were starting with different assumptions. One body of assumptions held that our economic system is still operating automatically under competitive conditions, which means the consumer has effective participation and control. Another set of assumptions, to which Mr. Sears subscribed, is "that this no longer accurately depicts the system we are now living in, and that we are going to have to work out new patterns of behavior by which there can be a different kind of participation and control than can be exercised through a free market that seems to some people to have been seriously eroded."

EDUCATION

When the chairman turned the conversation to practical measures that might be taken in the field of education, he called first on Mr. Huxley, who made three main points:

(1) Both management and workers, in their joint interest, should see to it that the public school system in every industrial community is maintained at a really high level.

(2) Some methods of education rob the student—especially the young boy or girl—of confidence in his own abilities, while others build confidence. For instance, some ways of teaching mathematics tend to make children feel that they are "damn fools at mathematics and probably damn fools at everything else." The right method, whether in mathematics or language or drawing or music or sports, draws the student out, develops his capacities, and gives him confidence.

(3) Adult education in a society like ours is a necessity. In this connection Mr. Huxley mentioned the need for relating the individual in the small community or in the industrial nation to world problems, the need to encourage opportunities for self-expression, and the need for recreational facilities which encourage people to make the best of themselves in their off time, through their hobbies, through travel, through sports, and in other ways.

MR. HUXLEY: I think it is extremely important that we should now begin, in our educational system, to pay more attention to universal history, meaning the history of mankind as a whole, to pay more attention to biological evolution as opposed to the physical sciences only, and to pay more attention to giving people the opportunity to get satisfaction through realizing their own capacities.

WORLD OUTLOOK

Mr. Krusé took up the point about the need for an education which gives people a world sense of belonging and some understanding of other cultures. The new conditions created by the rise of modern industry make this practically a necessity, especially for Americans. In the past we have confronted people largely on the basis simply of selling them some article or on the basis of fighting them in war. But now the time has come to seek some real feeling of understanding. Through literature, through philosophy, through religion, and in other ways, our education must help us to enter somehow into the minds and hearts of other peoples.

MR. KRUSÉ: I sometimes get the feeling that we do a much better job in kindergarten than we do in college. In kindergarten I notice they sometimes have a Japanese week or something like that, and the teachers make a brave start. But by the time we go to college, it appears as if it is only this little Western world that has any significance whatsoever. . . . I think that we in educational institutions have been remiss in that regard. I have taught the history of world philosophy. Now I realize that I taught just a tiny segment of world philosophy, and I see how important it is for us to enter sympathetically, understandingly, imaginatively, into the minds and into the hearts of such people as the Chinese and Japanese and Indians. I think that is a new responsibility and a practical one. . . .

CREATIVE ARTS AND CONFIDENCE

Mr. Huxley in his remarks on adult education had cited Devon, England, where he had recently visited, and he had noted that the two subjects most popular with adults in that agricultural county were drama and pottery making.

MR. HUXLEY: It is most interesting—self-expression through drama and self-expression through creative work with their hands. This would have been impossible twenty-five years ago before agriculture had been mechanized. People were just too tired when they came back from a long day in the fields. Now British agriculture has been highly mechanized, and the agricultural workers are getting more pleasure and more interest and initiative. That is giving them a feeling of confidence and a feeling of the status of the individual.

Mr. Calhoun, however, found himself "a bit uneasy" at this point.

Mr. Calhoun: Selecting as the most popular subjects in adult education, self-expression in drama and self-expression in pottery making suggests to me that what is wanted by the folks who are the recipients of this education is apparently not the development of critical habits of thought, not the development of skills which are directly pertinent to the main business of living, but rather the development of accessory activities which might have the character of an escape. A kind of opium for the people might conceivably be the outcome. . . .

At this Mr. d'Harnoncourt jumped in prepared to do battle.

Mr. d'Harnoncourt: May I protest the a priori association of creative activities with escapism?

Mr. Calhoun: Oh, please, let me correct the impression that I regret having given. . . . The comment of one of my old teachers is perhaps in point. To ornament construction is sound. To construct ornament may be very unsound. To find ways of beautifying the major structure of one's living through recreational and expressive outlets of one sort or another certainly is not escapism. But if these outlet activities should become a substitute for the efforts to learn the hard way, to understand better what one does and what one is called upon to do, then I say, yes, they are escapes.

Mr. Huxley: But you learn to understand what you are by understanding what you can do. I mean, these activities help you to realize certain capacities which you can't realize in the ordinary business of life.

Mr. Frank: I think Dr. Calhoun and Mr. d'Harnoncourt are bringing out the difference between an intellectualist approach and another type of approach. Maybe if we didn't talk so much about self-expression but thought of the arts as forms of self-discovery, we wouldn't be inclined to think that we grow up and learn only through intellectual activity. I think that is, at least, I hope that is, what Mr. d'Harnoncourt had in mind.

Mr. d'Harnoncourt: That is exactly what I had in mind. It is becoming increasingly difficult for the individual to find an opportunity for creative work. Television, radio, and film are an all too easy substitute for home dramatics and imaginative games, and the commercial production of objects serving innumerable purposes eliminates the need for nearly all manual work in the home. No wonder that the demand for creative activities is steadily growing in schools and community centers.

Creative work in any form and medium tends to make people aware of their individual ways of doing things. It helps them to discover their own personalities and by doing so contributes greatly to their sense of security. This was borne out by the success of occupational therapy in the field of the arts during the last war.

In this part of its discussion, as Miss Mead pointed out, the Roundtable on Confidence had crossed the trail of the Roundtable on Leisure, which was debating whether leisure should serve some useful purpose or whether it has values in itself. Should we take a part of life, such as artistic expression or leisure, and make it instrumental to another part, or should we simply regard it as living?

FAMILY LIFE AND REARING OF CHILDREN

As Miss Frenkel-Brunswik pointed out, it is within the family that we first learn interpersonal relationships. The child is confronted with people who are in authority, usually its parents; their attitudes and ways of rearing the child are basic in shaping the individual's subsequent confidence or lack of confidence in life.

Miss Frenkel-Brunswik: This is often not given enough weight in the family on the wrong assumption that children are small and so the problem of individuality doesn't yet enter. It can't be stressed enough that the child should really be accepted in his own individuality and his own need and not subordinated to the needs of the parent. If the parents mishandle the situation and expect subordination and conformity, then the child has to narrow down the possibilities of his own experience to please them; and this narrowing down has important implications. In our experiments we find that the child later repeats the attitudes which it has developed toward parental authority. Childhood problems of conformity vs. creativity, problems of self-acceptance and the like, are really the foundation for our confidence in life.

Mr. Cohen here called attention to the strains imposed upon family life under modern conditions. He offered the concrete suggestion that adjustments ought to be made in employment practices to allow women to work parttime. A working woman must make great sacrifices. If she cannot work eight hours a day like anybody else, then she cannot hold a job. Management, labor, government, must begin to look at some of the things that they are doing in terms of what the effect is upon the family. Mr. Frank later summed up this way:

MR. FRANK: If we are going to have the kind of personalities who are capable of maintaining a free industrial society, then we have to look at the whole process of personality development, which goes back, as we now know, more and more to family life. So you have a circular process. If people are dissatisfied because of their working conditions, they are going to take it out in their family life and their children. This perpetuates the inabilities of society—of people—to develop toward the very goals that we say we want to attain. Someone once said that the American family has been subsidizing business and industry for a great many generations. They have been taking up the slack in unemployment; they have been meeting all the demands of industry—hours, wages, layoffs, etc.—until recently when we said, "Look, they can't do it any more." . . . I don't think we can put more strain and stress on the American family and expect it to live up to the profound social obligations of today.

NEED FOR FURTHER EXPLORATION

From the first, Chairman Pierce had urged members to keep in mind that one outcome of these discussions might well be "a little clearer idea of where future studies could usefully be directed." Many suggestions emerged out of the general discussion and, in addition, the final hour on Saturday morning was largely devoted to the topic of future explorations. Here is a staccato summary of concrete projects proposed by various members:

(1) What are the goal values that we seek? Comparative, empirical studies should be made to determine what in fact people do value most highly, examining representative samples of people in many different backgrounds, and paying attention to their actions as well as their words. (Lasswell, Dennes)

Mr. Morris reported in this connection that he has been investigating the life ideals of young people in some twelve different cultures. When American young people (college students) are given a choice among a number of life patterns, the dominant choice, selected by about 40 out of 100, is a pattern which stresses an integrated personality, where action and enjoyment and knowledge are all emphasized in the good life. "This doesn't appear in any of the other cultures in anywhere near the same degree. It is a demand for psychological abundance, if you will, that is the corollary of the possibility of a society of abundance."

(2) Factual studies might be made to determine how many people in industry have a "family feeling" about the enterprise in which they work and how this varies as between people with many and few years of service. (Pierce)

(3) What relation exists between the dynamism in a civilization and its view of the cosmos? Are some absolutes essential to the well-being of any kind of society? (Masse) Father Masse called attention to the way in which the absolutes of Communist doctrine seem to inspire confidence and enthusiasm among Communists.

(4) To what extent are many of our values today dependent unconsciously on the Judo-Christian tradition, including values of the dignity of the human being, the value of freedom, and all the rest? Are we, in effect, living on borrowed ethical capital in our industrial society, retaining the ideals after having abandoned the beliefs that inspired them? How long can that go on? (Masse) Miss Mead endorsed this idea: "We do not know the conditions by which a civilization survives without some kind of abiding faith. We have lived on the residue of an age of faith, and we don't know what the conditions are. That is a primary problem for study today."

(5) Have we had a divorce between our religious beliefs and our economic practices? (Masse)

(6) Intensive exploration of individuals should be undertaken, to find in detail how they solve ethical problems in their different

areas of life, how satisfactory their various solutions are, and how the solutions change during life. (Frenkel-Brunswik)

(7) Most studies of developmental psychology stop at the age of twenty. Why not extend them to the age of seventy? (Frenkel-Brunswik)

(8) The relationship between ethical convictions and the factual basis of those convictions deserves study. "Some people think they can derive their attitudes from facts, and it is interesting to see the different ways of rationalization." (Frenkel-Brunswik)

(9) Studies on the awakening and development of a sense of identity, of uniqueness, and of a sense of the contribution of an individual to the group would be valuable. (d'Harnoncourt)

(10) It would be illuminating to study on an international scale the various degrees of compromise between central control, positive planning, or negative control, on the one hand, and freedom of individual enterprise, on the other. (Huxley) "Because, for instance, in my country we certainly shouldn't go back on certain government controls. They have given us confidence, for instance, in the health of our children. We wouldn't have got it otherwise, without government control. But the question is, how are you going to get the two sides of it balanced?—which seems to me is necessary in any modern civilization."

(11) Interrelations between living in the family and working in industrial enterprise need study—the kinds of satisfactions, the conflicts, the dissatisfactions. (Frank)

(12) Could not major industries (not companies, but industries) be stimulated to study what they may unintentionally be doing to create some of the difficulties and problems that undermine confidence? For example, the industry that makes labor-saving devices for the kitchen has created a problem of leisure time for women. Should this industry take some responsibility for helping women to make better use of their leisure time? (Frank)

(13) We should look critically at some of our traditional beliefs, asking which have persisted as folklore past the time when they were applicable, and we should attempt to translate the continuing aspirations of man into more modern terms. (Frank)

(14) It would be valuable to study people who change enormously through life—for example, those who come from Europe and become Americans, or the people from simple or possibly illiterate backgrounds who rise to importance on the international scene. "Changes in people through life, we don't know anything about." (Mead)

Mr. Kestnbaum observed that industrial technique, represented by the large-scale survey, seems to have captured the imagination of the academic profession. He hoped that the philosopher would not resign completely. (Mr. Dennes: "You can't stop us.")

Mr. Morris spoke in favor of a new approach developed in England and this country during the war called "action research" or "operations research." The important thing about it is that it unites scientific and humanistic concerns by enlisting the techniques of the expert in solving real value problems.

FOLLOW-UP TO THIS CONFERENCE

The Roundtable on Confidence formally and unanimously decided to inform the organizers of the Conference that, as chairman Pierce put it, "The generally expressed opinion here is that there should be some study of a continuing organization."

Mr. Lasswell had early suggested that "we may be participating here in a first step." In his view, "a significant contribution to the reorganization of our culture" might be made by a "continuing inquiry which would have much the same title as this Conference —on the problems of living in an industrialized world." Such an enterprise should formulate our goal objectives in terms of realization of human dignity, should keep abreast of the changing stock of scientific knowledge and insight into the factors affecting the realization of these goal values, and should examine the alternatives of strategy by which the preferred goals might in fact be approximated.

Mr. Lasswell: I should like to be part of a continuing process of inquiry, conducted by people with varied backgrounds such as are represented here: responsible decision makers, specialized intellectuals who are in touch with what we know and suspect about the development of human personality and the development of culture. I should like to be part of a continuing quest for clarification of what it is that we want, especially for provisional workable definitions and images of what sorts of people we find admirable, what sorts of characters we are talking about when we are concerned with persons who represent the confidence that we want. . . . I should like to participate in a continuing quest to find people who are approximations at different ages and in different backgrounds of what we are talking about. Then I would like to get a much better understanding, if possible, of how they came to pass and how it is possible to increase the likelihood that favorable conditions for such developments will occur. We need to clarify our goal values and to invent means of enlisting enthusiastic participation in the building up of a sort of life that we want.

As various members of the group rallied enthusiastically to the idea that the experience at Corning should be only a first step, the reasons they gave indicated three points of uniqueness and value which they saw in the Conference:

(1) Participation of people with quite varied backgrounds.
(2) The problem approach.
(3) The humanistic perspective.

Mr. Huxley suggested that one of the large foundations ought to be interested in carrying on the kind of enterprise the round-table had been exploring. He particularly emphasized the first two values, and in this he was supported by Mr. Dennes.

Mr. Huxley: It seems to me that this meeting has shown of what great advantage it is to have people of different sorts around a table studying a problem instead of a subject. I think that is the whole tendency now, isn't it, in modern life? I mean, the universities have tended to study subjects. Now we are beginning to realize that it divides your knowledge into compartments. . . .

Mr. Dennes: I feel that that suggestion deserves careful attention from a group like this. I have no doubt that groups of scholars and social scientists will be making proposals to foundations for studies in this field; and I think that if we could see ways by which representatives of labor and industry could participate in planning and in carrying out such studies, they might have a great deal better balance and scope.

Mr. Sears thought that the value of the Conference would be largely determined by what continued out of it. He was impressed with the wide gulf that separates those who are practically engaged in industry and those, like himself, who are theoretically engaged in examining industry. This is largely a matter of different assumptions. Would it not be possible, in connection with a continuing enterprise, to recognize frankly these profoundly different assumptions and see if we couldn't find out why they exist?

The unique stimulus and integrative value of the humanistic outlook that permeated the Conference was particularly stressed by Mr. Hiltner and Miss Mead.

MR. HILTNER: It seems to me that in a sense what we have been doing in this group is to say that the humanities are not to be understood merely in the traditional terms. Our discussion represents a kind of fusion of the interests of the humanities with some of the methods of study of the social sciences, supplemented by the philosophical modes of study. . . . I know of no previous gathering of this kind in which the humanities have been lifted up with the full traditional implications of the humanities, and yet tempered by this interest in the social studies. Is it possible somehow to use the stimulation of this Conference to redefine what the new element in the humanities is, so that there may gradually emerge a new sense of the importance of projects along this line? If you just talk about the humanities, people think it is the old traditional reading this and reading that, no creative work in it. If, on the other hand, you say the social sciences, you suggest to many minds narrow methods merely imitative of natural sciences, which many people do not believe is sufficient. Here in a sense is a merger. . . . Is there some way that this meeting can be used to stimulate such a redefinition of the humanities?

MISS MEAD: The unique thing about this Conference is that it has been keyed to the humanities, actually, and I would like to keep that very clear. I think one reason we have been able to talk the way we have—and at least once in a while say something that was intelligible all the way around the table—has been because we were within a wider structure. It wasn't just social scientists, on the one hand, talking with businessmen and engineers, industrialists and labor leaders, on the other, but we were talking about this whole question of confidence in life.

There is every danger that this will get lost again. We will have some nice studies in the best assembly line style, as Mr. Kestnbaum said, and will set up wonderful problems; and the whole question of value will get lost, because we will study values externally instead of studying them as parts of ourselves. . . . If we could keep the framework of the humanities sufficiently so we don't have people studying religion who have never said a prayer in their lives and are never going to—which is what we do now—and don't have psychologists studying creativity—who, so far as is known, have never manifested it—then we won't have people studying confidence in life who haven't got it.

CHAIRMAN PIERCE: You are setting a very high standard.

MISS MEAD: I am perfectly willing to have a few of those people in too, because they are a part of the world and we need them.

BETTER USE OF WHAT WE KNOW

The roundtable also recognized that, in addition to finding out more, we need to make better use of what we already know. Two angles of this problem were exposed: the need for better communication between the scholar-scientist-intellectual and the ordinary people whose problems they are trying to investigate and the need for bridging the gap between research and action.

COMMUNICATION

A philosopher and a labor leader agreed on the first need, and their characteristically different choice of words for putting nearly the same idea provided an illustration of the problem of communication:

MR. KRUSÉ: There is already a good deal of knowledge in all these areas, the cosmic area, as well as the social area, but somehow we don't communicate it.

MR. COOK: I think that in this group we are too far over the heads of the people that we are trying to do something about.

Mr. Krusé went on, as he said, to "put on the hairshirt." He confessed that academic people write too much for other specialists and not enough for the general mass of people. He applauded the farsightedness of the Department of Agriculture, which, some years ago, sent two philosophers throughout the nation giving extension courses in philosophy. These proved extremely popular. He added that adult education in industry might well be increased. Mr. Cook suggested that more people from the ranks ought to be brought into meetings like this Conference.

Mr. Cook: The big problem is, how are we going to span this gap between the thinking that goes on here and their thinking? From my observation, the only way you can do that with any degree of success is to get down to their level and find out what is running through their minds. . . . Even labor leaders, I am afraid, cannot convey as well as they should the real feelings of these people. . . . I wish it were possible to have more people right out of the ranks to participate in meetings of this kind. We would then get the story direct from them. And if you want to get it right, really right, then you should get down into the homes of these people and find out how they live and what they are desirous of. . . .

They are the same kind of people we are. . . . They are good citizens. They don't need to be made over. They are the right kind of people. They must be given an increased feeling of confidence in all things. I am in sympathy with the suggestion that we ought to continue our efforts here; we ought to try to create some agency or organization that will get down into this thing and make a more thorough study and get to the people we are trying to help and not merely those who speak for them.

FROM KNOWLEDGE TO ACTION

Mr. Kestnbaum stressed the importance of translating knowledge into action.

Mr. Kestnbaum: The practitioner is troubled by the fact that he has to make decisions today, and you gentlemen want to make studies to give us some information tomorrow, six months from now. I think that is useful, but in the meantime we must operate; we must operate with the best knowledge, opinions, that we have. And we must learn how to use these studies intelligently. . . . I am glad Mr. Cook said what he did—businessmen, labor leaders, foremen, are relatively illiterate people.

Chairman Pierce: Engineers.

Mr. Kestnbaum: I include engineers. They are relatively illiterate people. They don't read too well; they are sometimes unimaginative;

and they want to deal with the things that they call practical; but at least they want to deal with immediate factors. . . . So when you come to make proposals, to give us the benefit of this wisdom, someone has to take it and translate it into human action, at specific points, critical points; and that still involves the art of management and human relationships. . . .

While urging studies, Mr. Kestnbaum also directed attention to the reply of the farmer who was told that by going to the state fair he could learn better farming methods: "I don't farm now as well as I know how."

7

A Concluding Review

GENERAL SESSION

Eric Larrabee, rapporteur

The purpose of the final session had been to reunite in a single fabric the threads of study allotted to the several roundtables. Two representatives were to be selected from each by its chairman, to report on the roundtable's work and to initiate a discussion of the sum of the Conference before the entire membership. The previous evening, however, in an informal meeting of the Conference chairman Charles E. Odegaard, with the eight chosen voices of the four groups, it was found that none was anxious to usurp the function of rapporteur and to attempt a concise summation. Hence it was agreed that each might talk from his own vantage point, but that the names would be given Mr. Odegaard of eight additional persons he might usefully select (two from each roundtable) to add to the equitable variety of the opinions presented, in the limited time available.

"The gentlemen who are up here before you," began Mr. Odegaard on Saturday morning, "should be regarded simply as a kind of extension of the audience down there below. . . . None of the members of the respective panels here wishes to be regarded as having the necessity of giving a résumé of what happened." This meant that unavoidably there would be lacunae, that there would be no open free-for-all in which the complete Conference participated, and that this concluding record must thus devote itself to locating each speaker's view, in relation not only to what was said but to what was not said. Needless to add, a reading of the stenotype transcript of all the roundtables discloses that their representatives interpreted freely within the angle of their own perspectives, and it is likely that anyone who comes to this chapter after those of the four rapporteurs will observe the optical illusions at work which deceive the eye of even the most impartial witness.

No prejudice need attach to human fallibility, nor will the writer concern himself with the impossible task of repairing each omission and returning every shifted emphasis to the balance of perfect justice. The effort will be made, however, to relate each speaker's words to the major themes of the Conference as the rapporteur understands them and to select from these final speeches the elements which connect one roundtable with another. "One of the things which I observed as I went from one roundtable to the next," Mr. Odegaard continued in his introduction, "was that you people, as we anticipated in the planning group, couldn't stay on the reservation assigned to you, that you were bound to stray—and, as a matter of fact, it is perfectly proper that it should be that way."

The overlapping areas of interest that revealed themselves are bounded by identifiable preoccupations and defined in terms which the reader will recognize. The inherited dichotomies—between practical and theoretical, between production and "values," between men of action and men of thought, between material and spiritual—underlie these deliberations as they did the two opening addresses of the first general session, with initially the same deleterious results. But in this last session it became apparent that concentrated cultivation of these arid fields of investigation had borne unexpected fruit; by this time the authority embodied in the conventional contrasts between "mind" and "matter" had been challenged, and the atmosphere of questioning was shared—though often in terms of paradox and irony—by nearly every speaker. It was no longer sufficient to state that industrial civilization suffered from a specific need without adding the qualification "Are we sure it does?" A magnetic pull in the direction of existing evidence can be felt throughout, even where the Conference attempted to exercise objectivity on itself and its own functioning.

In the mood of self-analysis, here also was the occasion for compliments to the Corning sponsors. The fact that the most flowery bouquets will not appear in this account should not suggest that they lacked fragrance or sincerity, but only that they would be out of place in a volume devoted more to the substance of the Conference than to the fact of its existence. Let a paradox express the gratitude of the group. Speaking for labor, and suggesting that if "a conference of this sort . . . is good for big business [it] is good for big unionism, too," Mark Starr of the International Ladies' Garment Workers entered his reservation about the luxurious manner of life which the Conference had enjoyed. "Are we not," he asked, "getting an installment of the Welfare State in the way in which we have been so carefully looked after?"

One signal factor in the physical situation was the necessity for the chairman "to watch the clock here because of another event which is to take place shortly"—the formal opening of the Glass Center on the split-second schedule required by Governor Dewey's radio address. "I am not sure," said Mr. Odegaard, "whether the chairmen designated these individuals because they talk so easily, or because they talk with such restraint; and, not being quite sure of the principles that were operative here, we are laying down a house rule that they will be privileged to use no more than four minutes." With this introduction, Mr. Odegaard turned to the representatives of the Roundtable on Work, Sir George E. Schuster and James Worthy. "I thought it was five minutes, and not four," Sir George Schuster began. "Don't count that in my time."

WORK FOR THE KNIGHT IS COMING

The rapporteur of the Roundtable on Work has described how its members tended to follow Mr. Hayes and Mr. Price in basing their attitudes toward industry on the postulates of idealistic humanism. With the exception of Mr. Hayes' reservations that have already been noted—and a number of cynical asides by Everett Hughes* which mainly passed unnoticed—there was agreement

* Mr. Hughes, having the opportunity to check this text, makes the following comment: "I prefer to be thought skeptical rather than cynical. The rest

that work should deliberately, if not aggressively, be made more attractive in human terms to the individuals who engage in it. Sir George Schuster began by adopting this line of approach, possibly out of deference to the important role it had assumed for his colleagues, even though he himself, as it later devolepd, came at the same matter from a significantly different direction.

Within this near-universally acceptable border, Sir George Schuster framed the problem as one of making "a success of our society," of finding how "industrial employment—breadwinning— can be made the basis of a satisfactory human life . . . not as an evil burden to be reduced or escaped from as far as possible (and here I am looking at the thing from the worker's point of view), not as an evil burden which is increased by the incompetence or indifference of management, or by the greed of shareholders and financiers." All well and good, and noteworthy to have been said, if only as an index of how correct Mr. Price was in emphasizing "to what extent capitalism has changed in the past generation, the past decade, even the past few years." Yet when it came to the "right attitudes" which Sir George Schuster felt were necessary, he found himself in conflict with much that had been said at his roundtable, its other representative, Mr. Worthy, serving as spokesman for the opposition.

As the record shows, the Roundtable on Work spent much of its effort on the techniques of organizing work so that the "right attitudes" could find expression. There seemed to be some ambiguity: did the "right" kind of organization produce the "right" kind of people, or the other way around? But whichever it was, Mr. Worthy (aided by Chairman Douglas McGregor and, among others, George C. Homans of Harvard, who spoke from the floor in the final session) maintained that organization was of primary importance. Though Mr. Worthy, too, had been impressed—"I get about the country and talk to a great many people in a good many lines of

---

of the sentence would indicate that I am against having work made more attractive to people. I am not against having work made more attractive. I am only against trying to kid people into saying, whether they believe it or not, that unattractive work is attractive."

business"—with the "degree of good intentions on the part of business leaders which is very apparent," he felt that the chief reason for the failure to carry them out in practice was the fact "that the pattern or structure of the organization tends to get in the way of our efforts to effectuate the sentiments on management's part."

Mr. Worthy: Machine work can be just as interesting and just as satisfying as handicraft work. I think all of us who have experience in industry can recite many examples where working in the midst of machine technology can produce very real, very substantial satisfactions. But in order to do that, the machine work itself must be recognized as meaningful and be so treated by management. It is not merely a matter, too, of saying the job is important, but actually setting up jobs in such a way that they are important.

This problem is a question of managerial temperament. Certain types of management tend to develop certain types of organization. Largely, however, I think it is due to certain mistakes in concepts that we have taken over from "scientific management." I think one of the great needs of modern society is for the development of a more adequate science of management. After all, Taylor* was an engineer. He was very little influenced by the social sciences. As a result, his thinking developed along pretty mechanistic lines, and we have carried over that type of thinking in the ways in which we have organized our business.

Mr. Worthy is associating himself, of course, with Mr. Price's plea that we avoid regarding mechanical work as spiritually debilitating, yet he is sharply cutting himself apart from Mr. Price's conviction that "the unskilled worker has been correctly described

---

* Frederick Winslow Taylor (1856-1915), author of The Principles of Scientific Management and for many years a leading exponent of the term. Mr. Worthy is perhaps somewhat severe with Taylor, who described for a congressional committee in 1912 the "great mental revolution" that was required before his system could be correctly applied. Taylor also took up the question of which was more important, the man or the job; and his answer strongly favors the latter. Mr. Worthy clearly feels that here Taylor leaned too far on the side of "organization." Cf. Hearings Before the Special Committee of the House of Representatives to Investigate the Taylor and Other Systems of Shop Management Under the Authority of H. Res. 90, 62nd Congress, 2nd Session, Vol. III, pp. 1377-1508.

as an engineering imperfection," or that "the machine, which created the problem in the first place, is the answer." Perhaps this complexity can be simplified by referring to the remarks of Mr. Homans, who was equally concerned with the "organizational" as opposed to the "engineering" approach, because he believed the mechanical needs of life to be largely satisfied by our present high level of productivity. Now that industry is no longer preoccupied with "merely seeing that people have the goods and services they require for existence," it can turn its attention to "these more profound values" and the problem of "how to give people satisfaction . . ."

Both Mr. Worthy and Mr. Homans speak of "human values" as distinct entities, almost as though they had similar qualities to goods and services. Sir George Schuster carefully avoided any such position, and ahead of his light footprints around the perimeter it is possible to trace the earlier ones of Mr. Hayes, who had already found it desirable to reject management's assumption that it could "give" anything to labor. On this subject Mr. Hayes had spoken to his roundtable eloquently, with an intensity of feeling which seems to have taken many of his listeners by surprise, and the effect of his words of warning was perceptible in Sir George Schuster's summation. The last sentence of the quotation that follows has therefore been italicized, since (obvious as the reader may find the sentiment to be) it shows an awareness which was not anticipated in the agenda when the Conference began.

SIR GEORGE SCHUSTER: There are two dangers, or evils, to be shunned like the plague. The first is complacency, the second is paternalism. We must be adaptive and adjustable. We are dealing with a population which is becoming increasingly well educated, and unless one can find a basis on which all workers can feel that they are part of a living organism—which I distinguish from mere organization—unless they can feel they are parts of a human living organism in which they have a dignified part to play, I do not believe we will have the setup in industry which is necessary to solve our problem. If we try, as many of us do who hold managerial responsibilities, to set out a list of ideals which we are to aim at, or which we think are good for people for whose employment we are responsible, then I think again we are doomed to disaster. *We have to work with an intelligent population.*

THE STATUS QUO: "WHO ARE SOME OF THESE CHARACTERS?"

The same determination to reorient humanistic knowledge around the existence of a society more profoundly civilized than our means of apprehending it appeared in the reports of other roundtables, especially those on Leisure and Confidence, whose interests were legitimately philosophical and cultural. The former, for example, had been conceived in the understanding that leisure was a problem to a sufficient number of living Americans to warrant treatment on a par with "work" or "confidence." This touchstone had been firmly (and, it seemed, permanently) dislodged by Santha Rama Rau, who had doubted that as long as we regarded leisure as a "problem" we would ever solve it. The first speaker from the Roundtable on Leisure, Howard Mumford Jones, regretted that Miss Rama Rau's exceptional outlook on Western institutions "as a representative from another culture and another side of the problem," had not been fully exploited, since he had the feeling that "we could have defined the leisure problem in America . . . if we had placed it in contrast with the notions of life elsewhere." And this was true, even though the Roundtable on Leisure (certainly the least disciplined of the four) had followed many wide-ranging and superficially frivolous bypaths into the uses of leisure which have been elaborately conventionalized by industrial peoples on their own initiative—in ways less influenced by automata than Occidental thinking is accustomed to admit.

At least "nobody was opposed to leisure," and this, as Mr. Jones properly observed, was "a matter of more moment than a wisecrack, because it represents a complete reversal of values in American life, of the doctrine that 'Satan finds some mischief still for idle hands to do,' which reigned in this country until the twentieth century." Yet his description of the roundtable's progress was nonetheless an illustration of how, in the absence of sympathy with Miss Rama Rau's insistence on accepting leisure as a gift of the

gods, there ensued a riot of mismatched definitions and an intro-
spective Anglo-Saxon symposium on leisure, if not as Satan's play-
ground, as in any event a liability.

MR. JONES: At least seven meanings of "leisure" turned up during
the course of the discussion. There is leisure as mere idleness, there is
leisure as playing, there is leisure as relaxation (that is, in a vacation
sense), there is the idea of leisure as an avocation (the hobby idea),
there is leisure simply as spare time, there is leisure as the world of
fantasy (and that brought us into an extended argument about television), and leisure as enforced abstention from work (which brought
us face to face with the problem of old age and unemployment). . . .

Despite our difficulty about definition, two opposite meanings presently emerged from the fog of brilliance. One was leisure as a state
of being and the other was leisure as a state of doing. As a state of
being, leisure represented no problem at all . . . and most of our time
was concerned with leisure as a state of doing, or being done to—or,
shall I say, being done at? This got us into great difficulties about self-
improvement and civic improvement. The ghost of John Calvin
haunted us all day yesterday. . . .

The second speaker from the Roundtable on Leisure, Eric Larrabee, defended the Calvinistic attributes of his colleagues' discourse as "valiant efforts to fill the terrible vacuum" created by the
growing amounts of leisure earned by a given amount of work.
These he subdivided into "a number of suggestions of ways in
which we might isolate, or identify, socially useful purposes that
could be served by leisure." Yet the fact remained, he felt, that the
Roundtable on Leisure "tended to show a lack of confidence in the
capability of industrial civilization to generate leisure without stulti-
fying it, or without debasing the standards of leisure which we
already have, or without sacrificing the independence of the individual to potential leisure monopolies."

Some members of the roundtable held different views (as a
perusal of the statements of Walter Paepcke, David Riesman, Mark
Benney, or David Sarnoff will show). From these elucidations of
leisure as it is actually lived Mr. Larrabee argued that "the most
fruitful avenue we followed could be called that of the ecology of

leisure, as represented by our background paper, into such questions as the sources in childhood of habits of leisure consumption
—customs as shown, for instance, in different odds for gambling
and the attitudes they represent, in the extent to which they
demonstrate the individual's sense of his own 'stake' in an industrial world." From the interplay between these specific illustrations
had been deduced the need for "flexibility on the part of the individual," who must be prepared "to face the exhaustion of leisure
resources one by one and to shift rapidly to another."

MR. LARRABEE: There were implicit in these arguments some fairly
deep semantic difficulties, perhaps a representation of the difference
between a philosophy of abstract ends and one of process. . . . We
found ourselves on the edge of a new approach to socioeconomic
problems. . . . You might say that we need to treat the status quo—
the body of material that faces us—in terms of the total amount of
personal effort which it absorbs and which is needed to sustain it. We
tend to assume that the status quo was always there, always will be
there, unless we change it by intervening from the outside. Actually
that is not so. It is changing all the time; it will change whether we
touch it or not; it is not static but a product of the dynamics of
thousands of individuals. We know very little about that. . . .

Later the same characteristic of the Roundtable on Leisure was
reported from the floor by Mr. Starr, who remembered that he had
been the person who "suggested that nobody should worry about
having too much spare time on his hands while our social and
political life remains at so low a level." He had been "utopian
enough to suggest that maybe sometime we could make our industry so flexible that the workers could have as much freedom and
as much elasticity in their work as they need. We have been talking about leisure for the workers. Why not import a few and really
find out what they are thinking?" And, in recording his concurrence with Sir George Schuster's belief that "we must be adaptive
and adjustable," Mr. Starr condensed into six words another conclusion of the Conference which parallels Sir George Schuster's insistence on the "intelligent population" as a condition of inquiry.
"A word that came up again and again," said Mr. Starr, "was

'flexibility'—that is, we need to think, in terms of modern industry, about this strong trend toward mechanization and standardization, for *human beings are fighting back.*"

In the writer's opinion, no other single phrase spoken at the Conference is comparable in importance to this one for understanding the human consequences of industrialism. "For human beings are fighting back." So urgent is the necessity behind these words that it was reflected in the subjective reports from at least three of the roundtables. It was most impressive of all, since here was the logical source, when it came from the Confidence group, out of the mouth of Harold D. Lasswell, their second forceful spokesman. Mr. Lasswell talked emphatically of the "values" that underlie "human dignity" and of the need for "a great willingness to reconsider the specific details of character formation in environment, in industrial routine, and the rest of it." At a certain point, he continued, "we asked why we accepted this hypothesis about human dignity, so we began to ask how we grounded our opinions for this fundamental item; and some of our philosophical friends and some of our theological friends really stimulated us, I think, to a new awareness of the sorts of issues that present themselves when you get serious about this." But from his roundtable's discussion Mr. Lasswell also "had a sense that it might be a good idea if only we didn't have to stop and exchange so many abstract words, if we could only ask ourselves—who are some of these characters who have been thrown up in life who fit what we are talking about?"

TALKING ABOUT EACH OTHER: A PSYCHOLOGICAL INVESTIGATION

In the Roundtable on Leisure, said Mr. Odegaard in introducing Mr. Starr, he had noticed "that in addition to talking about leisure, the members of the panel were talking about each other . . . a sort of psychological investigation . . . each individual processing some of his colleagues as well as discussing the subject. "As the speakers from the third and fourth roundtables progressed into their subjects, they, too, spent a few moments on personalities and the strengths or weaknesses of the total performance. Mr. Jones, for example, had already indicated two significant characteristics of the

Roundtable on Leisure. "Some of our representatives," he said, "thought that we had got nowhere, but as Dr. Johnson said, 'At least we had a good talk.' " His other remark unfortunately held for the entire Conference: he deplored the "imbalance of the sexes, one woman and sixteen men. . . . The result was that a very important sector of the problem, the housewife, received inadequate attention."

The tonality of self-analysis was frequently ironical—as when Ralph Coghlan of the Roundtable on Community paid his respects to "an excellent background paper . . . and a most remarkable chairman, Mr. Witman, who—from time to time as we talked— would stop to recapitulate what we had just said. Well, it was hardly recognizable." This good-humored sniping was easily matched by Meyer Kestnbaum, of the Roundtable on Confidence, who thought it "fortunate that this meeting should end on a note of confidence." Mr. Kestnbaum, striking a chord of salutary parody, then swiftly recapitulated the accomplishments of his group:

MR. KESTNBAUM: The Roundtable on Confidence went at this problem in the most scientific and thorough manner that could be imagined. The subject was quickly broken down to its general areas. I assure you that all the comments were entirely pertinent and on the subject. There were no marked deviations and all the objections that were made were completely objective.

Here, reading backwards and between the lines, is a statement about the confidence of the Roundtable on Confidence in itself— an image in miniature of American self-confidence in the large, and perhaps an answer to Antonio Carrillo Flores's question: what has happened to our optimism? The paradox lies in the deprecating way the subject is by-passed, just as the unconscious omission of another topic indicates how secure an issue it is inwardly believed to be. Two things, said Keith S. McHugh of the Roundtable on Community, were scarcely mentioned: religion and the war. The slighting of the former disturbed Mr. McHugh, because "there is no other single influence on men's behavior that is as strong," yet he felt that the omission of the latter was a proof of strength for a reason which answers his uneasiness about the former. "Is it not," he said, "an extraordinary tribute to America that we can take three days to talk about how we are going to improve our *peacetime* civilization . . . ?" The fact that one heard "nothing about faith" was noted also by John E. Burchard, who went on to draw the conclusion which the observation justifies. "Certainly," he said, "we have a culture which is somewhat agnostic, perhaps the most agnostic culture which has ever been. *But there are other kinds of faith*, and I think we are reaching one of them, a faith by which—though it is going to be confusing, I know—we can live very well indeed."

Just as Mr. Burchard had refused to be impressed by an outward lack of "faith," Mr. Coghlan had not greatly concerned himself (the lines of this conflict are laid out in Mr. Rosecrance's background paper) with the traditional attributes of "community." "The roundtable," he said, "didn't waste a great deal of time in nostalgia. We did recognize that there were some ancient virtues that should be preserved, but for the most part we felt there was nothing much to cry about in our modern civilization. I think the general idea was: how are you going to keep them down on the farm, after they've seen Paree?" The same theme was echoed by Mr. Burchard, who wished to report from a dinner conversation which unhappily does not show in the record "the amount of twitting I have taken around here as to why we try to teach engineers any history."

MR. BURCHARD: If anyone in his senses knew anything about history, no matter what his role in America today—unless perhaps he would like to be a proconsul or Sir Francis Drake, and there may be some people of that kind—nobody in his senses in any walk of life would wish to change positions with his opposite number in Periclean Athens, or Republican Rome, or the High Middle Ages, or the Renaissance, or the days of Queen Victoria, or even of William McKinley. . . . This is a good time to be alive. . . .

"Is it not true, in part," Elliott Jaques had asked in the Roundtable on Work, "that we are using the workers to talk about ourselves?" Though previously the necessity to consider the individual had not been applied to present company, Mr. Burchard brought it home to his own kind and joined the major issue of academic vs. business man in the familiar backhanded fashion—by attacking himself. He began by describing an academic community as "a group of people who are believed to be intelligent and known to be neurotic," from whom the one thing to be learned "is that participation had better be planned by the people who are going to do the participating. The whole thing will fail if you just present some of these screwballs on the faculty with a wonderful idea which wasn't theirs; but, if on the contrary it is their idea, things will go very well even if you attempt to frustrate them." From the business side, Mr. McHugh responded with an equally extravagant apology for his own existence.

MR. McHUGH: When Am Houghton called me about three or four weeks ago, invited me to have a highball with him at the University Club, and then proposed that I join this distinguished group, I said to him, "For goodness sakes, Am, what can I contribute?" The very name "Learned Societies" scared the dickens out of me to start with. . . . You know, we read you gentlemen in the humanities—and there are doctors of philosophy here, professors of medieval history—we read you and enjoy it and get very much indeed from what you write. We are a little scared to talk with you, though. We are a little concerned that we won't understand all your words, or ideas, and that our comeback is going to be a little slow.

WHO'S ON THE HOOK?

Besides making every effort to praise the other by demeaning himself, the theoretical academic and the practical business man also came to general agreements about the industrial civilization that both inhabit. Though the Roundtable on Confidence, according to Mr. Kestnbaum, recognized that it is difficult to solve problems "through industrialization per se, which in itself is neutral," there were stray indications that D. W. Brogan's direct contradiction of this belief (he argued that the importation of American industrialism into other countries was anything but a neutral agent) had taken some effect.

"When I was growing up," said Mr. Coghlan, "the term 'soulless corporation' was common, and the abuses of corporations were a matter of political issue. Well, in my lifetime I have seen a remarkable change in this. I don't know whether it could be said that corporations have obtained souls, but at least they have obtained intelligence." Mr. McHugh agreed. "All during yesterday's program," he said, "it began to be admitted from time to time that perhaps the 'soulless corporation' had gradually become somewhat enlightened on this community problem, and, to my amazement, just before we adjourned last night, one of my academic associates actually suggested that we had better take the corporations off the hook. I knew that was too good to be true, because this morning we got back on again." Yet no matter how shaky the alliance, it assured, in Mr. Kestnbaum's view, a practical future for the theorists and freedom at least a short while longer for the businessman to remain unbusinesslike:

MR. KESTNBAUM: We had an interesting development in this roundtable. We found that our industrialists on the whole were trying to be theoretical and our academic people were trying to be practical. This produced some interesting and surprising results. I am glad to say that we found very quickly that we needed more knowledge—and this was hopeful. I think this contributed greatly to the note of confidence I have referred to, because once we agreed we needed more knowledge this satisfied the American Council of Learned Societies—they no longer faced technological unemployment. It also gave great satisfaction to the industrialists, because it is clear that for a while at least we can go ahead in our own mystical and mysterious way to handle these problems by instinct, rather than through reason and judgment.

The phrase Mr. Kestnbaum applied to the ACLS was picked up by Margaret Mead to prove the same proposition. Mr. Coghlan had denied "the rather ugly rumor that I heard around the corridors" that his roundtable had been "accused of sesquipedalianism," calling it a "base, canard remark" and maintaining that he himself "did not hear any word of more than eight syllables in length." This Miss Mead thought a fair point. "I don't think I have ever in my life," she said, "heard more of an interchange of patter—like 'technological unemployment,' for instance—thrown around from one side to the other with great facility." In a similar fashion, she had been "very much amused with the effort that had been made here to try to prove that business and the academic world don't understand each other."

MISS MEAD: I have never seen less signs of people not understanding each other. . . . Once in a while somebody remembered he ought to be misunderstood by the other side, but it took skill to do it.

Miss Mead, as Mr. Odegaard had said, "is worth ten men, so I think that our average, as far as the distribution of the sexes goes, is far better than a mere statistical count would show." Having shut off with one definitive statement any further discussion of the differences between the "material" and "spiritual" departments of activity represented at the Conference, it remained for her only to provide an appropriate moral on a closing note—and this she did. There were other remarks to be made thereafter; but when Miss Mead sat down, the Corning Conference to all intents was closed— and at its peak.

MISS MEAD: I like to go away from any conference with a new question, and we are also going to need a theme. We have come out of here without one, in a sense, and without anything definite. Now, as we see the American character, one of the things Americans have to have is another team to play against. This is awfully unfortunate in the world at present, because we seem to invest the other team with virtually all our own vices and virtues, and even go through life in a sort of Harvard-Yale position. Americans have never got along without either the devil or the other team, so that the problem that I am going away from here wondering about is this: when we get business and academicians working this well together, and they have to pretend so hard that they don't, what's the next step? What are we going to do for another team that we will be able to work with?

"ISN'T THERE SOMETHING NEW?"

To Miss Mead's question, and to Mr. David's of two days before, the Corning Conference suggests a tentative and only partially developed reply. There is no new team, but there are new teams; and they may be told apart by their attitudes toward the "something new" which the vast phenomena of industrial civilization in creation represent. The successful mixing of personalities from the study and the office may be an achievement—and may the custom prosper!—but it is only a parallel step to the admission quite widely made that colleges have become big business and that business is increasingly intellectualized. This enforced unanimity, which Mr. Brogan singled out as characteristically American, should not be allowed to hide the useful antipathies that shall exist. "Our conflicts," Mr. David had said, "lead to our dynamic way of life," and mercifully the roundtables showed that conflicts still are there, though metamorphosed almost out of recognition in partisanship and context.

The records of the roundtables reveal a number of these new teams in action. The members of the Roundtable on Work who were interested in "organization," for example, included a professor, a college president, a businessman, and many more; their opposition numbered at least two professors, a businessman, and a psychiatrist. The group in the Roundtable on Leisure who defended American mass culture against the accusation of "lowbrow" contained none of the commercial figures whose job loyalties might have been thought to dispose them in that direction. The attack on nostalgia for the small town which was conducted in the Roundtable on Community was led by a humanist who showed himself to be expert in studies of the past. In the Roundtable on Confidence, as a consequence of both its make-up and its assignment, the conflict took a turn which might have been pivotal for all the others. Here four or five voices were raised in chorus for the individual's creativity as the essential ground for humanistic studies of any kind and for abandonment of the outdated ideas (the word used was "Newtonian") that accompany the effort to ape the traditional versions of physics and chemistry in the proper study of mankind.

One of the conceptions over which a monumental disagreement rises is the idea that "human values" can be added to an institution that is already growing to maturity, as though they were bonuses or pension programs, whenever managers or the salesmen of humanities decide to give the word. If this is a fallacy, as many of the delegates to Corning claimed it was, then it is a fallacy shared alike among the occupations, "disciplines," and various walks of life the Conference planners drew upon. The legendary commercial belief that anything can be fixed by spending a million dollars is matched, if not surpassed, by the impulse of scholars to pose research problems in a manner meant to be attractive to the large foundations or to frame all questions in the language of "projects" and refer them to committees. The Conference offered far too many outlets for this tendency to be denied entirely, but certainly the most encouraging result is the absence of a list of concrete recommendations to "do" things which it would have been presumptuous (as Gwilym A. Price had noted) to claim the power to do. The recognition that a recommended change might come about regardless is preliminary to an understanding that industrialism contains its own built-in aesthetic, its own morality, its own "human" and "spiritual" penalties and rewards.

Since most of our effort was spent in arriving at the edge of this awareness that "human beings" have been "fighting back" for many years, the Conference did not make great progress in the direction of discovering what these industrial "values" really are. "Nobody is used to living in this new society at all," as Mr. Brogan admitted. "It's new to all of us." The investigation is hampered at the outset by a superfluity of data, and among the most disturbed and disturbing members of the Conference were those who found themselves compelled constantly to add a new bit of evidence, a new contradiction, a new paradox to the shaky structure under construction. To make self-consciousness "bearable," in the words of Miss Mead's definition, requires not only a scrapping of stereotypes and a new naïveté before the facts, but also (again Mr. Brogan's words came to mind) "more—shall I say?—humility before the job, more objectivity." One might add, "more willingness to admit that our present techniques of analysis, both academic and commercial, have revealed only a distorted and inaccurate picture of the life in industrial civilization that we actually lead."

Broadly speaking, there is under way on all the avenues of knowledge a healthy motion to break the boundaries of specialization and unite each "discipline"—an unhappy word for the cultivation of narrowness!—with its neighbor. But "unity," as Julian Huxley counseled the Roundtable on Confidence, "is not the same thing as uniformity." Whether a synthesis of the social sciences after the manner of an all-inclusive Einsteinian equation is achievable, or even desirable, the tendency shows itself in humanistic studies (as they were discussed at Corning) in cross-references—like the psychology of economics, the philosophy of engineering, or the sociology of cultural entertainments. These pursuits Everyman is indeed privileged to engage in, for out of his chosen field each expert is a layman—and this applies to businessmen as well as to professors, now that management is to be thought a specialty like any other, equally subject to the vices of academic obsolescence. A man must be born a geometer, to paraphrase Dr. Johnson, but we are all sociologists in our common self-consciousness over the creation of an industrial society in America. This civilization can best be comprehended through the amateur sociology which its citizens have already developed and of which this book may be called a manifesto.

Part II

Background Papers

8

The World of Work

by William F. Whyte

SONG ON THE ASSEMBLY LINE

Some years ago there was a group of men who sang while they worked on the automotive assembly line. They were led by a big, middle-aged Welshman, with a booming bass voice. They would work in silence for a while, then he would sound the first note, and they would all sing in rhythm to the repetitive motions of the line.

Then a new plant manager was appointed. The outgoing manager "oriented" his successor in the usual, formal manner. He explained the organization chart, the policies, and the procedures. He made no mention of the singing; that had no place in management's procedures or policies.

The new manager had hardly settled behind his desk when the sounds of song broke in upon him. He called in his assistant and demanded an explanation. The assistant replied, "Well, sir, the men just like to sing while they work."

The manager snorted. "This is no glee club. I'm running a factory. The men are here to work. That singing must be stopped at once."

The order went down, and the singing stopped. That is the end of the story—except to record that for months and years afterward that assembly line never attained the production it had made in the "glee club" period. Somehow, not as much work got done, even though the men were doing nothing but work.

PRODUCTION AND SOCIABILITY

The comptroller of a plant, who was responsible for its office force, was concerned about the social activity that took place during working hours. He put the problem this way:

You know, I've just come back from a visit to the main office, and I want to tell you, the contrast is really unbelievable. They have an office force several times as large as ours, and it's all in one big room. But you could stand in that room any time of the day and hear a pin drop. Now, down here the place is in an uproar a good deal of the time. Of course, I realize that people sometimes have to talk to each other to get their work done, but I know lots of times when they are talking it can't be just about the work. I wonder, Dr. Whyte, do you think I should ask them to quiet things down?

I asked him how well the work got done.

Oh, I'm more than satisfied with that. Two years ago when I came here we had 62 people in the office; we now have 57, and still we are handling 40 per cent more orders than we were when I started. Why, last week they put out a volume of orders that I didn't think was possible. Whenever we have an emergency, I only have to ask them to put out a little extra effort, and everybody pitches in. Now, I'll bet you that, man to man, the main office doesn't begin to put out the volume of work we do right here. . . . But I don't know. It doesn't seem right. The place is in an uproar. . . .

In this case, the comptroller took no action, so his office continued to be noisy—and productive. And he continued to worry because somehow it did not look businesslike.

CAN WORK BE FUN

These two stories—one from yesterday, one from today—illustrate one of the persistent problems of our time.

The manager who insists upon absolute quiet and rigorous attention to work may feel that he is being completely logical and businesslike, but these stories suggest that the manager often reacts simply in terms of a traditional conception of what work should be. There seems to be a deep-seated belief in our culture that work is a duty, that work is absolutely different from play, that man is obligated to work for money, and that if he enjoys anything but the immediate job operations it must somehow detract from his efficiency.

Of course, no one would state this argument explicitly any more. But we have only to look at industry and business all over the country to find again and again that men are expected not only to be busy but to look busy. Perhaps managers no longer enforce this demand as they did in the time of our first story, but they still are inclined to worry if people seem to be enjoying their work too much.

Those stories pose the question: Are work and enjoyment incompatible under modern industrial conditions?

A SOCIAL SETTING FOR WORK

According to one extreme point of view, mass production has taken so much interest out of work that man plods along, giving it far less than his full attention yet prevented by work from doing anything else. The solution proposed would be to carry mechanization and automatization so far that the worker could perform his job without any conscious attention at all. Then his mind would be completely free to wander onto pleasanter topics. Give him also attractive surroundings, music piped at him as he works, refreshments readily available, and periods of rest and sociability to break up the day, and life in mass production might become tolerable.

Some managements have built really handsome factories, and their claims that this has helped worker morale may well be true. It seems also plausible that music, refreshments, and chances to get away from the job contribute to worker satisfaction.

But note that these solutions treat the worker as a passive instrument. Things are done for him and given to him in order to make his life more endurable. Is there nothing he can do for himself?

Furthermore, music, rest periods, and refreshments all represent an escape from work. Such changes may well be helpful, but we must still ask whether it is possible to solve the problems of enjoyment in work through separating work from the rest of life.

The voluminous studies of fatigue, monotony, and boredom are pertinent here. While some progress has been made, the results have been disappointingly small. They have been small, perhaps, because it is impossible to treat work as an isolated physical or mental phenomenon. Work must be seen in a social context.

THE MEANING OF WORK TO THE WORKER

This is best illustrated in the studies of E. Wight Bakke (*Citizens Without Work*, Yale University Press, 1940) in the period when he and his associates were studying the human effects of unemployment. They were forced to conclude after hundreds and thousands of interviews with workers, employed and unemployed, that a man's job was not simply something that brought in money for family support; it was an activity that gave him a place in the social world and in large measure gave meaning to his life. In fact, Bakke describes the goals of workers in their jobs in the following broad terms: "To play a socially respected and admired role; to win a degree of economic security customary among one's associates, to gain an increasing amount of control over one's own affairs, and to understand the forces which make their impact felt in those affairs, and in all of these to experience satisfying and predictable relations with the members of the groups with which one is most intimately associated—these are the goals which our informants were most vigorously striving to reach."

To the worker, then, work has a broad meaning.

Work serves to define a role to be played both in the factory and in the community. It follows from this that we cannot understand the meaning of work to the worker unless we observe him in action both at work and in the community outside of work.

INDUSTRY-COMMUNITY RELATIONS

The work of W. Lloyd Warner and his associates (*The Social System of the Modern Factory*, Yale University Press, 1947) on the Yankee City study has clearly shown how changes within the work place affect the life of the community and how the factory activities themselves are affected by the social structure and life of the town. But these studies give us a broad general picture and tell us little in detail about the meaning of work in the community setting. They tell us what must be studied, but they leave the conclusion still to be found.

We must recognize that workers in modern industrial plants are subject to an exacting discipline. The discipline does not consist solely of the rewards and punishments administered in person by management. It consists more importantly in the requirement of playing a narrowly specified part in a complex and coordinated set of activities, of work for eight hours at a highly repetitive task, conforming to standards set by other men.

Certainly man does not "naturally" take to this sort of discipline. Where factories are built in a nonindustrialized society, this discipline is exceedingly difficult to inculcate. Even in our own society, the tendency of young workers to jump from job to job before finally settling down may be due in part to the strain of adjusting to this discipline.

In our society most workers do learn to take the discipline—but at what cost? Some have claimed that the exacting controls of industry lead workers to want to kick over the traces when they get outside of the plant or leave them apathetic and hopeless before the tasks of family and community life. At one time or another, most of the ills of American society have been attributed to the human stresses of mass production.

I know of no published research that explores the impact of industrial discipline on life outside of the plant, so we know nothing for sure here—except one thing: there must be a connection between life outside and life inside the workplace. A man does not park his personality at home when he goes to work. What industry does to him inside the plant must necessarily have effects upon his behavior in family and community, and the community life will show its effects within the plant. The work satisfaction problem, then, requires us to explore the industry-community relationship.

THE SOCIAL SYSTEM OF THE PLANT

In comparison to the industry-community area, our knowledge of life within the plant is highly developed.

It does not seem to be true, as some have supposed, that mass production methods have reduced most of the work force to the level of unskilled labor. In fact, the results have been to increase greatly the proportion of semiskilled labor, at the expense both of the totally unskilled and of the craftsman. Most people in our work force today are performing repetitive operations for which there is some learning period required, but the period is short. At the top end of the scale the craftsman is giving way more and more to the skilled operator whose job is to service machines or to stand by while they operate, watching charts and controls, and occasionally making an adjustment.

However we divide men as to skill, it is evident that the craftsman of old who made the whole product himself, who gained the satisfactions of developing his initiative and exercising his imagination in creating something new, is hardly to be found on the industrial scene today. These satisfactions of craftsmanship are gone, and we can never call them back. If these were the only satisfactions men could get out of their immediate work, then work would certainly be a barren experience today.

There are other important satisfactions today: the satisfactions of human association and the satisfactions of solving the technical and human problems of work.

We now look upon the factory as a social system involving people at all levels of the organization, constantly seeking to work out the problems of their relations with each other and with their work. There may be little scope for the semiskilled worker to introduce changes directly into his job; but there are innumerable ways in which work and the relations among men may be organized, and those problems of organization must be solved by people. For the workers, what is done in this area is not a matter of indifference. As one of them said to us about his work in the factory: "This is where we really live. We spend more time in this plant on the job than we do anywhere else except home in bed."

SATISFACTION IN SOLVING HUMAN PROBLEMS

More and more, managers are recognizing that this complex set of human problems cannot be simply brushed aside in order to get on with the production job. The problems are complex, to be sure, but they are also fascinating and challenging. In my observation, one of the greatest satisfactions men in industry gain today comes from the skillful working out of these human problems. Men who acquire this skill enjoy their work. Men who do not possess the skill experience never-ending frustration.

But if we grant that the exercise of skill in human relations in industry brings with it deep satisfactions, we still must ask how many people really have opportunities to exercise such skills. How widespread can this participation be?

THE PROBLEM OF PARTICIPATION

Researchers in group dynamics have shown that men do not work effectively or gain real satisfactions from their work when they are simply told what to do and have no feeling of participation. Most of the studies have been done on small groups outside of a context of large organizations. They have shown in a general way how the sense of participation may be developed, and they have shown that it makes an important difference to the participants. But even in these small group studies there are many unsolved problems concerning the nature of leadership and the nature of the relations among leaders and other group members. My experience at Bethel, in the National Training Laboratory for Group Development, clearly showed not only the possibilities of work with small groups but also the primitive nature of our present knowledge of group processes.

Even if we did know much more than we do today concerning small group process, we would still have the large unsolved problem of relating the participation in small groups to the experience of people in large hierarchical organizations. We would also have to solve the problems of relating the expert and his technical knowledge to the participation process.

SCOPE FOR DECISION-MAKING

The small informal group may be free to carry on its discussion and arrive at a decision thoroughly accepted by all its members, and not determined in advance by any single individual. Clearly, the process here cannot be carried over without major modifications into the industrial or business setting where the organization is composed of dozens or hundreds or even thousands of small groups. The requirements for coordinating activities make it impossible to allow each group wide latitude in determining what it shall do. If we see participation only in terms of actual decision making, we must be disappointed.

To be sure, there is still some scope for work group decision making in most modern industrial plants. Skillful managers have learned to distinguish between the setting of the production *objective* and the determination of the *means* of reaching that objective. They have learned that the work proceeds more efficiently and with greater satisfaction if they allow the work group some scope in finding the best *means* for doing the job. The worker who has his every move spelled out for him is neither happy nor efficient.

PARTICIPATION BY BEING CONSULTED

At the same time we must realize that the scope for such worker decision making is rather narrow. We must see participation not simply in terms of decision making but also in terms of consultation. The manager may lay out an objective and a tentative plan of action without putting the decision up to the work group. He may then consult with individuals or groups and find that, on the basis of such discussion, his own plans are influenced and changed. This sort of consultative participation is going on constantly in industry today; and when it is practiced, the people involved in it gain greater satisfactions from their work.

Such participation can arise only if the managers have a genuine respect for the people working in the plant. Science and technology have advanced so far that there is a natural tendency of the scientifically trained or the business-school trained manager to think that it is possible to specify the best way of doing the job in full detail, on the basis of scientific and engineering knowledge. Research has demonstrated that this point of view is false. We know now that the worker's claim to acquired know-how through years of experience with machines is not entirely a matter of his imagination. We find that even with machines built to exactly the same specifications there will be variations in machine performance, and this range of variability grows with the age of the machines. The worker who works day by day with the machine or equipment is in the position to know some of the details of operations better than any supervisor or technical man.

KNOW-HOW OF THE MAN ON THE JOB

This point was vividly illustrated to me in my first study in an aviation gasoline plant. At that time union representatives were bargaining with management, trying to get a higher rate and classification for the top operators in the plant. The representatives argued that these operators must possess an especially high degree of skill and should be rewarded more amply for it. The management representative, in seeking to answer this skill argument, committed a striking blunder. As the union representative reported to me, "Did you hear what he said about us? He said that we were only watchmen. He said, 'Down there in that plant you have got automatic controls and charts. If anything goes wrong with the meters, you just call a meter man. If anything goes wrong with the engines, you call a repair man. If anything goes wrong with operations, you call an engineer and he tells you what to do. There is no skill in that work, you just have to watch the charts.'"

That statement was not only exceedingly undiplomatic (it stirred up more resentment against management than any other single statement in my experience); the statement also was simply untrue, as various members of management themselves told me. The following day an engineer came into the plant to ask the operators what was wrong with fractionating column number 4. They shrugged their shoulders and replied, "You're supposed to tell us." The engineer was embarrassed. He didn't know what was wrong with number 4. He had, in fact, only the vaguest idea. Number 4 had been built according to the same sort of specifications as other fractionating columns. It was supposed to work like other columns, but in fact it never had. It always had given the operators trouble. However, in the course of long experience, they had learned to live with it, to adjust to its peculiarities, and to control its performance within limits. They couldn't explain in scientific terms how they did it; but they knew how, and the engineer did not.

The point is obvious when we speak about the petroleum industry, which requires a rather high level of skill and technical knowledge for many of its jobs. The point is not so obvious—but it holds—when we speak of jobs requiring much less skill. Even on the most unskilled jobs I have ever seen I have always found that the worker still knows something—something that the manager does not know. In fact, the skillful manager recognizes this. He knows that if he can get the worker to contribute not only his physical effort but also his knowledge, the result will be increased productivity and increased satisfaction in work. The feeling of participation grows as men are encouraged to contribute their ideas on both technical and human problems.

TECHNICAL SPECIALTIES AND HUMAN ORGANIZATION

I have been saying that effective participation depends upon developing the appropriate relationship between the technical specialist and the men who do the production work. In part, this is a problem of integrating technical knowledge with the knowledge of experience—but only in part. We are dealing also with the feelings and attitudes and social adjustments of people.

The technical specialty is not simply a set of scientific tools. It is also a way of looking upon the world of the factory and an outline of the expected ways of behaving. It is a view of the world—a very partial view of the world.

WHAT ENGINEERS OFTEN OVERLOOK

Roethlisberger and Dickson (*Management and the Worker*, Harvard University Press, 1939) have effectively analyzed the engineering approach to production problems so often found in the factory. The man with conventional engineering training tends to look upon production in terms of the capacities of machines, in terms of the most efficient physical layout, and so on. Only after he has set up the technical requirements for the job does he bring human beings into his thinking. The human beings are then expected to adjust to the machines and to adjust to any changes in machinery or production methods that efficiency seems to dictate.

Such a point of view has worked untold havoc in industry. The engineer tends not to recognize that nearly any change in machines or process involves changes not only in the physical activity of men but in their social relations, including their relations to management and to each other. Research has demonstrated the satisfactions that the worker derives from close association with fellow workers—and not just any fellow workers. Wherever he works, he tends to build up membership in a group. The engineer, in introducing a new machine or process, may not be aware that he is breaking up the social groupings of the workers and removing one of the main bases of their satisfaction on the job, but they are well aware of it even when they don't put it in that language.

How can we resolve this conflict? Certainly in modern industry we cannot dispense with the engineer, but neither can we dispense with the worker. Engineering changes will continue to be made, but already we find they are not made with the same reckless disregard for human adjustment as they were in the past. Research has shown, and some managers have long recognized, that people can adjust to marked changes in their work so long as they are taken in on the planning and carrying out of those changes. When the changes are simply imposed upon them, they fight back, trying to restore the basis for their personal security in a world of work that is familiar to them.

COST ACCOUNTING AND HUMAN RELATIONS

We see a similar problem when we look at the accounting organization of a large company. We might say that American industry is characterized by the high development of its accounting methods almost as much as it is by the organization of machines and technical processes. Cost control is an essential activity, but cost control also tends to be its own peculiar way of life, involving a special view of the organization. In a study we have been making at Cornell we have found the activities of the accounting and cost control department giving rise to some of the most serious frictions and dissatisfactions within the organization. And this was not that the cost control specialists themselves were maladjusted personalities; in fact, it seemed to inhere in the very nature of the accounting and cost control activity as it is customarily practiced.

The cost control man, as he freely confessed to the researcher, is a fault-finder. If he doesn't find something wrong with the way operations are going, then he is not doing his job. He worries about this himself. He recognizes that when he points out faults to higher management, somebody down the line is going to be punished, and he is going to be considered a so-and-so for bringing out the evidence. He sees this as the nature of his job. It puts him in a conflict situation, and he puts other people in a conflict situation also. When the manager acts upon these cost figures, by cracking down on work groups or departments that seem to be out of line, we find supervisors exercising remarkable ingenuity in trying to shift responsibility onto someone else. So the superintendent in Department A tries to unload an unpleasant cost onto Department B, and the deterioration of relations between A and B can readily be imagined. Thus we have a situation in which superintendents spend a good part of their time and their best ingenuity in trying to manipulate the cost control records. The struggle of department against department, and production department against cost control, leads to emotional tension and friction throughout the organization. It is felt primarily by people within management, but the effects are passed on to the workers.

The modern manager cannot dispense with cost control any more than he can with engineering. But he is coming to realize that cost control, while having a logic into which all plant activities fit, is still only a specialized part of the whole system of activities and human relations. It is his job to fit those specialties together and to fit them together also with a systematic view of the requirements of human relations in the social system of the plant.

He can get measurements of the efficiency of machines, and he can get all sorts of figures from his cost accounting department. Even though these figures are not actually so precise as they appear to be, they nevertheless do give a neat and useful view of one part of the system of activities. One of the great needs today is to develop a systematic means of assessing the state of human relations in an organization. Until this can be done, there is an almost inevitable tendency for the manager to place first the requirements of engineering and cost accounting since those requirements are more or less well known; while the requirements for maintaining the system of human relations in a state of dynamic equilibrium are not nearly so well known or so readily subject to measurement. Important steps already have been taken in providing this systematic assessment, and we may hope that research in the near future will do much to fill in this gap.

THE DESIGN OF ORGANIZATION

I have stressed the importance of developing a sense of participation in industry. I have argued that building this sense of participation requires coping with two difficult problems. The first discussed was that of relating the technical specialties to the requirements of the social system. The second involves the problem of integrating small group participation with the large hierarchical organizations that we find in many industries today.

We cannot leave to the foreman the job of stimulating participation on the part of his work force. The foreman is simply the last man down in the line of authority. He tends to react to the behavior practiced upon him by higher management. Higher management may talk eloquently and sincerely about the values of worker participation in the activities of the enterprise; but if, in the foreman's experience, his superiors control him narrowly, do not discuss his problems with him on a man-to-man basis, and simply expect him to be a good soldier, then he in turn can hardly build up the sort of democratic work group that is coming to be more and more the ideal.

This is not simply a problem of the executive personality. It is also a problem of design of the organization.

TALL VS. FLAT ORGANIZATION

Here, in the terms of Gardner and Moore (*Human Relations in Industry*, Richard Irwin and Co., 1950), we can contrast the tall with the flat organization. In the tall organization, we find many levels of authority between the worker and top management, and we find each level exercising detailed supervision over the level below. In the flat type of organization, by contrast, we find few levels of authority and only general supervision.

The tall sort of organization seems to develop naturally when people do not have the skill and make the effort to avoid it. For example, we find that the superintendent has more to do than he can keep on top of, so management gives him an assistant superintendent. Then we find that the general foreman has more than he can supervise in detail so he is given an assistant, and so it goes. As the problems become more complex, more levels of authority are added.

The tall type of organization also has one common justification; that it is in line with the principles of scientific management. I refer here to the question of the span of control. It has been pointed out by various authors that the number of people, engaged in interrelated activities, who can be supervised in detail by a single individual is strictly limited. Authorities may differ as to the exact number, and they are willing to allow differences in terms of the number supervised at different levels in the organization, but they emphasize that only a small number can be given detailed supervision. There is nothing wrong with this argument, if we accept its underlying assumption. That assumption is, of course, that people need detailed supervision, that the organization will break down unless people are closely watched.

Proponents of the flat type of organization argue that men do not need as detailed supervision as is commonly supposed. They feel, in fact, that under detailed supervision not only is the work less effectively done, but people are denied the opportunity to develop their capacities and find out what they are actually capable of achieving. They are allowed no initiative in solving their problems, so they can hardly be expected to develop initiative. Proponents of the flat organization would then argue that if men are adequately motivated, they can be given a good deal of scope for activity and should not be directed in the details of their jobs. The executive with this conception expects to hold his subordinates responsible for *results*, but he does not expect to dictate in detail the methods whereby those results are to be achieved.

JOB SATISFACTION AND ORGANIZATION DESIGN

This is not simply an argument over principles of administration. We are talking about job satisfaction, and the design of the organization is crucial for that problem. We find when people function in the tall organization under detailed supervision they become preoccupied with complying with the directives of their work and in jockeying for position within the political structure of the organization. Such a type of organization makes it impossible to develop consultative management and group discussion to increase the sense of participation of workers or of anybody else. In other words, we can't consider the job satisfaction of the worker on the bottom of the pyramid without considering the structure of the pyramid itself.

Sears, Roebuck & Co., Johnson & Johnson, and various other organizations have shown the possibilities of operating effectively with relatively decentralized controls and a short, flat organization. We know it can be done, but how it is done we know only in the most general way. We can see the importance of such a structure in providing job satisfactions and opportunities for growth of the members. We need to learn much more than we now know concerning how such a structure can be built and maintained.

DECENTRALIZATION

There is another important question related to the design of the organization: how large should the operating unit be? In some types of industrial activity, the nature of the technology and processes requires bringing together large numbers of people on one site. For other activities, management has a choice between building up a number of small plants or centralizing its operations in one or a few large plants. What difference does it make which course management takes?

Sears, Roebuck & Co. organization surveys have demonstrated that the morale or satisfaction with work within the Sears organization is definitely higher in the smaller stores than it is in the largest department stores. Why so? The answer seems to run along these lines: Job satisfaction is importantly related to the identification of the individual with the organization. Does he feel really a significant part of it, or does he just work there for a living? Does he take pride in its performance? The studies seem to show that the individual cannot identify himself effectively with a large organization without intermediate identification groups. He can much more readily identify with an organization when the unit that he is working in is small enough so that he has some face-to-face contact with all of its personnel. He does not have to be on intimate terms with the top executive, but it seems to be important for him to recognize that individual as a real personality instead of just a remote power symbol.

Our industrial civilization is necessarily one of large corporations. From the standpoint of human satisfactions, the danger inherent in this sort of development may be counteracted by building the large corporation into small operating units. Where this is not possible, we need to experiment further with decentralization management controls within the large unit.

THE ROLE OF THE UNION

So far we have been discussing problems of work satisfaction with little reference to unions. This may have been necessary to avoid overcomplicating the problem as we first examine it. But, obviously, any discussion of work satisfaction today must provide a prominent place to consider the role of the union organization.

The role played by unions in controlling speed-ups and other pressures that would tend to overtax the strength and endurance of workers has been widely recognized. This service has been of obvious importance, for certainly little job satisfaction can grow where the work is such as to endanger the health of the workers.

UNIONS AND THE SOCIAL SYSTEM OF THE FACTORY

Unions have played a much less obvious but also a vitally important role in the administration of the social system of the factory. Traditionally, we tend to view the union as a protest organization. According to this picture, management has the complicated job of deciding what actions should be taken in a wide variety of situations, and the union officers simply raise protests when their constituents seem to be hurt by what management does.

Research shows that this picture is not simply an oversimplification. Actually, it is totally misleading. In work now being done on the human relations problems of unions, we have been impressed by the remarkable complexity of the problems faced by local union officers, not even to mention the higher officials. Most grievances that are raised within the union, even when they are officially directed at management, involve possible disadvantages as well as advantages to individuals or groups of workers.

In cases we are now studying we find that the local officers spend far more time in discussion among themselves and with rank-and-file members—trying to decide what action they should urge management to take—than they do in actually arguing the grievance with management. We have seen, in fact, many cases where management is prepared to accept almost any proposal the union brings up as a grievance, but the real problem is for the union officers to agree among themselves as to what proposal to make. Coming to this agreement involves a complicated balancing of advantages and disadvantages to individuals and groups, plus an estimate of the reactions of such individuals or groups to a whole range of possible actions.

To handle such a job effectively requires a high degree of intelligence, social skill, and understanding of human relations and economic problems. No longer is leadership in our industrial institutions confined to the management hierarchy. Unions have made an exceedingly important contribution through multiplying the numbers of people in the workplaces who are given opportunity to develop social initiative and exercise leadership.

GOVERNMENT BY CONSENT AND FREEDOM OF EXPRESSION

Unions also have brought about important changes in the status of workers in the social system of the plant. Research has shown that workers did not and do not join unions simply to improve their wages. In part, they join in reaction against the unpredictability of their world of work. Where a man may be transferred or fired according to the personal judgment of his boss, where his work may be radically changed without prior notice or consultation—in short, where he cannot predict from one day to the next what his world of work will be like—he tends to support an organization which is working with management to develop a government by consent and through understanding, instead of by fiat.

The right of free speech is of great importance here. Americans of all classes learn at home and at school that free speech is one of the most vital rights in our way of life. A man who has the courage to express his convictions is widely admired. We all like to think that we are free to say what we really think and feel, without fear of punishment. We must recognize that before unionization, this right simply did not exist in many industrial plants. Today that right is much more widely recognized. That does not mean that in all unionized situations workers feel completely free to express their opinions. Fear of management and uncertainty over how management will exercise its powers is still prominent in many plants. Furthermore, we have seen cases in which workers hesitate to express their opinions for fear of incurring the displeasure of union officers. Nevertheless, the over-all balance shows that there is today considerably more freedom of expression in American industry than there was years ago, and this sort of atmosphere is, of course, necessary in building up the social participation upon which job satisfaction in major part rests.

PARTICIPATION IN THE UNION

In pointing out the role of unions in increasing the proportion of people in the plant that can actively participate in working out the solutions of social and economic problems, we should not assume that unionization automatically leads to widespread worker participation. Even if we disregard certain unions which are well known for their autocratic controls exercised from the very top, and look upon those organizations whose leaders make conscientious efforts to develop member participation and a decentralized responsibility, we find that there is an ominous tendency in the other direction.

In part, this is a response to the growing centralization of management controls. In response to pressures from the union, management tends to limit the freedom of action of foremen in dealing with the union, so that the important matters may be handled at a top policy level. If the foremen cannot give any answers, then the steward whose job it is to deal with the foremen is also stymied, and the importance of this bottom level of union leadership declines.

The technical nature of many of the problems the union has to deal with also makes it difficult to develop a high level of member participation. We have seen this same problem in looking at the company organization. For example, in many plants the problems of union-management relations seem to revolve around the incentive system. A knowledge of industrial engineering alone is far from sufficient to cope with these problems, but some knowledge of industrial engineering appears to be essential. The worker, or even the local union officer, who does not possess this knowledge tends to step aside and call in the expert. On these and other technical problems, we find many of the local union officers refusing to make their own decisions and expressing dependence upon higher levels of the union, not because those higher officers demand obedience but simply because great stakes are involved and the local officers do not have sufficient confidence in their knowledge to be able to take the necessary risks on their own.

To meet this situation, more and more unions are developing their own technical specialists who come in to work with the local officers. However, while this may meet the immediate technical problem, it does not solve the problem of participation. The union, like management, has the problem of developing an effective relationship between the expert and the working people.

THE PROBLEM OF APATHY

We see another aspect of the participation problem as we observe the history of a union from the militant organization phase into the period of contact administration. The drama of the period of organization and strike for union recognition makes it easy to stimulate membership interest and participation. This is the period when the "colorful personality" comes to the fore in union leadership and rallies people around him. Still today in periodic crises, the members turn out in large numbers. But as union-management relations become more humdrum (even when there is some underlying conflict) and as these relations are handled more and more by higher officials, member apathy grows. The union cannot be considered a "way of life" for many people in the plant as some union philosophers would like it to be. The union local may even have difficulty in getting men to take the positions necessary to make the organization function.

The annual round of contract negotiations may still stir member interest, and the economic gains may be gratefully received by the members; but negotiations generally come once a year or less, and the union organization must function every day if it is to play a vital role in the lives of its members.

AN AREA FOR UNION-MANAGEMENT COOPERATION?

There is a world of difference between passive acceptance and active participation. Economic gains are certainly important, but we may ask whether they alone are enough to give meaning to life.

To an impressive degree, we find the same human problems within both union and management organizations. That raises the question: is it possible for union and management officers to develop a cooperative program in working on these problems?

THE PROBLEM OF LOYALTIES

It is commonplace now to recognize that man is a social animal. He needs to belong to some group; he needs to feel group loyalties.

But modern industry complicates the problem of loyalties. A man may feel that he belongs to a work group, but he is also a member of a department, of a plant, perhaps of a corporation. He is also a member of a departmental group in the local union, of the local itself, and of the international too.

Where there is conflict within industry, the worker may have to take a stand with one group or another, but most of the time he lives with an uneasy adjustment of divided loyalties. We see these tangled loyalties all over industry today. People struggle to resolve the conflicts within themselves, and all too often do so with a cynical rationalization that there is nothing they can really believe in; each man must just look out for himself.

A CHALLENGE TO MODERN INDUSTRY

Is the problem of conflicting loyalties inevitable where union and management exist together? The evidence of various studies suggests that it is not. (See, for example, Whyte's *Pattern for Industrial Peace*, Harper & Brothers, 1951.) In some situations, we find that men can sincerely express loyalty to both union and management and not feel any conflict about it. This does not mean that no disagreements exist. It does mean that people have found mutually satisfying ways of working out their disagreements.

Where the problem of divided loyalties has been resolved, people have come to see union and management as organizations mutually dependent on each other, each carrying out different but interrelated functions. They don't think only of what their own particular group must achieve. They come to think and act in terms of a philosophy of how the whole union-management system should operate. Their loyalties then are channeled toward a way of solving the human problems of the whole union-management community. Loyalties to the immediate group remain, but those loyalties are integrated into the larger system.

This is possible. We have seen it happen in a few cases. The possibility presents a challenge to modern industry: can union and management, working together, make of the industrial system an integrated human community to which individuals can give their unreserved loyalty? The human satisfactions connected with work in an industrial civilization will depend in no small degree on the answer to this question.

WHAT NEEDS TO BE DONE

EDUCATION AND RESEARCH IN HUMAN RELATIONS

Progress in this complicated field will depend upon coordinated effort in both education and research. The effective development of either area of activity requires close collaborative efforts among management, union, and university groups.

Our civilization has been marked by exceedingly rapid development of the natural sciences and technology in industrial work. We all recognize today that if we are to use the fruits of science and technology in building human satisfactions, we need to speed up the development of knowledge and skills in human relations.

EDUCATION FOR HUMAN UNDERSTANDING

This need is now generally recognized, but too often educators try to meet it by simply adding "the human element" to a standard curriculum in engineering or business management. Treating human relations in such a separate compartment is of dubious value.

We need to train people in the development of a greater sensitivity to the thoughts and feelings of the people with whom they live and work. We need to train them to see a pattern in the social world around them, so that they do not try to solve social and economic problems through one narrow approach, whether it be cost accounting, engineering or some other specialty. We need to train them to a better understanding of their own personalities, so that they will not go about blindly satisfying their own unrecognized personal needs at the expense of other people.

Finally, we need to give them practice and guidance in developing skill in handling human situations.

That is a large order indeed, and yet it would not be too much to say that some of the essential methods for such training are already known and already being applied on a small scale.

METHODS

To give students some idea of the complexities of human problems and some ability to think in terms of patterns instead of simple cause-effect relationships, the case discussion method has been found particularly useful and is used at Harvard, Cornell, and many other institutions. Instead of presenting the students with abstract principles which they find difficult to apply to life situations, they are given cases to analyze, stemming directly from field research.

Whether he is to be a union or a management official, the individual gets most of the information he needs, in order to function effectively, from the people with whom he works. He must be able to learn not only what they are thinking, but he must also sense how they are feeling in any given situation. For this he needs to develop skill in drawing others out. The interviewing method developed in the Western Electric research program can readily be adapted to accomplish this sort of training.

The effective man of action also needs to be able to observe group behavior. It is not enough, as some personnel men claim, to be able to treat each man as an individual. We must also be able to perceive the relations among individuals, so that we will not treat people as if they were isolated units. The training methods for skill in social observation have been highly developed in sociology, anthropology, and social psychology.

The man of action must learn through acting. He cannot tell how he would behave simply through writing the answers to pencil and paper questions. He needs to try out his approach to problems in situations approximating real life. The technique known as role-playing is particularly helpful here. Here several individuals have the opportunity of acting out before a group how they would handle a common problem situation. This seems an ideal way to diagnose the individual's problems in relating himself to other people and to increase a man's sensitivity to the thoughts and feelings of others. Here the experience of Moreno, Bavelas, and MacGregor is particularly pertinent.

Parts of this program are already being tried out on union and management officers, and other parts have been applied to college and university students. But if the need is as important as we think it is, fragmentary and tentative efforts must be supplanted by a broad, intensive program.

RESEARCH NEEDS

Our survey has shown that work satisfaction is not one problem but rather a series of interrelated problems. It follows then that any attempt to treat a single aspect in isolation will be fruitless. We need first to recognize the parts, but then we need to put them together in building a rounded research program.

At least these problem areas seem important:

1. *The worker in relation to the job operation itself.* While isolated studies of fatigue, monotony, and boredom have been of dubious value, nevertheless workers are concerned with the questions such researches raise. They talk about jobs being interesting or dull, easy or tiring. They sometimes enjoy the sheer physical activity of the job, and they are always concerned with the freedom of action the job allows or denies them. These aspects will take on increasing significance when they are seen in proper perspective.

2. *The worker in the social system of the plant.* His relations with supervisors, with other management personnel, with fellow workers. Does he feel himself a cog in a machine or a member of a production team?

3. *The worker in the social system of the union.* His relations with union officers and with other members in union activities. Does he look upon the union simply as an instrument that may or may not do something for him, or does he feel himself part of a significant social movement?

4. *The worker in the family, church, and club or group life of the community.* To what extent does his job tend to place him in

the community? How does it affect his social activity and satisfactions in the community? How does his community life affect his place, behavior, and satisfactions within the plant?

Similar questions could be asked for management people also. We must recognize that they, too, have problems of work satisfactions.

INTERRELATED STUDIES REQUIRED

When we ask how a worker feels about his job, about management or the union, we are not satisfied with a simple descriptive picture of his sentiments. We must seek to determine, through an analysis of the events and conditions of his experience, how he came to feel as he does. Furthermore, we cannot be satisfied with a different explanation for every man. We must seek some underlying uniformities in the reactions of men to work.

Each of the problem areas noted must be studied in relation to the other areas. We are dealing with systems of human relations that are interlocking and mutually dependent upon each other. To understand the problems of individuals and groups, we must therefore study them in action in the significant areas of their activity.

This means that we cannot be content with studying one group of workers in terms of the immediate job, another in terms of community activities, and so on. If we are to fit the parts together, we must study the same people in relation to the job, to management, to the union, and to the community.

That calls for concentrated study in a single plant—a plant having a variety of job operations and skills, for purposes of contrast. It means also work within a single community, so that we will not have to study a new community for each new group of workers we observe. And, finally, it means a long-range research program, for obviously the complex and interrelated problems outlined here are not to be resolved with a quick survey.

PROGRESS BY TACKLING SIGNIFICANT PROBLEMS

Is such an ambitious program beyond the present capacity of social research? If we are thinking of final answers to all the questions raised here, then of course we are attempting the impossible.

But if we have the more modest aim of pinning down a few definite propositions and gaining leads toward further knowledge, then the situation is much more hopeful.

Some of the essential methods of research already have been developed in community and industrial studies. Other essential methods are still to be devised. But the history of science suggests that we do not progress through tailoring the problems studied to the research methods we have ready at hand. We must first define the significant problems and then stretch ourselves to devise the methods that will enable us to cope with those problems.

The problems surrounding work are crucial to our society. An intensive exploration of the world of work may help us to meet the challenges of our industrial civilization.

SELECTED BIBLIOGRAPHY

No attempt will be made to present a comprehensive bibliography. References in the text are cited again here for purposes of convenience.

Bakke, E. Wight, *Citizens Without Work*. Yale University Press, 1940.

Gardner, B. B., and D. G. Moore, *Human Relations in Industry*. Richard Irwin & Co., 1950.

Roethlisberger, F. J., and W. J. Dickson, *Management and the Worker*. Harvard University Press, 1939.

Warner, W. L., and J. O. Low, *The Social System of the Modern Factory*. Yale University Press, 1947.

Whyte, W. F., *Pattern for Industrial Peace*. Harper & Brothers, 1951.

For a general background for the study of human relations problems, the writings of Elton Mayo are invaluable. See *The Human Problems of an Industrial Civilization* (Macmillan, 1935), or *The Social Problems of an Industrial Civilization.* (Harvard Business School, 1940).

The most useful theoretical framework for the analysis of problems of human relations in industry seems to me to be provided by George C. Homans in *The Human Group* (Harcourt, Brace, 1950). This also contains an analysis of two case studies taken from industry.

9

Leisure in Industrial America

by Reuel Denney and David Riesman

NEW-RICH IN LEISURE

Mass leisure has hit us so suddenly that we tend to think about it by drawing on the stereotypes of an earlier era. Thus, we take much the same view of modern leisure that people in Jefferson's day took of industry. But, whereas in Jefferson's day there were some hopeful ones, like the Englishman Samuel Ure, who looked to the coming of the machine with enthusiasm, the tone of most contemporary comment about the coming of leisure for all views it as a calamity.

Certainly, it is arguable that we have got too "rich" too fast, in our quantities of time off, and behave with the discomfort and lack of grace common to parvenus. And it is evident that many people, consciously seldom but unconsciously often, flee back to artificially strenuous work—or even to war—in order to escape the perplexities of choice presented by abundant leisure.

These are the pangs of transition—though obviously, in such matters as the preference for war, overabundance may be the purgatory that leads to hell and not to heaven. All we can say is that a more hopeful outcome is conceivable.

DEFINITIONS

The discussion that follows is about American leisure in general. It is a large subject with many facets and many definitions. Among these, for instance:

play, which may mean games or may mean the general animal
   capacity for enjoying the useless;
recreation, which appears to be, in some cases, a teacher's or
   social worker's definition of what play should be;
off-time sociability, which is the background of much of our play;
intensely private pleasures of the connoisseur or hobbyist;
intensely public and conformist pleasures of many sport and
   media fans.

Our discussion is concerned with all of these within the context
of the larger issues of the use of leisure in modern industrial life.
We employ the term "leisure" not only to refer to the time away
from the workplace or the work-hours and from home obligations,
but also to refer to certain demands which are made on us not to
squander unimaginatively the resources which industrialization has
opened up for us. Leisure, in that sense, implies a quality of life
which we seek to capture or recapture as an element in all of our
activities.

THE PRODUCTION AND DISTRIBUTION OF LEISURE

"TIME ON MY HANDS . . ."

We need to remember certain historical developments that
provide a background for the better understanding of contemporary leisure.

The industrial work-week declined from an average of 64 hours
in 1860 to an average of 42 hours in 1930. This, of course, does not
take account of such recent institutions as the midmorning coffee
hour—nor of such old but steadily elaborated ones as the slow-
down and the loafing time made available in most offices and
shops.

Paradoxically, the relative scarcity of labor in the United States,
from the beginning, helped promote the mechanization that made
reduction of hours look reasonable. Mechanization, given this
impetus, more than caught up with labor scarcity, even though the
scarcity artificially continued by the shutting down of immigration
after World War I. Thus, scarcity of labor led eventually not to

long and exhausting hours but to short if not sweet ones. That this has not happened with doctors and other professionals who have made themselves scarce—and then have forced themselves to keep up with demand by working 70-hour weeks—may be due not only to the difficulties of mechanizing the professions but also to the emotional difficulties the active middle class would encounter if not allowed to work more than, say, railroad hours.

Man-hour productivity—despite the "conscientious withdrawal of efficiency" practiced by labor and management alike—has been going up in the United States every decade for eight decades of growing industrialization. If we were willing to accept the standard of living of 1870, most of us could presumably get by with a five-hour week.

KINDS OF WORK AND PATTERNS OF LEISURE

The accent on industrial productivity needs also to be understood in the light of the shift of the past quarter century in the types of employment. As a percentage of the total labor force, industrial workers and, of course, farmers have declined. The "new middle class" of the small clerical, the service trades, the professionals, and the managerial class—including all the people engaged in the growing education and leisure industries have made the gains. This markedly affects the *kind* of work done. And, as we shall see, the patterns of leisure differ very much depending on the kind of work done or on whether any work is done at all.

Indeed, one question of this sort, where leisure and type of work interact, must be touched on at the outset. It is argued in *The Lonely Crowd*, by David Reisman with the collaboration of Reuel Denney and Nathan Glazer (Yale University Press, 1950, chapters 6 and 15), that rising industrial productivity and the shifts in type of employment it has brought about have moved so fast that some of the "extra time" has gotten lost in the industrial process itself. Thus it may be that the multiplication of so-called overhead functions within industrial management is in one aspect a partial response to surplus time created within modern industry. More generally, current concern for industrial teamwork and, beyond that, for emotionally meaningful work may symbolize the time that has been absorbed in this way in the very process of its creation.

LEISURE IN THE LIFE CYCLE

Just as matter in the wrong place becomes dirt, so time at the "wrong" time becomes waste, enforced idleness, unemployment.

The same forces which have reduced the work-week have lengthened the life span and have made it compulsory for the young to wait it out in school until the labor force will make room for them. For many of the young this turns out to be simply a prison, with rather inefficient and wholly unhappy jailers. The denizens of these jails have little more pleasure in their free time than prisoners usually do who exercise their ingenuity in outwitting and tormenting their guards.

JUVENILE DELINQUENCY

One set of responses to this situation is labeled by society as "juvenile delinquency"—activities in which gregarious theft and gang warfare by the boys and gregarious sex by the girls appear to be channels for the playful, sociable, and conformist impulses of the lower-class youth. If, in many areas, we find a lower-class boy or girl who is not delinquent in this sense, we can be fairly sure that he or she is either headed up the class ladder or is psychologically deviant or both, being unwilling or unable to join in the group activities sanctioned by his peers. This paper has some things to say about this area and about lower-class leisure generally, but it is largely concerned with the middle- and upper-class leisure patterns that almost all Americans are aware of as models.

THE PROBLEM OF THE ELDERLY

If leisure constitutes a problem for the idling young just prior to their employment (see William F. Whyte's description of unemployed New England youth in *Street Corner Society*, University of Chicago Press, 1937), there is perhaps an even greater problem for the elderly just following their disemployment. Studies show that forcible retirement operates more destructively on men than on women. Even the housewife whose children have all grown and flown has a less difficult time of it than her husband, most of whose self-esteem, fantasy, and sociability have clustered about his job. These haunt his postemployment life like ghosts, and they are the more ferocious the more intangible the job from which the man has been retired. The retired railroader with his cronies and neat cottage and lot and his hunting and fishing gear— all of which absorbed his semiretired hours during his short working day and life—may be better off than Willy Loman in *Death of a Salesman*, whose work was never so real to him nor so separate from his sociable play.

Surely some more sensitized awareness that sociability is a human need makes our society increasingly uncomfortable about the isolation of the elderly. We realize that the pension money paid them, even if it is financially adequate—which it rarely is— does not absolve us from some responsibility toward their feeling themselves surplus in an industrial age.

A case in point. An anecdote suggests this feeling.

A Midwesterner engaged in adult education recently regularized his meetings of older men and women at the same room in a club building and on the same night of each week. Banking on their knowledge of the place and time, he stopped sending cards to the oldsters to notify them. The next week he was overwhelmed with angry protests. "But you know the time and place by now," he protested. "Yes," they replied, "but it's so nice to get the mail."

Several of the Conference consultants have called our attention to the mushrooming "Golden Years" and "Senior Citizens" clubs which have sought to provide sociability, craft hobby facilities, and guidance for older, and especially retired, persons. Many of these persons have had the bad luck to be born in an age which admired hard work and savings-bank deposits, and now grow old in an age which not only ridicules the inhibited player but also redoubles the insult by decimating his savings by inflation. True, there are many elderly men who have never thought it became them to work so hard that they could not adjust to compulsory play. A retired Franklin Roosevelt would have been quite content with his boats, his stamps, his acres, and his memoirs.

CHANGING PROBLEMS OF LEISURE

Yet all this sounds as if time were no problem for people in the society that preceded ours. Then, the leisure perplexities were indeed rare in a nation of early-rising, hard-working farmers and factory hands who were apt to regard leisure like a gold or oil strike, as a windfall uncomplicated by emotional excess-profits taxes.

It appears that until the Age of Taft, the "leisure class" held something of a monopoly on the problem; it could occupy itself with perfecting the game of leisure, in ways so admirably satirized by Thorstein Veblen in *The Theory of the Leisure Class* (Viking Press, 1899) because of its leadership and the high visibility of its leisure pursuits. In other words, the leisure class took on itself the task of playing on behalf of the whole overworked society; and the very inequality of this distribution of leisure paradoxically gave the leisure class a certain amount of justification for its activities. Yet, in the case of many sensitive and intelligent men and women, this justification sometimes broke down; there was often a pathetic feeling of aimlessness and social imprisonment.

Since no society changes all at once, a good many of these older justifications remain, both in the upper and in the lower classes. If we search far enough, we can find the Huck Finns whose river adventures are truant but not delinquent, and we can find gilded youth and wealthy aged folk for whom idleness is not discomfort. Time does not move evenly for everyone, even in our allegedly standardized industrial culture. But it is this very fact which leads often to tragedy. *Tragedies of leisure occur for the individual when his life cycle fatefully gets mixed up with some larger social cycle (e.g., of unemployment, or of suddenly lowered retirement ages, or of the more general shifts we are discussing) which is at odds with his own development.*

TYPES OF LEISURE—CHILDHOOD TO MATURITY

We see that youth, maturity, and age pursue distinct types of leisure when we notice that we do not speak of children's leisure but of their play. By speaking of play, we imply the relatively unproblematic, but by no means uncomplicated, nature of the activity. *Leisure* has much more ambiguous connotations.

In the young child, work and play are not yet independently organized. Play is viewed by the observant society as preparation for work and, in the investigations of Jean Piaget (*The Moral Judgment of the Child*, 1932; Glenco Free Press, 1947), for political roles, quite as much as for future leisure.

Children's play, in fact, is simply given. While it has aspects of artifice which the ever-renewed child's culture elaborates, it is something which we find in all cultures. The great horror of the early stages of industrialization was the harnessing of very young children—often literally harnessing—to factory work, and the consequent destruction for these generations of this great, natural resource of childhood play and curiosity. Today, at any rate, the child's right to play is so fully established that few adult exploiters can stand out against it. Here, at least, industrialism has more than restored to us what it once took away.

CHILD'S PLAY A MODEL

We can say, in fact, that the child's play serves as the model for all later efforts to free leisure from its burdens and to cope with the puzzling availability of adult time.

Here, too, our imagery can easily succumb to nostalgia. Studies of children's play by the psychoanalyst Erik H. Erikson (*Childhood and Society.* Norton, 1950) show that it is not always free of terror and anxiety and morbidity; our own unclouded recollections often tell us as much. Whatever extra problems are created in the realm of leisure by conflicts betwen the individual's one and only life cycle and the social developments of his time, we must conclude that leisure—like life itself, of which it is so great and characteristic a part—will never be free of ambiguities, of haunting self-consciousness, of sheer miserable existence.

COMPETENCE IN PLAY

We can, however, take from studies of childhood play one important lesson for the adult: that children appear to derive their greatest satisfactions from experiences of mastery and control. Could it be that the dissatisfactions with contemporary leisure might be reduced if we did more with the problem of sheer competence, if we enabled people to become more "workman-like," and at the same time more imaginative, players?

A case in point. Erikson's work sees children's play as a series of fictions that establish experimental connections with the real world. Part of this world is the child's own body, maturing at different rates and with different sensations, and Erikson seeks to relate play to the zones of muscular and psychosexual development. While we have hardly any studies as sophisticated as this dealing with adult play competence, there come to mind the two satirical studies of adult play by Stephen Potter (*Gamesmanship* and *Lifemanship*—the titles are revealing). Potter, in his spoofing studies of British middle-class life, assumes that sociability is itself a game, played for the sake of a felt superiority in any situation. He studies conversation as a contest in which the ability to lie, to indulge in ellipsis, in confusing innuendo, and so on, becomes a glorious achievement of human resource in mastering difficult situations—and in making others rather than one-self uncomfortable. Perhaps a line can be traced between the solitary craftsmanship of a child learning to master the Yo-Yo—with far more zeal than he will employ learning to hang up his clothes at night—and the social craftsmanship of Potter's devotees of aggressive sociability.

TIME AND EXPENSE BUDGETS FOR LEISURE

What are the facts and figures on the cost of leisure in time and money?

One of the most important studies, made in the early thirties, found that the average citizen of a Westchester community spent half his leisure time visiting other folks and watching or participating in sports. (Lundberg, Komarovsky, and McInerny, *Leisure: A Suburban Study*, Columbia University Press, 1934.) The other two biggest single blocks of weekly time were spent for radio listening and reading—about 10 per cent of total leisure time each. Movies accounted for something like 5 per cent of spare time.

As one might expect, the highest dollar expenditures per hour fell under the head of sociability. The lowest were those devoted to reading. In view of these hour-to-dollar ratios, it is significant that many "hard-cover" book publishers feel defensive about the allegedly high price of their product, though in hour-entertainment cost books are still the best leisure buy.

There are, unfortunately, few studies of this sort, though George Gallup has stated that he is planning a survey of a 24-hour day in the life of Mr. Average American. An earlier study by Sorokin secured time-diaries of people in Massachusetts. Dallas Smythe has obtained some leisure diaries in connection with his as yet unpublished studies of television.

Even at best, however, such data are merely suggestive. They go only a little way toward answering such questions as that of Lynn White, jr.: whether leisure may not be destroyed and rendered meaningless by its abundance. (We believe abundance may be rendered meaningless if there is no leisure!) Or Lawrence K. Frank's: whether leisure pursuits do not often serve simply to distract people from unpleasant reveries, so that people return to work with only a negative accomplishment to show for their "recreation" time.

DOLLAR TOTALS UNREVEALING

The dollar figures for leisure are, if anything, even less revealing than the time-budgets—except for those few instances where we can get comparative data and thus have some idea of recent historical changes in leisure. We know, for example, that in the year 1946, when total consumption reached $143 billion, the calculated expenditures for recreation were $7.9 billion. (How this squares with recent guesses before the Kefauver Committee that the annual "take" on gambling is around $20 billion is anyone's guess.) The Department of Commerce figures are general and loose.

The economists have found no way of estimating many types of recreation. They cannot allocate consumption expenditures for house, clothes, car, and food as between recreation and subsistence, because such an allocation would require a subtle analysis of motives. Nor can they allow for all the recreation that gets smuggled into what is socially defined as work—though national totals on expense accounts, by industries and regions, would be a help.

TRENDS IN EXPENDITURE

More fruitful is an historical survey of recent changes in American leisure, based on the category "Recreation" in the Commerce Department's national product figures. (Frederick Dewhurst et al., *America's Needs and Resources*, a Twentieth Century Fund publication.) Sports equipment sold as well in 1929 as in 1909, as a percentage of consumer outlay. But reading, hobbies, and pets fell off from 24 per cent to 18 per cent in the same 20-year span. Total recreation expenses declined in relation to club dues—possibly suggesting the greater importance of business and professional "promotional" leisure. From 1929 to 1941, gambling increased in volume about one thousand per cent—as the world itself became more chancy—while theatre and opera declined 65 per cent and books 15 per cent. (For another study of dollar trends, see Julius Weinberger, "Money Spent for Play: An Index of Opinion," *Public Opinion Quarterly*, Vol. II, No. 2, April 1938.)

THE LEISURE INDUSTRIES

Such essentially static approaches to the leisure economy, by way of dollar totals, may neglect the dynamic aspects of leisure in its impact on the whole economy. It may be that the sectors of the economy which cater to leisure have a disproportionate opportunity to influence the health of the economy as a whole. We can, for example, think of a house as shelter and view the housing problem in terms of minimum shelter needs. Alternatively, we can view the house as a great consumer of leisure—the housewife's spare time, the father's puttering, the children's away-from-school pastimes and chores, all of which in turn can consume further dollars by efforts at efficiency and mechanization. The house allows people to accumulate play-tools as well as work-tools: books and records, TV, toys, games—the whole gamut of play materials.

The circle of home activities is only one example of leisure activities which may have a far more important influence on general economic expansion than we are even now willing to recognize. Leisure spending is conceivably more sensitive than any other kind as an index to society's changing demands on the allocation of resources. The very fluctuations in recreational spending, as well as other factors in the occupational structure, make the leisure economy alert and sensitive to change, despite monopolistic tendencies.

All this suggests that expansions and contractions in leisure lines need to be studied not only as effects but also as causes of the general prosperity structure. Thus, an economist who wanted to find a full-employment substitute for war production could begin his search for antideflationary "multipliers" with the leisure trades. He could begin his work by thinking of the endless group-leisure activities which can absorb dollars: from national parks to local pools, from free books in the library to free fireworks in the sky.

VULNERABILITY TO CRITICISM OF LEISURE INDUSTRIES

Such economic approaches, however, may today be inhibited by the fact that industries which cater primarily to leisure are vulnerable to public criticism—movies and TV are prime examples—in a way that industries which cater primarily to "production" are not. Our feeling that the media, for example, need more and better criticism, should take account of this. The high visibility of the entertainment industries opens them to political and aesthetic criticism that is rarely applied to the building trades or the auto industry. Yet, in the latter industries some of the same underlying issues of policy and art are equally important.

CULTURAL AND EMOTIONAL FRONTIERS OF LEISURE

Can we say that leisure cash and time are well distributed in America today? While obviously there are still people who work too long hours under conditions not of their choosing—some residual domestics and agricultural laborers on factory farms, for instance—wage and hour laws have much reduced these abuses. Likewise, though inflation has imprisoned many fixed-income people in leisure strait jackets, those who suffer from inadequate leisure spending money may be fewer than those who suffer from inadequate leisure spending-motives.

Many hardships of leisure lie more on the social, cultural, and emotional frontiers than on the simpler economic and hourly frontiers. What keeps over half the American people from going to the movies is not the absence of cash but the cultural definitions of moviegoing which will lead them to muster the energy to go. (We do not think, incidentally, that people fail to go because movies are so "immature" or bad or filled with false values, or because in most cases they have better, more "active" things to do. We feel that many American as well as European movies are stimulating and artistic experiences which are perhaps beyond the ability and sophistication of that part of the population over thirty which never had or has lost the movie habit. Here again the problem may be one of competence on the part of the movie audience, that is, the ability to control the play materials.)

CLASS-MASS LEISURE

MARKET RESEARCH INFORMATION ON LEISURE

Very likely, the most refined information we have on American leisure exists in the files of market research agencies. There we can discover the fictionally typical consumer: the thirty-three-year-old male who owns three and a quarter golf clubs, goes to two movies a week, drinks Scotch but not beer, and bought a television set in mid-1950. (The standardization of these figures tends to give the impression that leisure and consumption are themselves standardized—a point we shall return to.)

Market research provides easily ascertained sex, age, and income categories, partly because advertising expenditures are planned with a purchasing-power approach, partly because it is usually less difficult to estimate an interviewee's income than his social position, his character, or his temperament—though these might be much more important variables from the point of view of a theory of leisure. Furthermore, market research focusses on leisure products rather than on leisure processes, though of course the two cannot always be separated. Despite these limitations, there can be no doubt that market research experts possess some of the most detailed statistics, and the shrewdest hunches, about what goes on in leisure.

THE FACTOR OF SOCIAL CLASS

While this research, like the Department of Commerce national dollar totals, emphasizes consumer classifications based on *income*, the studies of Lloyd Warner and his assistants analyze the consumer market indirectly, by a method that emphasizes the classification of people in terms of *social* class rather than *income* class. This is important to the student of leisure because it demonstrates that membership in a social class is defined today less by earning power than by spending habits, less by occupation than by friendships which cluster about leisure activities.

In his *Yankee City* studies (4 vols., Yale University Press, 1941-1947), Warner noticed that people of similar income, but divergent social class, subscribe to different periodicals, join different clubs, vacation in different ways. This is not news to most literate Americans or to readers of John Marquand's *Point of No Return*. We have Warner to thank, however, for a systematization of our folklore on this topic and for rounding out our picture of class behavior by studying its emotional expression in play, as well as in the previously studied areas of work and politics.

Indeed, Warner's work has become part of the folklore of our educated classes. Observers sometimes worry that Warner will freeze the very classes he describes and that leisure habits, class-polarized by envy and snobbery, will drive Americans further apart.

Though a class war between highbrows and middlebrows, with the lowbrows looking on, hardly seems imminent, it can be argued that common leisure interests serve to unite Americans of all income classes. Sports, *Lil Abner*, the Hit Parade, and politics viewed as entertainment hold the United States together by offering at least some class-free themes for talk and attention. What if only the weather were left as common conversational coin for upper-upper and lower-middle? To be sure, Warner has studied mainly the divergencies, the cutoff points, that serve to locate his people in class terms; he has not studied directly the unifying topics and pursuits.

SHAPING OF LEISURE HABITS

Warner's work deals not only with leisure habits as they appear fully formed in the adult but tries to discover how these are inculcated in the family and at school, particularly in high school.

Free public education to an advanced age—itself a product of our industrial abundance, including our ability to spare a million teachers, and the teachers of teachers, from productive routines—means free exposure to class models of appropriate leisure behavior. That is, teachers are themselves part of the social class system and (as A. B. Hollingshead's *Elmtown's Youth*, Wiley, 1949, shows) they tend to judge their pupils in terms of their amenability to class-dictated standards of appreciation. Many teachers assume that sensitivity to literary values is necessary to the full use of leisure, but they have no better way of insuring this than by forcing the more docile pupils to grasp the plot-structure of one of Shakespeare's plays. This procedure—ritualistic for many, ornamental for a few—often resembles the old-time piano lesson in its crudeness and banality.

SCHOOLS VS. MEDIA

The school's anxieties over these matters of class-bound taste are in part reflected in their desperate and losing battle with the media. The schools—and with them many middle-class parents—regard the media, and particularly the newest one, TV—as unfair competition for the pupils' free time and as evil portents for their eventual leisure tastes.

We suggest that the battle is not a productive one. On the one side, the schools overvalue the differences between lowbrow and highbrow art. They take it as self-evident, for example, that print is more aesthetically significant than film; that *The Raven* is superior to most B-movies; that a poorly acted play by Shakespeare is better than a good Fred Astaire musical; that heavy-handedness about literature is the same thing as seriousness; and so on. On the other side, the schools tend to overestimate their failures to open up artistic possibilities (including the movies) for a few, because they believe they owe something to everybody and have limited ways of discovering their contributions to the few.

BATTLE OF THE GENERATIONS

The result of these tensions is to compel the adolescents in every generation to become involved in a battle over the uses of their leisure. Their use of leisure, with its class and "brow" overtones, becomes a major factor in their struggle toward adult independence; and whether they join battle with parents or flee, they are caught in anxiety and defensiveness. When they are in turn parents, they tend to fight the same battle with a new vocabulary.

Thus, fifty years ago the issue was joined over the moralizing novel, which was supposed also to be the artistic one. Twenty-five years ago, as the Payne Fund studies testify, it was joined over the discovery that children were using movie stars as models for behavior. (The possibility was overlooked that movie stars, on the screen and in life, were not worse models than other adults and, since their modeling was mediated consciously and unconsciously by the conditions of art, were conceivably better ones.)

HYGIENIC STANDARDS FOR LEISURE?

Today, in some quarters, we are faced with the same sort of polarity in the form of an increasing emphasis on the emotionally hygienic aspects of participative uses of leisure. Television is decried because of the alleged passivity of its audience, as well as, more appropriately, on account of its frequent banality.

A case in point. A bookseller recently observed that, in her experience, 90 per cent of the parents who come to buy books for their children are wholly dependent on the bookseller's advice and an age-bracket formula. "I want a book for an 8-year-old girl." Or, sometimes, "I want a cowboy book for a 10-year-old boy—he doesn't go for fantasy." These parents are closer to Aunt Agatha than to their children when it comes to buying a book: they have not taken the trouble to try to pierce the veil between the generations. It is these same parents who, the bookseller agreed, scold TV because their children do not read as much or as well as the parents would like.

Added to the YMCA concept of strenuous muscular leisure (useful in sublimating sex) is the more subtle notion that mentally challenging leisure is useful for emotional growth. The truth of all these assumptions, especially the more sophisticated recent ones, should not lead us to overlook the fact that no such "useful" or simply hygienic assumptions can contain the final truth about art, including television art. The media men as well as the media audience are likely to be damaged by these pressures. The leisure tensions engendered by the battle over the media may stand as a warning that the leisureful use of art, and the artful use of leisure, are tenuous things, easily destroyed by challenging them constantly to stand and deliver social values.

LEISURE AND ETHNIC GROUP

Except for some detailed studies of Negro leisure (for example, in Myrdal's *An American Dilemma*, chapters 42, 43), we know little about the important ways in which ethnic background directly influences leisure, both in its production and in its distribution.

True, we can trace the boundaries that separate the "folk-dance" culture of the Anglo-Saxon heritage, the bebop culture of the Negro, the "Catskill culture" of the Jewish-influenced screen and airways, the garlic food culture of the Eastern and Southern Europeans. Likewise, contrasting the movies with the comic books, we can see that the movies provide a wide range of ethnic physical and cultural types as models for emulation—Italians, Swedes, Jews, etc.—while the comics confine themselves to square-jawed heroes and oafish Mediterranean villains.

Furthermore, it seems evident that people struggling for emancipation from Puritan backgrounds tend to make use of the cultural contributions of non-Puritan ethnic groups—indeed, often use these groups as "fronts" in their own cultural battles for a less conformist life style.

Nevertheless, apart from some reportage found in novels, we

know almost nothing about these matters. We do not know, for example, how much the variety and quality of American leisure has been dependent on successive waves of immigrants contributing leisure themes from their folk cultures and finding influential positions in the industries catering to leisure—from Greek and Chinese restaurant keepers, with their use of characteristic interior décors, to German fishing-reel makers and Jewish comedians. Just as we drew skilled workmen from Western Europe for a hundred years and broke their skills down into assembly line techniques which the semiskilled could copy, so it may be that we have drawn many of the crafts of our mass leisure industries from Eastern and Southern Europe. If so, we need not expect that we can—or should—subdivide these skills in order to employ them in a mass-assembly manner. For one thing, the skills of the leisure industries may be far less amenable to the process of substituting mechanical for human skills.

ETHNIC SANCTIONS

Ethnic stereotypes on the leisure scene have on their negative side much the same effect as the social class tags: they tend to imprison people at play within the limitations of the group they are, willy-nilly, identified with. There are Negroes, for instance, who are "forbidden" to like jazz or, indeed, any aspects of Bohemian leisure, because this has been identified in public stereotype with "the" Negro. Conversely, there are Jews who dare not dislike Israeli folk songs.

Since ethnic sanctions come out to a greater degree in play than in work—partly because of our ideology, more work is impersonal—these sanctions and compulsory reactions against them are more stifling in the leisure field. Just as, in an older culture, people had to be wary of breaking the rules of class etiquettes, so in America they must be sensitive to ethnic ones.

A case in point. One of our students made a brief study of attitudes toward their respective ethnic cuisines on the part of Polish, Lithuanian, and other East European housewives in the Chicago area. She found that these women typically went through a phase of Americanization when they could not socially afford to eat their native dishes.

Then, if they moved a bit up the class ladder, they found their new friends intrigued by "exotic" foods and went back to their mothers to learn how to cook their native dishes—even if they did not like them.

LEISURE AND SEX

We are not concerned with sex itself as a pastime. Kinsey's work can be interpreted to show that in terms of time-budgets spent in actual sexual activity, there is not too much difference on a class or ethnic basis. What the middleclass and the more religiously inhibited groups lose in number of times of intercourse, they more than make up in the amount of time spent in fantasy, courtship, and play. Yet this very investigation is as good an indicator as any that budgets of leisure in terms of time and expense barely tap the significant emotion—or affect—budgets of people. For the number of physical "outlets" (Kinsey term) for sex obviously bears little enough relation to the fantasy or work patterns to which sex and its cultural embroidery give rise. (See *The Lonely Crowd*, chapter 7, for a discussion of sex as the "last frontier" in a society of abundant commodities.)

SEX-TYPED LEISURE ACTIVITIES

Rather, our concern here is with the way in which various leisure activities other than sex get identified with men or women and are thus pre-empted from the opposite sex. There are many subtle problems here. "Modern dance" appears to have become a field for women, allowing them to gain a control over bodily motion which men, perhaps, do not gain equally well from football or baseball. (Perhaps men have more than made up for this through the services of Arthur Murray and his numerous competitors!) Horseback riding appears to be in transition, becoming increasingly a field for women; their refinements of dress and dressage may be their revenge against their exclusion from the cowboy culture of little boys, as well as a response to the dated notion that horsemanship is high-class.

Whenever a leisure activity gets sex-typed, it throws up barriers

against the other sex and thus inhibits the recapture of those childhood play patterns which, up to three or four years of age, are
relatively free from sex cues. As compared with fifty years ago,
there is doubtless a great deal more liberty of choice in leisure,
especially for women. But the greater psychological knowledge of
our day has made it difficult for people to protect their sex-
crossing leisures from anxiety. The boy who reads "too much,"
the girl who rides "too much," may be told, or self-told, that their
masculinity or femininity is threatened.

MANDATORY LEISURE

Notice also that two social themes have combined to make
leisure, as it were, mandatory, and mandatory along certain lines.
On the one hand, our loss of psychological innocence means that
people can no longer employ certain older, socially supported
alibis for their difficulty in having fun. On the other hand, our
heightened gregariousness means that people cannot protect by
privacy those escapist pursuits which do not pass muster among
their peers. One's leisure even more than one's work becomes an
area of personal effort toward emotional unity and sexual competence. In that sense, as we have elsewhere put it, there is *no
escape from leisure.*

A case in point. One of the syndicated advice columns recently
carried a headline: "Hubby who works too hard may be escaping from
wife." The column explored in detail the telltale clues by which the
wife could detect the signs of such escape and the methods by which
she could batter down the defenses of her spouse.

LEISURE AND CHARACTER STRUCTURE

The classifications discussed so far—by age, social and income
class, ethnic group, and sex—have been until recently the principal
ones used by social scientists and market researchers for cross-
sectioning the American population. The size of town and region
(rural-urban) are additional classifications about which we say
little here since our major concern is with the urban industrial
scene. In the past few years, however, emotional categories of

various sorts have been proposed by psychologists and anthro-pologists engaged in the study of "national character."

Thus, we find Wolfenstein and Leites analyzing movie content in American, British, and French films in order to obtain a com-parative picture of family structure, attitudes toward sin and sex, toward secrecy and showing off, in each of these three countries. (*Movies: A Psychological Study*, Free Press, 1950.) Donald McGranahan has made similar studies of German and American drama, and a good deal of other work of the same sort is now under way.

Such investigations into "social character" throw only an in-direct light on the media and on leisure, since their concern is with the audience. Yet because they show, no matter how tenta-tively, that the audience can be divided into psychological types, they establish that social categories such as class and age fail fully to tap the dynamics of leisure—the drives and impulses that people seek to release, control, or observe in their free time. The difficulty then becomes a research one: what psychological types shall we employ for the study of leisure, and what methods can we use to "type" a person? As to both these questions we are still pretty much in the dark, but we have a few clues worth noting.

PERSONALITY TYPES AND CAPACITY TO PLAY

Recent and ongoing studies of American character at the Uni-versity of California have been preoccupied with the problem of authoritarianism in people and in the social structure. (See Adorno *et al., The Authoritarian Personality*, Harper, 1950.) People have been divided into authoritarian (antidemocratic) and nonauthori-tarian (democratic) types, with various subcategories of each. While these studies have been mainly concerned with attitudes, they have hit on one theme which bears directly on people's capacity to play.

It has been found that the authoritarian type is rigid, hostile to fantasy, and "anti-introceptive" (unwilling to look into himself). Conversely, most nonauthoritarian types are easygoing, capable of some fantasy, and willing to look into themselves. There are some rigid "democrats" too, but they are less typical. Thus, these studies uncover some of the political and social dynamite hidden underneath a society's capacities and incapacities for play. (While we ourselves have a number of criticisms to make of the political angle of the Berkeley work, this is not to the point here.)

More important, perhaps, is the evidence from this work that simple interview questions can be framed which (when tested against a background of psychoanalytic interviews and such instruments as the Rorschach or Thematic Apperception Test) shed light on underlying character structure. Thus it becomes possible, in principle, to "type" the population at large and not only a few individuals rounded up for a battery of complicated tests. Hence our research question becomes: what sort of psychological categories would be most useful if our main interest were not in authoritarianism but in leisure?

Categories drawn directly from psychoanalysis (for example, "oral" or "anal") are not notably useful because they are insufficiently social and historical. Categories drawn directly from sociology (for example, those based on class and region) are not notably useful either, since what needs to be discovered is whether these social categories are also psychological ones. What is required, therefore, is a set of types which is at once social and psychological. This is the merit of the Berkeley types; it is also their drawback, if one does not share the research assumption that authoritarianism is the main problem facing American society today.

In a recent article, Robert K. Merton suggests a distinction, based on his study of communications behavior in a small town, between those he calls the "cosmopolitans" and those he calls the "locals." ("Patterns of Influence: A Study of Inter-personal Influence and of Communications Behavior in a Local Community," in Lazarsfeld and Stanton (eds.), *Communications Research 1948-1949*, Harper's, 1949, pp. 180-219.) For him, this is a distinction between types who are tuned in to the national and international scene—reading *Time* magazine is a good key to this—and those who are preoccupied with the personalities of their own community.

The former are more likely to be interested in the doings of the school board, the latter of the police force. We can all recognize these types once they have been pointed out to us. Now the possibility suggests itself that these types not only behave differently but are different types of people in their internal design; that they use their leisure differently; and that, even if they appear to use it in the same way, they draw different meanings from it. That is, when locals and cosmopolitans attend the same movies, it is a deeply different experience for each type.

"INNER-DIRECTED" AND "OTHER-DIRECTED" PEOPLE

In *The Lonely Crowd*, Riesman and his coworkers have inaugurated another effort to link these two approaches by describing a set of character types which appear to be useful in the study of leisure. In short, we possess an experimental framework for comparing recreational behavior in the historically earlier "era of inner-direction" (the job-minded society) with that in the historically recent "era of other-direction" (the people-minded and leisure-minded society). Inner-directed people are "gyroscopically" guided from childhood by internalized goals implanted by parents and other imposing adults. In contrast, other-directed people are less influenced by their parents. They learn early to accept their directions in the game of leisure and life from their peers—that is, their age-mates, job-mates, and play-mates—to whom they respond with "radar" sensitivity.

It should be clear that these two psychological types are abstractions: we are not going to find concrete individuals who are exclusively inner-directed or other-directed. The inner-directed person is seldom if ever completely immune to his peers; the other-directed person, though socialized to a high degree among peers, is still the child of his parents and has been heavily influenced by them. Other-directed people have existed prior to the twentieth century, while inner-direction perhaps remains the orientation of the numerical majority of Americans even today. Nevertheless, other-direction appears to be increasing in the upper-middle class of the metropolitan areas.

Play and leisure, we suggest, perform different functions in the *shaping* of these two types in childhood and then in their *persistence* in adulthood. Thus, the other-directed person learns as a child to take cues from others in the very forms of his play. As an adult, he continues to engage in a characteristic type of play sociability, whatever the objective content of his leisure. To take a simple example from audience psychology: the inner-directed person learns as a child to identify himself with heroes in fiction who zealously pursue workmanlike goals. One result is that, as an adult reader, he prefers detective stories in which he works with the detective to overcome obstacles and solve a crime.

A case in point. Study tends to show that two distinct types of detective story serve the emotional needs of the two different types of character. The inner-directed person is apt to prefer the old-fashioned (Sherlock Holmes) type of detective story, because he enjoys joining in the rational solution, through hard work, of a merely temporary puzzle. The other-directed reader may prefer the genre of "suspense," by which he enters at once into a mood shared by the stories' characters—a mood, ordinarily, of anxiety and terror—but hopes for rescue by a *deus ex machina*.

Plainly enough, since no one person is purely inner-directed or other-directed, we cannot type him by his taste in mysteries; but we can get a clue which, combined with many similar clues, may give us a rough basis for judgment.

We do not want to argue the merits of one or another character type or the merits of one or another system of constructing such types. Rather, we have simply wanted to introduce the importance of character as a variable in society which is now open to research.

CHARACTER TYPE STUDY AND APPLICATIONS

The study of character types is an especially good tool for discovering and explaining much that is going on in our society. It enables us to see, for example, how and why, with the emergence of new character types, attitudes toward the spheres of work and play are changing, and attitudes toward politics, sex, education, and so forth, also are changing. It enables us to see why there is such a struggle between the old ways and new ways and to see that this is not a superficial struggle but a profound character-ological struggle.

Aesthetic and moral judgments of leisure and its by-products and aesthetic and moral prescriptions for its use have, in turn, to take character types into account. To suggest to newer, more other-directed people that they should return to the pastimes of their grandparents does not usually make sense; there is no point in trying to cramp the style of a bobby-soxer by making him into a second-rate craft hobbyist or gardener. Conversely, it is equally foolish to make snobbish attacks upon the slower-moving tastes of older character types. They learn only fear or resentment when, for example, modern painting is forced upon them. This is not necessarily a difference in age. It is a difference of character, where some old people may be new types, and some young people may be carry-overs of old types.

LEISURE AND WORK

All that has been said so far points toward an increasing self-consciousness that attends leisure activities in an advanced in-dustrial society. People acquire images of themselves which lead them to say such things as, "Now I'm not working," or, "Now my time is my own," "Now I have nothing to do, and must enjoy it by doing something." We believe that many people, talking to themselves in these terms, are confused; our culture no longer provides us with clear and emotionally secure distinctions between work and leisure.

THE SMALL GROUP AT WORK AND PLAY

It may well be that the people who make the best use of leisure with each other are those who are related through their roles as co-players and in no other way. The men who meet one a week to bowl or play golf, and don't have the time or business occasion to see each other during the week, are saved from the risk that the roles may get confused with each other. They can count on the fairways and alleys.

Obviously, much of American leisure suffers from the reverse situation.

A *case in point*. The company bowling team is an example of the leisure group which is recruited—save for a ringer or two—directly from the work group, making no major addition or deletion of personnel as the shift from work to play takes place. If it is argued that this is good for the work relations of the men involved, then the argument may imply a certain exploitativeness toward leisure as such. The dramatic final example may be the Office Party, an institution most people rather like in some senses and are deeply ashamed of liking in others.

Housewives suffer from unclear and shifting distinctions between work and play. Should they enjoy themselves together with women as women or as women brought into social affairs with their men? Whatever the answer, women's worst fate is to be dragged along with their men and then separated into their own kind, to talk only to other women who feel equally superfluous and who have equally little reason to be together.

WORK GROUP SOCIABILITY

Analogous problems appear by implication in the study of industrial work motivations by Elton Mayo and his group. (See, for example, Mayo, *The Human Problems of an Industrial Civilization*, Harvard Business School, 1946.) They have seen the degree to which reveries arising in the nonwork sphere enter into the problem of industrial productivity, and they have sought to exorcise the demons by making the work sphere itself more sociable and, through counseling services, more cathartic as well. Now, the older paternalism of the industrial tycoon sought to create company towns in which any non-Puritan or nonuplifting leisure activity would be off limits. Today, the newer paternalism of the Harvard Business School-trained manager seeks to make the factory itself a company town, replete with services not so easily available in the industrial metropolis. One of these services is the encouraging of small-group sociability. (For a brilliant re-examination of Mayo's work and its implications for the ways in which groups create a nonwork or leisure agenda while at work, see George C. Homans, *The Human Group*, Harcourt, Brace, 1950, which also contains material bearing on leisure drawn from studies by social anthropologists.)

LEISURE AND THE OCCUPATIONAL STRUCTURE

It is perhaps significant that these studies of factory life and its morale have generally been concerned with mass industries occupying a stable place in the economy (e.g., telephone, electrical equipment), though more recently the Survey Research Center and other groups have tackled some of the more heavily white-collared trades, such as insurance. In these industries and services, in a full-employment economy, labor relations tend to replace consumer relations as a focus of managerial concern.

EXTRACTIVE INDUSTRIES

By comparison, the extractive ("primary") industries like mining and farming have taken little interest in the problem of work morale. In these same industries, leisure tends to have a traditional quality. The day's work is hard and varied, and play has some of the old-time windfall aspect—catch as catch can. That is, farmers, miners, and lumbermen have in the past accepted the simpler forms of play in part because they may need less play, in part because less is available to them. To the degree, however, that the media now bring them into contact with more complex leisure fare, the workers in this primary sector come face to face with a sophisticated and elaborated leisure for which they have not always had the training. Some of them may feel disproportionately excluded from the American society as a whole because of inability to comprehend and make use of its leisure side. This may, in turn, influence their political and economic demands.

Meanwhile their wives, daughters, and sons are seeking to enter into their American birthright by adopting the appropriate attitudes toward leisure and consumption. The stabilization of agricultural prices and mine wages has created a new, somewhat isolated group with a stake in time off; the women and children who are currently engaged in seeking to urbanize their leisure, without much visible guidance in their experiments. Partly for this reason, the sons no longer find in their father's work its ancient appeal; and if they stay at the pit or on the farm, a strain is put on their new uses of leisure by the dissatisfactions they now discover in their work. (See e.g., the article by George Saxon, an observant coal miner, on the attitude toward competitive sports on the part of miners' children—and also their feelings of ethnic disadvantages—in "Immigrant Culture in a Stratified Society," *Modern Review*, Vol. II, No. 2, February 1947.) The result may be that the work itself is seen as creating problems of morale which have many of their roots elsewhere—and a new set of clients for industrial relations techniques will enter the market.

SERVICE TRADES

At the other end of the industrial process, in the so-called "tertiary" industries (the service trades, mass media, transport, etc.), jobs appear to be less physically difficult than in the extractive fields and less routinized by minute divisions of labor than in manufacturing. At the same time, these are the occupations in which workers meet many people as customers and clients. The workday of the airline stewardess is a glamorized example.

This variability of effort and process may itself become a form of routinization of the individual, as in the case of the department store salesperson. Since, however, routinization by contact with people is rated by the society as less lowly and less wearing than routinization by contact with machinery, many people enter the service trades just in search of this personalized quality. Milkmen need not be excluded from this motivation and certainly not icemen—a dying form of free love in the few regions still unsaturated by the electric ice box.

More significant for our purposes are those more lucrative service trades where people make a good living by doing what they enjoy doing in their free time. A good example is the woman fashion designer who satisfies fantasy directly in her job and is well paid and well regarded for it.

A case in point. Such a professional woman, who has turned a talent for décor into a job and a wider view of society, will tend to live away from the shop as she lives in the shop. Work and play are both luxuries in the sense that they involve people, goods, and tastes. The leisure of such specialists tends to become a search for experience that confirms the idealizations of their own advertising copy. In many cases, the search is crowned by "success," and what appears to the nonmerchandiser as a life built on illusion proves to be a real route to love, board, and fame. Whatever diffuseness of human relations remains is often concealed by the glamour of the profession in the eyes of other women.

STRATEGIC IMPORTANCE OF "VARIETY" INDUSTRIES IN LEISURE

We have gone into some detail here to drive home the point that the leisure of those who recruit themselves into the "variety" industries elaborates itself in ways quite different from that of workers in the broad band of manufacturing or extractive industries. At the same time, it is the people of the variety industries who, to a large degree, set the pace and develop the commodities for everybody's leisure. Despite their numerically disproportionate power, we think it no more likely (or desirable) that a crimp be put in their power to innovate leisure styles than that a crimp be put in the production of other social inventions whose consequences may be at once liberating and discomforting. Rather, it makes sense to establish as many centers of innovation as possible, drawing on as many styles and traditions in leisure as possible, so that people in a fluid society may find their way to styles that fit them.

RELOCATION AND LEISURE

Such suggestions lead to the further observation that Americans may be moving around the country increasingly in search of good neighborhoods for leisure rather than in search of the "right job." Astute companies, in their relocation programs, recognize this and have either moved to the centers of glamour and design or to the suburbias within reach of other leisure consumables such as grass and sunshine. The service industries, such as movies and, to a degree, education, have always been free to move (though when the physical plant gets big, they find it hard to do so)— and this very fact has given them part of their quality of mixing work and play. Manufacturing industries have only recently been freed from their river and rail sites by electrification, trucking, and better highways. It will take atomic power and tank agriculture to free the extractive industries. Until this comes about, we can expect different leisure profiles to prevail in the various sectors of industry and different tensions to be set up within industry as a result.

MENACE OF STANDARDIZATION?

These last considerations may well raise in the mind of the reader the image of some "Brave New World" where everybody's leisure—at least, class and ethnic group apart—is just like everybody else's. Indeed, Aldous Huxley's *Brave New World* (Harper's, 1932), like so many European antiutopias, was itself doubtless written largely as a satire on the contemporary U.S.A., whose allegedly standardized consumption patterns have been the butts for both right-wing and left-wing European writers and, in part derivatively, of American writers. While "the" Detroit car has not escaped criticism, "the" Hollywood movies, "the" radio weeper, "the" bestsellers, "the" soft drink have been thought of as inviting menaces which threaten to Americanize the world. How much truth is there in this picture?

Some, of course, as with any stereotype. But the paradoxical result of this kind of highly generalized criticism is to prolong a situation in which detailed criticism of American leisure commodities is much less mature than the commodities themselves. A single John Crosby, taking radio and TV seriously, is worth more to the improvement of the American leisure horizon than any number of English satirists on American safari. A single James Agee, criticizing movies (and now making them) is worth more than many facile writers who have scored easily off Hollywood's vagaries. Serious criticism of the popular arts and of mass-produced commodities from an aesthetic point of view, as, for instance, in John Kouwenhoven's *Made in America* (Doubleday, 1949), is one of our greatest needs.

MASS PRODUCTION MAY MAKE VARIETY POSSIBLE

Furthermore, it is our belief that the very growth of mass production leads to a decline in standardization. It is only in the early stages of industrialization that handicraft production and consumption are driven out by inferior machine-made processes. Later on, industrialization permits the enhancement of variety because new machine tools and distribution channels (e.g., quick freezing) permit a much more adaptable meeting of various nuances of consumer demand. The class market of precapitalist days gives way to the mass market, and this in turn gives way to what we might term the class-mass market, which is large enough to allow modern machinery and small enough to encourage modern variety.

True, inadequate use has been made as yet of these potentialities. We have more variety in canned goods then in canned entertainment. But the one hue and cry of "standardization" covers both the advancing and the retrograde fields and helps blind us to the existing possibilities for creating still more flexible leisure and consumption patterns.

In terms of research, what we need are some good, intensive studies of the "leisure profiles" of individuals of different class, ethnic, age, sex, and character groups. We believe these will reveal considerable variety. True, the variety will be composed of selections from a fairly standardized set of available commodities and recreations, though one might by the same token define mosaics or sonnets as standardized. We are caught here, as previously indicated, by the market research or economistic orientation of the bulk of our researches into leisure and consumption thus far. It will require a more individualized approach to research to discover a more individualized picture of leisure in America.

LEISURE AND CONFIDENCE IN LIFE

We ask: "What are the outstanding gains and losses, from the point of view of human values, arising out of leisure time and its uses in modern industrial society?" The question has some interesting implications. For one thing, it is strange that leisure time could be considered a loss. Traditionally, civilization has been based on the freeing of men from routine economic production in order to enable them to pursue refinement, cultivation, and statesmanship. If men, then, use their leisure in ways that are considered vulgar or unstatesmanlike, there appear to be some who would prefer to send these culprits back to their toil, where they would at least be out of sight. Sometimes it is the very lightness and casualness with which many factory workers accept their new-found leisure which annoys those more ascetic critics whose own leisure is scarcer in quantity and more problematic in quality. (Conversely, there is a tendency among social scientists today, not mitigated by Kinsey, to think that the lower classes have all the fun, the middle classes all the miseries and inhibitions—not a very original version of pastoral!)

LEISURE: MEANS OR END

The question above has still another aspect: its implication that the uses of leisure time are to be valued by reference to a larger human world of which leisure is only a part. There is a danger, already seen, of regarding leisure as a means even to a very broad "something else"—as any kind of value beyond itself. Since the dilemma of means and ends in human action can never be entirely escaped, we will tend to come up with different research and policy suggestions for the leisure sphere depending on whether "leisure" is the major premise or whether the "something else" is. Hence, it is not surprising that this dilemma goes back at least to Plato and Aristotle, the former of whom tended to regard leisure in the form of art as instrumental, while the latter was prepared to grant it a wider autonomy.

In the latter view, man's humanity consists partly in his ability to react to Nature by enjoying the coinage of artificial natures: the game, the mathematical formula, the poem or painting. A later philosopher, the romantic Schiller, went so far as to argue that play is the area of the distinctly human—the psychological domain in which men value indeterminacy and freedom for their own sakes. Reviewing this historical argument of philosophers and students of aesthetics, it is apparent that much of what men are likely to conclude about the use of leisure springs from their own and their culture's philosophic commitment.

DOES CONFIDENCE GO WITH PLAY?

The question arises, however, whether we cannot limit somewhat this relativity of judgments if we can compare groups and cultures which give leisure a high priority and a reasonable autonomy with those which turn leisure into something like a "strength through joy" movement or try to banish it altogether. Will the hypothesis stand up, for instance, that those societies marked by high confidence in life (Pericles' Athens, for example) also tend, other things being equal, to be those which have elaborated the leisure culture in spontaneous and interesting ways? Is it perhaps the case that play constitutes a sort of growth hormone for the society at large? If a psychologically disturbed child is typically one who suffers from what Erikson calls "play disruption," may not a sick society be one whose play has either been suppressed or has become a means to other ends?

In answering such questions—and in the present state of our knowledge they may not be answerable at all—we cannot of course assume that we can always recognize play and players. This follows from our analysis of the overlaps between leisure and work. The Puritans, for example, are supposed not to have known how to play, and certainly they have cast a pall over some kinds of play. Only now are we recovering from it. But such a man as Calvin may well have hidden his "play of the mind" within the folds of his elaborate legalistic arguments, while among his followers prophetic interpretations of the Bible often took on the character of a parlor game. Conversely, a glance at some aspects of

American competitive sport suffices to show that players are often the hardest kind of workers, so that college football under a coach like Blaik is more like the assembly line than the assembly line itself.

Even if we can learn to recognize play, can we learn to recognize confidence in life? In one of the first and most famous efforts at creating an index for such a topic, Emile Durkheim tried to use comparative suicide rates as a measure. Studies of absenteeism or accident rates in factories and Army units follow in his lead, in tying an objectively measurable and quantifiable index to a subtler mental state of confidence or morale.

One danger of such work lurks in the possibility that situations which drive some to suicide are precisely those which allow others to achieve an exalted confidence. Negroes, we know, have a lower suicide rate than whites, but have they—perhaps they do—a higher confidence rate? Durkheim's researches led him to a critical estimate of modern industrial society, which, compared with pre-capitalist patterns, had a higher rate of suicide, especially among the leading professional and business groups. His negative view has been echoed by social critics and social scientists for the past fifty years. Yet obviously many of these writers, had they lived in the precapitalist era, would have succumbed to the high mortality rates and thus not lived long enough to contemplate suicide! And we ourselves believe that the same individualistic tendencies which lead some to suicide also lead others to those innovations in ways of living which can make abundant leisure less of a threat and more of a promise.

GAMBLING

Looking only at those who fall by their own hands, Durkheim's index is therefore inadequate as a test for a more than merely conventional and customary confidence in life. Studies of gambling and attitudes toward gains and losses in the several social and psychological categories might turn out to be a better index. Some seem to gamble from despair, others from casualness, still others from hope.

A case in point. How little we know about the economic and the social motivations of gambling is an index of how little we know about leisure in general. While anthropologists have studied gambling in primitive tribes and have suggested that it may take its rise when movable goods become part of the economic order, we have no comparable studies for the various social classes in America. Mark Benney, of the London School of Economics, has suggested that the amount and kind of gambling in a social group is an indication of that group's attitude toward its life-chances in the larger society. For the lower-class person, his job is a gamble, his economic security is fictitious; so, losing all the big chances, he takes the little ones. In the lower-middle class, hard-working people believe that, if they cumulate all their little chances, they may have the big chance of moving a step up the social ladder; and they seldom gamble. Still higher up, there is a surplus with which to gamble, and a new set of motivations takes over. If this pattern is borne out by the studies Benney has inaugurated, it would be a further indication that work and leisure—and, more broadly, life and leisure—exist in terms of tensions and polarities.

Gambling, however, unless it turns into the kind of capitalist caricature of those who try to win at roulette through a "system," comes close to the extreme case of a leisure activity which is fundamentally passive and unconducive to growth. It can vary the rhythms of life; it can provide escape and excitement; but it seems to have its strongest hold on those who—like the Chinese laundrymen, who are said to gamble away their laundries in a night—have very impoverished resources either for work or play. We would expect that in a full employment, wide abundance society, gambling would become a mild diversion and lose its narcotic quality. For an index of confidence in life that will, so to speak, grow with the country, we must turn elsewhere.

DEVELOPING CONFIDENCE IN LIFE THROUGH COMPETENCE IN LEISURE

We have no answer to this problem, but we believe that shrewd analysis of leisure trends may lead to an answer. In a society in which competence in work is no longer a self-evident requirement either for individual or for social advance, competence in leisure may have to take over much of the justificatory quality previously found in work. That is, by developing ability in leisure skills, people may be able to circumvent social tendencies that make their work skills obsolete. With time on our hands, we can educate people for their leisure in ways that we have only begun to do; we need greatly to expand the panoply of those we may call the "avocational counselors."

Moreover, with the developments that have taken place in America in the past few years, we need not be entirely visionary and utopian—though we need to be much more visionary and utopian than we have been—in contemplating the possibilities for greatly developing leisure competence and hence, by our hypothesis, confidence in life. Having frequently been curious about the decline of the little-theater movement from an experimental avant-garde to a retelling and retailing of Broadway hits (some of these, to be sure, of interesting quality), we recently discovered right in our own Chicago neighborhood three different amateur groups who have been putting on "theater in the round" of unusual drama, based on a few rehearsals but no memorization of lines. Players and audience alike enjoy themselves. The spread of Sunday painters, of chamber music amateurs, of movie art theaters—these developments are well known to readers of Harper's excellent "After Hours" column, a column which is itself (like its fellow, "Accent on Living," in the Atlantic) a sign of increased curiosity about American leisure. Most of these developments have occurred without much assistance from organized educational and recreational agencies.

Indeed, such assistance has, as we have pointed out, a two-edged aspect: it may rob leisure of the very freedom and spontaneity which make leisure valuable. However, if we are alert to this danger, we can begin to explore ways of making leisure competence more widely available through communal action.

ACTIVITIES OF UNIONS AND ADULT EDUCATION AGENCIES

As one consultant points out, labor unions are increasingly on the lookout for spheres of action other than their traditional jousts with management. (See further on this, C. M. W. Hart, Report on Windsor—an account of union, extraplant activity in this Ontario town.) Having read Mayo too, they are indeed beginning to concern themselves with some of the same areas of worker dissatisfaction that perplex conscientious managers, and they compete with management in offering workers a life outside the plant.

While workers' adult education continues to be a pious preparation for union stewardship or civic right-mindedness in the intention of its sponsors (and a quiet preparation for mobility out of labor's ranks for many of its students), there seems to be some awareness that adult education, even for workers, can be treated as a luxury, as an exercise in intellectual and discursive pleasure.

Similarly, some public libraries are sponsoring discussion programs, music programs, and many other cultural activities that help channel leisure interests into challenging and skill-requiring pursuits. A critical survey of such developments throughout the country would be of considerable help to students of leisure and to those in search of models for their own practical contribution to the enhancement of the leisure arts.

CRAFT HOBBIES

Another set of new developments has been called to our attention by Lynn White, jr. He points to the way in which people have in many places begun to use their leisure to develop craft hobbies, such as pottery making, which have then turned into minor sources of income and have actually increased the variety of consumption commodities on the market. He sees this process, if greatly expanded, potentially as leading to satisfying leisure for the hobbyist and to the advancement of the taste and décor of the clients. (We will add to his long list of items which are now being produced in this way the enormous number of homes which families, especially veterans, have been building for themselves with little help and great feelings of competence in the post-World War II period.) As we have already implied in this paper, this view may tend to underplay the qualitative aspects of less strenuous leisure activities and to exaggerate the suitability for all character types of craftsmanlike leisure patterns. Still, for many this will be one good highroad to competence. The principle here should be: to each his own.

SELECTED BIBLIOGRAPHY

General

Bothoul, Gaston, "La durée du travail et l'utilisation des loisirs," *International Labor Review*, vol. IX (January-July, 1949).

Dulles, Foster Rhea, *America Learns to Play*. Appleton, 1940.

Huizinga, J., *Homo Ludens*. Roy, 1949.

Lundberg, George A., Mirra Komarovsky, and Mary A. McInerny, *Leisure: A Suburban Study*. Columbia University Press, 1934.

Lynd, Robert S., and Helen Merrell Lynd, *Middletown*. Harcourt, Brace, 1929.

Riesman, David, Reuel Denney, and Nathan Glazer, *The Lonely Crowd*. Yale University Press, 1950.

Rowntree, Benjamin Seebohm, *Life and Leisure*. Longmans, 1951.

Veblen, Thorstein, *The Theory of the Leisure Class*. Viking Press, 1899.

Weber, Max, *The Protestant Ethic and the Spirit of Capitalism*. Scribner's, 1948.

The Media

Huxley, Aldous, *Brave New World*. Harper & Brothers, 1932.

Legman, G., *Love and Death*. Breaking Point Press, 1949.

Leites, Nathan, and Martha Wolfenstein, *Movies: A Psychological Study*. Free Press, 1950.

Children

Dewey, John, "Play," *Cyclopedia of Education*. Macmillan, 1911-1913, vol. IV, pp. 725-729.

Erikson, Erik H., *Childhood and Society*. Norton, 1950.

Social Forms

Whyte, William F., *Street Corner Society*. University of Chicago Press, 1937.

Economics

National Income Supplements, *Survey of Current Business*. U.S. Department of Commerce.

Social Class

Warner, Lloyd, and Associates, Yankee City Series, 4 vols. Yale University Press, 1941-1947.

10

The Community in Industrial Civilization

by Francis Chase Rosecrance

Modern technology and power probably constitute the most disturbing fact of this age. While they have resulted in almost unbelievable contributions to man's means of production, transportation, communication, and ease of living, great dangers can be clearly seen. The dangers arise from our failure to meet the demands of the new technology and to make the changes in our society which it requires.

We can fly almost anywhere in the world in sixty hours. The telephone, radio, and television give us almost instantaneous communication. High-quality products at relatively low prices are available to the common man in more and more areas. Thus, technology is drawing the whole world together in one vast community and making it possible to provide the comforts of life in ever-increasing quantity.

Few people today would go back if they could to the "good old days" of backbreaking labor, monotony, and narrowness of outlook. The very scope of today's problems and the fact that men are seeking their solution make this an exciting, challenging time to be alive.

Unfortunately, the new technology is also responsible for many less desirable features of modern life. Economic depressions and unemployment occur, sometimes followed by migrations and class conflicts which confuse and divide people who formerly lived and worked in harmony. Although we know how to release the full power of technology in modern warfare, we do not yet know how to release this power in peacetime, and war is due in part to this fact. Individuals are confused concerning issues of right and wrong. Is it right to have machines idle when their products are needed? Is it right for one community of workers to destroy crops when another community of persons goes hungry?

One important present-day leader declares that the central problem of our time is how to eliminate poverty without undue concentration of power in the hands of management, labor, or the government. Another insists that the preservation of freedom—freedom of the press, freedom of thought, freedom of religion, freedom to own property, freedom of enterprise, and liberty under due process of law—is our most important responsibility. Which shall it be, security or liberty—or can we have both?

SENSE OF BELONGING

Perhaps the most serious evil resulting from industrial civilization is the loss of the sense of meaning of life for the individual and his fellows. Life has creative meaning for men only when they see that what they are doing is so connected with what others are doing and with social progress as a whole that they can see their contribution to the whole ongoing process. If they do not feel a part of it, their activity seems to be a dead-end, and they say, "What's the use?" Distress, anxiety, discontent cut deeply where this sense of belonging does not exist.

What has happened in modern industrial society to the satisfactions which come from feeling a part of some community? Have communities and the relations of individuals to them changed in such ways that many people lack that vital sense of belonging? What can we do to recapture, under modern industrial conditions, some of the human values that may have been lost in this way?

DEFINITIONS OF COMMUNITY

It is proposed in this paper to use the word "community" in two ways. First, it will be used in the neighborhood or geographical sense and, second, in a psychological, emotional, and philosophical sense. Readers will understand that it is possible for an individual to live in a community and not have a "sense of community" with any person or group in this social structure. They will also understand that the social structure without a community of spirit cannot long survive; the latter must undergird the former.

A community has been defined as "a population aggregate, inhabiting contiguous territory, integrated through common experience, possessing a number of basic service institutions, conscious of its unity, and able to act in a cooperative capacity." (Cook, *Community Backgrounds of Education.* McGraw-Hill, 1938.)

While the focus of this definition is on the local community—the village, town, or city; the township, parish, or county—one would like to believe that wherever individuals have a feeling of interdependence there a community exists; hence, that a region —the state or a regional grouping of states, a nation considered as a whole, and the earth itself, the only truly integral area— have potentialities for becoming a "community" as here defined. Within each of these communities are so-called specific interest groups, such as the family, church, school, labor union, business, intercultural and recreational agencies, whose effect on the individual's sense of community must also be appraised.

Therefore, it is proposed to examine the effect of our industrial civilization (1) on the individual's sense of community in various kinds and sizes of community structural organizations and (2) in specific interest groups found therein. A sense of community involves not only an individual's feeling of identification but a feeling of being respected by others, a willingness to adjust personal purposes to desirable group purposes, sharing in decision making, participation in group endeavors, and a commitment to work for common ends.

INDUSTRIAL CIVILIZATION AND GEOGRAPHICAL COMMUNITIES

RURAL COMMUNITIES THEN AND NOW

The closely knit rural community groups of the early 1900's in the United States are rapidly disappearing. In these groups the same people met at church, conversed around the "cracker barrel" of the country store, went to singing school, voted at the school meetings, worked on the road together, attended husking bees, exchanged labor, teams, and equipment at threshing time, discussed the problems of running their farms, borrowed from one another, and celebrated the Fourth of July together.

Not only did most individuals participate in social functions but their desires were almost identical with the social code. Youths understood also the various economic activities which were a part of rural life and could forecast quite accurately their own place in that sphere.

In the older rural community the neighbors would drive by the land and comment on the height of a neighbor's grain, the straight, clean rows of cultivated corn, the number, size, and quality of his cattle and horses. Here a man's work and his purposes were easily discernible; his attitude toward "keeping up the road" was quickly assessed by the man's own actions. If he did not do his part, he did not "belong." While commonality of purpose could be discerned and participation appraised, in many ways such rural communities on outlook. Often support for the Foreign Missionary Society of the church was the sole avenue of outreach. Likewise, emerging new ideas were few. The automobile and the tractor were strongly resisted; newer methods of the fertilization of the soil, of crop seeding and rotation were adopted only after some "outlander" had demonstrated by results that they were superior.

Modern transportation and communication have greatly enlarged the radius of rural life. The farmer has shifted his business from the nearby general store to a town chain or department store, where he is able to purchase household necessities at bargain prices. As a result, stores in small trading centers have often been forced out of business.

The farm family, once dependent on nearby neighbors for human association and recreation, now travels long distances on good roads to visit friends or attend the movies. The farmer meets with one group to discuss the best ways of raising poultry, with another to discuss soil conservation, and with another dairy farming. This may enlarge his outlook and undoubtedly it improves his farming methods, but it frequently results in segmentation and disintegration in the community.

Thus, in the old farm area a large degree of unity and understanding was present, but new ideas and outreach were pretty much absent. In the new rural community, new ideas and outreach are likely to be present; but because of segmentation and disintegration, some of the unity and understanding formerly present have departed.

THE SMALL TOWN

The effect of industrial civilization on the individual living in an American village or small town (population, say, 5,000) differs largely in degree from the effects on rural people. Near the close of the nineteenth and in the early twentieth century, life in the small town was closely integrated and ingrowing as well as hard-working and uneventful. Because there were relatively few opportunities for cultural recreation, nearly everyone went to all the events—a lecture and concert series in the town opera house, the commencement address by an outside speaker at the high school graduation exercises, and a Chautaqua program during the summer.

Though the owners of the carriage factory and two or three other small concerns occupied larger homes and sent their children to expensive colleges, they were part of the town life, interested in what happened in its government and frequently serving in such important positions as that of mayor. Thus, there was a minimum of class distinction and much common interest and activity throughout the town.

In the small town, standing between country and city, there was loyalty not only to friends and kin but to the community as a whole. Here were traditions of the town meeting, the good neighbor, and action for the common good. As a rule the population contained more women than men, more oldsters than youngsters. Perhaps it is the preponderance of older people that explains the conservatism of the small town and the unwillingness to spend more for so-called "frills" in education, for a swimming pool or a community house.

THE NEW SMALL TOWN

In the small town, as well as in the rural community, advances in transportation and communication have brought many changes.

The nearby city has grown into a larger center with attractive shops and commercialized amusements, and the drive there takes the individual but a few minutes. Thus, most articles other than food are purchased there. The factories in the town are much larger and use modern assembly line methods; but they have been purchased by bigger corporations in the largest city in the state, so that the owners no longer live in town or have much interest in it or their workers, save that of profit-making, labor turnover, efficient production, and access to raw materials and markets. Consequently, the citizens of the town sometimes regard the new factory owner with resentment rather than with a sense of pride.

Most of the men and women who operate the machines live in the town or nearby. New conditions have increased class consciousness and brought conflicts. Though the rise in the standard of living has brought labor-saving devices, modern plumbing, and shorter hours of work, there is less contentment and much less of integrated community life.

Thus, with the development of modern transportation, communication, and industrial conditions, the locality bonds are giving way to special interest ties. Here it may be stated again that the shift from locality to special interest tends to divide a once-unified whole into a number of different parts. Locality loyalties devoted to the public good are replaced by pressure groups who believe that the promotion of their own special interests is the way to promote the good of all. Whether or not this is true, the techniques of social and political action change from the town meeting, with its face-to-face discussion and show of hands, to the processes of organized promotion and propaganda.

Modern science and technology are changing the small town, as they have changed rural life. The form and sense of community, too, have been altered; whether this is for good or ill is not yet clear.

THE SMALL CITY

The effects of industrial civilization became evident even earlier in the small city. Early in the twentieth century sidewalks, streetcars, street lights, brick or cobblestone streets, fire engines horse-drawn, livery stables, hitching posts and rings, and an occasional auto-wagon were all visible evidence to the individual of a different, if not more advanced, kind of community. A few neighborhood stores catered to local trade of those who bought in small quantities,

MORE PEOPLE HAVE MOVED TO THE CITIES

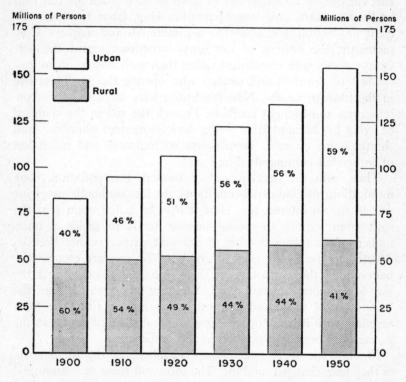

but in the downtown district specialism, though not so great as today, was already in evidence. Grocery stores, dry goods stores, drugstores, shoe stores, boys' and men's furnishings, hardware stores with attached sheet metal shops, "palaces of sweets," piano and furniture stores, bakeries, and scores of other kinds of commercial enterprises accented the change from the multipurpose store of rural areas.

It did not take a keen observer to discover that the small city was located usually at the site of some access to power—water provided by a river, or coal provided by a railroad—or at the intersection of some trade or commerce route. Here were the magnets that attracted factories, providing employment for local residents for small-town or farm boys who wanted to get away from home, and for cheap labor imported from other sections of the country or from abroad.

At the beginning of the century only 40 per cent of the total population of the U.S. lived in the cities. With greater industrial development this percentage has increased to 59 per cent, as shown by the preceding chart. This trend and its effect upon the community and a sense of community are significant.

THE SAME SMALL CITY TODAY

The midwestern city, described above as it was soon after the turn of the century, has developed from these beginnings of industrialization into a modern business community, known throughout the United States for its products. It has numerous large factories now, many of which have strong ties with outside associations, some of which are parts of national industrial concerns with the center of control in New York City. The city has modern hotels, fine stores, many amusement places. In spite of the excellent stores, a large number of the well-to-do go to a large metropolis some distance away for the bulk of their shopping.

Class stratification, the beginnings of which were indicated in the early 1900's, has become much stronger. There is the dominant country-club set composed of high-salaried, conservative business executives as well as bankers, owners of commercial establishments, and some professional people. There is a large group in the middle-income brackets who live comfortably. There are also the skilled workers and the unskilled laborers. Unionization has progressed to a marked degree in spite of the paternalistic attitude of many of the employers toward the workers, and there is some conflict between labor and management.

Though there are some apartment houses, most people live in

homes, and a high percentage own their own homes. There is no real slum district. There are the usual service clubs, lodges, women's organizations, and churches. Cultural opportunities are present but somewhat limited.

It is easily apparent that the specialism found in cities in commercial and industrial life is paralleled in social intercommunication. Though belonging to different churches, women may be together in a Woman's Club, separated in auxiliary societies, send their children to different schools, be interested in the same charities, but belong to different political parties. Men in the business class likewise tend to be divided not only from their own fellow businessmen but from the great majority of workers. Workers live in separate sections of the city, belong to their own labor unions, bowling teams, and social groups. Because they live "across the tracks," they feel apart from, if not inferior to, the business group, even though their children may attend the same high school.

This separation is reflected in the groups which represent different interests in the community. There is the Council of Social Agencies, concerned with family and child welfare; the health council concerned with preventing epidemics and promoting good health; the recreation commission which agitates for playgrounds, parks, and athletic fields; the housing authority which insists that good health, high moral standards, and the prevention of juvenile delinquency cannot be achieved without good living conditions; and the chamber of commerce, which tends to believe that the welfare of all the aforementioned depends on the economic health of the community which, from its vantage point, means lower taxes and less public service.

Often, too often, the separation in cities, fostered by industrial civilization, has so divided communities that both the sense of direction and the will for united action have not developed. The total problems of the community go unsolved; citizens develop a sense of futility and look to the state capital or Washington, D.C., for the solution of their problems.

THE METROPOLIS

In the great metropolitan areas we have at once the highest concentration of advantages of industrial society and the greatest evils of it. The larger the city, the more it is likely to be dominated by industrial and commercial activities. Since professional people like to live close to their work, towering apartment houses and skyscrapers have become identified with the metropolis. In one of the latter as many as 30,000 people work; in one of the former are housed as many people as are found in an average village. These concentrations of people both at work and at home present great opportunities and problems.

In the metropolis there is both natural and artificial segregation: natural when commuters choose to live outside the city or when workers live near their work in the city, and artificial when ethnic groups voluntarily or by compulsion live in certain prescribed areas.

The metropolis has all the problems of the city and more. Anonymity is frequently sought, and in some cities to seek to know your neighbors is to be resented. While the problems of the slums are great, the development of a sense of community in any part of a metropolis is a staggering task. Yet Cook says,

The metropolis is a community because it functions as one. It collects taxes and revenues; it makes ordinances and enforces laws. It provides a host of indispensable public utility services. It protects life and property, establishes relief and welfare agencies, provides free public education, and organizes recreational activities for needy children. It zones the city for building purposes, regulates commercial concerns, advertises the area's resources and advantages, and plans for its future expansion. If the concept of community is not to be discarded as outworn, it must be applied to corporate undertakings of this nature.

Difficult though the development of the structure and the sense of community may be in a metropolitan area, yet, if it is attacked with all the media now available, even this problem may yield to solution.

Since there can be no turning back to the life of an earlier and simpler day, no alternative appears to exist but to work for social cooperation in rural areas, small towns, cities, and metropolitan regions. Already years of neglect and internal competition have led to disruption and disorganization.

Collaboration in an industrial society cannot be left to chance. Historically and traditionally social cooperation was inherent in the situation, and hence it was easily achieved. Mass production and its attendant specialization have produced a different kind of situation. It, too, calls for cooperation but a form of cooperation that is not inherent in the situation. It will be much more difficult to achieve, yet if we would avoid disaster, we must work at it.

Industrial civilization, as has been noted, has created many groups, some of which may appear to have conflicting interests. Among these are some of long standing, like the home, the church, and the school; others of more recent origin, like labor groups, business groups, recreation agencies, and intercultural bureaus. Before examining the fundamental questions of how a sense of community may be developed and how a community may organize itself to solve its problems when it is composed of groups which have conflicting or even antagonistic interests, some attention should be given to the impact of industrial civilization on each of these groups.

INDUSTRIAL CIVILIZATION AND THE INDIVIDUAL'S RELATIONS TO SPECIAL GROUPS

THE FAMILY

Many authors have pointed out that the family once had many more functions than it has today. Indeed, probably the most truly revolutionary effect of the Industrial Revolution has been its impact on the family. In it formerly was centered not only the biological function of race survival, but it was the primary social carrier of love and affection, the chief institution of economic production, the main educational agency, the center of recreational activities, and the fountainhead of religious training. These various functions served to bind the members of the family together. Except for the biological and psychological functions, other institutions have grown up to take the family's place—the factory, the school, the recreation center. In the early days mother, father, and children shared in the activities and work of the family as an economic producing unit. With industrialization the father goes to work in a plant or office miles from home, and the wife and children often do not know about nor appreciate his work life. Likewise, the father does not understand the problems of the mother, who too often has been bequeathed the sole responsibility of caring for the home and children.

The transfer of the production of economic goods from the home to stores, offices, and factories has not only weakened the family bonds of activities but it has opened up new work opportunities for women. In World War II women became skilled welders in airplane factories and in many other occupations new to them, working in many instances alongside of men. Not only single women but married women are holding jobs in factories, stores, and offices. "Door-key children" were well known during the war, and some evidence indicates that today more and more women are attempting to have both a home and children and a career. While such occupations release women from the drudgery of housework and baby tending and give them a feeling of being part of important affairs, in too many cases the child feels neglected and his sense of security in the home is threatened. Hence, though industrialization has given the family a larger income, it has contributed in still another way to the weakening of the ties that have held the family together.

Up to the beginning of World War II, all these factors had a depressing effect on the birth rate. Formerly children had been an economic asset because their help added to the productive unit. With urban living, mechanization of industry, and restrictive labor laws, they have become an economic liability. However, it seems safe to assert that no civilization has developed an adequate substitute for the role of the family in providing love and affection, which appear to be absolute necessities for the building of wholesome personalities. Nevertheless, in the last forty years this function has been threatened by the marked increase in separation and divorce.

THE HOME AND HOUSING

It has been asserted that it is far more difficult to develop a real community life if the majority of people in a neighborhood are tenants. Home ownership seems to go hand in hand with a predisposition for education and the building of good communities and democratic citizenship.

In the early thirties the President's Committee on Recent Social Trends reported that in large cities and their suburbs there had been a general increase in the percentage of dwelling units found in apartments. This seemed to be changing the manner of life of people. Here families live side by side, often never knowing each other's names and not speaking in the hallways or elevators. Janitorial and sometimes maid service are provided. There are few, if any, "chores" for children to do; often there is no place for them to play. These "cliff dwellers" who live in skyscraper apartments seem severely handicapped in building a sense of community among themselves. Their roots in community life are not deep.

It is encouraging to learn, according to data released by the Housing and Finance Agency (New York Times, March 3, 1951), that more American families now own their homes than ever before in history. According to these data, 53 per cent of all the houses in towns and cities and 65 per cent in the farming areas were owned by their occupants. The number of owner-occupied homes in the U.S. rose 71 per cent between 1940 and 1950, "the largest increase for any decade on record."

These favorable figures, however, should not cloud the fact that hundreds of thousands of families live in crowded quarters in small apartments, in unsanitary conditions in tenements which ought to be condemned, and in neighborhoods so crowded that delinquency and crime are fairly commonplace. The kind of living accommodation is a big factor in the way people feel about their homes and determines in large part whether they enjoy being at home or want to escape from it.

THE CHURCH

The Renaissance and the Protestant Reformation, the development of science, the Industrial Revolution, the development of modern capitalism, the creation of a great middle class, and growth of political democracy and its *sine qua non*, compulsory, free, tax-supported education, provide the backdrop for an understanding of the church and its place in the community today.

In the past the church, more than any other institution except the family, has stated the standards and values of life. Even though the value of church property has increased and church membership has kept pace with the general growth in population, yet with the development of industrial civilization religion claims much less attention and the church has found its influence and authority challenged or ignored. One may wonder if a decade of cold and hot wars with the attendant increase of brutality, aggressiveness, anxiety, and dependence upon materialistic values may not drive society to an increased emphasis on moral and spiritual values in the years ahead.

In the early part of this century, church membership compensated the individual in some measure for the growing "humdrum" of occupational life. Even if he worked as a finisher in the furniture factory, he might achieve status by joining the church and becoming an usher, then a teacher, superintendent of the Sunday school, member of the official board, and perhaps, though not likely, a member of the board of trustees. Today it is no longer true that the individual acquires such status by joining the church or holding these offices. Indeed, he may find none of his business associates or neighbors in his community at his church or any church. From the point of view of social status in the eyes of those who count in his life, there is not much to be gained by church membership. Indeed, it may even cause him to be regarded by some as a trifle naïve.

"Nowhere does the modern church fail more dismally," says Swift (*New Frontiers of Religion*), "than in its sincere and often Herculean effort to make itself the center of the social life of the community." As in the case of the small community and the home, the impact of science and technology has been to keep people away from church. Too many commercial interests compete successfully for the citizen's leisure time.

It is true that religion offers the individual important values apart from social ties, and these will be dealt with in another roundtable; but it is also true that the church most strongly influences the beliefs, ideals, and activities of individuals when it has many opportunities for a close relationship with people. In remote parts of the United States, not so fully affected by technological developments as the large metropolitan areas, the church still ministers in an effective way to individuals whose interests and hazards of life are quite fully shared. As has previously been indicated, however, the rural community and hence the rural church have not escaped the impact of industrial civilization. The latter, too, has been pushed toward the circumference of the social circle.

With the apparent need in mid-twentieth century for a resurgence of emphasis on moral and spiritual values and the possibility of decentralization of industries and cities, one may well speculate how these movements, if they occur, will affect the church. Like the home, the church has been the passive recipient of the industrial age. Both have been the beneficiaries and victims of improved means of transportation, the development of mass media of communication, and the productive power of the economic system. It may be prophesied that the home and the church, both the standard-bearers of moral and spiritual values, must abandon the role of passive recipients and become prime movers in promulgating these values.

THE SCHOOL AND COLLEGE

From 1616, the date of the founding of Harvard, the first college in America, to the present day, faith in education as an indispensable prerequisite to democratic government has been strong.

Perhaps one of the best early affirmations of this faith is the statement of Congress in the Ordinance of 1787 providing for the government of the territory lying north of the Ohio River:

Religion, morality, and knowledge being necessary to good government and the happiness of mankind, schools and the means of education shall be forever encouraged.

In harmony with this view, the states, through compulsory attendance laws and financial grants-in-aid to school districts, encouraged everyone to finish elementary school. More recently we are approaching the goal of a secondary school education for all American youth; and up to the period of the current international emergency, higher education seemed on the verge of an expansion that might parallel that of elementary and secondary education. Without the productive power of our economic system and the higher standards of living flowing therefrom, this growth would not have been possible.

Educational development in this country has been essentially democratic in spirit. It did not follow the class lines of European schools but has been open to all the children of all the people. It has been the one common core of experience which has tended to preserve, defend, and extend our American heritage and culture. Perhaps it may be said that in an important sense free, public, nonsectarian education has provided the social cement which has tended to hold the bricks of our democratic society together.

Like the home and the church, the school has been definitely affected by our industrial civilization. From industry was copied the specialization of labor, so that schools, particularly in large cities, were run like factories. At the sound of a bell, senior high school boys and girls pass from classroom to classroom where different subjects are taught them by trained and certified specialists in these fields. This plan was extended downward to the junior high school, when it came into existence in the second decade of this century. In some school systems the departmental or platoon plan, in modified form, was extended as low as the second grade.

The aggregation of population in large cities resulted in huge school organizations with as many as 9,000 or 10,000 students per unit in some instances. Impersonalization of the school and mass production of the output were almost inevitable. Under such a factory system of education it was possible that a youth might graduate from a public school system having had as many as 100 different teachers in twelve years, none of whom knew him intimately. This form of educational organization made it unlikely that the individual student would feel that he was understood or that he would develop a real sense of belonging to his group.

FRAGMENTED EDUCATION

Cowley asserts that prior to the Civil War colleges and universities were concerned with the all-round development of the individual. With the importation of the research emphasis from German industries and German universities and the development of the factory system in America, college administrators and professors became interested primarily in subject fields and in the academic accomplishments of students and less and less interested in the total growth of mind, body, and spirit of the college student. This fragmentation of knowledge, of personal contacts, and of experience carries with it many implications which cannot be discussed here.

As a reaction against such fragmentation, one professional organization (The Foundation for Integrated Education, Inc.) has made the following statement of beliefs:

(1) American culture stands in greatest need of being saved from disintegration. The factors producing disintegration are not only external, but they are internal as well.
(2) In a democracy, integrating efforts must come from men whose concern it is to produce and to propagate cultural values.
(3) General education, various forms of which are now wide-spread in American schools and colleges, is designed to offer types of knowledge that are deemed unifying. Its effects are salutary and are already felt.

Despite these statements, there are too many schools and colleges in which the dignity and worth of each individual, regardless of creed, color, intelligence, and economic status, are not respected. There are too many where young people have no chance to share in making decisions. There are too many in which valuable bits of knowledge are taught without relation to other bits of knowledge or to the realities of the world in which we live. Moreover, the tendency has been to stress competition among students at the expense of cooperation. Though the school and college, like the church and home, have been the passive recipients of the effects of our industrial society, these deficiencies cannot be attributed solely to this cause.

LABOR GROUPS

It is a truism to say that had there been no industrial revolution followed by mass production, there would have been no labor unions as we know them today. As long as "hired men" worked alongside of or had personal contact with their employers, they had a sense of purpose and dignity in their work and there was little need for labor organization. With the formation of the corporation, the development of huge factories, and the consequent loss of personal contact of the employer, no matter how benevolent, with his employees, the need for a feeling of unity among the workers grew.

As another roundtable will examine the effect of work on the individual, it is not proposed to discuss the features of unionism here. Rather, the purpose is to consider the effect of the existence of labor unions on the individual's sense of community.

In an industrial system where the tools and materials of production are entirely owned and controlled by management and the worker has only his labor to sell, membership in an organization which aims to improve the conditions under which he works, as well as to increase his paycheck, gives him a sense of security he would otherwise lack. The seniority system provides job protection and makes him feel confident of advancement. In meetings of his union, his vote counts and he feels that he has shared in decisions. If his union provides recreational, educational, and other welfare benefits, his sense of belonging to a group is strengthened. When union leaders make all the decisions, the worker's sense of participation ceases to exist, and he loses interest and often pays his dues unwillingly.

BUSINESS GROUPS

If it is true that unions have emphasized security, entrepreneurs have stressed freedom—freedom of competition, freedom of enterprise. The energy of the American capitalistic system resulting in the highest per capita income and wealth in the world has been tremendous.

In the early 1900's small businesses could be started and, with good management, had some chance of success. With mass production, nation-wide advertising, and national distribution through chain stores and huge mail-order and department stores, it has become more difficult for an individual to start to make a success of business. So-called heartless corporations, which froze out competitors and were run by absentee owners, were the subject of sharp criticism in the 1920's and 1930's. Whether this criticism was justified or not, in recent years a high sense of community responsibility is emerging on the part of the executives of some great corporations. An illustration of this new attitude is the recent statement of Frank Abrams, chairman of the board of Standard Oil of New Jersey: "The corporation bears the same relationship and should discharge the same responsibility as an individual in taking an active interest in the welfare of the community."

The Cooperative Movement represents an example of business groups which have joined together for purposes of production or distribution or both. While not all business organizations containing the word "cooperative" in their business titles operate on the Rochdale principles for cooperatives, those that do provide the opportunity for a real sense of community between buyers and sellers, producers and consumers.

INTERGROUP TENSIONS

Intergroup tensions were greatly increased in the early days of industrialization when large industries brought thousands of immigrants into the country in order to secure a cheaper labor supply. Workers in these plants naturally resented the "foreigners" who took over their jobs and lowered the standard of living for all workers. However, with the passage of immigration laws, such importation of workers was reduced, and the American labor force became more stable and the workers more secure.

The beneficial effects of industrialization on relations between races is best seen in factories, offices, and commercial establishments where one observes members of different races working together cooperatively and on a basis of equality both in kind of job and rate of pay. While these ideal conditions are not too generally found, and though we must admit they are frequently as much the result of an FEPC bill and pressure from other sources as of the policies of progressive management and unions, we still must recognize that there are few facets of American life where interracial and intergroup barriers are breaking down as rapidly as in the modern industrial plant. When men of different groups work together, they grow to appraise and respect each other as individuals rather than as representatives of a race. Many studies that have been made indicate that when individuals of different ethnic groups have the opportunity really to know each other, antagonistic attitudes tend to disappear.

RECREATIONAL AGENCIES

Organized recreational agencies were practically unheard of and for the most part unneeded in the days before the Industrial Revolution. Though the hours of work were long, work was not so monotonous as in a modern factory, and the worker had the satisfaction of carrying through the process of the completed product.

Though women's work was arduous also and afforded little time for fun, women knew that their work was necessary to the well-being of the family and consequently derived satisfaction from it. Moreover, being a member of the large family of that day was in itself a socializing experience, and the close-knit community life in the country and the small town provided considerable opportunity for contact with one's fellows in work and play.

The urgent need for organized recreational facilities coincided with the development of large industries with their mass production methods and the crowding of large populations into city areas. Here the need for social centers, playgrounds, and such character-building agencies as the Boy Scouts, the YMCA, and YWCA are too obvious to require elaboration. The problem is that these agencies are all too few and too poorly financed to give the amount of service that is required and that the need for such agencies in small towns and rural areas has not been sufficiently realized.

MASS MEDIA OF COMMUNICATION

Reference has already been made to the fact that the United States and the other nations of the world have been drawn into one big community by modern methods of transportation and communication. They are also linked together by commercial interdependence. It seems appropriate at this point to examine in particular the effects of the mass media of communication. From the point of view of influence, it has already been indicated that they are pushing schools and churches into a corner. Roughly speaking, here is a numerical count of the extent of their coverage in the United States:

1,800 newspapers with 51,000,000 readers
2,000 magazines with 200,000,000 readers
  250 comic books with 40,000,000 readers
1,900 movie houses with 90,000,000 patrons
  250 television stations with 15,000,000 viewers
2,000 radio stations which are listened to 3½ hours a day by the
       average American

It would appear that this is communication's golden age, but are we making the most of the scientific advances represented by these media? More particularly, are they or can they be of use in developing a sense of community among those who read, listen, and watch? News broadcasts have made the names of faraway places familiar to all Americans and have contributed to our general information about distant lands, but does such information of itself contribute materially to our sense of community with those who live in such countries?

WHAT IS BEING DONE?

An awareness of what was happening to people and communities as a result of the new industrial processes began to develop almost as soon as the processes themselves became widespread. In the beginning there were demands and proposals for the protection of the individual against bad working conditions in most factories, lack of sanitation in crowded urban areas, excessive hours of work, effects of prolonged unemployment, and many others. As early as 1912 a few cities conducted surveys to learn what most needed to be done; and the Country Life Commission, established by President Theodore Roosevelt in 1911, was the results of a growing awareness of the changing conditions, particularly in rural America.

VARIED ATTACKS

Since these beginnings there have been many and varied attacks on the problems until, according to Wayland J. Hayes (*Revolution—Community Style*), by 1947 about one-fourth of the communities in the United States were seeking to develop and control some of the most signficant relationships of men and women by means of formal community organization other than government. Moreover, the agencies working to bring about such community organization are legion—health and welfare associations, churches, state and local boards of education, state universities and private colleges, agricultural colleges, state committees, planning associations, labor unions, and farm bureaus, to name only a few. Frequently a successful community movement has been the result of the vision and leadership of one person.

This being the situation, it would be impossible within the scope of this paper to do more than briefly summarize the achievements of a few of the better known and more successful experiments in developing better communities through cooperative action and in the promotion of a sense of community in our country. The inclusion of one case and omission of another does not mean that the latter is less well known or less successful, only that it was desirable to illustrate different types of cases and that a selection had to be made.

RURAL

The Carroll (Georgia) Service Council, operating on a country-wide basis, has individuals working on agricultural, recreational, religious, educational, and industrial committees. Some of the outstanding results have been a recreation program, employment of a country health nurse, a regional library, and a country-wide fund raising campaign for social agencies.

SMALL TOWN

In Kingsport, Tennessee, conferences on the social and economic problems of democracy caused a group of young people in one of the churches to take the initial steps in forming the Kingsport Christian Youth Association. This group made a careful survey of living conditions among the Negro population of the city, with the following results, among others: a government low-rent housing project for Negroes to replace the houses in the worst area; a day nursery for small Negro children, which was operated efficiently for four years under the direction of the group and then taken over by the school board; an extension library in the high school, for Negroes; a city-sponsored recreation program with playgrounds for both races and year-round indoor activities; and joint meetings of white and Negro Christian Youth Associations.

SMALL CITY

In Henderson, Kentucky, the community in which the Committee for Kentucky began its work, the Committee for the City and County of Henderson studied local problems in many areas and began action on a pressing health problem—the need for sewers. Through the development of public understanding, the bond issue for sewers was voted, and the Committee applied the same techniques in meeting other problems. What Dahir (Communities for Better Living, Harper, 1950) called the "religious fervor of this movement" is well expressed in its Credo:

The Committee for the City and County of Henderson is more than an organization. It is a faith. It is a faith in the ideology of democracy. It is a physical embodiment of the belief that men and women—citizens of the same community—can assemble from different interests and occupations, from different racial stocks and religions, from different social and economic positions and, by subordinating special interests to general interests, can thereby achieve a richer, fuller community life than is separately attainable. It is a belief that the areas of agreement and unity are more important than the areas of disagreement and disunity. It is the belief that our biggest problems are held in common—that we hold the problem of disease and health in common, that we hold the problem of ignorance and enlightenment in common; that the problems of poverty and prosperity, of bad government and good government, of bad citizenship and good —all of these are problems and projects in which all citizens hold a common responsibility and for which solutions can come only through community-wide cooperation. . . . This is the statement of our faith, resting in the ancient ideals which gave birth to the United States of America. It is the credo of our democracy.

The Committee for Kentucky's radio program "Wake Up, Kentucky" did much to make people all over the state ready and eager to get together and do something to improve their own communities.

METROPOLITAN AREA

In *Kansas City, Missouri,* a city-wide program of local community organization is sponsored by the Municipal Department of Welfare. A special feature of the plan is the "community worker" who acts in the same way with respect to social problems as a county agent with respect to agricultural problems. He lives in the district, has his headquarters there, knows the people, their temperament and problems. His interest is in the over-all picture of the community and in the development of leadership and responsibility on the part of the citizens. Smaller neighborhood councils form part of the larger community council serviced by the worker. Children are involved through a Junior Citizenship organization.

The Committee for Kentucky, the New York State Citizens' Council, the Central-Illinois Community Betterment Program, the Montana Study, the Georgia Citizens' Council, the Arkansas Plan, the Ohio Farm Bureau Advisory Councils—these titles and others are indicative of the many state-wide organizations, both government and voluntary, which are concerned with the community problem and doing something about it. Space permits a brief summary of only one of these.

The purpose of the *New York State Citizens' Council* is to stimulate the formation of local councils and to assist them in an advisory capacity. The state body helps in forming local councils, advises on planning and program and on the services available by state departments and other agencies, aids in research into community needs and promotes publicity through radio, press, and films. The council also holds an annual state-wide Institute of Community Leadership as well as occasional regional meetings and publishes a monthly pamphlet called *The Community Forum*.

REGIONAL PROJECT

The results accomplished by the Tennessee Valley Authority in a large southern area embracing parts of seven states indicate what can happen in an entire region when a major multipurpose development is undertaken by government. The greatest achievement has been the raising of the general economic level of the people, first because of the wages paid to the thousands of men who worked on the project, and then through the development of cheap electric power and the manufacture of phosphates to improve the worn-out soil. But there have been other factors of "community" improvement.

The same benefits have been extended to Negro as to white farmers. As demonstration farms throughout the area proved the value of the use of phosphates, more and more farmers started using them. The consequent increases in farm incomes have lessened the racial tension, which is in large part the result of economic pressures. The feeling of accomplishment which came from many people working together—engineers, mechanics, and laborers—to produce a magnificent result also contributed to a sense of community. The TVA has encouraged rural cooperatives and community-owned refrigerators and harvesting machinery. Libraries furnished in the work camps have, in many cases, been continued by county or town. The demand for better public health services has resulted from the control of disease in the camps.

One of the important factors in achieving citizen cooperation was that early in the project the TVA stopped doing things for people and instead helped people to do things for themselves. In relation to this policy the TVA report of 1936 said, "The planning of the river's future is entrusted to the TVA. The planning of the Valley's future must be the democratic labor of many agencies and industries, and final success is as much a matter of general initiative as of general consent."

A spirit of unity in the region was evident in the way the Valley rallied behind the project when it was in trouble with Congress. People have found in TVA an agency and influence favorable to men's happiness and well-being in the Valley. Duffus and Krutch (The Valley and Its People) say: "All over the Valley little men have been growing into bigger men because they have had bigger things to do."

NATIONAL ORGANIZATION

An outcome of the National Conference on the Community held in October, 1947, was the formation of the Committee on the Community under the temporary sponsorship of the National Planning Association. The organizers of the conference listed three signs of a growing community movement in America: (1) the community movement is a swing away from overemphasis on special interest blocs and toward unity, putting loyalty to the whole ahead of loyalty to the part; (2) the democratic idea of wide citizen participation is growing; (3) the conviction is growing that the community's government must be flanked by the citizens' volunteer organizations. A fact-finding study showed that in 1947 some nine to ten thousand of our twelve thousand communities in the nation possessed none of the following organized community services: planning, welfare, community councils, human relations councils, adult education councils, economic development councils, public education councils, and good government councils.

For over a year this committee held meetings in Washington, appointed working committees on Training, Field Service, Research, Exchange and Information, and Finance. At the end of that period most of its members were involved in launching the American Council on the Community.

The *American Council on the Community* is a general-purpose national organization. It has an office in New York with an executive secretary and an office staff. It has held three conferences—one in Garden City, New York, in 1949; another in Columbus, Ohio, in 1950, and a Fontana Conference in the fall of 1951. Thus far, its program has been largely that formulated by the NPA Committee on the Community. This organization is the only one that is grounded in democratic support of persons of diverse interests and regions of the United States. While some moneys have been received from membership fees, its chief source of funds is a private donor.

WORLD AFFAIRS

Community councils on world affairs have in some places been effective in bringing local groups into closer touch with our world responsibilities. Cleveland has been a pioneer in this respect.

In the world as a whole, the basis of a sense of community is being laid through the *United Nations*. The General Assembly, Security Council, Economic and Social Council, International Trusteeship System, the International Court of Justice, International Labor Organization, Food and Agriculture Organization, UNESCO, International Civil Aviation Organization, International Bank for Reconstruction and Development, International Monetary Fund, Universal Postal Union, International Telecommunication Union, World Health Organization, International Refugee Organization, and International Trade Organization, together with a score of committees and commissions, are slowly laying the foundations for a world community and stable peace. However discouraged one may be at this moment of history, some evolution toward world law and order does seem to be taking place.

The industrialized world has contributed much to improve the means of communication between distant parts of the world, thus laying the foundation for world understanding; it has done much also to increase the terrors of war. It is our job to see that our science and technology are used for constructive and not destructive ends. Peace and goodwill cannot exist where there is hunger, disease, and fear of the scourges of poverty, war, and starvation.

Thus it may be noted that the structure of a community and the sense of community have been gradually enlarging—from the small group to the larger, from the small town to the city, state, and nation. Some will say that the next logical step is a world state. The question is here raised as to whether the super-structure at any level can long survive unless the sub-structure—call it the community—is alive, alert, and attacking the problems which it can solve. Emphasis should be placed on revitalizing democracy at the grass root, on sensitizing and involving each individual citizen to his responsibilities as well as to his rights and privileges. These involve not only voting and paying taxes but actual participation with his neighbors in doing as many things as can be done in the local setting.

SPECIFIC INTEREST GROUPS

Space is not available to include descriptions of what is being done to develop a sense of community in schools and colleges, business groups, labor unions, churches, and other specific groups. Brief attention will be given to what is being done in community planning and in the use of the arts.

COMMUNITY PLANNING

Only in the past twoscore years has much attention been given to the physical planning of the community. In the early part of the century the location of a new town or village was determined by an artery of transportation, river or railroad, and the "team haul" of the surrounding countryside. One needs only to drive through most of our cities to realize that they, too, grew up without adequate forethought.

Planning bodies have suffered from two handicaps. First, they have often been volunteer groups brought together to formulate a zoning ordinance or a city plan; and when they had more permanence and substantial continuing responsibilities, they were usually at the periphery of local government instead of at the heart of it. Second, such bodies have been restricted largely to the physical elements of city planning, which include zoning, streets, parks, transit, transportation, and civic art. Too seldom has planning been done in terms of the total community life of the people.

Examples of comprehensive community planning are to be found in Radburn, New Jersey, and Levittown, Long Island, both of which were planned by private corporations, and in Greenbelt, Maryland, and Greendale, Wisconsin, planned and built during the depression by the federal government.

Another phase of planning which involves the community are the huge low-rental housing projects erected both under the auspices of private business and governmental agencies. The mere settling of 1,200 families in such a project involves community relations among these families and with those surrounding the housing project. However artificial this situation is, it provides a splendid opportunity to develop both the structure of a community and a sense of community.

Recognizing this fact, the Federal Public Housing Authority stated in 1947 that the resources of the community and its agencies and those of the residents of the project should be fully utilized in planning, operating, financing, and appraising community activities, that democratic principles should be observed in self-government among the residents, that to the greatest extent possible the needs of the project residents should be provided for through a well-balanced program, and finally that project activities and services should be integrated with those of the neighborhood. As a result of these policies, Citizens' Clubs or Tenant Councils have been established in a number of projects. Recreational programs, project newspapers, measures designed to improve the appearance of buildings and grounds and to secure better public transportation are typical of their activities.

THE ARTS

From the point of view of developing a feeling of community and a sense of belonging, the arts—music, drama, the dance, painting, and sculpture—provide unusual potentialities even though they are not used specifically for these purposes. They appear to constitute not only an international language of communication but a medium of fellowship for groups within nations. Brownell (*The Human Community*; Harper, 1950) tells of the "singing group" in Fairhope, in which thirty-five men and women, lovers of music but no experts in the art, sang until "the compulsion of their singing filled the room with a greatness of its own," and then they forgot their leader, and forgot themselves, while the music captured all.

He also tells of a community drama which was written by members of a community group in Lonepine, Montana. Of it Brownell says:

The parts in many cases were taken by the historical characters themselves. First the son or daughter took the part as the parent had lived it during the early days of Lonepine. Then, as history moved down toward the present, the parents took their own parts in the show. . . . It was a friendly and a thorough success.

Through this drama more than one thing was accomplished. A history of the community was developed, young and old learned to work together, and the sweep of the production in its final performance created a sense of belonging which hitherto had not existed.

Similarly, no one can witness a performance of a professional dance troupe or of a skillfully directed local square or folk dance on Saturday night without realizing that not only is this an art form which demands creativity, rhythm, muscular coordination, and skill but that in the doing there develops a feeling of unity and fellowship.

While painting and sculpture are more individualistic in production, great art catches the common interests, attitudes and aspirations of mankind and enshrines them on canvas or in marble.

FACTORS CONTRIBUTING TO SUCCESS

DEVELOPING A SENSE OF COMMUNITY

Early in this paper it was asserted that a person might live in a community without developing a feeling of belonging to it. At this point it is desired to suggest some factors which tend to hinder or increase this sense of membership.

Among the people who seem to lack a real sense of community are the uprooted and isolated, the disadvantaged and segregated, the confused and disillusioned, and the sectarian. Those who seem to possess a feeling of belonging are the socially secure, the active participants, the altruists, and the integrated personalities.

Community workers have discovered that the best sense of community cannot be developed (1) if people spend an inadequate amount of time working together, (2) if there is a denial of freedom to community members to indicate their interests and needs and to make choices and judgments about them, (3) if the group does not have some common experiences such as visits to community institutions or attending such community affairs as school board meetings, and (4) if the relationships of the members of the group are confined merely to talking about things instead of doing things together, such as conducting fact-finding surveys or engaging in subsequent community action.

Conversely, a feeling of belonging may be increased (1) by serious meetings and social affairs which produce rapport and understanding, (2) by enlisting friends and neighbors to work together on common problems, (3) by undertaking a commonly agreed-upon challenging community enterprise, (4) by fostering the desire "to solve our own problems," and (5) by achieving a genuine sense that the group association is their creation, with purposes formulated by them and decisions that are their own.

GENERALIZATIONS REGARDING EXPERIENCES IN COMMUNITY WORK

From a study of what is being done in various local, state, regional, and national areas to vitalize the community in the structural sense, several principles and problems seem to emerge.

The beginnings of community projects do not follow any special pattern. A traffic problem, the health needs of children, a lack of recreational opportunities for young people, a serious situation in the schools of an area—these and countless other problems may serve as the springboard for cooperative action by members of a community. It may be safe to say that for long-range growth, work on problems which would tend to be divisive should be postponed until communication, confidence, and a sense of unity and devotion to public welfare have been built up.

A community may decide to embark on a developmental program as a result of the interest generated from inside sources or from the stimulation of an outside source—state, regional, or national. Such a program cannot long survive, however, unless an indigenous movement develops.

Early in the process, exploration and thought should be followed by gathering of facts before action is taken. In this respect the practices of the League of Women Voters on the local, state, and national levels serve as an excellent example for other groups. Their "Know Your Town" studies are particularly outstanding in this regard.

A sense of community grows through group participation. The reverse also is true, namely, that it is shattered as groups which once provided it are torn down. A sense of community is also developed by showing people ways in which their special interests may actually serve the interests of all members of the community.

While there are many examples to be found of successful community work which has been initiated by or is related to some area of government, broadly representative councils which are independent of government tend in the long run to be more successful. Such an organization can avoid being enmeshed in partisan politics, continue its work even when there is a turnover of office-holders, and work on projects upon which general agreement of various political and nonpolitical groups can be achieved. It seems increasingly clear that government needs to be flanked by voluntary, nonpartisan groups which are devoted solely to the public interest. Such groups act as an independent check upon public authority and help to mobilize public opinion to support community improvement whether it is sponsored by governmental or by private agencies.

FINANCING COMMUNITY PROJECTS

While examples have been given in this paper of government-supported community programs, fiscal independence seems a desirable goal toward which to work. However, the question of finance is one of the biggest problems now interfering with the development and continuance of general-purpose community programs. In this area in particular research is needed. How can community councils be financed without obligation to governmental or private interests?

Meanwhile, the alternatives that appear to be open to groups requiring financial support are these:

(a) Ask the schools to employ a "community man."
(b) Try to secure private support from individual organizations, foundations, unions, corporations, and community chests.
(c) Ask the city, county, or state to make an appropriation. This means incorporating as a public agency to receive tax money.
(d) Join in a nation-wide movement for funds patterned after the Red Cross drive.

GROWING DEMAND FOR BROADLY TRAINED WORKERS

There is evidence that the birth and death rate of local community councils is high. In almost every instance this can be traced to lack of leadership or lack of finance. What is the role of leadership? The general-purpose, professionally trained, all-round community leader hardly exists in this country. City managers who might be thought to exemplify such leadership are quite often either engineers, who are interested and skilled in the physical phases of city life, or political scientists, who are likely to be concerned with administrative, personnel, and legal phases. Gradually an effective demand is emerging for a more broadly trained professional worker. If and when such leaders are to be had, their chief function will be to work with lay citizens, stimulating their interest, helping them to secure facts, helping them to formulate policies and to carry them out, but never to weaken the interest or support of lay citizens by doing most or all of these things for them.

WHAT NEEDS TO BE DONE?

Several times in the foregoing pages it has been pointed out that industrial society has been the prime mover in social change. The home, the church, and the school have been the recipients of the effects of this direct action. The assumptions are here made that it is impossible as well as undesirable to attempt to return to a preindustrial order and that our present "mixed economy," which contains elements of private enterprise, cooperatives, and some government ownership or operation will be continued.

DECENTRALIZATION OF INDUSTRY?

Does it seem unreasonable to ask whether or not, within this framework, some limitation in size of industrial and commercial units should be considered? Should there be decentralization of industry, not from the viewpoint of defense against an external attack, but from the viewpoint of defense against internal weakness? Would the development of smaller communities whose workers traveled to scattered large productive units tend to preserve some of the advantages of mass production and of small-community life as well? Should every worker in a large plant thus become a "suburbanite"?

Do we reach a point of diminishing returns, from the social point of view, when larger and larger factories beget larger and larger communities and more and more segmentation? Even though assembly lines in huge factories discharge goods at a very low price, is such economy bought at too dear a price if workers feel no sense of community, if communities become too large for people to maintain wholesome human relations? While these questions are not intended to promote an argument for a return to preindustrial society, they do suggest the need for a fundamental study of the optimum size of industrial units in relation to size of communities. This study would seem to be important not only for formulating wise business and social policies in this country but also in relation to the problems of economically less-developed countries that are striving to become industrialized and which we are helping.

NEED FOR RESEARCH

One of the greatest needs is research into the various problems of social disorganization—research which will point the way to and be followed by effective action. No one of the following proposals can be developed fully, but several questions in a number of areas will be raised.

With regard to the home, what has been the specific effect of industrial society on the family as a unit, on the father, the mother, the children? Have ties of loyalty and affection been seriously weakened? Has the home lost its influence as an inculcator of moral and spiritual values? With data at hand to diagnose causes, what specific action could be recommended? Should home ownership be made easier? Should parent education be strengthened and spread more widely?

Similar searches for facts, to be followed by action, should be started in relation to churches, schools, and colleges. How much influence do these social institutions have in inculcating human values today? Do people who attend churches actually display higher standards of conduct than those who do not? If not, how can the influence of churches on conduct be increased? In what ways are churches effective in developing higher standards of values?

It has been asserted that when schools and colleges contain more than 750 or 800 students, the sense of "belonging" among youth is lost. How can these institutions, most of them at the upper levels and highly departmentalized, present a rational, coherent system of values to young people—or is it better that diversity of such standards prevail?

Has the segmentation in education produced a generation of young people who lack integration, consistency, and integrity? Has the emphasis on "objectivity," on "the scientific point of view," on the separation of church and state robbed our youth of a sense of moral values?

While management and labor must maintain the productive

machine, do they also have a responsibility for contributing to the protection, defense, and extension of human values? Does not industry have an educative function in this sense just as surely as it has a productive function? Is "enlightened self-interest" in economic life the best way to assure public interest and public welfare?

COMMUNITY COUNCILS

It is commonly recognized that many communities are over-organized, that they have too many single-purpose groups. Hugh R. Pomeroy, director of planning for Westchester County, said in a speech delivered before the Institute of Community Leadership of the New York State Citizens' Council:

Clinics on individual phases of community developments continue to cut toenails for corns, trim hair for migraine headaches, put poultices on broken legs and run hell out of the patient with a weak heart. It is about time that we held a clinic on the community as a whole.

What is needed is a general-purpose community council, flanking elective officials, which is concerned with the total problems of the community. The birth and death rates of community councils seem to be high. A badly needed research is a careful study of all the general-purpose councils in the U.S. with some reference to similar experiences in other parts of the world. How can such councils be brought into being with the best chances of success? What principles of organization and functioning can be derived? How can they be financed? How important is the professional community leader to the survival of a community organization?

Action flowing from such research might necessitate the establishment of several pilot projects to be undertaken in local communities, each to be carefully staffed, planned, and evaluated. If the outcome of such projects in community cooperation were favorable, how could more projects be brought into existence? Should there be state or regional citizens' councils? How should they be encouraged? Is there need for a national organization to stimulate state and local community councils, to provide for exchange of experience, to engage in continuous research?

SMALL COMMUNITIES FOR NEIGHBORLY COOPERATION

Is it true, as Brownell insists, that the only "human community" is a small community? If this is so and human values are to survive, what steps should be taken to decentralize metropolitan areas? How can we preserve both the benefits of industrialized society and the values of small-community life?

The answers to these questions are urgently needed. Already evidence of the people's abdication are available. Only 50 to 60 per cent of eligible voters vote in a national election. A sense of futility has enveloped many local citizens who separately have tried to solve local problems. Feeling that they are being manipulated, they have given up and look to the state capital or the District of Columbia for the solutions. Evidence of the ties between the underworld and some city politicians, as uncovered by the Kefauver Committee, gives even greater emphasis to the need for citizen participation in government.

While there is no evidence that a "man on a white horse" is about to take over in any of the seats of government, this feeling of failure and helplessness provides just the kind of soil out of which such a movement could develop. And the soil in which such a movement would have least chance is one in which, all over the nation, people in neighborly communities have learned the advantages and derived the satisfactions and happiness that come from working together to solve their common problems.

TRAINING FOR COMMUNITY PARTICIPATION AND LEADERSHIP

A factor which becomes increasingly evident to anyone who is concerned with this whole subject is the need for two types of training.

First, there is the training that all students, whatever their special interests or vocational ambitions, should receive if they are to become effective citizens of communities. This paper stresses the fact that the only permanent solution of various problems is that which emerges from the thinking and experience of the people involved. The Earlham College Program of Community Dynamics, now in its fourth year, provides an excellent example of this type of training for community participation and leadership.

Here students in a liberal arts college become observers and participants in the activities of men and women seeking the general welfare in local communities. Interested in the all-around development of students. Earlham believes they will become better citizens by working with local people who are producing better communities. In selecting projects with which their students are to be associated, first consideration is given to those which promise students opportunity to participate in policy making for over-all community growth.

Second, there is the type of training required by a professional community counselor—a generalist in community service. While every university is likely to have in its program phases of training that would be useful in the preparation of such community counselors, the Garden City Conference of the American Council on the Community reported the lack of any adequate comprehensive curriculum for professional preparation in this field in any university. Accordingly, it suggested a plan for such preparation, about half of which would be devoted to on-campus training and half to supervised field experience. The principal lines of campus training were multiple-discipline training in insights, personal counseling, training in working knowledge of community problem areas, training in the arts, training in community methods and techniques, and training in research.

FOR A SENSE OF COMMUNITY

In the early pages of this paper a sense of community was said to involve not only a feeling of identification, but also a feeling of being respected by others, a willingness to adjust personal purposes to desirable group purposes, sharing in decision making, participation in group endeavors, and the commitment to work for community goals. Our civilization cannot be allowed to destroy itself. The process of self-destruction will take place if this sense of community is not nurtured in every club, society, church, school, hospital, business, and labor union. It should be the urgent concern of every person interested in preserving a free society to see to it that in whatever occupation he works, whatever leisure he has, whatever formal or informal group he is a part of, this sense of belonging, of being a partner, of being respected, wanted, and desired is fostered. Only an unrelenting and wisely developed effort can restore the sense of community which we once had but now seem to have lost. It comes through democratic procedures initiated by personalities sensitive to the interplay of other personalities.

The sense of community may be developed in an integrated way or in a hundred specific ways. While the latter process may not be desirable as the former, it may be more practical. Further, some sense of community is better than none at all, providing always that it is not provincial or selfish. Community chest drives, fund-raising campaigns for hospitals and clinics, alumni fund campaigns for colleges, every-member canvasses for churches, subscriptions for the opera, contributions to the World Student Service Fund—all these are means of cooperation action. When they do not work at cross-purposes, they are good.

What appears to be needed is more imagination and creativity in opening up new avenues for building a sense of community, in both integrated and segmented ways. What is also needed is to secure the participation of a larger and larger number of citizens in the work of community groups, rather than limiting such work to a few people who meet with a hospital board one day, a welfare committee the next, and a YMCA group the following day. No person today should have the sense of being a good citizen if, when asked what contribution he has made to American life, he is able to answer only, "I pay my taxes."

CONCLUSION: TWO KEY ISSUES

The individual is the unit of energy of the human race. This unit of energy would scarcely have a personality, a being, if he were not born into a social world. Life is a social affair. To live more adequately is to live with others. To learn to live better one must learn to share more fully in the thoughts and feelings and interests of others. In one sense "community" means more of my mind, feelings and interests in yours and more of yours in mine. According to Dewey (*Democracy and Education*), "Democracy is more than a form of government; it is primarily associated living." Indeed, respect for the dignity and worth of all individuals and confidence in the process of sharing the decision-making power have been key points in our democratic faith.

But the development of the whole individual and of a whole democratic society has been complicated in modern industrial society (we will not say retarded, since diverse forces playing on each individual may result in positive good) by segmentation. A single individual may belong to many groups. His development as an individual is not truly fulfilled by his being partially included in multiple groups.

Similarly, industrial civilization has created many publics, with conflicting interests. If a given community has within it certain labor groups, management organizations, public housing committees, tax-reduction leagues, and church, school, recreational, and intercultural groups, some of which have conflicting interests and may even be antagonistic to one another, how can the community organize itself to reconcile them and to solve its pressing problems? In a simple, primitive community it might have been possible to achieve a total inclusion of all personalities in all segments of community life, but under the complex conditions of modern society this cannot be done.

Two key issues, then, arise: (1) Will more and more vigorous participation in the segmented activities of a democratic state achieve unity for the individual? (2) In view of what appears to be the inevitable increase in the number of segments of community life, how can a total inclusive community program be achieved?

SELECTED BIBLIOGRAPHY

Brownell, Baker, *The Human Community*. Harper & Brothers, 1950.
Cook, Lloyd A., *Community Backgrounds of Education*. McGraw-Hill, 1938.
Dahir, James, *Communities for Better Living*. Harper & Brothers, 1950.

Drucker, Peter F., *The Future of Industrial Man*. John Day, 1942.
    The New Society. Harper & Brothers, 1949.

Golden, Clinton S., and Harold J. Ruttenberg, *The Dynamics of Industrial Democracy*. Harper & Brothers, 1942.

Hayes, Wayland J., "Revolution—Community Style," reprint from *Social Forces*, vol. 28, No. 1 (October, 1949).

———, *The Small Community Looks Ahead*. Harcourt, Brace, 1947.

Hicks, Granville, *Small Town*. Macmillan, 1947.

Hillman, Arthur, *Community Organization and Planning*. Macmillan, 1950.

King, Clarence, *Organizing for Community Action*. Harper & Brothers, 1949.

Lippitt, Ronald, *Training in Community Relations*. Harper & Brothers, 1949.

Mayo, Elton, *The Social Problems of an Industrial Civilization*. Harvard University, 1945.

Morgan, Arthur E., *The Small Community*. Harper & Brothers, 1942.

Ogden, Jean and Jess, *Small Communities in Action*. Harper & Brothers, 1946.

Patterson, S. Howard, *Social Aspects of Industry*. McGraw-Hill, 1943.

Poston, Richard W., *Small Town Renaissance*. Harper & Brothers, 1950.

President's Research Committee, *Recent Social Trends*. McGraw-Hill, 1933.

Sanders, Irwin T., *Making Good Communities Better*. University of Kentucky Press, 1950.

Sanderson, Dwight, and Robert A. Polson, *Rural Community Organization*. Wiley, 1939.

Schacter, Harry W., *Kentucky on the March*. Harper & Brothers, 1949.

Swift, Arthur L. Jr., *New Frontiers of Religion*. Macmillan, 1938.

Warner, W. Lloyd, and J. O. Low, *The Social System of the Modern Factory*. Yale University Press, 1947.

Warner, W. Lloyd, and Paul S. Lunt, *The Social Life of a Modern Community*. Yale University Press, 1941.

———, *The Status System of a Modern Community*. Yale University Press, 1942.

Whyte, William Foote, *Industry and Society*. McGraw-Hill, 1946.

11

Personal Morale Today

by Robert L. Calhoun

A UNIVERSAL PROBLEM

The problem that concerns us here is universal and entirely familiar, though not easy to define. It is the problem of personal morale, working faith, active confidence that human life is worth living. One reason it cannot easily be defined is that in major part such confidence is not an object of conscious attention or affirmation but something much more deep-going. In daily relations to my friends, my business associates, my fellow citizens, if I find myself constantly needing to remind myself that my friend is honest, my bank is sound, and so on, such conscious reiteration is a sign of some lack of confidence rather than its full presence. When I genuinely trust a person or an institution or a social group, my actions take for granted, with perpetual conscious assertion, that a solid basis for confidence exists. So it is also in my basic assumptions about human living.

Such working faith should no doubt involve rational inquiry and reasoned conclusions, but it cannot consist entirely nor even mainly of reasoning processes. Without them it is blind and undependable. But in its fundamental character it is dynamic rather than analytic, pervading the whole active set of one's personal existence rather than confined to a particular part of it. We are concerned with the problem of confidence not simply in one or another portion of ourselves and our world, but in what is most fundamental and far-reaching in the whole of reality as it involves us, confronts us, and bears upon our living.

SECURITY FOR CHILDREN AND FOR MATURE PEOPLE

Our concern, furthermore, is with the problem as it confronts mature, perceptive, and realistic people. Doubtless there are sorts of wishful thinking which can provide for an uncritical person a sense of security that the facts do not warrant. We have no concern here to defend or try to produce any such glossing over of unpleasant realities.

It is important to keep clear two sharply contrasted patterns of personal security, each appropriate in its own place. One is protection from the all-out challenge of adult living. This is the security proper to the infant, the immature person, or the helplessly dependent. Unless security of this sort is provided for very young children, their lives are warped by premature pressures and they may never achieve a basic and durable confidence at all.

On the other hand, such protection from challenge, if too complete and too long continued, can prevent or grievously damage a young person's growth to maturity. What the adolescent must discover and develop, to become adult, is a body of resources to meet challenge. This provides the security most appropriate to fully mature and competent human living, and in this discussion we shall be concerned primarily with grounds for confidence in this latter sense. We want for ourselves and our fellows the security of the sailor able to cope with storms, of the swimmer not afraid of strong currents; not the security of the timid or lazy person who seeks protection behind the labors, ventures, and perils of others.

BROAD INTERRELATIONS OF CONFIDENCE

In obvious ways, the problem of this roundtable involves intimately the problems of the other three. Confidence in life cannot be separated from the relationship of the individual person to his work, to the opportunities and activities of leisure time, and to the various communities in which his life goes on. But over and beyond all these, it includes also the individual person's relations to the whole universe in which work, leisure, and community life have their place. At bottom the question of confidence in life is a question of man's working attitude toward what he takes to be most fundamental, most ultimate in the whole of his real world.

Partly because it cannot be confined to a specific, well-marked area of inquiry, and because much of its subject matter is normative—that is, involving value judgments—rather than factual or directly observable, this paper even more than the other three must resort often to interpretative appraisals that go well beyond any observable facts. Such interpretations must, of course, be compatible with whatever facts are known. But at best they are more open to debate than straight reporting need be. Such judgments not merely examine a common problem; they illustrate a particular person's working faith.

BASES FOR CONFIDENCE IN LIFE

Personal morale may be regarded perhaps as resting upon grounds of four main sorts: a sense of personal adequacy, of social validity, of economic security, and of the ultimate meaningfulness and worth of human life.

INDIVIDUAL ADEQUACY AND MORALE

Differences among individual persons make almost any kind of generalization about the sense of personal adequacy dubious or even dangerously misleading. But one may say that ordinarily a sense of personal adequacy involves some combination of such factors as physical fitness, mental competence, and emotional integrity.

Physical fitness need not and should not mean the specialized powers of an athlete. It does mean at least a tolerable amount of the energy, endurance, and skill that are required by one's job and the responsibilities of one's social living. It goes without saying that physical handicaps of many kinds can be absorbed and taken in stride by a person whose mental and emotional maturity is what it ought to be. But any one who is compelled, through malnutrition or disease or other pervasive weakness, to live continually below par in his capacity for physical response will find it exceptionally hard to maintain an attitude of basic confidence in life. Where such conditions of subnormality are chronic, obviously a part of our problem is to seek their elimination.

Mental competence includes capacities for learning, possession of relevant knowledge, endowment with practical sagacity or judgment that can make knowledge a living and not merely a formal part of one's personal existence, and many more such favorable factors. Again it goes without saying that what we are talking about is not the possession of college degrees nor the development of technical and specialized intellectual skills, except where these are required for a particular individual's living. We are talking about the kind of knowledge and judgment that makes the difference between a man who knows his job and the beginner or bungler, between the parent, the businessman, the citizen who has enough understanding of himself and his neighbors to carry on relationships with them in such fashion that both are the gainers, instead of repeatedly damaging human relationships by innocent blunders and ending in perpetual frustration. Mental competence, like physical fitness, is indispensable as a base for over-all personal morale.

Importance of Emotional Integrity. Finally, emotional integrity, without which a person cannot very well be a distinctive and recognizable human self at all, is in some respects even more deep-going and indispensable. It is, moreover, of all these factors the one most directly affected, for better or for worse, by nurture in early childhood.

Emotional integrity must include the steady responsiveness that enables a person to recognize and be guided by the desires, purposes, intentions of his human neighbors and to appreciate the sources of beauty and other sorts of satisfaction in the world of nature. It includes the stability that makes a person keep a consistent direction in his life through both favorable and stormy times, in presence of both approval and disapproval from those about him, in success, and in temporary failure. It requires especially the elusive but essential sentiment usually called self-respect: the ability to accept oneself realistically, without conceit and without humiliation, one's personal assets and personal liabilities alike frankly acknowledged. The man of self-respect and self-confidence is not the egoist, the aggressively cocksure person who too often is trying hard to conceal a deep-seated sense of insecurity by bold talk. He is the man of sober, mature understanding of his own strength and weakness, who is ready to affirm, for better and for worse, his right and duty to be himself.

At all these points we are of course talking not simply about the existence of physical fitness, mental competence, emotional integrity. We are talking about the active attitude of a person who sees himself as one whose physical, mental, and emotional endowments are in fact sufficient for productive living.

The distribution of emphasis among these several factors can vary from individual to individual without limit. What one man may regard as inadequate for himself, another might find quite tolerable. What one man lacks in intellectual equipment he may well make up in physical vitality, or the other way about. A person who is modestly endowed with both physical and mental resources may nevertheless have in outstanding measure the sort of emotional integrity that makes him a dependable and admirable member of human society. Any attempt to apply a rigid blueprint or yardstick in these matters is both absurd and unjust. The one thing that can be said with some emphasis is that a first indispensable base for any person's confidence in life is a sense of personal adequacy.

SOCIAL VALIDITY AND BASIC CONFIDENCE

There is need, in the next place, for a sense of social validity. This means something quite different from a need for the liking or approval of one's fellows. Essentially, it is the social counterpart to what we have called self-respect. As such, it has two correlative dimensions:

One is the perceptible attitude of the group to which one belongs or desires to belong. The sense of social validity is maintained when one has the sense of being accepted, of belonging as a full-fledged member to one or more of the communities, large and small, that crisscross in the area of one's personal life.

To be liked or disliked, to be approved or disapproved by one's fellows is no doubt a source of satisfaction or dissatisfaction. But much more fundamental for personal morale is the sense of being accepted or rejected, of being included or shut out, of having one's place as a recognized member of a group or being everywhere treated as an alien.

The other dimension of the sense of social validity is actual loyalty and cooperation by the individual person himself. To be counted in as a member of a group will give one lasting satisfaction only if one can feel that one is in fact contributing positively to the group life and so, in one's own way, worthy of inclusion. To be solidly grounded in social living, to be assured of personal status in the network of human relationships and activities without which no one can live as a person, means at once to be regarded by others as a dependable and acceptable member, and to be regarded by oneself as deserving that sort of appraisal.

Here, again, as at so many other points, the most important part of the groundwork must exist below the surface of conscious attention. The man who finds it necessary to remind himself constantly that he is accepted, or that he does deserve to be counted a friend and companion, is showing a more or less radical insecurity about his social status. The man who is socially secure is one who takes it for granted that he is welcome and who can act freely and confidently in the presence of others, not seeking always with anxious care to avoid doing or saying what may irritate his neighbors but assuming that their acceptance of him is sufficiently fundamental so that they will take in his conduct both agreement and disagreement, conformity and dissent, with full recognition that these are the words and acts of one who, whatever his personal variations, is a genuine member of the group.

The "Private" and "Public" Orders. At this point there are important differences between a democratic and an authoritarian tradition and pattern of life in the social group itself. There will be need to examine this point more carefully in a moment. Meanwhile, we may notice that there are two closely associated but differing areas of social relationship in which each person needs to find himself at home. Professor Hocking has labeled these two areas "the private order" and "the public order." The private order, consisting mainly of one's family and friends, is that region of social relationship in which what a man *is* counts for more than what he *does* or can do. In this area of relationship the dominant patterns are largely noncompetitive. Gaiety, responsiveness, tolerance, generosity, kindliness—these are the characteristics that are likely to be most highly prized in private relationships. There is need here, too, for dependability, frankness, readiness to pull one's weight, but primary stress is laid upon the contribution one can make simply by being oneself in the relatively informal and uninhibited give-and-take of intimate personal relationship.

The public order, by comparison, consists of the larger community of work, citizenship, and public responsibilities. Here the dominant pattern is necessarily more competitive and impersonal, determined by the exactions that arise from the inescapable need to get necessary jobs done and to maintain at least a minimum of social efficiency with the complicated traffic of modern life moving steadily and smoothly. Here the acceptability of an individual person must depend much more obviously upon his competence to do work, to succeed in competitive struggle with others in economic or political activity, to achieve recognition and success as a man who has proved that he can take and fulfill responsibility.

These two areas of social living obviously cannot be separated in the lives of most people. Success or failure to be accepted and acceptable in either is likely to affect a person's sense of adequacy and at-homeness in the other. But again, in different individual lives, widely differing patterns of private and public validity may be attained. The primary requisite is that in both areas a person shall achieve at least a minimum of fellowship and acceptability, or his basic confidence in the meaningfulness of his whole life must suffer.

Feudal Pattern. A fact of great importance for our basic problem is that the social pattern of Western civilization has developed during the past thousand years in a way that has altered significantly the relationships between private and public order. In medieval

society, with its basically feudal organization, the private order of
family and person-to-person relationships set the basic pattern
for public organization. The essential scheme of feudal order
rested on individual loyalty of vassal to liege lord and the individual obligation of the lord to fulfill responsibilities toward the
vassals who depended upon him. From the humblest serf to the
greatest prince, the social pattern reflected the order of the human
family: father and child, master and servant, authoritative ruler
and obedient dependents. This pattern is often called quite accurately, paternalistic. Its model is indeed the private order of
family life.

With the rise of modern nation-states and of industrial society,
the medieval pattern has undergone more or less far-reaching
change, so that today great diversity exists in the areas that have
become highly industrialized. In some places and in some institutions the feudal or paternalistic pattern is continued. The assumption is that the employer stands to his employees, or the
political ruler to his subjects, in a position not unlike that of the
father and head of a household. This was in fact the familiar
relationship of ruler and subject in feudal society and of employer
and employee in the earlier and simpler days of hand craftsmanship. In the far more complex and impersonal world of machine
tools, absentee ownership, and mass production, its appropriate-
ness is more difficult to maintain in either industry or government.

Democratic Pattern. A second pattern, which in varying degrees has begun to replace the traditional one, differentiates much
more sharply between the order that is appropriate to family life
and that which is appropriate in business, industry, and politics.
Instead of attempting to carry over into public life relationships
of father and children or of master and servants, the democratic
impulse that has played so large and dramatic a role in the past
four hundred years of Western history has sought to introduce,
especially in the public order and to some extent in the home, a
pattern in which the typical relationship is a relationship of adult
with adult. The underlying assumption of democratic theory and
practice is that, in spite of diversities of ability and of function,

mature and socially responsible persons should maintain economic and political relationships that recognize and safeguard the maturity and responsibility of every participant. The relative freedom of the wage worker as compared with the medieval serf, the extension of political freedom and responsibility through the steadily widening franchise, the encouragement of venturesomeness and diversity in economic activity in the context of what we know as free enterprise—all these familiar developments mark a more or less radical change from the assumptions and the patterns of feudal life.

Gains and Losses. The change has brought evident and invaluable gains in the widespread development of chances for personal maturity in the public order. At the same time, these new opportunities have brought with them the loss of much of the traditional grounds for security in social status. In the feudal order, whether in the medieval period of the West or in various regions of Europe and Asia today, each individual's place in the social scheme was pretty definitely fixed for him by inheritance and by social convention. There was no reason for him to feel uncertain of either his rights or his duties. The pattern to which he was expected to conform was the familiar and natural pattern of dependence upon a superior, while maintaining responsibility for those dependent upon himself as children upon a father.

With the spread of more democratic and free patterns of life, however, both the intimate personal quality and the definite social structure of feudalism have given way to a much less well-defined diversity in which the responsibility for finding or making his own place in the scheme rests much more heavily upon each individual person. Moreover, the situations in which the individual may need to find or make his place are much more largely situations defined by impersonal forces and institutional structures than by face-to-face personal communication. It is not surprising that in our own time, a time of bewilderingly rapid and far-reaching transition and of large-scale organization, there should be widespread emotional insecurity and wistfulness over the threat to personal integrity and to the more intimate personal relations.

Authoritarian Pattern. Partly in reaction against this threat of uncontrollable disorder, there have been notable attempts in our own day to re-establish in the contemporary scene authoritarian patterns of public life. Superficially they have some resemblance to the traditional patterns of feudal society. But fundamentally their temper is different. Both facism and contemporary communism accept without question the tools of industrial living and the large-scale patterns of organization which the use of those tools makes necessary. They seek to impose, then, upon this industrialized and largely depersonalized social order a pattern of rigid control from the top. The result is not really a return to the warmth and personal security of feudalism at its best. It is rather a caricature of that order, in which ruthless controls through such impersonal agencies as propaganda ministries and secret police have taken the place of the old personal loyalties and responsibilities of genuine feudalism.

The problem of modern man who must seek to achieve a sense of social validity in a world as full of conflicting and uncertain development as ours can scarcely be overstated.

ECONOMIC STABILITY AND PERSONAL MORALE

One factor in the social orientation required for basic confidence is so important that it calls for special notice: a sense of economic security. This does not mean assurance of a lifelong vacation with pay. Few vigorous people want that. It means assurance of continuing opportunity to maintain for oneself and one's dependents a fairly stable or improving standard of living, with safeguard against economic disaster through illness or accidental disability, prolonged unemployment, or old age. Bare subsistence is not enough. What is needed, over the long haul, is the physical basis for a life with self-respect, with enough comforts, diversions, and opportunities for growth to keep life interesting, and with hope, not oppressive anxiety, for the future.

In this area, also, industrialization has brought drastic changes. When the economy of the West was based mainly on agriculture and handicrafts, both work and its products contributed directly to maintaining the customary standard of living. Food, shelter, clothing, and other concrete equipment for humane life were produced and either used for the immediate benefit of those who produced them or exchanged more or less directly for other wanted goods. A farmer with his land, a craftsman with his tools could be fairly sure—barring wars, plagues, droughts, or other major disasters—of a tolerable living in good times and bad. When production and consumption were so closely connected there was always work to do, and it resulted in concrete benefits. Overproduction was hardly possible, and inflation was a problem for money-lenders rather than for workers. There was depressing hardship and constriction of living for unskilled laborers and unemployables, both on the land and in towns and cities—and that means for much too large a part of the whole population. But there was economic stability and a place for everybody.

New Situation and Problems. When exchange of work and its products for money, instead of for usable goods, became the rule, and when high-speed power-driven machinery replaced journeymen's tool kits and crofters' oxen, the direct, concrete correlation of work and human needs was replaced in large measure by a system far more complex, abstract, and liable to periods of acute instability. Money became the universal, impersonal symbol of economic value, for which both labor and goods came to be sold. Money wages and prices varied widely as supply and demand shifted to one side or the other, for reasons that had little to do with the needs of the workers. Labor became a commodity, bought and sold often as impersonally as hogs or cotton. Economic security now seemed to mean primarily possession of surplus money, not possession of skill, tools, and a recognized place in a working world. And this new situation involved new difficulties for the man with only his work to sell. For him it was difficult to acquire enough surplus money for a rainy spell, because when wages were high, prices for daily necessities were likely to be high also. If prices went down sharply, wages, too, were likely to drop or to disappear in a glutted labor market.

This is by no means to say that industrialization has brought only insecurity. Both gains and losses will be noted later. It is to say that economic security has to be conceived and sought now in more complex and impersonal situations than those of pre-industrial society, although the basic need is still for assurance of humane living.

ASSURANCE OF ENDURING SIGNIFICANCE AND WORTH

For the sort of confidence we have been discussing, there is need, finally, of some assurance of the ultimate meaningfulness and worth of human life. Talk of what is ultimate, or fundamental, or all-inclusive is likely to seem to us presumptuous and even a bit impertinent. Normally we are immersed in activities that go on from day to day and objectives which we can set up and actually attain year after year. To suggest that there is any point in trying to look beyond these manageable or at least intelligible factors in our living is likely to seem confusing rather than helpful.

But the problem that concerns us here cannot be dealt with in terms of short-range objectives alone. The distinctive character of that most basic working faith which runs through the whole of a human life, and which refers to the whole reality with which our life is concerned, cannot be understood at all without reference to long-range perspectives and man's need for at least some guidelines that hold steady generation after generation.

In the midst of activity, there is indeed little chance for deliberate seeking of ultimate meanings. But even for the busy person at the height of his powers, there are times of leisure and solitude in which it may be impossible to shut out questions about the meaning, or lack of meaning, of the whole enterprise of human living. For men and women who are growing older, whose capacity for steady, active work is diminishing, and whose achievements are increasingly in the past rather than in a future still to be lived, questions concerning the worth of what has been done become increasingly urgent. At the other end of the scale, for young men and women whose outlook upon a troubled and largely chaotic world-epoch is deeply disquieting, the need for long and inclusive vision is scarcely less evident. If it be true that the mind of our time has lost its sense of the significance of such deliberate effort to see life steadily and whole and to appraise it fairly in the light of some trustworthy standard, this fact may well be a particularly damning indictment of what modern civilization has done to its children.

Need for Stability of Values. One major side of the demand for assurance concerning ultimate meanings is the need of a sense that values to which men devote themselves and for which they are ready to live and die have the kind of stability that can justify such devotion. We have learned much that is sound and helpful concerning the diversity and the relativity of human value judgments. We know a great deal more than once was known about the extent to which moral and aesthetic standards are bound up with the whole life of a particular culture and time. Social anthropology, history, cultural sociology, and social psychology have brought wide illumination to our understanding of ourselves and our preferences. But when all this has been said, there is need still to be assured that some standards of worth are authoritative not only for those who happen to like them, or for those who happen to live in a particular time and place, but for all rational human persons.

Not Particular Institutions, but Basic Truth and Right. This need for universality and permanence in primary values should not be confused with a demand for permanence of particular institutions or social patterns. It is not vital that any particular value judgment, or any detailed system of values, shall be guaranteed permanent and universal. But it is vital that the attempt to make discriminating judgments of better and worse shall be assuredly a significant effort. If there are no permanent lines of direction, then the effort to make value judgments becomes absurd. Unless there is a genuine difference between truth and falsehood, justice and injustice, generosity and callousness, then the effort to discover truth, to achieve more nearly perfect justice, to practice human decency loses all rational meaning. Unless the world is the kind of world in which there is an intrinsic order of truth and right that is not wholly dependent upon human preference or decree, the essential character of human life must logically be conceived not in terms of truth seeking and rational self-devotion, but in terms of arbitrary references among shifting, transient satisfactions.

Unless something is really thus or so, whether we know it or not, there is no truth to seek but only more or less persuasive fictions to make. Unless in human relationships one course of action is really more just than another, whether we like it or not, there seems no rational ground for rejecting expediency as our best guide to moral action. But if moral action is, in fact, nothing more than opportunism in evening dress, human life loses one of its most familiar and convincing claims to dignity and self-respect.

THE UNIVERSE AND MAN

Besides the need for assurance that there are some value standards of universal human significance, there is need of the further conviction that such values stand in a positive relationship to the order of existence itself. However noble and indestructible truth, equity, and decency may be as ideals, it is a wholly reasonable and mature question whether they are grounded in whatever forces make the universe go or whether they stand apart as splendid but ineffectual shadows without real power. The affirmation that somewhere in the universe supreme goodness and supreme power are united is in principle the affirmation of belief in God. The primary point here is not to inquire whether, along with other existing beings, there is also one that fits my idea of God or some particular philosophic or theological formula. The primary question is whether what is actually fundamental in the actual universe is a powerful source and sustainer of good.

Instead of such affirmation, many able and devoted men and women today urge the superiority of religious humanism. In their view, man himself is the chief—perhaps the only—source and sustainer of good in a universe whose unwitting support of values consists essentially in its support of human life. Apart from man, the world of nature has no independent realization of good, nor inclination toward it, nor power to produce it. But mankind has all these characteristics, and deserves the trust and devotion of all men of goodwill. Theism, which affirms belief in God as

Supreme Being, surpassing man in power and goodness, on whom man depends for his present existence and his best hopes for a better future, is rejected. For such belief is regarded as diverting attention and effort from the potentialities in man himself and from his duty to improve by his own exertions the lot of all men present and to come.

This need not be so. When thoughtful men have affirmed wholehearted belief in God and have lived in accordance with that belief they have found in their more discerning moments not primarily a source of comfort and a warrant for complacency or indolence but rather a source of judgment, challenge, and powerful assurance calling for vigorous action. There is a familiar kind of religion which has deserved to be contemptuously called "the opium of the people." It is most likely to go with the immature demand for protection against challenge, the perpetuation of sheltered infancy. But there is another and very different sort of theism—a religion for mature minds and hearts—in which the believer finds himself as often as not compelled to re-examine and revise his most dearly cherished achievements and aspirations. He finds himself not lulled and protected by his trust in God, so much as constrained to put forth new efforts and to seek new ways of life in the presence of height and depth in reality that defy any human expression.

In the being of such a God many have found the most significant ground for ultimate confidence in life, because in such conviction there is assurance that whether a man's best efforts succeed or fail in terms of particular short-term objectives, it remains fundamentally worth-while to go on giving himself with the utmost strength and courage of which he is capable. Such a believer can say, with the ancient poet, "The grass withereth, the flower fadeth, but the word of our God shall stand and forever."

BALANCE SHEET FOR HUMAN CONFIDENCE TODAY

It goes without saying that the indirect effects of industrialization are even more important, for our present problem, than its direct effects in speeding up and expanding the production and distribution of goods. Industrialization implies and involves highly developed technology and scientific disciplines, changes in individual and social behavior, and complications of social and political structure. All this has far-reaching effects on men's working presuppositions—their basic assumptions with respect to themselves and their world. When we talk, therefore, about the impact of industrialization upon men's fundamental confidence in life, we are concerned not only with the processes of industry but with the whole cultural context in which modern industry has developed and is carried on.

EFFECTS OF ADVANCING TECHNOLOGY

A first major aspect of the development of modern industry is, of course, the provision of an extraordinary body of technological equipment for human living. If one were trying to define the main areas in which this development has proceeded, one might distinguish between equipment devoted to the maintenance and conduct of life and equipment devoted to the protection of life, especially against natural enemies and pressures. There is no need here to attempt to say in detail what belongs in each of these major areas. In the first, presumably, we should place the newer procedures for providing food, clothing, shelter, and the whole physical basis for civilized pursuits; in the latter, the development of techniques for improving public health, the elaborate apparatus of the medical sciences and arts, the utilization of knowledge of building materials and of the resources of sanitary engineering to make life safer and more secure.

Gains for Confidence. From all this development in technology there have come clear gains for men's ultimate confidence in life. Most obvious and familiar, perhaps, is the startling improvement in respect of physical security, fitness, and life expectancy. In as far as a sense of personal adequacy depends upon the maintenance of a tolerable level of physical vitality and freedom from anxiety about one's chance to continue in good health, men of the Western world in our day have an almost unimaginable advantage over most men of the past.

A similar improvement has extended to what is loosely called our standard of living. Superficially, this phrase is likely to suggest physical comforts and luxuries, which thoughtful men might well be inclined to discount. But more fundamentally a superior standard of living is the provision of opportunity for personal fulfillment in many directions—intellectual, aesthetic, social, as well as physical—which only a thoughtless or ignorant critic could brush aside as without long-range significance.

One of the most fundamental gains through the development of modern technology and industry is a real promise that this sort of opportunity can someday be extended to all human beings. In a time when the work necessary to provide for mere subsistence occupied most of the waking hours of a majority of the people, it was literally impossible to look forward to the extension of comfort and opportunity to the masses of mankind. But now the transfer of the heaviest sorts of drudgery, in industrialized civilizations, to power-driven batteries of machines holds out for the first time in all history the hope that if our resources are rightly directed a tolerable standard of living for everyone is, in principle, within our range of vision.

This same consideration points in another direction. Our modern technology has supplied the requisite physical basis for worldwide human communities. When the physical isolation of peoples in secluded pockets of the earth's surface made free intercourse among them difficult or impossible, the chance for the advance of mutual understanding and cooperation on a large scale was small. Now our systems of communication and transport have overcome those physical handicaps. By themselves they by no means assure that we shall go on speedily to achieve world community. But, at least, such achievement is no longer physically impossible. In as far as the ultimate meaningfulness and worth of human living are associated with the achievement of global understanding and cooperation, and the diminishing of the threats of destructive conflict, the equipment of modern industry has at least opened doors that for millennia of human history remained tightly closed.

New Perils. On the other hand, we have no need to be reminded that the new equipment has brought new threats to our confidence in life. On the one hand, the very fact that the whole world is now open to us, thrusting itself upon our attention whether we will or not, has subjected us abruptly to more complex, urgent, baffling demands for understanding and cooperation, for which in many respects we are unprepared. In ancient times the contact between diverse cultures was likely to come either through the slow processes of trade, individual travel, and gradual cultural intermingling, or else abruptly by invasion, conquest, and assimilation of one group by another. In either event there was no such demand as we now confront for overnight adaptation of our thought processes and our patterns of behavior to requirements posed all at once by a dozen diverse cultures, none of whose peoples we expect or desire to conquer and rule, yet all of whom we find difficult to understand and to work with in partnership.

We are experiencing on a vastly greater scale something like what the Greek world underwent when Alexander conquered the Near and Middle East. Then for the first time Greek-speaking citizens of the proud but now subject city-states found themselves constrained to recognize as fellow subjects in the Macedonian Empire the Persians and Parthians, the Syrians and Egyptians, and the whole diverse array of peoples of the eastern Mediterranean world. One result of this sudden subjection and absorption into the motley populace of the new empire was what Gilbert Murray called in a widely known phrase, "a widespread failure of nerve." The conquered Athenian or Spartan or Theban found his confidence in himself and the destiny of his city undermined. He was made to feel pitifully small and helpless in the sprawling new world, which he could not control nor even understand. And if at the same time his mental horizon was stretched to include ways of life that he had never hitherto been compelled to confront seriously, so that his sense of the magnitude and variety of human living was enlarged in the new setting, his bewilderment and sense of inadequacy were on the whole stronger than the elation that comes when one finds oneself identified with a bigger world than one had ever known. Something of that sort has been happening to the peoples of the Atlantic community in our time. It has happened to us, moreover, at dizzying speed and with a threat of global disaster in case we fail to meet the challenge thus thrust upon us.

Technology and Despotism. The threat of disaster presents itself, of course, as another manifestation of the impact of technology and industry upon our way of life. We have devised new and more efficient ways to destroy both existing life and the basis for life. Modern industry and, especially, modern warfare have become enormously wasteful of natural resources, some of them irreplaceable. The techniques of modern warfare have developed now the ability to devastate huge areas of industrial installations and the means of transportation upon which modern life so largely depends. Perhaps most fundamental as a threat to our living, the devastation of industrial regions is likely to result in the disruption of economic, political, and social relationships that are indispensable to civilized order. The tools that offer us new hope for life are balanced by new weapons that threaten a more speedy obliteration of life than ever before was possible.

At the same time, both new weapons and new tools enhance the power of modern dictators to control their own subjects, as well as to threaten their neighbors. Successful revolt is harder to plan and to achieve against modern secret services, motorized police, and machine guns. Closely held means of mass communication—press, radio, television—make possible an unprecedented hold on popular thought and emotion. Centralized basic industries —electric power, steel, transportation—make possible dictatorial control of the main structure of an industrial society. (At least, this is true temporarily. It may well be that in the long run such tight control from the center is self-defeating, through lowered efficiency in economic activity and diminishing returns in popular fitness and morale. For the immediate future, it looks as though the despots are making shrewd use of modern equipment.)

Large-scale Society and Feeling of Helplessness. More far-reaching and more difficult to regard as abnormal or avoidable consequences of our immense industrialization are new modes of enslavement and dehumanizing of life that characterize even normal operations of large-scale production, whether in war or in peace. The relevant facts here are perfectly familiar and often emphasized—sometimes overemphasized. On the one hand, the logic of improving machine production involves the need for steady acceleration of output and distribution by processes reduced as far as possible to mechanical routine. In as far as many individual workmen are essential parts of an assembly line, the tendency is to utilize in the industrial process not the whole of their personal powers but primarily a tiny fragmentary skill, so that they become in some sense interchangeable parts of the ongoing machine.

The greatly increased productivity that results and the need for a steadily broadening market for the goods produced are likely in our economic system to result in periodic gluts of the market, the need to cut back production, and the real or apparent demand for intervention and control by the government or by some other agency—cartel, authority, or what not—to direct and rationalize both production and distribution until the crisis can be survived. At the moment we seem to many observers to be avoiding major economic trouble by devoting a large share of our industrial power to the production of armament. That is scarcely conducive to an increase in security on the part of thinking men. But, in any event, whether during the alternation of active production with deflation and unemployment or during a period of increasingly tight central control, the effect upon the individual employer or employee is likely to be the development of a more or less acute feeling of helplessness in a situation unmanageably large and pervaded by impersonal drives that disregard the requirements of individual living.

Shifting Social Patterns. Quite as disturbing, though less directly referable to the rise of modern technology and industry, is the dislocation of traditional social patterns and their replacement by forms of social organization in which many of the dependable personal values seem to be in peril. We have noticed the change from the person-to-person pattern of feudal society in the direction of a more individualistic social order more consonant with our industrial plant and processes. In this new order there is greater need for easy mobility of labor and more rapid turnover of processes of work. There is a changing unbalance of age groups in the population, with a larger and larger proportion of men and women who are regarded in ordinary times as too old to hold up their part of a swift-moving competitive industrial organization. The habituation of both younger and older folk to rapid and frequent change of habitation and of occupation contributes to a widespread loss of familiar grounds for a sense of social validity. Perhaps most fundamental in this group of changes has been the altered status of family life, with a strong tendency to atomistic individualism and destruction of the organic cooperative patterns which in an older culture made one's place in the household, on the family farm, or in the small home industry a secure base for a sense of personal identity and worth.

Whether the gains or the losses in this trial balance of the effects of modern technology must be judged the larger, I confess I am not able to say with confidence. At all events, both gains and losses are evident, and the threats are sufficiently frightening to demand most serious attention.

EFFECTS OF NEW WAYS OF UNDERSTANDING MAN AND THE WORLD

Correlative with the development of modern technology has been development of new theoretic pictures of nature and of man. The most distinctive constituent in this new intellectual outlook has been the rise of the modern sciences and modes of thought closely associated with them.

In trying to characterize the modern scientific temper, there is need to take account both of its essential nature and of the aberrations or distortions to which it has proved especially vulnerable. In its essential character, the scientific temper seeks to employ precise quantitative methods for observing, reporting, and interpreting perceptible events. Its temper is governed by the ideal of objective empiricism. It seeks, that is, to see as steadily and clearly as possible what is actually before the observer's eyes and to avoid permitting his own bias, preference, or hope to warp his vision. This is a difficult attitude to acquire and to maintain. Actual human beings are never simply calculating machines. But to keep the ideal constantly in view is essential for one who attempts seriously the practice of scientific inquiry.

Science and Philosophy of Life. The desire for simplicity and precision of results and the extraordinary successes that have attended the application of scientific technique in many fields have not unnaturally attracted the allegiance of many folk who lacked the specialized training and careful discipline of first-rate scientific minds. Not infrequently, the temper of the trained scientist is more or less imperceptibly changed into the temper of a speculative philosopher who may regard himself and represent himself as a scientist pure and simple. Such a man may assume that the world of nature and of human society, as far as knowable at all, must be interpretable through and through in the simple and precise terms that have proved largely applicable in physical research. The aim of such an assumption, whether explicitly stated or tacitly assumed, is to interpret the whole realm of perceptible reality as reducible to uniformly simple terms. One familiar outcome is a world view that construes all reality as analogous to physical events governed by the relatively simple patterns which nineteenth-century physics supposed to be universal. Twentieth-century physics is far more sophisticated, complex, and fluid, and is already contributing to world views much less intent on reduction of everything to mechanical simplicities. But the need is permanent to distinguish between the methods and findings of the sciences and a full-scale philosophy of life.

Among the special sciences which have risen to immense competence and prestige during the past two centuries, the physical sciences—intent upon analyzing, measuring, and interpreting the shifts of energy units of one sort and another in the areas with which physics, chemistry, and their several branches and developments are concerned—have come to occupy the place of type specimens. The exact sciences, as they are often called, have become a kind of standard by which inquiry in other fields than physics and chemistry often seek to be judged. The physical sciences serve at once as guides to the practical control of physical nature, in the interest of human understanding and power, and as clues to a working philosophy which often takes the form of physical naturalism, mechanistic or organistic. Machine of living organism, nature is all; and all is physical reality open to purely physical interpretation.

In somewhat similar fashion, the special studies of living structure and behavior in individual organisms, the biological and psychological sciences, have supplied at once the basis for many sorts of significant practice and a point of departure for philosophic generalizations about the nature of life and of man. One of the most widely accepted and significant findings in the philosophic area touched closely by biological research is the conviction that life is continuous on this planet through all the stages of simple unicellular living things through plants and animals in all stages of complexity. Man, like all the others, had his place in the scheme of terrestrial life, and must be understood in the light of principles that apply to all life.

Among the inquiries that have contributed most directly to this evolutionary understanding of human life, the impressively careful work of students of genetics and the still more popularly striking work of the students of environmental conditioning occupy especially conspicuous positions. Evolutionary philosophy and comparative psychology, whether it be of the behavioristic type developed by Pavlov and his disciples or the depth psychology associated especially with the work of Freud and his successors, has done much to spread the conception of man as essentially a complex and especially adaptable animal.

Newer Insights—"Field Theory." The difference in outlook and in implication for the over-all understanding of man and his world that sets off the newest physics, biology, and psychology from the earlier views of Newton, Darwin, and Freud deserves special emphasis. Eighteenth- and nineteenth-century scientific thought, and the philosophies that most closely reflected its influence, were predominantly mechanistic. The physical universe and the bodies that compose it were conceived more or less literally as an enormously intricate clockwork, with each part driven by neighboring parts according to Newton's simple laws of motion. Freud's picture of man as actuated by diverse natural drives and hidden "complexes" resulting from collisions between such drives and socially imposed restraints, and Pavlov's account of behavior as a system of mechanically "conditioned"—modified and reconnected—automatic reflexes, fitted fairly well into the nineteenth-century scheme.

But the discovery and study of radioactivity, the restudy of gravitation, electricity, magnetism, and light, and new experimentation with living embryos have led to an immense and exciting change of perspective in physics and biology. This change is carrying over also into psychological and social studies. Instead of laying exclusive stress on the interacting separate parts—of bodies, behavior systems, social groups—it has been found necessary to give at least equal stress to the inclusive fields—gravitational, electromagnetic, organic, cultural—in which the interaction can go on. Development of these newer insights is only well begun and gives promise of far more fluid, subtle, and inclusive understanding of man and nature. Whether such understanding logically points beyond a world view bounded by the data and findings of the sciences is now warmly debated.

Studies of Social Behavior, Cultural Relativism. Finally, the systematic study of social behavior and developments in the several fields of anthropology, sociology, economics, government, and various departments of history have helped to round out a naturalistic picture. The results of these studies, by and large, have been less fully translated into direct technical applications than the findings of the physical and biological sciences, and have therefore affected somewhat less obviously the ordinary run of popular thought. At the same time, they have contributed directly to the rise of politically powerful social philosophies. Liberal democracy, Marxism, and fascism all have drawn in different ways on the findings of the social studies. These studies, moreover, have helped gradually to spread among people without technical training some of the assumptions concerning man that have emerged during the development of social anthropology and the work of cultural sociology.

The concept of cultural relativism, which focuses upon the particular patterns of life in a certain time and place and seeks to interpret each aspect of the life of the community studied in close interrelation with the entire culture pattern, has become more and more widely accepted into our working assumptions about ourselves, even when it is not explicitly stressed. The conception of social evolutionism, whether or not the analogy with biological evolution is applied in more or less literal fashion, and the related "idea of progress" as a basis for evaluation and prediction of lines of social development, have likewise become a part of much popular thinking about society. Direct practical application of our findings in these fields is as yet by no means systematic or widespread. But changes in our understanding of ourselves have been prompted largely by the systematic effort to discover common factors and predictable sequences in social behavior.

Science and Gains for Confidence. As in the area of technological development, so here there have been definite gains for man's confidence in life. Growing knowledge has helped to eliminate or reduce many traditional fears directed toward processes of nature that were not well understood. Abnormal behavior of individual persons, no less than physical ailment, has come to be understood much more fairly and fully during the past fifty years, and there is promise for yet better understanding and perhaps better prevention and control of such psychopathic behavior. Perhaps most widespread of all, there has been provided an apparent basis for optimism in the philosophy of evolutionary progress, with its frank and unabashed encouragement to human self-reliance. The notion of "the survival of the fittest" has been applied in many uncritical ways to the appraisal and interpretation of all sorts of human phenomena. The conviction that man has made discernible progress and is making more rapid progress generation by generation has become for many a heartening and confident philosophy of life.

Threats to Confidence. On the other side of the balance there are new threats to this same fundamental working faith. The discovery in biological and psychological research of new grounds for affirming that man is essentially an animal has been accompanied in terrifying fashion by rediscovery in actual life that savagery and irrationality lie near the surface, even in "normal" human behavior. There has been undermining of moral imperatives and of confidence even in the most strongly held human values, as an increasing acceptance of social relativity and an increasing practice of moral and political opportunism have become a part of the climate of the modern mind.

Along with this change has gone a waning of faith in God. This has resulted in part from the discovery of plain errors in particular theological beliefs, which conflict with the procedures and the findings of the sciences. It has resulted in part, moreover, from increasingly clear recognition of moral inadequacies in specific ecclesiastical practices. The official spokesmen for religion bear a heavy load of responsibility for the failure of their stewardship to keep pace with the demands of the swift-moving modern world. On the other hand, a considerable part of the change of sentiment with respect to religion has resulted from the offer of a substitute basis for human confidence, a basis of naturalistic optimism and secular activism that professes to offer a sufficient basis for all legitimate human needs. That this substitution has been premature and ill-considered seems to me clear. At any rate, it has contributed substantially to the shift of confidence away from traditional religion to what professes to be a better modern substitute.

Science and Religion. At the same time and on a more fundamental level, though with far less popular concurrence, there is among thoughtful people a questioning of the propriety of religious commitment of any kind. The temper of scientific objectivity, which stresses the need to withhold judgment until convincing evidence makes affirmation rationally inescapable, has been understood to mean that the whole of man's life should be lived within the austere limits thus defined. Once again this judgment appears to me overhasty, and in practice untenable. Yet its influence in undermining the basis for confidence in the ultimate meaningfulness of human life cannot be disregarded. As a critical caution against irrational dogmatism it is salutary and welcome. As an alternative kind of dogmatism it must itself be continuously criticized.

WHAT MUST BE DONE?

It is impossible here to do more than hint at the direction in which effort may be applied to the problem of making the fullest use of the gains and seeking to offset the losses for man's basic faith in life that have come with industrialization. That problem may well have a major place in our roundtable's discussion.

PERSONAL ADEQUACY

In the first place, it seems almost obvious to say that there is need to extend the best means now available for restoring and improving man's sense of personal adequacy. This involves provision for sound nutrition, proper medical care, and increasingly effective education for work, leisure, and life in community. Confidence in life does not exist in a vacuum, and it can be restored and maintained only if the indispensable conditions for its persistence are recognized and maintained.

BETTER BALANCE IN SOCIAL LIVING

There is need, secondly, for a determined effort to restore a better balance of personal and impersonal factors in contemporary social living. It has been noted that the sense of social validity is an indispensable basis for man's ultimate confidence in life, and to the degree that industrialized society has undercut the conditions that once existed for the individual's sense of being accepted and being worthy to be accepted as member of a living group, there is need for reconstruction. Perhaps the most obvious need is a new and systematic effort to safeguard significant family life, and to improve the nurture of early childhood and youth. There is need for the encouragement of diverse social groups within the main framework of society—interest groups of many sorts within which individual persons may find themselves more fully at home than it is possible for anyone to be in a world grown so large and complex that he finds himself overwhelmed in its presence.

DEMOCRATIC TEMPER AND PRACTICE

In this larger social order there is need for development of democratic understanding and practice. To a considerable extent this is another way of saying what has already been said: that diverse constituent communities and a growing sense of membership in the larger community must be encouraged and maintained. But something more is intended. Fundamental in the rise of democratic patterns of national life in the Western world has been the assumption that there are common standards of obligation, universal duties and imperatives ingrained in the nature of the world and of man, to which both individuals and societies are properly subject. The British parliamentary leaders who helped to oppose and destroy the autocratic Stuart government, the framers of the American Declaration of Independence, the French intellectuals who helped to shape the Declaration of the Rights of Man and of the Citizen were all convinced of the existence of such a common frame of reference for human law and human life. There is need to recapture and extend in our world, at both national and international levels of relationship and organization, that fundamental democratic faith. Without it we are reduced to the essential anarchy of competing interest groups, in which conflict can be resolved in the last analysis only by a trial of strength. Re-establishment of a secure basis for the individual sense of social validity in this modern world of high speed and complex organization depends in a scarcely calculable measure upon the achievement of democratic temper and practice.

REDISCOVERY OF MORAL AND RELIGIOUS FAITH

There is need, lastly, for rediscovery of a basis for the most ultimate sorts of moral and religious faith. One requisite for such rediscovery is refusal to be stampeded by the familiar fact that during the past century and a half the hold of traditional religious forms upon men of the West has greatly diminished. There is need to remember that throughout the history of Judaism and Christianity in the West there has been recurrent ebb and flow of religious conviction and moral devotion. There is need to recognize the familiar character of this repeated rhythm and to reject, on the one hand, the paralysis of despair and, on the other hand, the appallingly destructive alternative of idolatry. Idolatry is a word that seems peculiarly out of place in the modern world, but its primary meaning is relevant now if it ever was. When men turn way from a God worthy of their worship, it is likely to be not long before they transfer their unanchored cravings to gods unworthy of their worship—to deified emperors, political systems, races, or economic class organizations.

To aid in maintaining the stability and balance of outlook that is urgently needed, it is necessary that we seek more adequate appreciation of the real character and implications of the sciences and technology, that we get them into a suitable perspective in which their benefits may be frankly and gratefully accepted and their aberrations may be as resolutely put aside. But there is need that we seek more adequate understanding and practice of the moral and religious convictions that actually exist and their closer integration into everyday living. The quest of security through the discovery or establishment of some new religion or new morality is likely to be disappointing. Religions, like languages, grow in their own way. They cannot be constructed to order. But the religions deep-rooted in the life of the West need and deserve to be understood as most men do not now understand them. Their rediscovery and reinterpretation is an urgent task for churches, schools, and all men of intelligence and goodwill.

Needless to say, this is not meant as a defense of uncritical conformity. New knowledge, new insights, new demands call for continual rethinking of both moral and religious convictions. There is every reason to explore unbeaten paths and to attempt fresh formulations of what seems to oneself in one's own situation true and basic for life. At the same time, what each of us can know and actively believe now is largely determined by the heritage in which we have grown and which lives more or less consciously in us. To rediscover and reclaim it, and to make its resources more fully understood and accessible for hard-pressed people is a major part of our job.

SELECTED BIBLIOGRAPHY

Bennett, John C., *Social Salvation*. Scribner's, 1935.

Calhoun, Robert L., *God and the Common Life*. Scribner's, 1935.

Frank, Lawrence K., *Nature and Human Nature*. Rutgers University Press, 1951.

Fromm, Erich, *Psychoanalysis and Religion*. Yale University Press, 1950.

Hocking, William Ernest, and Others, *Preface to Philosophy*. Macmillan, 1946.

Mannheim, Karl, *Diagnosis of Our Time*. Oxford University Press, 1944.

Paton, H. J. (tr. and ed.), *The Moral Law*. Barnes and Noble, 1950.

Pound, Roscoe, *Law and Morals*. University of North Carolina Press, 1926.

Whitehead, Alfred N., *Science and the Modern World*. Macmillan, 1926; Mentor Books, 1948.

More detailed and technical works

Cochrane, Charles N., *Christianity and Classical Culture*. Oxford University Press, 1944.

Hallowell, John H., *Main Currents in Modern Political Thought*. Henry Holt, 1950.

Horney, Karen, *Neuroses and Human Growth*. W. W. Norton, 1950.

Kelsen, Hans, *General Theory of Law and State*. Harvard University Press, 1945.

Niebuhr, Reinhold, *Faith and History*. Scribner's, 1949.

Orton, William A., *The Liberal Tradition*. Yale University Press, 1945.

Perry, Ralph B., *Puritanism and Democracy*. Vanguard Press, 1944.

Appendix

LAWRENCE A. APPLEY: President, American Management Association. Former vice-president and director, Montgomery Ward and Vick Chemical Co.; was adviser to U.S. Civil Service Commission on administrative organization, expert consultant to Secretary of War on civilian personnel and training, executive director and deputy chairman of War Manpower Commission, member personnel policy committee of Hoover Commission and other government commissions; has been in field of personnel since 1930.

WELLS BENNETT: Dean, College of Architecture and Design, University of Michigan. Past president of Association Collegiate Schools of Architecture, Michigan State Board of Registration, Architects, Engineers, and Surveyors, and fellow of the American Institute of Architects (Detroit Chapter); writer of many articles on architecture and housing; instructor in and practitioner of architecture since 1912.

MARK BENNEY: Author and social scientist, London School of Economics. First book, *Low Company*, was an essay in criminology written from personal experience; wrote novels and films; during war worked as bench hand in factories and as industrial relations officer; author of *Over to Bombers* and *Charity Main*, dealing with attitudes to work in mines and factories; directed the Greenwich Election Survey, a study of political behavior; conducted survey of the English prison system, which was published under the title *Gaol Delivery*.

THEODORE C. BLEGEN: Dean of the Graduate School and professor of American history, University of Minnesota. Member board of directors, ACLS; past president of Mississippi Valley Historical Association; during war director of Historical Service Board and GI Round Table; author of *Grass Roots History*, *The Land Lies Open*, *Norwegian Migration to America*, *The American Transition*, and other books on American history.

HAROLD BOESCHENSTEIN: President, Owens-Corning Fiberglas Corp., Toledo. Chairman of the board of Fiberglas Canada, Ltd.; director of Owens-Illinois Glass Co., National Distillers Products Corp., Weco Products, and Financial Press Cos. of America; served on War Production Board during World War II; has been in administrative and sales-manager capacity since 1921.

DENIS W. BROGAN: Professor of political science, University of Cambridge, England. Fellow of Peterhouse, Cambridge, and of Corpus Christi, Oxford; author of *The American Political System, The Free State, The Development of Modern France, Politics and Law in the United States, The American Character,* and other books and articles on political science.

HARCOURT BROWN: Professor of French language and literature, Brown University. President of History of Science Society; editor of *Annals of Science,* author of *Scientific Organizations in 17th Century France* and of articles on the humanistic relationships of various scientific figures and organizations; engaged in making persons and aspects of humanistic past available to present age of technology and industry.

BAKER BROWNELL: Professor of philosophy, Northwestern University. Former newspaperman and editorial writer; director, The Montana Study, a project in community stabilization and enrichment; his books include: *The Human Community, Earth Is Enough, Art Is Action, Architecture in Modern Life* (with Frank Lloyd Wright), *Life in Montana* (in collaboration), *The New Universe;* edited numerous books on the community.

YALE BROZEN: Professor of economics, Northwestern University. Conducting research on economics of technological change; consultant to American Telephone and Telegraph Co. and to State's Attorney's Office, Cook County, Ill.; author of *Social Implications of Technological Change* and many articles on related subjects including, "The Social Impact of Technological Change" and "Technological Change in Backward Areas."

ELSE FRENKEL-BRUNSWIK: Research psychologist, Cowell Memorial Hospital, and lecturer in psychology, University of California. Co-author of *The Authoritarian Personality,* author of *Motivation and Behavior* and technical papers on personality problems.

JOHN E. BURCHARD: Dean of Humanities and Social Studies, Massachusetts Institute of Technology. Experienced in industrial housing, and was director of The Albert Farwell Bemis Foundation for housing research at M.I.T.; served with OSRD as leader of various projects and as chief of military-scientific missions to several foreign countries during war; co-author of *The Evolving House, Combat Scientists,* and editor of *Mid-Century: The Social Implications of Scientific Progress.*

TEMPLE BURLING, M.D.: Professor, New York State School of Industrial and Labor Relations, Cornell University. Served as psychiatrist with Institute for Juvenile Research, Chicago, Winnetka Public Schools, R. H. Macy & Co.; medical director of Providence Child Guidance Clinic; field director, Division of Vocational Rehabilitation, National Committee for Mental Hygiene; co-author of *Vocational Rehabilitation of Psychiatric Patients* and writer of articles on industrial and child psychiatry.

HAROLD S. BUTTENHEIM: Editor, *The American City Magazine*. Organizer, American City Bureau; chairman of the board, American City Magazine Corp., American Council for the Community; honorary president, Citizens' Housing and Planning Council of New York; director, American City Bureau, Inc., American Association for the UN, N.J. Federation of Official Planning Boards, Civic Films, Inc.

ROBERT L. CALHOUN: Pitkin professor of historical theology at Yale Divinity School, fellow of Saybrook College. Has taught and lectured on theology at various schools; author of *God and the Common Life* and *What is Man?*; co-author of *The Meaning of the Humanities* and *Religion and the Modern World*.

ANTONIO CARRILLO FLORES: Director-General of Nacional Financiera, an agency in charge of financial aspects of the development program of Mexico. Formerly dean of the National School of Law, Mexico City; professor of theory of law and administrative law; member of board of Bank of Mexico and other public institutions; has represented Mexico in Inter-American Economic and Social Council and as economic delegate to UN General Assembly and recent conference of Western Hemisphere foreign ministers; author of studies in law and economics.

RALPH COGHLAN: Office of the Defense Mobilization Director. Former editor of editorial page, St. Louis *Post-Dispatch*; former reporter and editorial writer for other newspapers; director of Pulitzer Publishing Co. and the American Society of Newspaper Editors; vice-chairman of National Conference of Editorial Writers.

WILBUR J. COHEN: Technical adviser to the Commissioner for Social Security, Washington, D.C. Former research assistant to executive director of President's Committee on Economic Security, which drew up the original Social Security Act; closely associated with subsequent amendments; studied and wrote on operation of European social security systems; represented U.S. government at international social security meetings and at the International Labor Conference; editor of *War and Postwar Social Security* and *Readings in Social Security*; writer of articles on social security.

HARRY H. COOK: International president, American Flint Glass Workers' Union, AFL, Toledo. Started work in glass factory at age ten;

learned glass-blowing trade and became highly skilled mechanic; a union member since 1901, served in all local union offices; was international assistant secretary and first vice-president before being elected president in 1940.

LOU R. CRANDALL: President, George A. Fuller Co., New York. Director of Curtiss-Wright Corp., Savoy-Plaza, Inc., and other firms; erected many notable structures, such as the Aetna Life Insurance buildings in Hartford and New York, State Capitol buildings of West Virginia and Louisiana, National Episcopal Cathedral, and Supreme Court building in Washington, D.C.; contributor to magazines on engineering and industrial subjects.

DONALD K. DAVID: Dean, Graduate School of Business Administration, Harvard University. Past president of Royal Baking Powder Co., and American Maize Products Co.; a director of Standard Brands, Inc., R. H. Macy & Co., General Electric Co., Federal Reserve Bank of Boston, and other business organizations.

WILLIAM RAY DENNES: Dean, Graduate Division, and professor of philosophy, University of California, Berkeley. Past president of Pacific Division of American Philosophical Association; has taught and lectured on philosophy at various universities throughout the country; worked on Manhattan District Los Alamos project; author of *Conceptions of Civilization, The Meaning of Individuality, Civilization and Values, Conflict, Methods and Presuppositions of Group Psychology*, and other books and articles on philosophy.

REUEL DENNEY: Assistant professor of social sciences, University of Chicago. Former assistant editor of *Time* and *Fortune*; author of *The Connecticut River* (verse) and co-author of *The Lonely Crowd*, editor of "Materials on Popular Culture and Leisure"; poems and reviews in various periodicals since 1932.

WILLIAM C. DEVANE: Dean, Yale College, and director, University Division of the Liberal Arts, Yale University. Former chairman of board, ACLS; editorial board of *Yale Review*; teacher of English literature since 1922; trustee of General Education Board; past president, College English Association; author of several books on Browning, in addition to *Tennyson* and *Charlotte Brontë's Legends of Angria* (in collaboration).

RENE d'HARNONCOURT: Director, Museum of Modern Art, New York. Chairman of Indian Arts and Crafts Board of U.S. Department of the Interior; organized art exhibits such as "Timeless Aspects of Modern Art" and "Modern Art in Your Life"; member program committee of U.S. Commission for UNESCO; author of *Mexicana*, co-author of *Indian Art of the United States*, numerous articles.

JOHN W. DODDS: Professor of English and Director of Special Programs in Humanities, Stanford University. Chairman editorial board of the *Pacific Spectator*; teacher of English since 1927; author of *Thomas Southerne, Dramatist* and *Thackeray: A Critical Portrait*; at present is engaged in preparation of *Biography of a Decade: England 1841-1851.*

FREDERIC W. ECKER: Executive vice-president, Metropolitan Life Insurance Co., Director of St. Louis and San Francisco Railroad Co.; an executive with Metropolitan Life Insurance Co. since 1925; during World War II was special assistant to administrator of Lend-Lease and headed the Lend-Lease mission to India.

CHARLES B. FAHS: Director for the Humanities, Rockefeller Foundation. Formerly was teacher of Oriental affairs, Pomona and Claremont Colleges; during World War II engaged in research on the Far East for the U.S. government; with the Rockefeller Foundation since 1946.

MARION B. FOLSOM: Treasurer, Eastman Kodak Co., Rochester. Was director House of Representatives special committee on Postwar Economic Policy and Planning, 78-79th Congress; former member, Regional War Manpower Commission; employer delegate to International Labor Conference, Geneva; active in National Advisory Defense Commission, and many other government commissions on social security, merchant marine, etc.; former chairman, Research and Policy Committe, Committee for Economic Development; writer of articles on social insurance, industrial relations, and business.

LAWRENCE K. FRANK: Author; member, Board of Leaders, New York Society for Ethical Culture. Former president, National Council on Family Relations, Gerontological Society; former chairman, Society for Research in Child Development; chairman, International Preparatory Commission, International Congress on Mental Hygiene, 1948; former director, Caroline Zachry Institute of Human Development; books include: *Society as the Patient, Nature and Human Nature: Man's New Image of Himself,* and *How to Help Your Child in School.*

JOHN M. GAUS: Professor of government, and chairman, Committee on Higher Degrees in the History of American Civilization, Harvard University. Past president of American Political Science Association; teacher of political science since 1920; administrative service with states of Massachusetts, New York, and Wisconsin and various departments of U.S. government; author of *Great Britain, A Study of Civic Loyalty, Reflections on Public Administration,* and other books and articles.

WALLACE K. HARRISON: Architect, firm of Harrison, Abramovitz and Abbey, architects, New York. One of group of architects of Rockefeller

Center, of Corning Glass Center; director of planning, United Nations Headquarters; formerly director, Office of Inter-American Affairs.

DOUGLAS HASKELL: Architectural editor, *Architectural Forum*. In the field of architectural criticism and architectural and planning journalism since 1925; articles in U.S. professional magazines and the *Architectural Review* of London and in general publications; formerly associate editor of *Creative Arts* and associate editor of *Architectural Record*.

A. J. HAYES: International president, International Association of Machinists. Cochairman, United Labor Policy Committee; special assistant to Assistant Secretary of Defense; started as apprentice and worked as machinist for 17 years; was chairman of shop committee, president of local union, president of Machinists District 7; subsequently grand lodge representative, vice-president and president of International Association of Machinists; during World War II was labor member of Sixth Regional War Labor Board, Chicago.

HENRY B. HIGGINS: President, Pittsburgh Plate Glass Co., Pittsburgh. President, Pittsburgh-Corning Co.; with Pittsburgh Plate Glass Co. since 1905, beginning as stenographer; director, Westinghouse Electric Corporation, Mellon National Bank, A. M. Beyers Co., Westinghouse Airbrake Corp., Union Switch and Signal Co., the Pennsylvania Co., the Pennsylvania Railroad Co., Hobbs Glass, Ltd. (Canada), Murphy Paint Co., Ltd. (Canada); trustee, Dollar Savings Bank, University of Pittsburgh; president of Board of Trustees, Elizabeth Steel Magee Hospital.

SEWARD HILTNER: Associate professor of pastoral theology, Federated Theological Faculty of the University of Chicago. Former member secretariat, Federal Council of Churches; pastoral consultant to *Pastoral Psychology* magazine; currently engaged in study of "Religion and Personality," an exploration of the interrelationship between religion and the sciences of man; author of *Pastoral Counseling, Self-Understanding, Christianity and Mental Hygiene*, and other books.

GEORGE C. HOMANS: Associate professor of sociology, Harvard University. Has done research in the field of industrial sociology, notably on technological unemployment and the social organization of clerical workers; among his publications are: *An Introduction to Pareto, Fatigue of Workers, English Villagers of the 13th Century*, and *The Human Group*.

EVERETT C. HUGHES: Professor of sociology, University of Chicago. President, Society for Applied Anthropology; conducting research in contacts of cultures at work and other problems of work behavior, especially in professional occupations; books include: *French Canada in Transition,* and articles: "The Knitting of Racial Groups in Industry," "Work and the Self," and "The Study of Ethnic Relations."

GEORGE M. HUMPHREY: President, M. A. Hanna Co., Cleveland. Former practitioner of law; chairman of the boards, Susquehanna Anthracite Co. and Pittsburgh Consolidation Coal Co.; director, Phelps Dodge Corp.; chairman executive committee and director, Industrial Rayon Corp.; chairman executive committee, National Steel Corp.; director of other companies.

JULIAN HUXLEY: Author. Past director-general, UNESCO. Past president of Association of Scientific Workers and the Institution of Animal Behavior; former secretary, Zoological Society of London, and advisory editor, *Zoo* magazine; former executive secretary, UNESCO Preparatory Commission; among his publications are: *Scientific Research and Social Needs, We Europeans, The Uniqueness of Man, Evolutionary Ethics,* and *Man in the Modern World.*

ELLIOTT JAQUES, M.D. Tavistock Institute of Human Relations, England. Associate member of British Psycho-Analytical Society; member of Management Committee of the Tavistock Institute; director of one of its projects in industrial relations covering a wide range of executive and consultative problems, and the way these are affected by intergroup and intragroup relations; a first report appears in his book *The Changing Culture of a Factory.*

HOWARD MUMFORD JONES: Professor of English, Harvard University. President, American Academy of Arts and Sciences; former educational consultant Provost Marshal General's Office; teacher of English literature since 1919; author of poems, plays, books, including: *Ideas in America, American and French Culture (1750-1848), Education and World Tragedy,* and *The Theory of American Literature.*

MARTIN JOOS: Professor of German, University of Wisconsin. Studied electrical engineering and worked as an engineer of manufacture in Western Electric plant; language teacher since 1938; during World War II was technical consultant in secrecy of communication, U.S. War Department; among his books are: *Word-Index to Joyce's Ulysses, Acoustic Phonetics,* and *Middle High German Courtly Reader;* writer of articles on linguistic theory, culture, and literature.

MEYER KESTNBAUM: President, Hart Schaffner & Marx, Chicago. Chairman, Research and Policy Committee of the Committee for Economic Development; director of Chicago and North Western Railroad Co.; past president of Council of Social Agencies of Chicago and Chicago Council on Foreign Relations; adviser to the Office of the Quartermaster General.

JOHN A. KOUWENHOVEN: Professor of English, Barnard College, Columbia University. Contributing editor, *Harper's Magazine*. Author of *Adventures of America, 1857-1900* and *Made in America: The Arts in Modern Civilization*; contributor of articles to *Harper's Magazine, Atlantic Monthly, Yale Review, Reader's Digest*, and others.

CORNELIUS KRUSÉ: Professor of philosophy, Wesleyan University, Middletown, Conn. Past chairman of board of officers and past president of American Philosophical Association (Eastern Division); chairman of Second Inter-American Congress of Philosophy; former foreign service secretary of American Friends Service Committee; former executive director and present chairman of board of directors, ACLS; co-author of *The Nature of Man, His World, His Spiritual Resources and Destiny*.

ERIC LARRABEE: Associate editor, *Harper's Magazine*. Served with the Military Intelligence Service in European Theater (during World War II); contributor of articles and book reviews to *Harper's* and other publications.

HAROLD D. LASSWELL: Professor of law, Yale Law School. Has taught and done research in political science at several universities; director of War Communications Research, Library of Congress; member Research Advisory Board of Committee for Economic Development; advisory editor of *Ethics, Public Opinion Quarterly*; among his publications are: *Psychopathology and Politics, World Politics and Personal Insecurity, Politics Faces Economics*, and *Power and Personality*.

WILLIAM E. LEVIS: Chairman, Executive Committee, Owens-Illinois Glass Co., Toledo. Director of New York Central Railroad, Ohio Bell Telephone Co., and Clinton Foods, Inc.; during World War II was assistant to chairman, War Production Board.

DAVID E. LILIENTHAL: Consultant to Management, New York and Washington. Past chairman, Atomic Energy Commission and Tennessee Valley Authority. Served as chairman, Board of Consultants on International Control of Atomic Energy, U.S. State Department; author of *TVA: Democracy on the March, This I Do Believe*.

LEO LIONNI: Art director, *Fortune* magazine. Painting, advertising, and design work in Italy; former art director, N. W. Ayer & Son, and of Container Corp. advertising account; has exhibited at Norlyst Gallery, New York, and Philadelphia Print Club; art and design consultant to government agencies and private societies; contributor of articles on architecture, art, and the cinema.

BENJAMIN L. MASSE, S.J.: Associate editor of *America*, National Catholic Weekly. Executive editor of the *Catholic Mind*; lecturer in industrial ethics, Xavier Labor School, New York City; associate in Columbia University Seminar on Labor; member, Industry Panel, American Arbitration Association; lecturer and writer, with special interest in trade-unionism and industrial relations.

DOUGLAS McGREGOR: President, Antioch College. Formerly taught psychology at Harvard and M.I.T.; one of founders and former director of Industrial Relations Section, M.I.T.; former director of industrial relations, Dewey and Almy Chemical Co.; consultant to twelve companies and unions in the East and Midwest since 1939; member, panel of arbitrators, American Arbitration Association.

KEITH S. McHUGH: President, New York Telephone Co. Former vice-president and director, Long Lines Department, American Telephone and Telegraph Co.; member executive committee and director, Air Reduction Co.; vice-president and member executive committee, American Management Association.

MARGARET MEAD: Associate curator of ethnology, American Museum of Natural History, New York. Former executive secretary, Committee on Food Habits, National Research Council; former director, Columbia University Research in Contemporary Cultures; many field studies in ethnology; among her books are: *Coming of Age in Samoa, Growing Up in New Guinea, And Keep Your Powder Dry*, and *Male and Female: A Study of the Sexes*; contributor of articles on oceanic ethnology and relationship between psychology and culture.

DON G. MITCHELL: President, Sylvania Electric Products, Inc., New York. Formerly in executive posts with American Seal Cone Corp., American Can Co., Marshall Field & Co., Pepsi-Cola Co.; director, Colonial Radio Corp., Wabash Corp., and other firms; member board of directors and executive committee, American Management Association; director, member executive committee and national vice-president, National Association of Manufacturers; member, panel of arbitrators, American Arbitration Association.

CHARLES MORRIS: Lecturer in philosophy, University of Chicago; lecturer in social relations, Harvard University. Associate editor of *International Encyclopedia of Unified Science*; currently engaged in study of preferred "ways to live" (value patterns and value orientations) of college students in various cultures; principal publications: *Paths of Life, Signs, Language, and Behavior* and *The Open Self*.

WALTER P. PAEPCKE: Chairman of board and chief executive officer, Container Corp. of America, Chicago. President, The Aspen Co.; director, Aspen Skiing Corp., Sefton Fibre Can Co., K. W. Battery Co., U.S. Gypsum Co., Fund for Advancement of Education (Ford Foundation); chairman of Advisory Committee, Institute of Design; trustee, University of Chicago and Chicago Orchestral Association.

SIDNEY PAINTER: Professor of history, Johns Hopkins University. Member, board of editors, *Medievalia et Humanistica*; former councilor of Mediaeval Academy of America; president, board of trustees, Roland Park Country School for Girls; among his publications are: *French Chivalry, History of the English Feudal Barony,* and *The Reign of King John.*

FRANK W. PIERCE: Director, Standard Oil Co. (New Jersey). Schooled in engineering; entire career spent in the field of industrial relations; former personnel manager, Goodyear Tire and Rubber Co.; joined Standard Oil (N.J.) 1924 as assistant to head of industrial relations, later in charge, and has been closely identified with development of the company's employee programs; former director and chairman of the board, Imperial Oil, Ltd. (Toronto).

GWILYM A. PRICE: President, Westinghouse Electric Corp., Pittsburgh. Former practitioner of law and state representative in Pennsylvania; former president and director, Peoples-Pittsburgh Trust Co.; director, National Union Fire Insurance Co., Blaw-Knox Co., The Hanover Bank, Peoples First National Bank & Trust Co., Baldwin-Lima-Hamilton Corp., Union Switch & Signal Co., Waynesburg & Washington Railroad Co., Westinghouse Air Brake Co.

SANTHA RAMA RAU: Author; student of Asian and Western cultures. Books: *Home to India, East of Home;* short stories in *New Yorker,* articles in *Mademoiselle, United Nations World, This Week,* and other magazines; worked for Office of War Information during World War II; was official hostess for her father when he was ambassador of India to Japan and to the U.S.; recent two-year trip through many countries of Asia.

PHILIP D. REED: Chairman of board, General Electric Co. Chairman of board, International General Electric Co.; director, Canadian General Electric Co., Metropolitan Life Insurance Co.; Honorary president, International Chamber of Commerce; joint chairman, U.S. Section, Anglo-American Council on Productivity; trustee, Committee for Economic Development, and former chairman, Research and Policy Committee; member of many business and government advisory groups; war service included War Production Board, deputy chief, Harriman Mission, London, and chief, Mission for Economic Affairs, London; commandeur, Légion d'Honneur.

DAVID RIESMAN: Professor of social sciences, University of Chicago. Former practitioner and instructor of law; a year as law clerk for Mr.

Justice Brandeis; worked for Sperry Gyroscope Co.; co-author of *The Lonely Crowd: A Study of the Changing American Character*, to be followed by "A Gallery of American Types"; contributor of articles on personality development and social structure and on popular culture.

FRITZ J. ROETHLISBERGER: Wallace B. Donham professor of human relations, Graduate School of Business Administration, Harvard University. Former practitioner of engineering in chemical industry; teacher and researcher in human problems of industry since 1927; author of *Management and Morale* and co-author of *Management and the Worker*, based on pioneering experiments at Hawthorne plant of Western Electric Co.

FRANCIS CHASE ROSECRANCE: Associate dean, School of Education, New York University. Former chairman, Committee on the Community of National Planning Association; former consultant, War Department, Commission on Teacher Education; present consultant, Department of Defense and U.S. Office of Education; member, committee surveying 44 colleges related to Presbyterian Church; co-author of *General Education in the American Secondary School* and *Guidance in Educational Institutions*.

IRWIN T. SANDERS: Head, Department of Sociology, University of Kentucky. Former dean, The American College, Sofia, Bulgaria; former agricultural attaché, U.S. Embassy, Belgrade; member editorial board, American Sociometric Association; member executive committee, Southern Sociological Society; director, University of Kentucky Social Research Consultation Services; director, Committee for Kentucky; author of *Balkan Village*, *Making Good Communities Better* and other books.

DAVID SARNOFF: Chairman of board, Radio Corp. of America. Former messenger boy, wireless operator, radio inspector, and engineer; chairman of board and director, Radio Corp. of America and RCA Communications, Inc.; director, RCA Institutes, Inc., NBC, Armed Forces Communications Association, Netherland American Foundation, National Foundation Infantile Paralysis, Metropolitan Opera, and other organizations.

CHARLES H. SAWYER: Director, University Division of the Arts, and dean, School of Fine Arts, Yale University. Former director, Worcester Art Museum, and Addison Gallery of American Art, Andover, Mass.; former chairman, Department of Art, Phillips Academy, Andover; special fields: art education, American art, and social history.

SIR GEORGE E. SCHUSTER: Director, Westminster Bank. Member of Government Committee on Industrial Productivity and chairman of the Committee's Panel on Human Relations. Director, Commercial Union Assurance Co. and other companies; former member of Parliament; former finance member of executive Council of Viceroy of India, and numerous other appointments in the public service; president, Multiple Shops Federation; member of Council of the British Institute of Management; treasurer, Medical Research Council; author, *India and Democracy, Christianity and Human Relations in Industry*.

LAURENCE SEARS: Professor of American political philosophy, Mills College. Part-time visiting professor of American political theory at University of California, Berkeley; former professor of philosophy, Ohio Wesleyan University and instructor, U.S. Army University, Biarritz; author of *Development of American Philosophy* and articles for journals.

MILLARD O. SHEETS: Artist; professor of art, Scripps College. Teacher of art since 1929; represented permanently in Metropolitan Museum of Art, Chicago Art Institute, Whitney Museum of American Art, Los Angeles Museum, Cleveland Museum of Art, and many other galleries; recipient of major art awards; artist for *Life* on Burma-India-China front; consultant in design to industry.

TED F. SILVEY: Staff executive, Congress of Industrial Organizations, Washington, D.C. Secretary, national CIO Community Services Committee; union printer, member International Typographical Union; early organizer for CIO in Ohio; formerly secretary-treasurer and legislative representative, Ohio CIO Council; since 1944, on national CIO staff; specialized in work with nonlabor organizations and with government agencies.

MARK STARR: Educational director, International Ladies' Garment Workers' Union, AFL. Worked in mines of South Wales; taught economics and labor history; former vice-president, American Federation of Teachers; member, U.S. delegation to set up UNESCO, 1945; member executive boards, American Labor Education Service and other civic groups; chairman, Public Affairs Committee; member, U.S. Advisory Committee on Educational Exchange; his books include: *Lies and Hate in Education, Labor Looks at Education, Labor Politics in U. S. A.,* and *Labor in America* (with Harold U. Faulkner).

ROBERT T. STEVENS: Chairman, J. P. Stevens & Co., Inc. Chairman, Business Advisory Council, U.S. Department of Commerce. Class C director and chairman, Federal Reserve Bank of New York; director, Association of Cotton Textile Merchants, General Electric Co., General Foods Corp., New York Telephone Co., Alexander Smith, Inc., Pan American World Airways System, Owens-Corning Fiberglas Corp., member staff, NRA, 1933 and in wartime civilian and military government posts.

JOSEPH R. STRAYER: Dayton-Stockton professor and chairman, Department of History, Princeton University. Teacher of history since 1929; member council, American Historical Association; former member, board of directors, ACLS; served on historical advisory committee, Army Air Forces; author of *The Administration of Normandy under St. Louis*, co-author of *Studies in Early French Taxation* and *The Middle Ages*, co-editor of *The English Government at Work*, 1327-1336 and other books.

EDWARD R. WEIDLEIN: President, Mellon Institute of Industrial Research, Pittsburgh. Former president and director, American Chemical Society and the American Institute of Chemical Engineers; former member of council, AAAS; member, executive committee American Section, Society Chemical Industry; member, advisory committee, National Association of Manufacturers; technical consultant, War Production Board and other government agencies during World War II; co-author of *Science in Action* and *Glances at Industrial Research*; contributor of articles on industrial research.

LYNN WHITE, JR.: President, Mills College. Formerly professor of medieval history; member board of directors, ACLS; member executive committee of World Affairs Council of Northern California, board of deYoung Museum, advisory councils of American Association for the United Nations (Calif.) and the Family Relations Center; member educational advisory council, National Association of Manufacturers; author of *Latin Monasticism in Norman Sicily* and *Educating Our Daughters: A Challenge to the Colleges*.

LANCELOT LAW WHYTE: Philosopher of science, Great Britain. Has engaged in development of new inventions; was chairman and managing director of Power Jets, Ltd.; former director of statistical inquiries, British Ministry of Supply, specializing in labor conditions; principal publications are: *Critique of Physics, Unitary Principle in Physics and Biology, The Next Development in Man*, and *Everyman Looks Forward*.

WILLIAM F. WHYTE: Professor of industrial and labor relations, Cornell University. Member of executive board, Industrial Relations Research Association; former executive secretary, Committee on Human Relations in Industry, University of Chicago; author of *Street Corner Society, Human Relations in the Restaurant Industry*, and *Pattern for Industrial Peace*, editor of *Industry and Society*; contributor of articles to professional journals.

LANGBOURNE M. WILLIAMS, JR.: President, Freeport Sulphur Co., New York. Chairman of Board, Virginia Central Railway; director of B. F. Goodrich Co.; member, Business Advisory Council of U.S. Department of Commerce; member of board of governors, Society of

New York Hospital; vice-chairman, National Industrial Conference Board; trustee, Bank of New York and Fifth Avenue Bank; trustee, American Church Institute for Negroes.

Louis Wirth: Professor of sociology, University of Chicago. President of International Sociological Association; past president of American Sociological Society; has served as director of planning, Illinois Postwar Planning Commission and as consultant to Federal Public Housing Authority, Office of Price Administration, National Resources Planning Board, and other government agencies; books include: *The Ghetto, Contemporary Social Problems,* co-author of *Urbanism as a Way of Life, Urban Government,* and other works; contributor of articles on sociology and social research to professional journals.

Shepherd L. Witman: Executive director, Cleveland Council on World Affairs. Associate professor of political science, Cleveland College of Western Reserve University; member, Adult Education Panel of UNESCO; member executive council, the American Association for Adult Education; member board of directors, American Council for the Community; member Advisory Committee, International Business Relations Council.

James Worthy: Personnel Department, Sears, Roebuck and Co., Chicago. President, Industrial Relations Association of Chicago; former president, Library of International Relations; former assistant deputy administrator, NRA; author of *What Employers Want,* and papers for professional journals on such topics as "Factors Influencing Employe Morale," "Organizational Structure and Employe Morale," and "Democratic Principles in Business Management."

FROM CORNING GLASS WORKS

Amory Houghton: Chairman of the board, Corning Glass Works. With Corning Glass Works since 1921; director, Steuben Glass, Inc., Blue Ridge Glass Corp., Pittsburgh-Corning Corp., Metropolitan Life Insurance Co., National City Bank, Erie Railroad Co., Dow Corning Corp., Investors Management Co.; member national executive board and honorary vice-president, Boy Scouts of America.

Arthur A. Houghton, Jr.: President, Steuben Glass, Inc. Director, Corning Glass Works, D.L. & W.R.R. Co., Investors Management Fund, Fundamental Investors, Inc.; member-at-large, ACLS; formerly curator of rare books of the Library of Congress; trustee of New York Public Library, Pierpont Morgan Library, Metropolitan Museum of Art, Institute of Contemporary Art; member, Advisory Councils of Harvard, Princeton, and Folger libraries; president, Shakespeare Association of America; vice-president, Keats-Shelley Association of America.

GLEN W. COLE: Vice-chairman of the board, Corning Glass Works. With Corning Glass Works since 1919; director and vice-president, Pittsburgh-Corning Corp.; vice-chairman, board of directors, Corning Glass Works of Canada, Ltd.; director, Dow Corning Corp., Corning Trust Co., Corning Building Corp., Corhart Refractories Co.

WILLIAM H. CURTISS: Vice-president and secretary, Corning Glass Works. With Corning Glass Works since 1920; former vice-president and secretary and present director, Blue Ridge Glass Corp.; secretary-treasurer and director, Corning Fibre Box Corp.; director, Corhart Refractories Co., Corning Hotel Corp., L'Electro Refractaire, Corning Glass Works of South America, Pittsburgh-Corning Corp.

WILLIAM C. DECKER: President, Corning Glass Works. President and director, Corning Glass Works of Canada, Ltd.; formerly chemical engineer, Western Electric Co.; sales engineer, Brown Co.

CHARLES D. LaFOLLETTE: Vice-president and treasurer, Corning Glass Works. Former assistant dean, Graduate School of Business Administration, Harvard University; director, Corning Fibre Box Corp., Steuben Glass, Inc., Corning Glass Works of Canada, Ltd.; director and treasurer, Dow Corning Corp.

GEORGE D. MACBETH. Vice-president and controller, Corning Glass Works. Former president and general manager, Macbeth-Evans Glass Co.; director, Corning Fibre Box Corp., Corning Hotel Corp., Corning Hospital, and Pittsburgh-Corning Corp.

RUSHMORE H. MARINER: Director of Centennial. Oil field worker, Humble Oil & Refining Co.; later regional manager with Tide Water Associated Oil Co.; became associated with Corning Glass Works in 1945 as assistant manager, Apparatus Factory, and subsequently administrative assistant to director of research, and manager, New Products Division; at present, sales manager, Standard Products.

EUGENE C. SULLIVAN: Honorary chairman of the board, Corning Glass Works. With Corning Glass Works since 1908; was chief chemist, director of research, organized laboratory which produced "Pyrex" laboratory and household ware and various special glasses; president, and director, Dow Corning Corp.; vice-president and director, Corhart Refractories Co.; director, Pittsburgh-Corning Corp., Dow Corning, Ltd. and Societe Industrielle des Silicones; former member editorial advisory board, American Chemical Society; author of papers in various fields of chemistry and glass.

FROM EXECUTIVE OFFICES, ACLS

CHARLES E. ODEGAARD: Executive director, American Council of Learned Societies. Formerly professor of history, University of Illinois; member, U.S. National Commission for UNESCO; adviser to U.S. delegation to Fifth General Conference of UNESCO, Florence, Italy, 1950; member, Scientific Advisory Committee to director of Selective Service System; author of *Fideles and Vassi in the Carolingian Empire*; contributor of articles on medieval history to journals.

DONALD H. DAUGHERTY: Assistant to the director, American Council of Learned Societies. Formerly in Department of Philosophy, Ohio State University and University of Missouri; author of articles and compiler of bibliographies in fields of philosophy, history, education, and musicology.

EUGENE STALEY: Special assistant for Corning Conference. On loan from Stanford Research Institute, where he is senior economist. Taught and did research in international economic relations at various graduate schools; served as economist in government war agencies, member 1st UNRRA mission to China, consultant, Economic Department, United Nations; executive director World Affairs Council of Northern California; chief economist of recent World Bank mission to Cuba; books include: *War and the Private Investor, World Economy in Transition, World Economic Development*, and forthcoming *Technology and Human Values*.

J. F. WELLEMEYER, JR.: Staff adviser on personnel studies, American Council of Learned Societies. Formerly economist, labor market research, U.S. Employment Service and War Manpower Commission; research interests: studies of personnel problems in humanistic and social science fields.